# UNTITLED.

## STREET ART IN THE COUNTER CULTURE

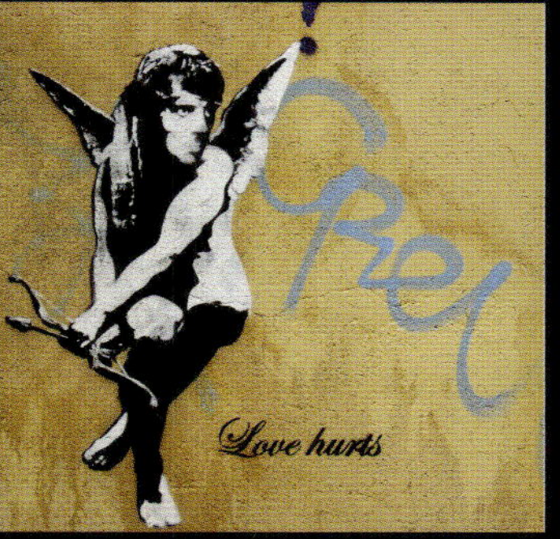


# UNTITLED.

## STREET ART IN THE COUNTER CULTURE

This is our Punk Rock

Published by Pro-actif Communications. Curated by Gary Shove

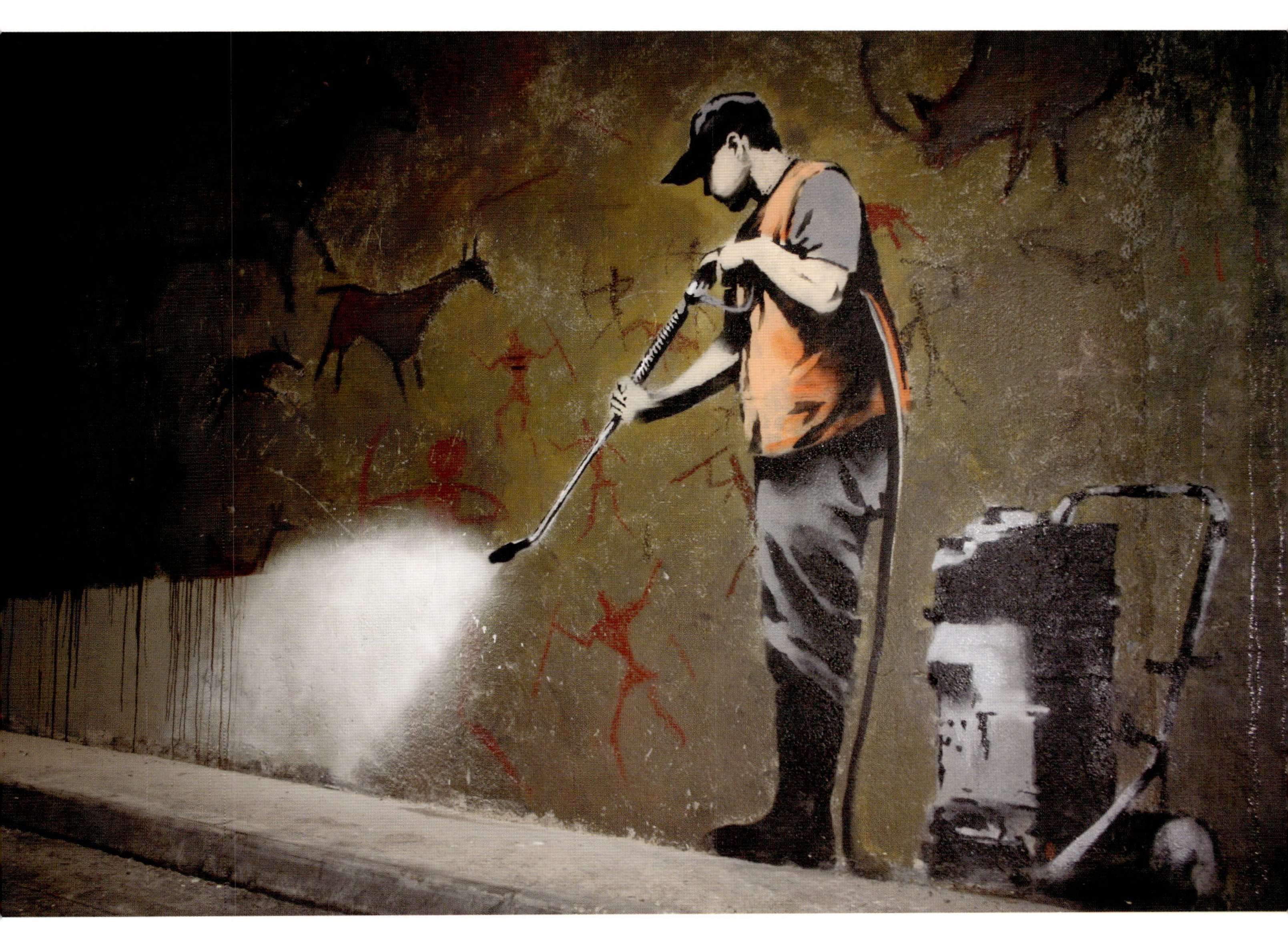

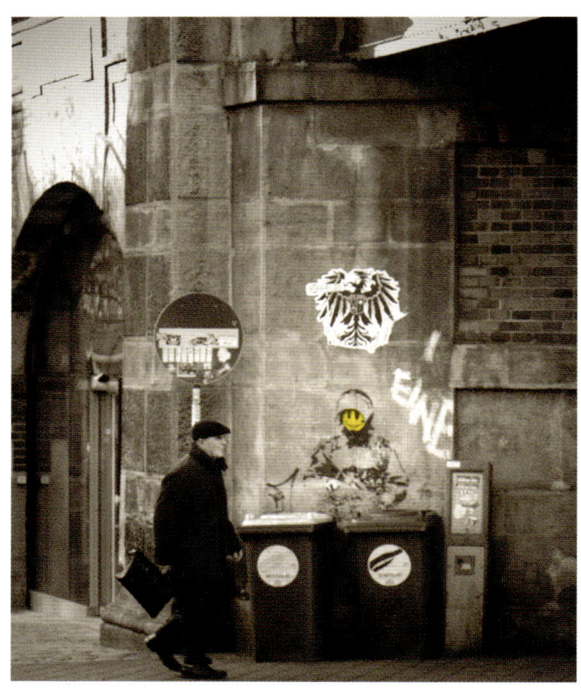

# How to Survive an Art Attack

Art rarely attacks human beings except when it is starved by environmental circumstances. Most species of art prey on thematic concerns such as time, death or shoals of fleeting emotions and idea crabs. However, when Art is driven by existential hunger into the shallows of everyday life where we swim and frolic, the best thing to do is remain calm. Art will only attack you if it thinks you are lame. Do not splash about on the surface of human experience like a dying kipper. Swim toward shore using strong regular strokes and Art will usually pass you by seeking weaker prey. If Art does attack you then kick against it as hard as you can. Gouge its eyes out and paint a picture of your own face on the surface of the water with its guts.

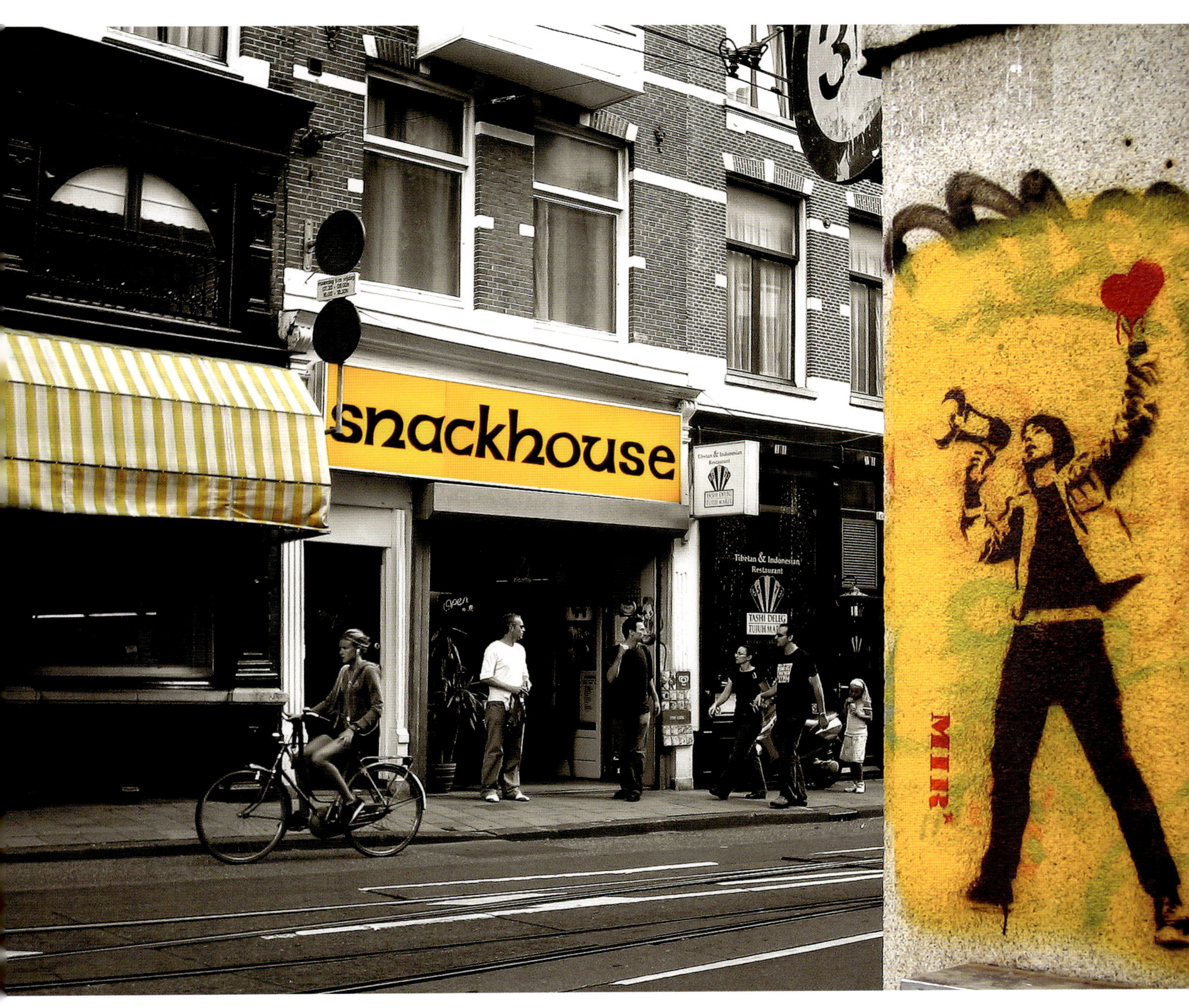
snackhouse
Tibetan & Indonesian
Restaurant
MIR

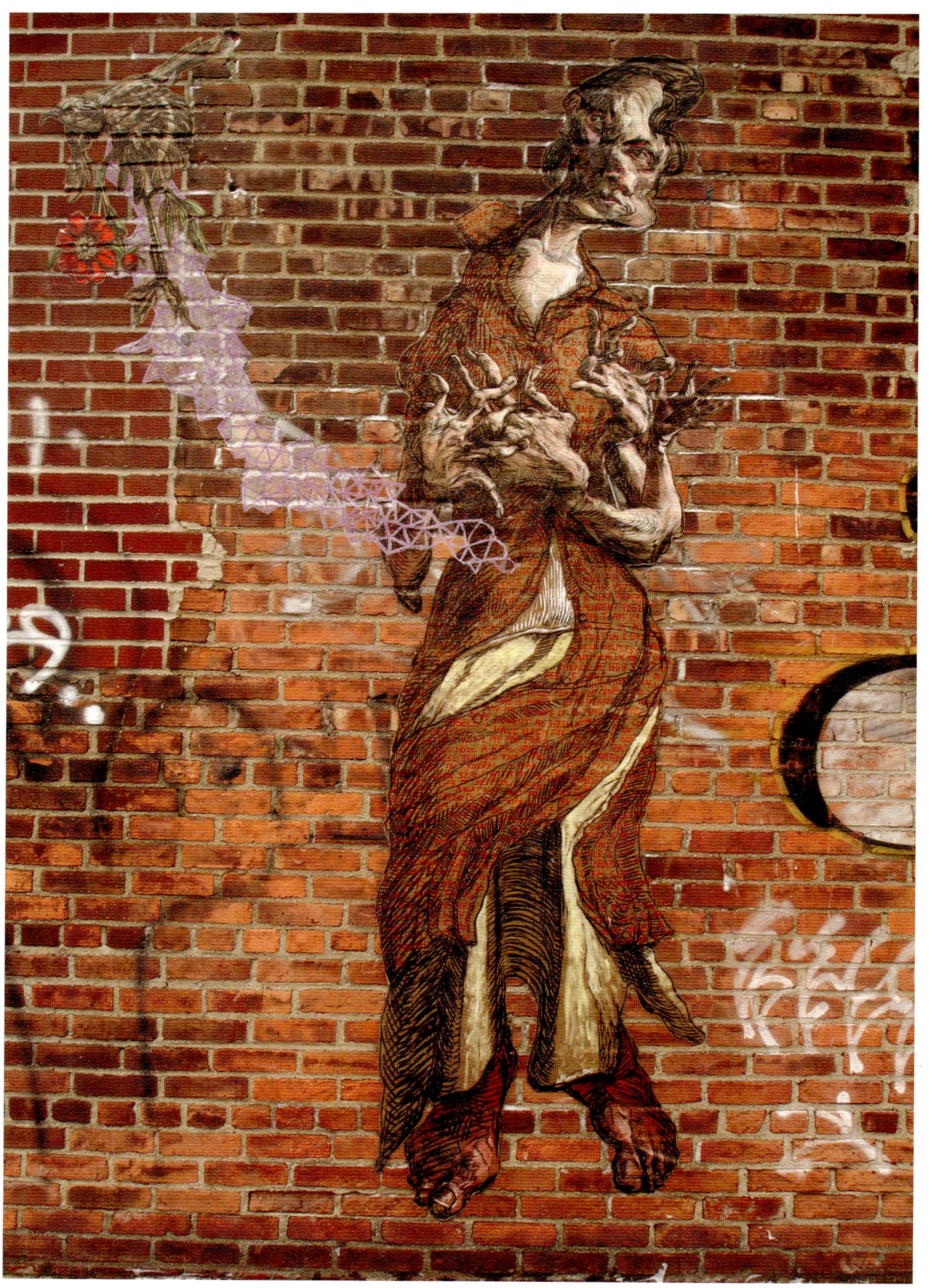

# Spring Street, NY

11 Spring Street in NoLIta, New York was indeed a building where many folks over much times painted and stuck and such, all manner of things and pictures and words and it became a 'big deal' and a 'landmark' which the people came to love.

It was like the haunted house that you dared each other to go to when you were kids. There were mysterious curtains and candles in the windows and no-one knew what was inside. All sorts of stories were told. Lou Reed did a poem. Someone proposed to his wife with a message on the wall. It used to be a stable.

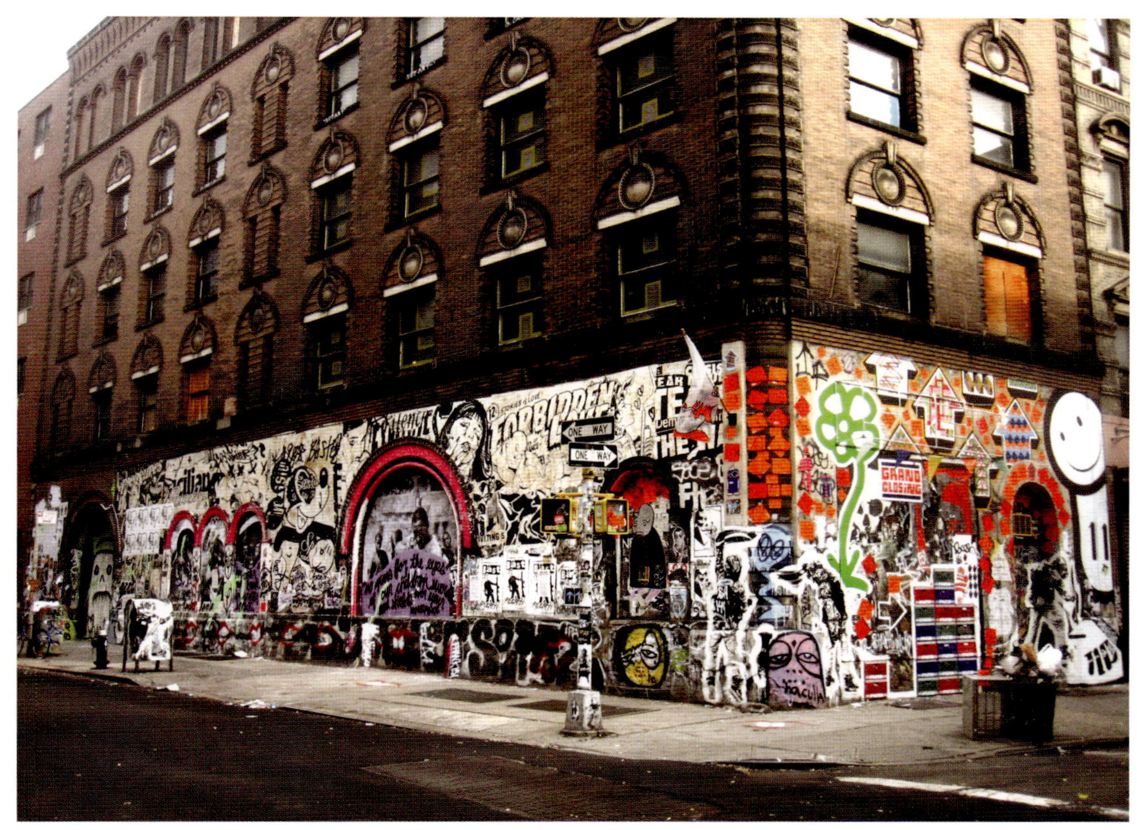

So this lady who is basically a property developer, chips in with an event to celebrate the art before they paint over it all and redevelop the site.

*"We are sensitive to the street-art issue."*

Caroline Cummings

However, one could not be mad at Caroline because she was nice about it all. In any case what can you say to these things? Why do we love these half-life places so much?

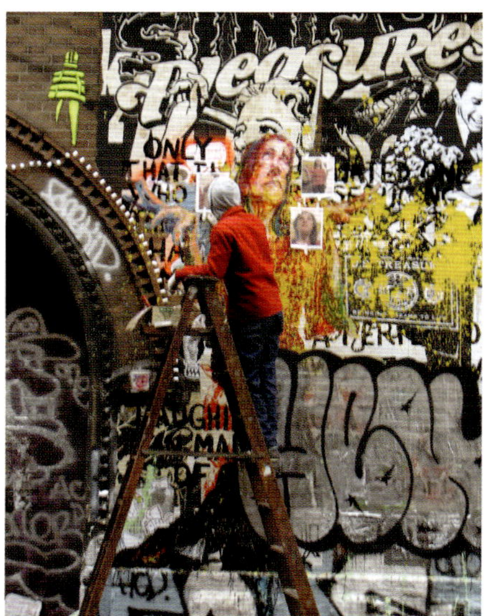
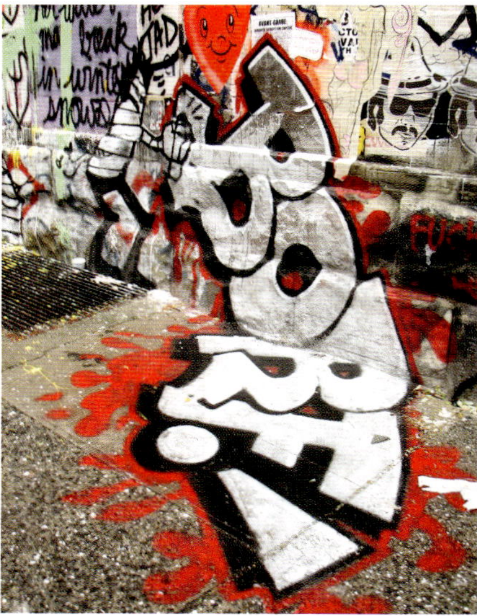
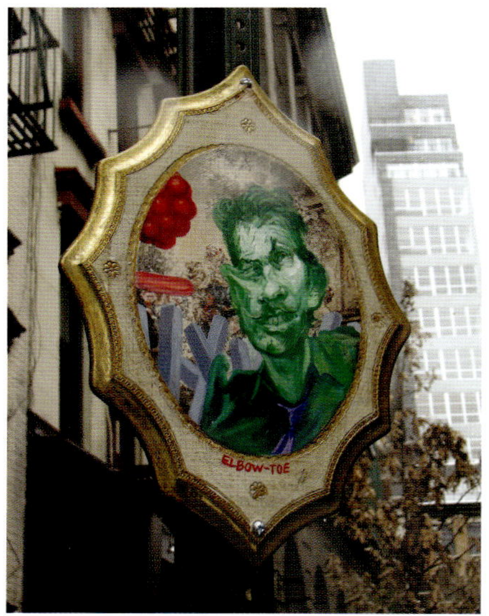

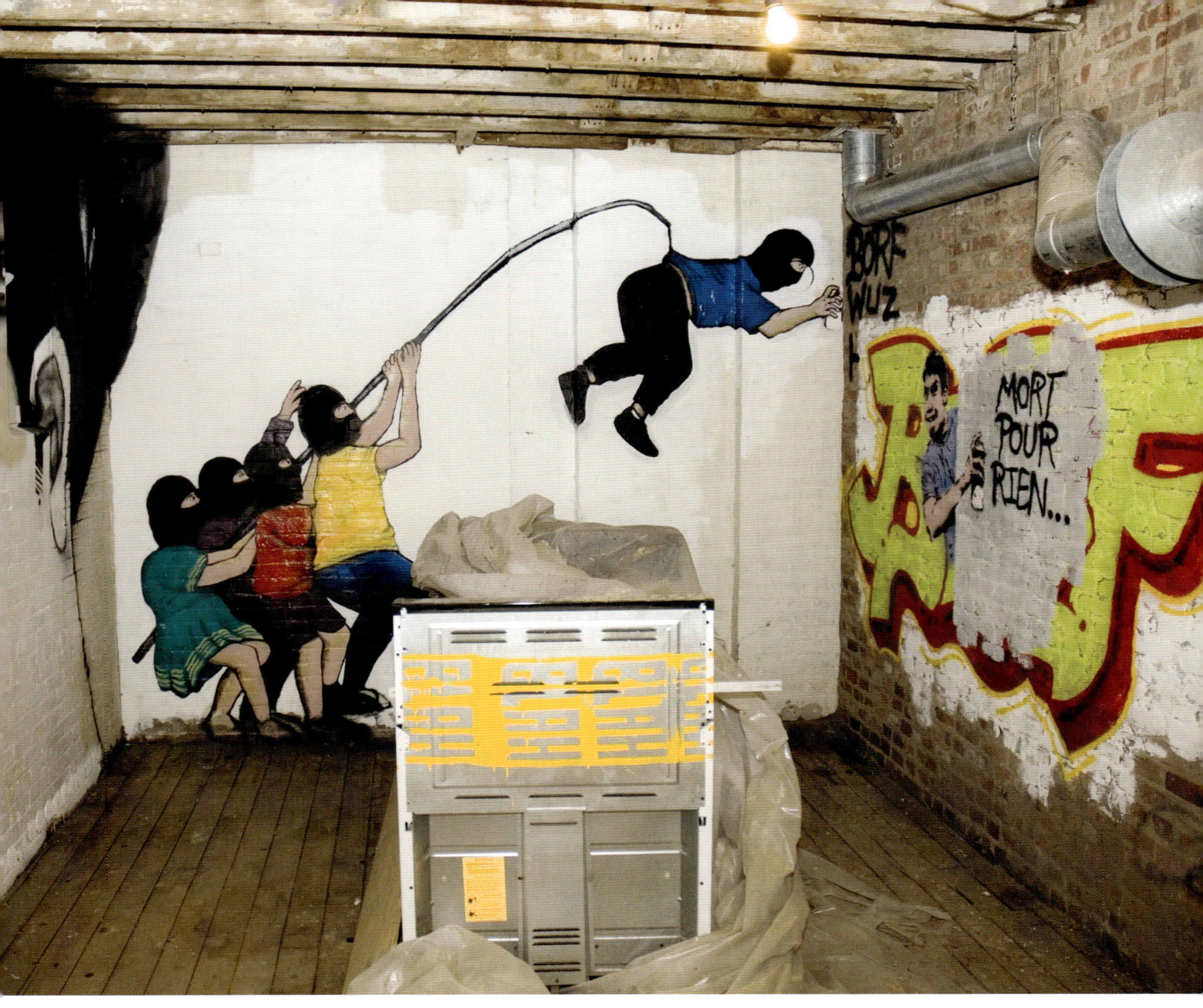


We are sensitive to the street-art issue

Caroline Cummings

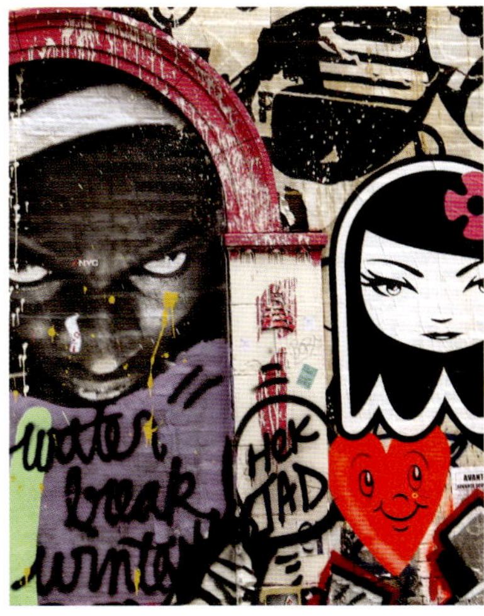
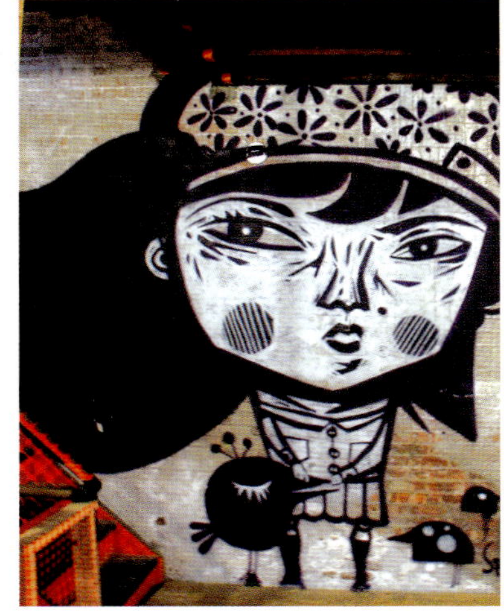
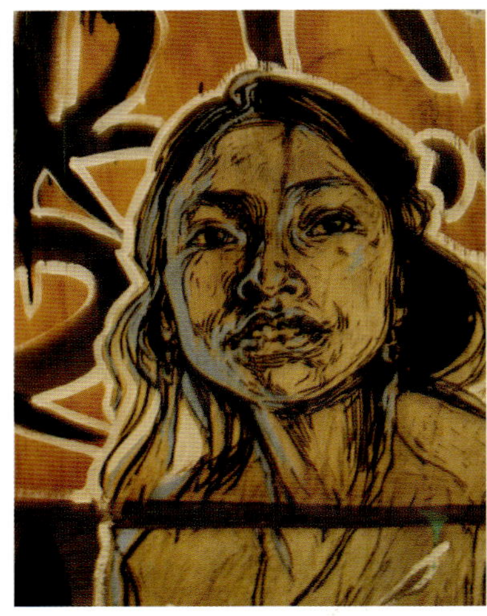
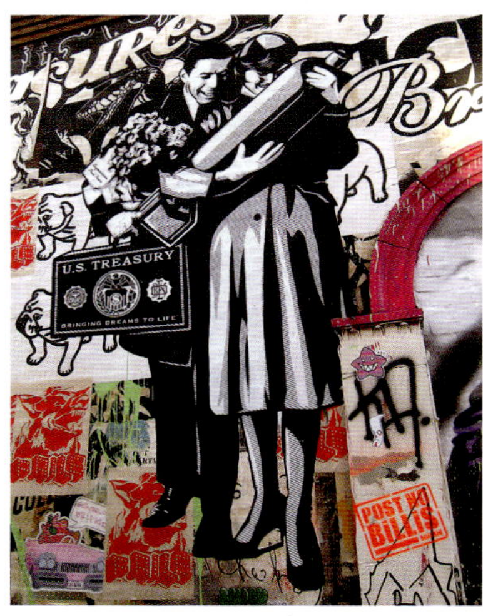
U.S. TREASURY
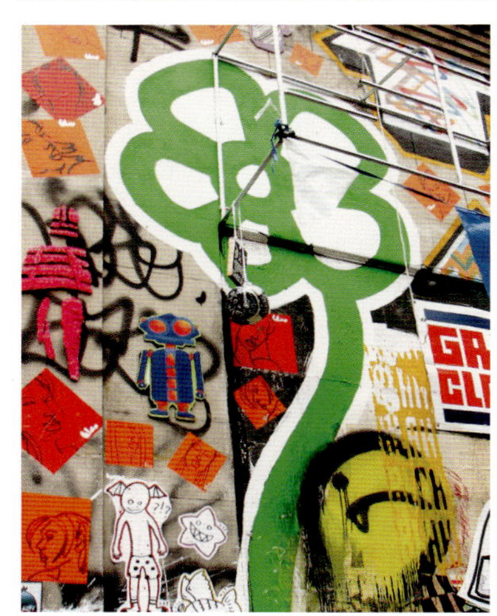
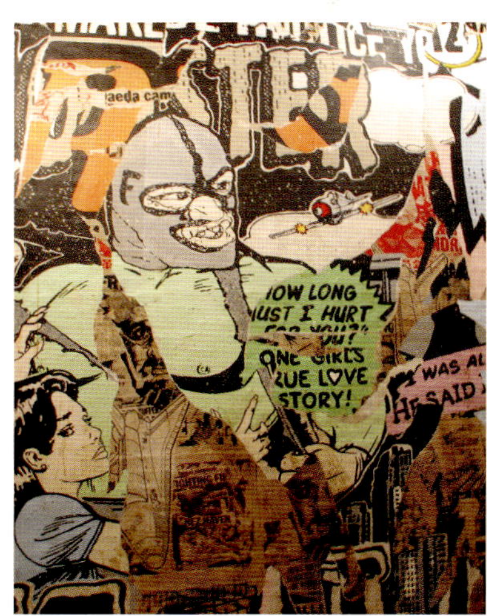
HOW LONG MUST I HURT FOR YOU? ONE GIRLS TRUE LOVE STORY!
WAS AL
HE SAID
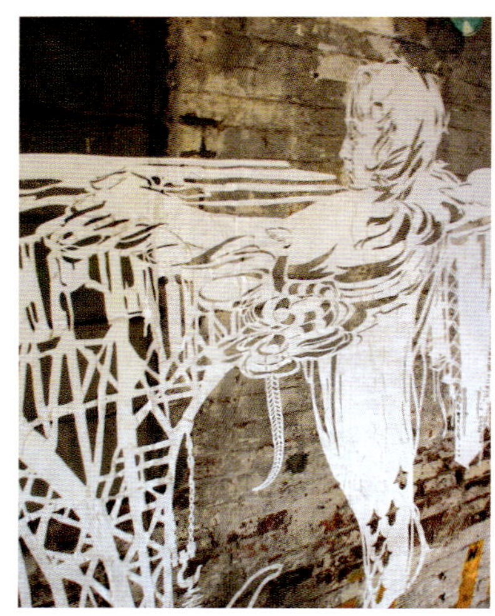
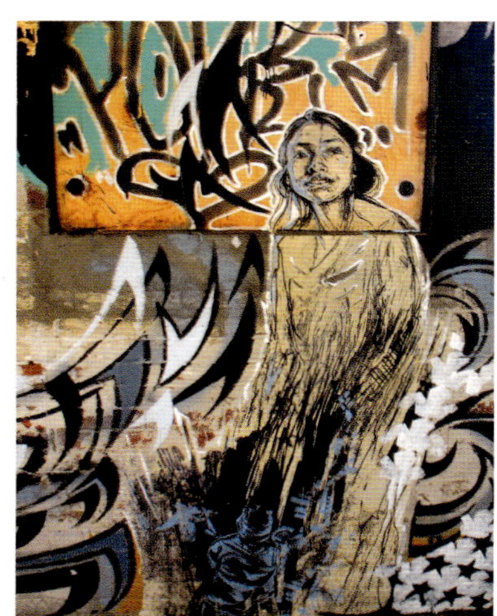
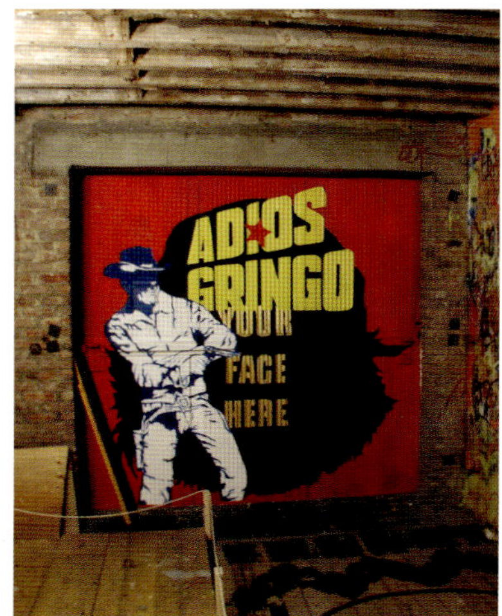
ADIOS GRINGO
YOUR FACE HERE

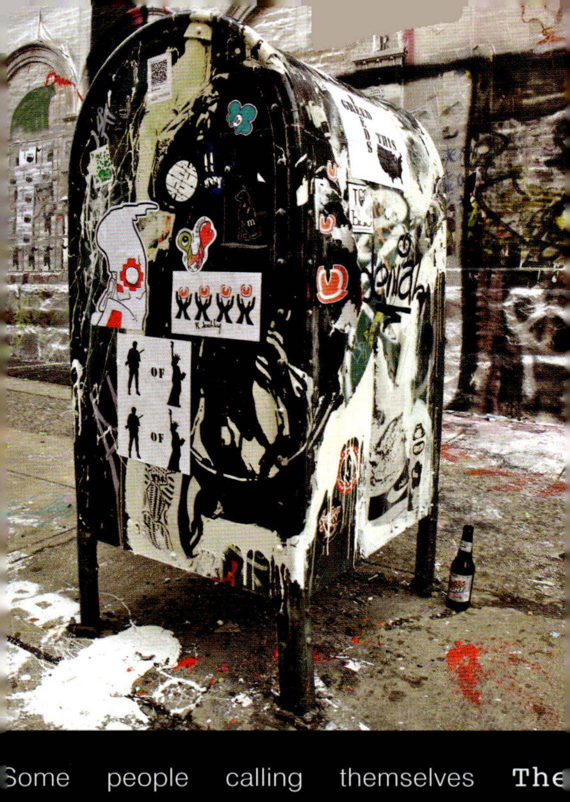

Some people calling themselves **The Wooster Collective** organised the event and loads of arty people came from all over the world to paint every inch of space within the treasured edifice and then they had a show and people came to see all the pictures.

The New York Times said it was all a tremendous laugh while studiously avoiding showing any images that were controversial. Such as the fantastic Rene Gagnon suicide graffiti bomber or the huge Obey spread of a copper threatening to

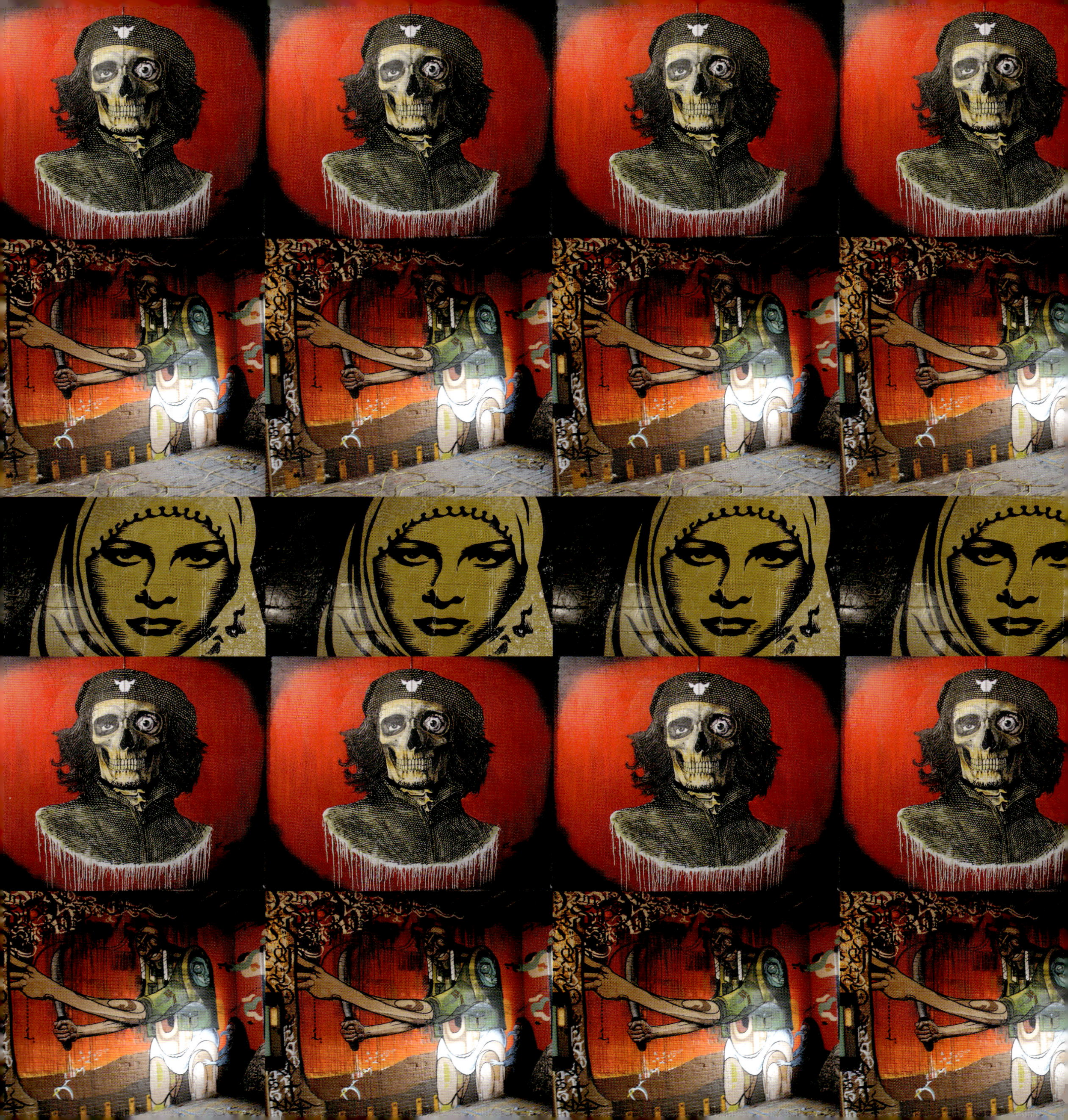

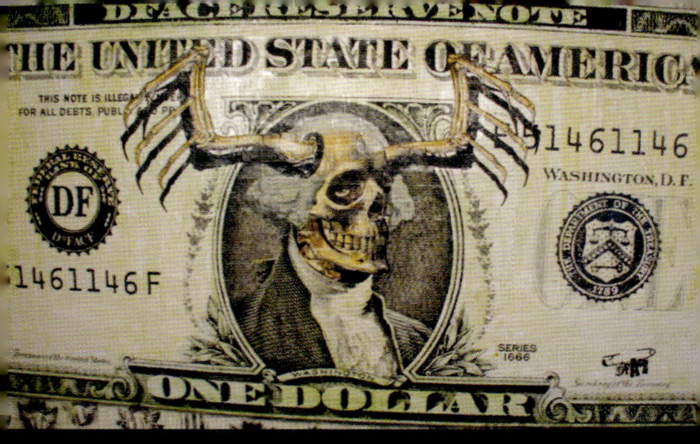


## My Hood?

So Spring Street means a thing because i
means a thing to a neighbourhood. Whateve
equivalent you have had you will have had one
Maybe there was no culture where you grew up
but you must have a Spring Street right? Sure
everybody does. Don't they?

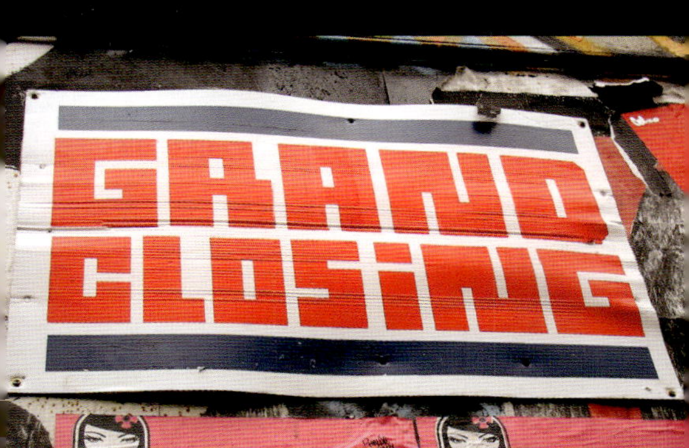

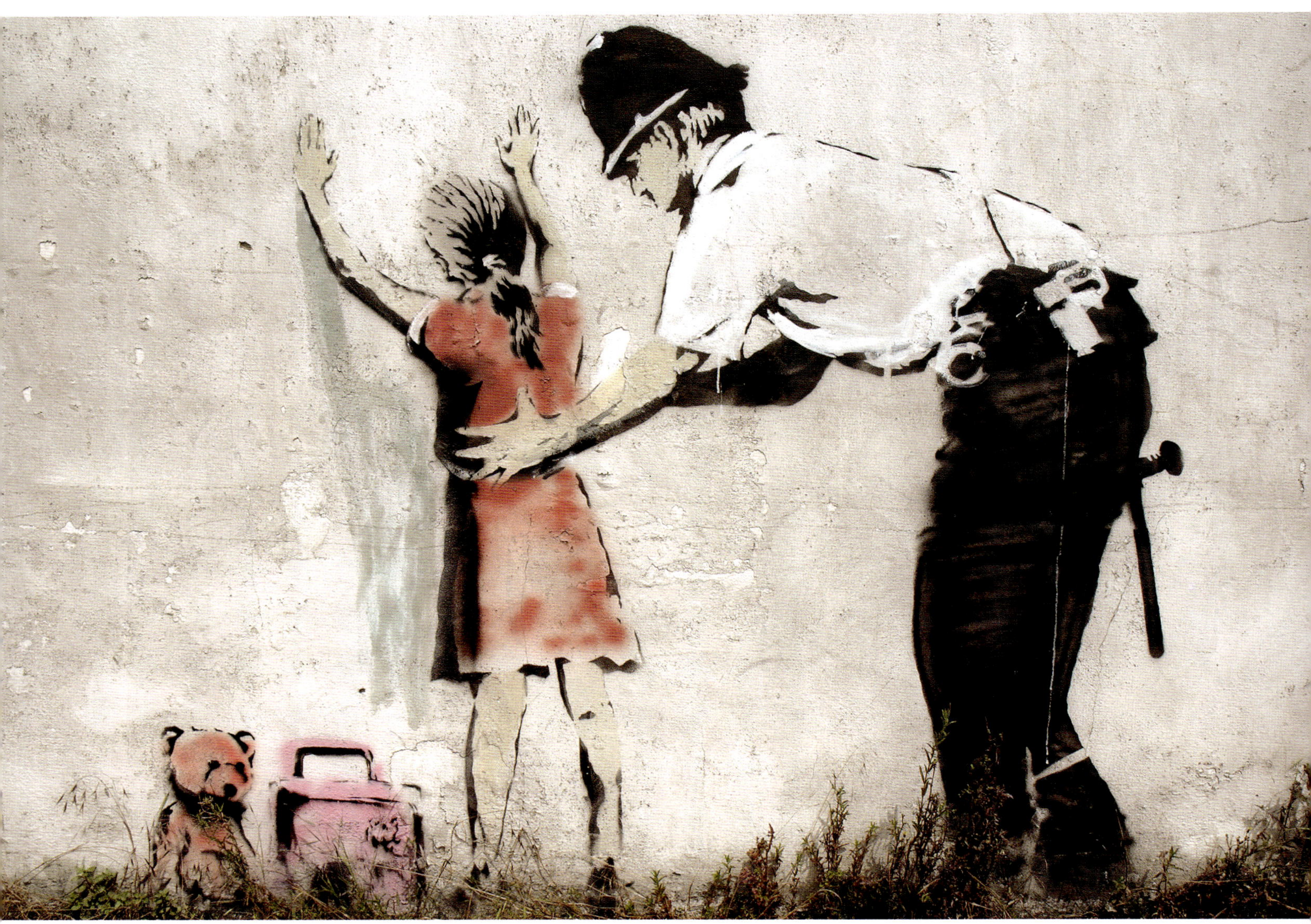

There are a number of major brands hidden in this book.
Why not try and find them all? Answers on P194.

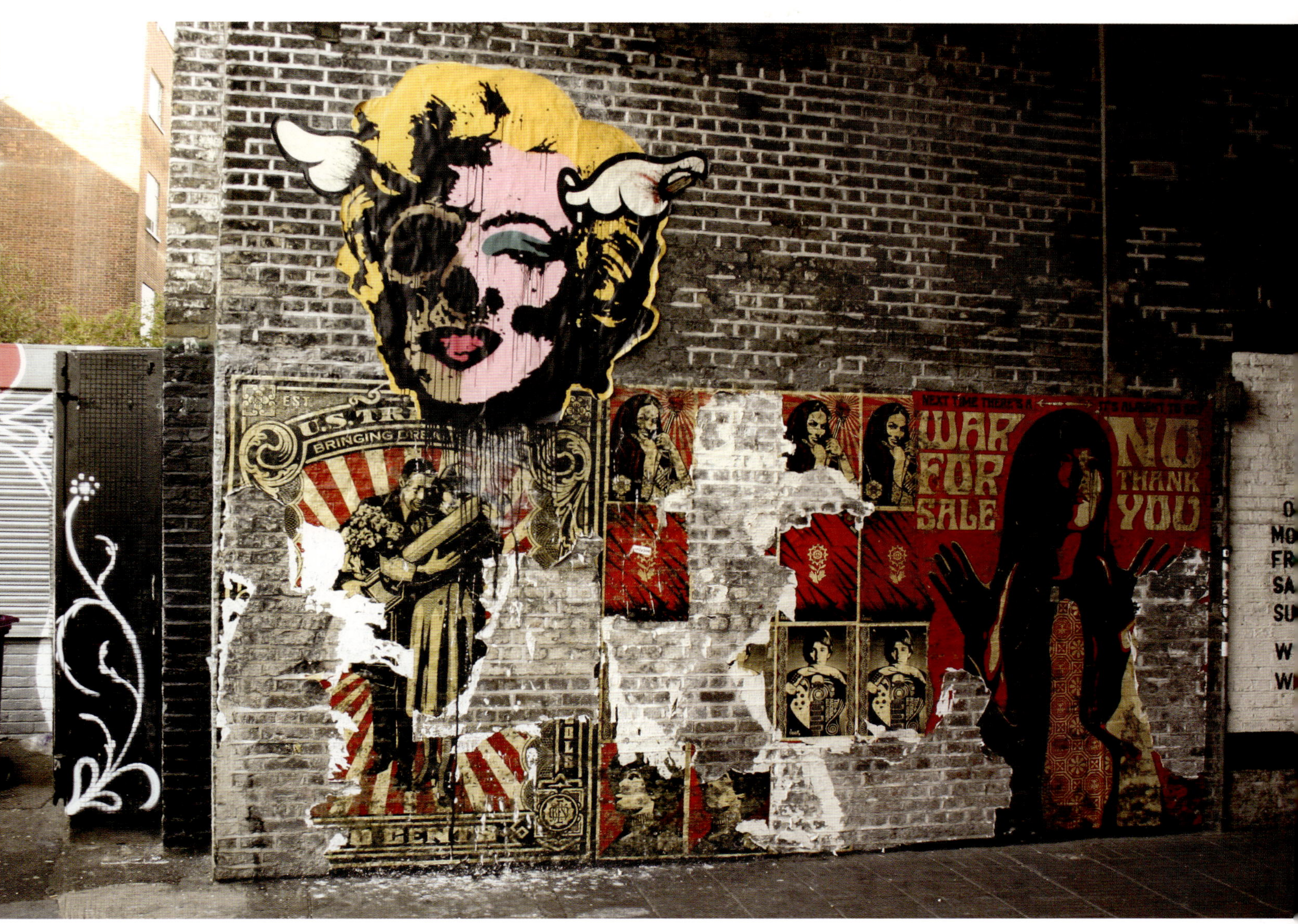
U.S. TR
BRINGING DREA
EST.
WAR
FOR
SALE
NO
THANK
YOU
NEXT TIME THERE'S A
0 CENTS
OBEY

# Career Advice

So the kid comes home with his first pay cheque from a guerrilla street art auction at Christie's and his dad sits him down, you know, for 'the talk'. He starts in with

"Son I'm proud of you but you got to promise me this. Whatever you do with this talent, even if you find yourself starving in a squat in Leytonstone, don't take a job in advertising. I'm begging you son."

So the son turns away and tuts and sighs and says,

'But Dad you don't understand, marketing guys spend four months a year snowboarding and banging Swedish teenagers!"

Dad looks away into the middle distance, a tear forms in his eye, almost inaudibly he mutters after what seems an eternity…

"Do they do friends and family discounts at Val d'Isere?"

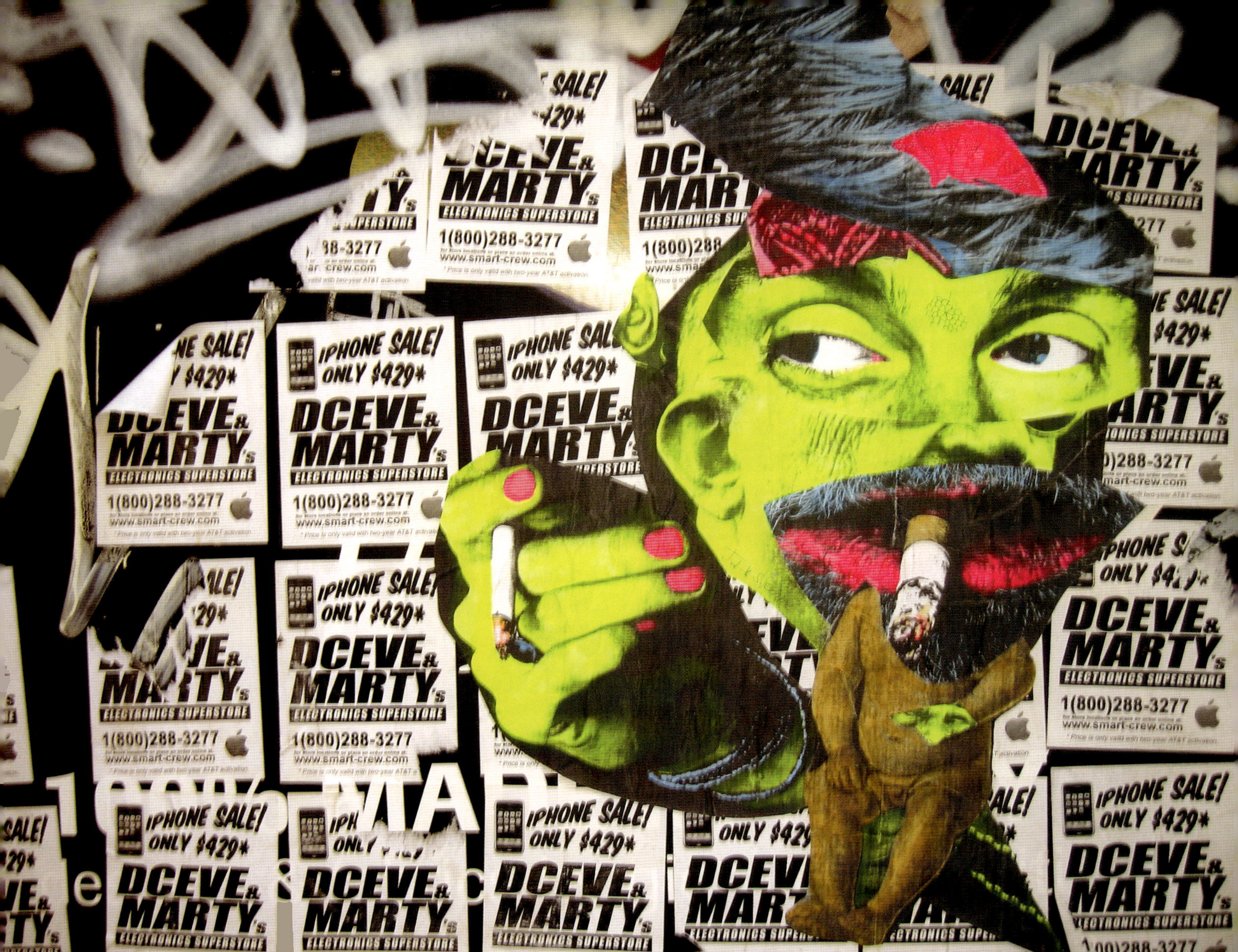

IPHONE SALE!
ONLY $429*
DCEVE &
MARTY's
ELECTRONICS SUPERSTORE
1(800)288-3277
for store locations or place an order online at:
www.smart-crew.com
* Price is only valid with two-year AT&T activation

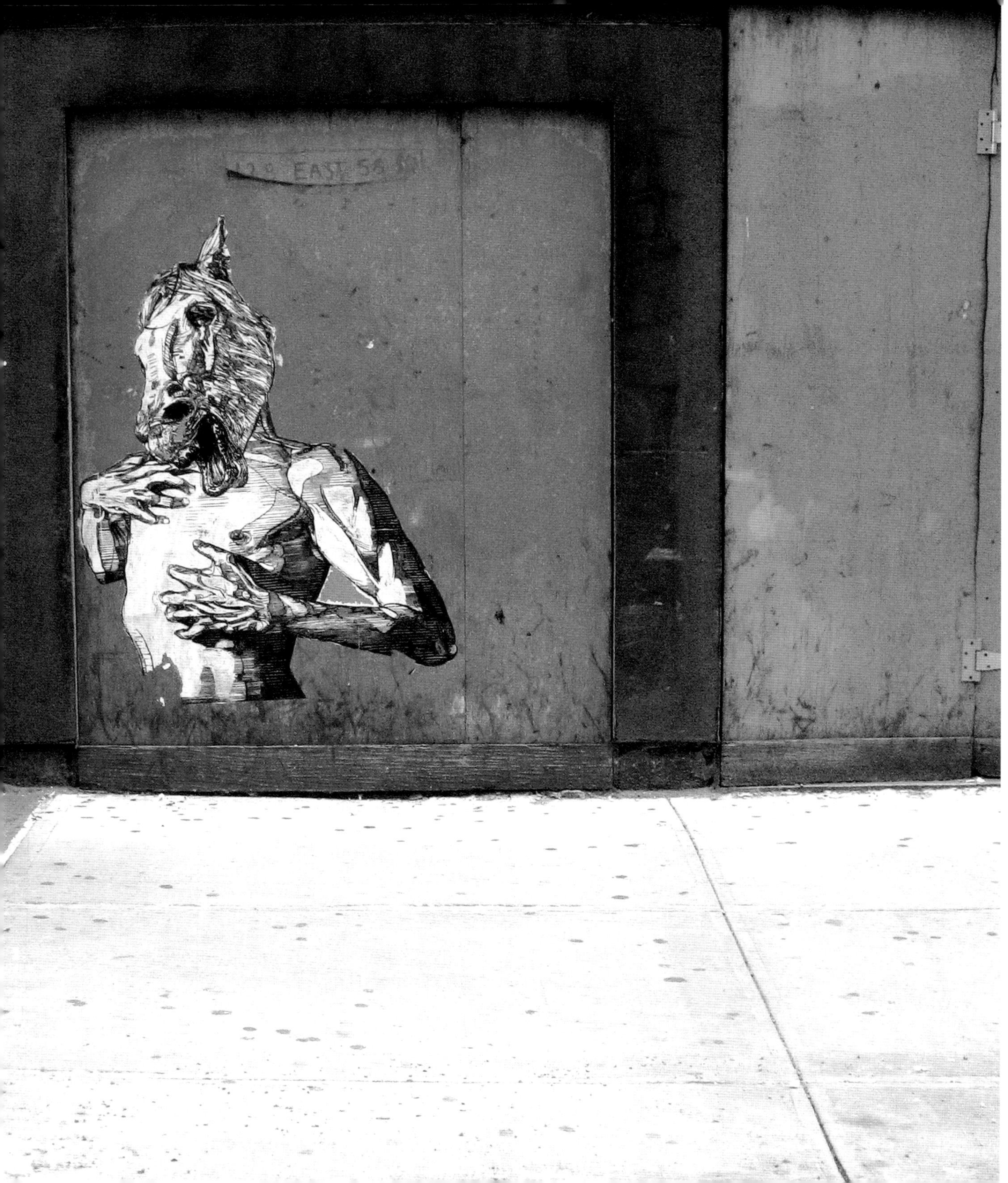
EAST 56

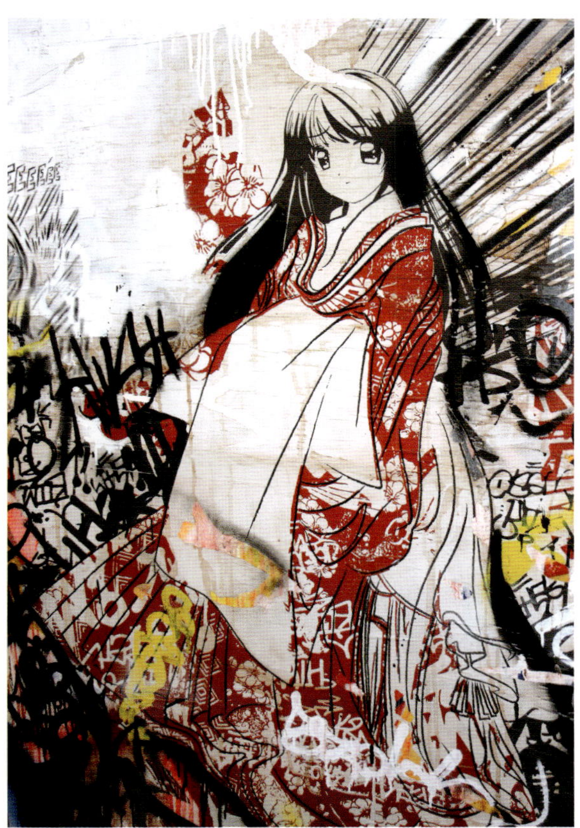

Graffiti and sports have long been associated. Of course it all started with 'Graffoxing'; a version of boxing in which combatants had to tag their name on their opponent using a big marker pen during a bout. Later 'Ghettokhana', a sport wherein well bred young ladies would jump show horses over walls heavily decorated with sick graff, became immensely popular. And who could forget last year's round the world 'YACHTAG' race? Victory went to the Norwegian team for successfully tagging a blue whale.

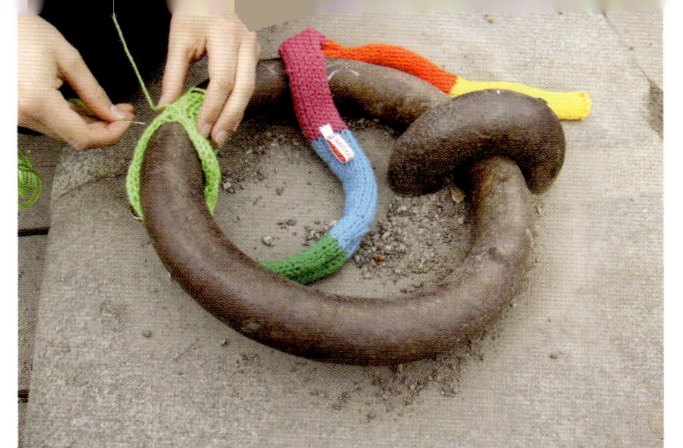

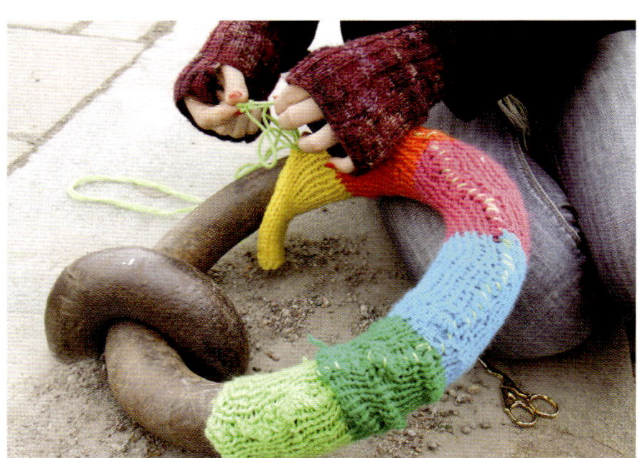

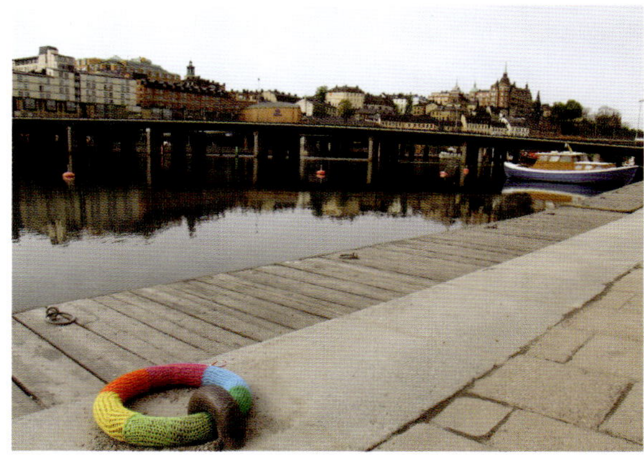

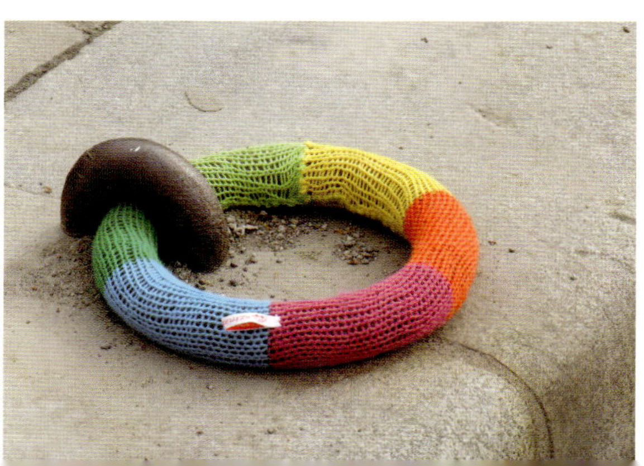

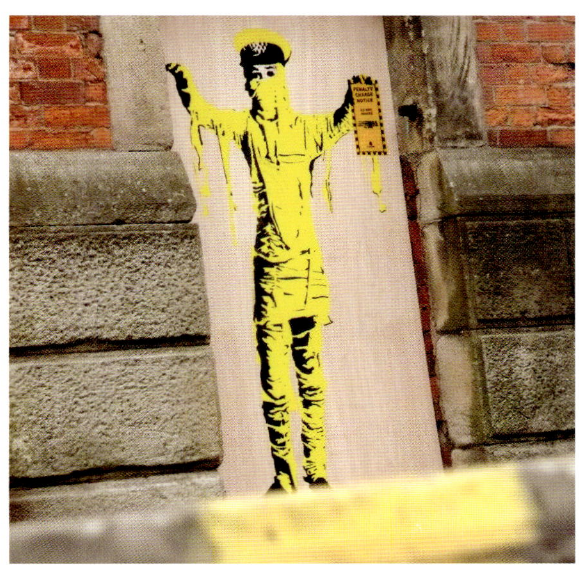

## Ghosts

Get hold of a projector on loan from an institute of education. Get a friend to film you from a bedroom window. Stand in the middle of the street, completely still, for ten minutes. Now project the footage from your bedroom window onto the buildings opposite. Banksy is right, people don't look up. But your ghost will be there. Even if only one person sees it, that street will never be the same. Many experiments are possible in this theme. Alter reality.

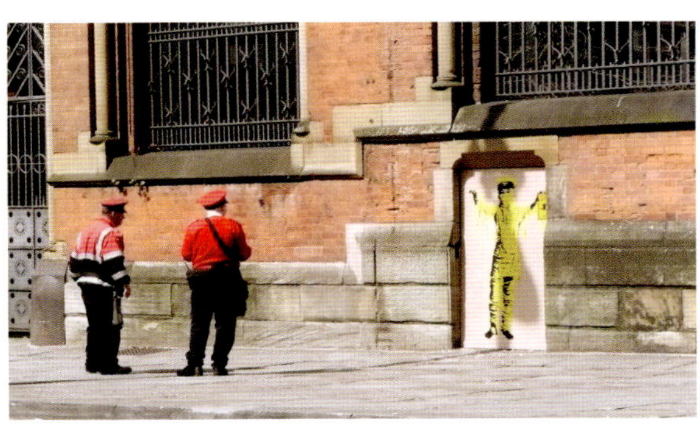

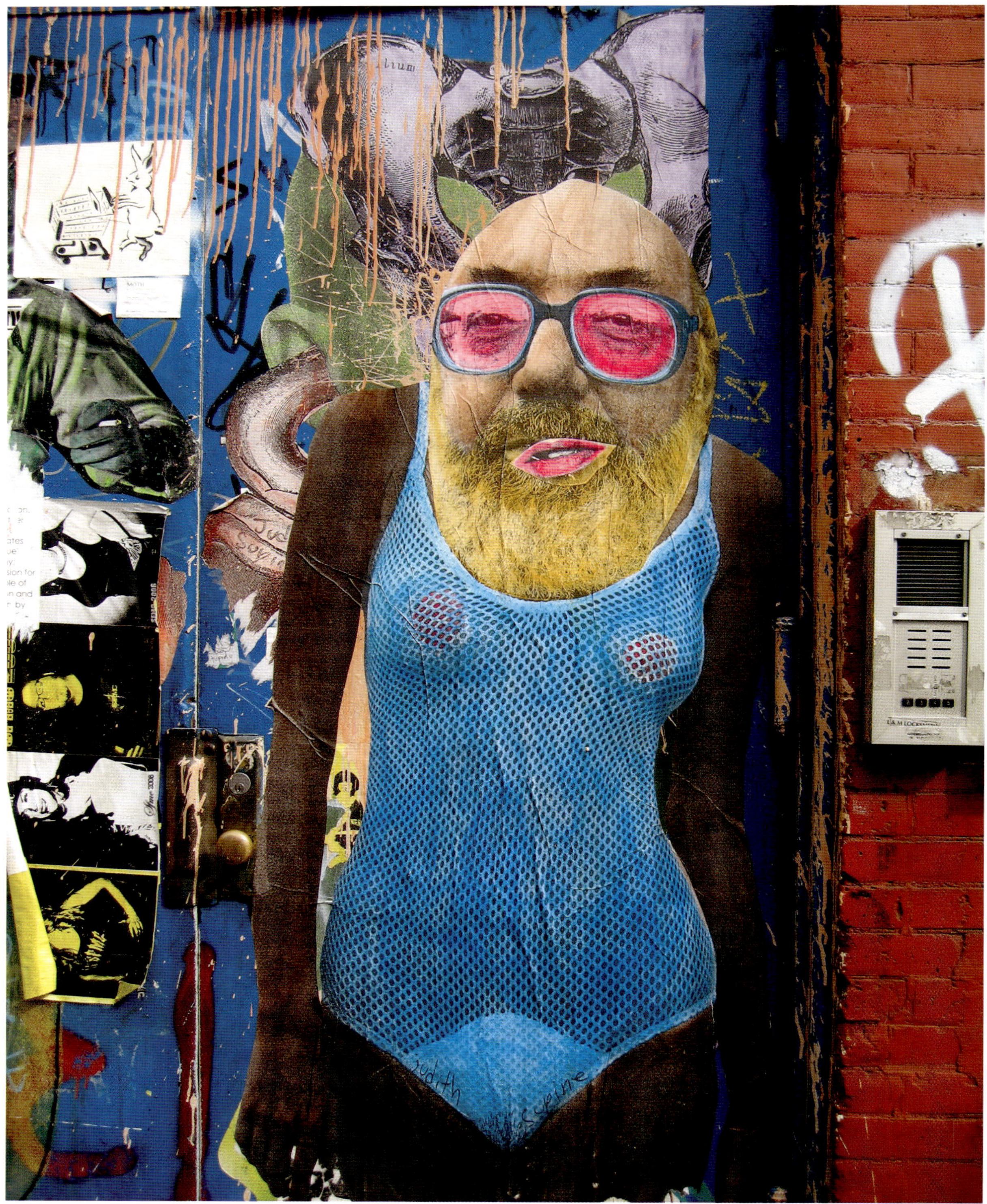

# You are...

...an acceptable level of threat

And if you were not you would know about it.

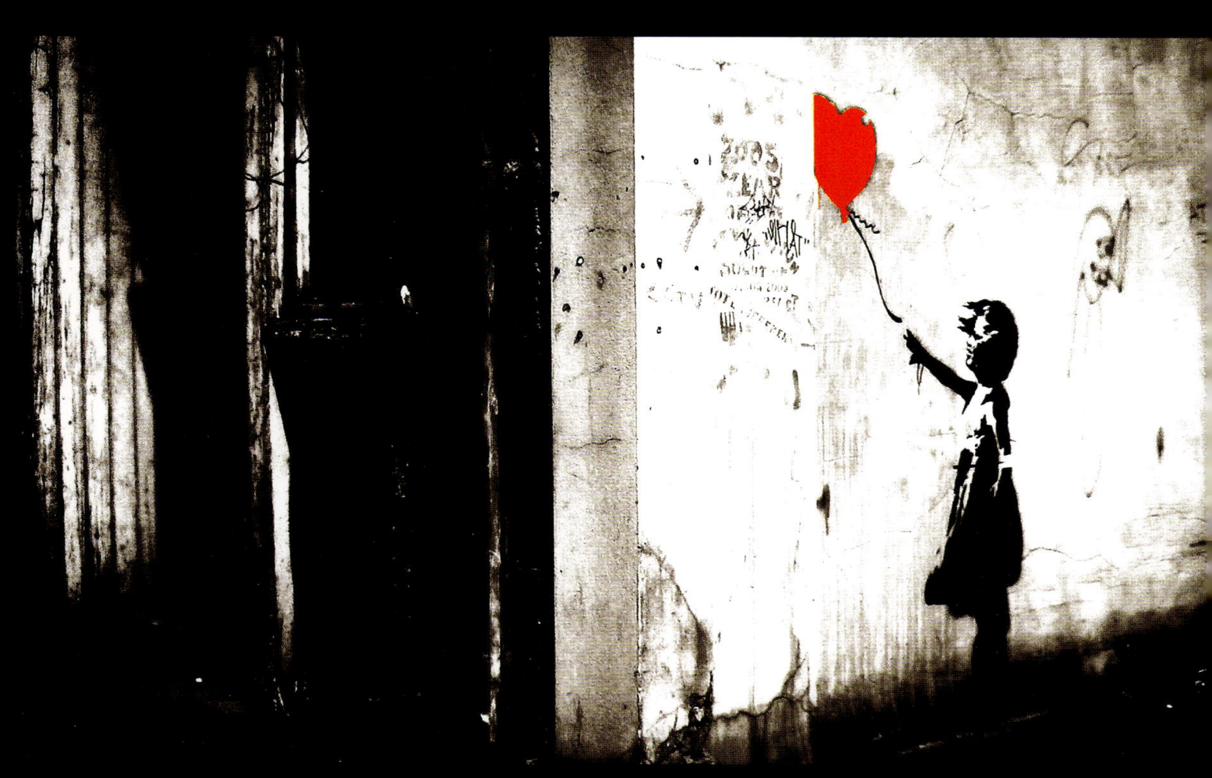

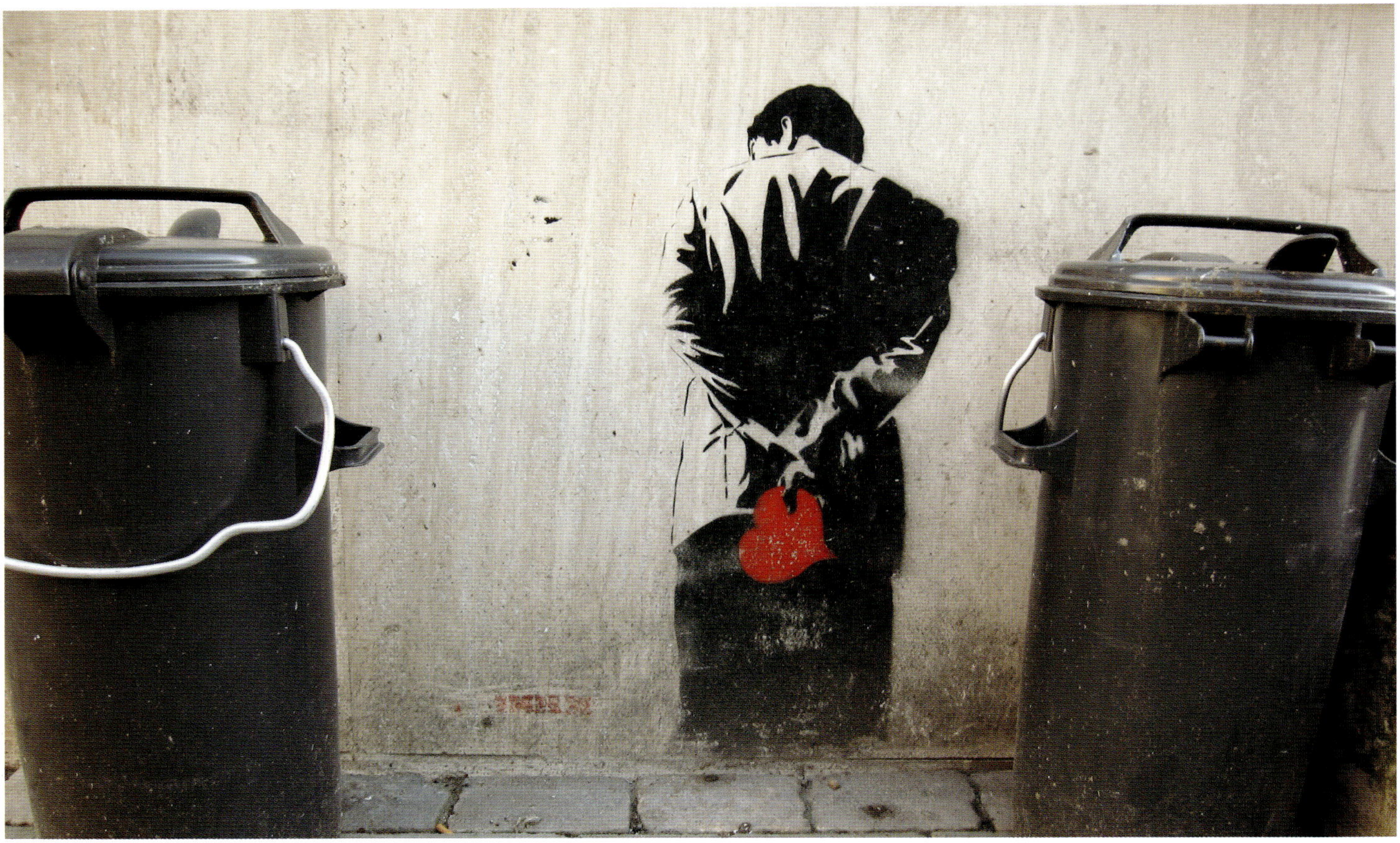

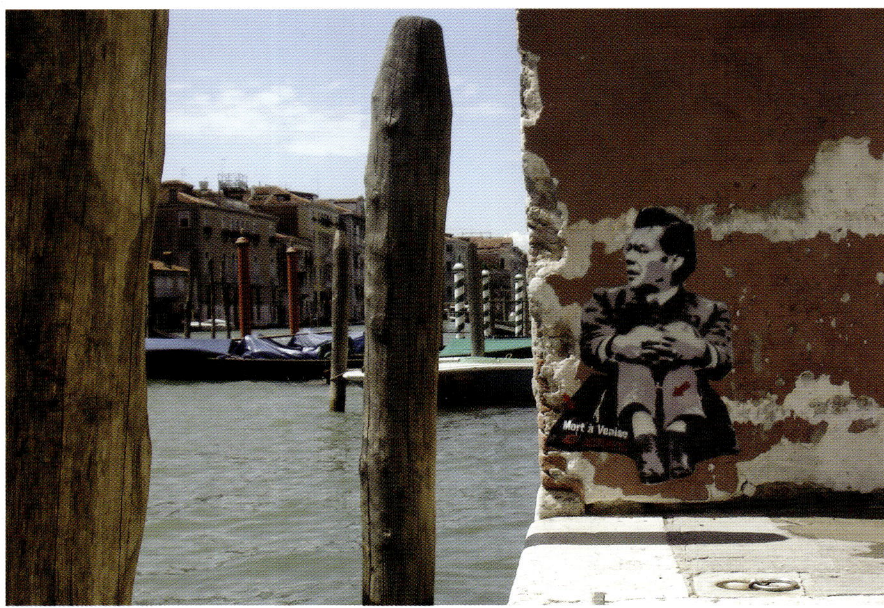
Mort à Venise

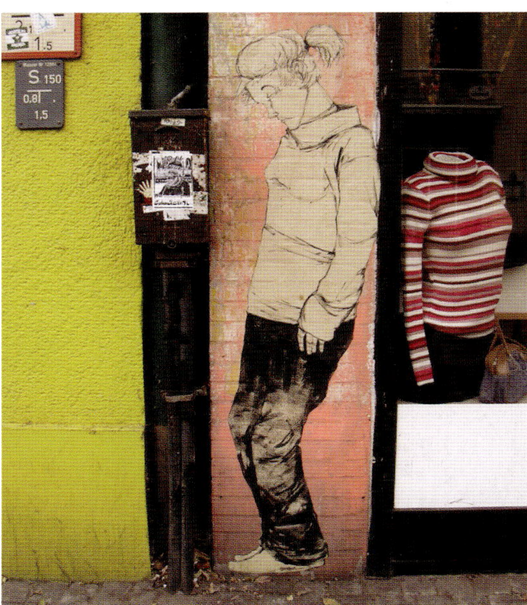
S 150
0.8T
1,5

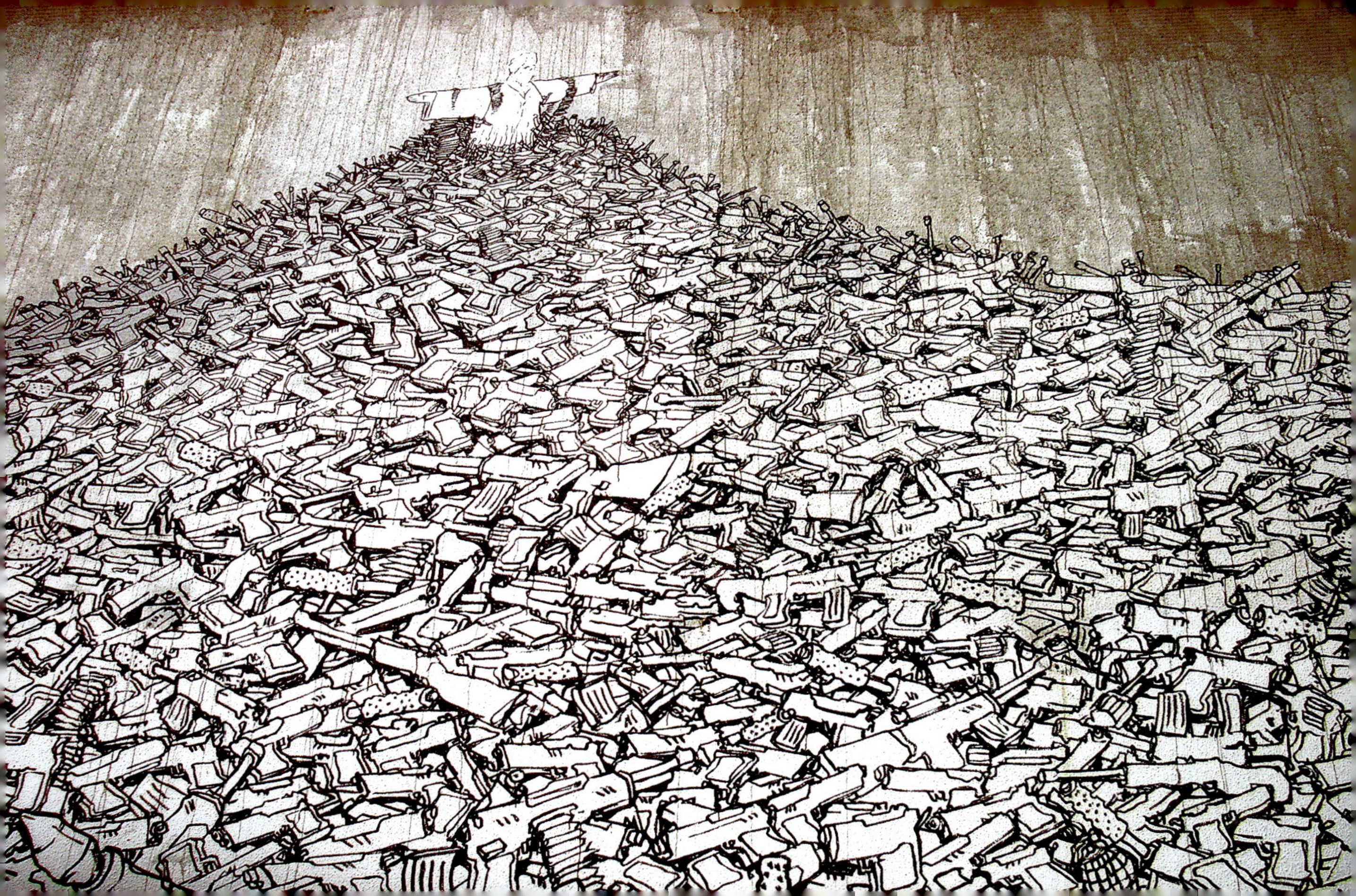

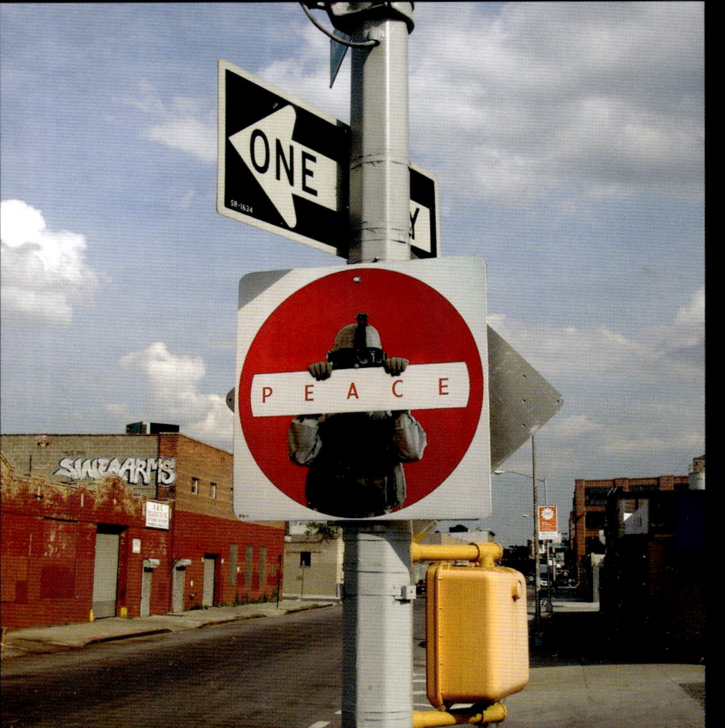


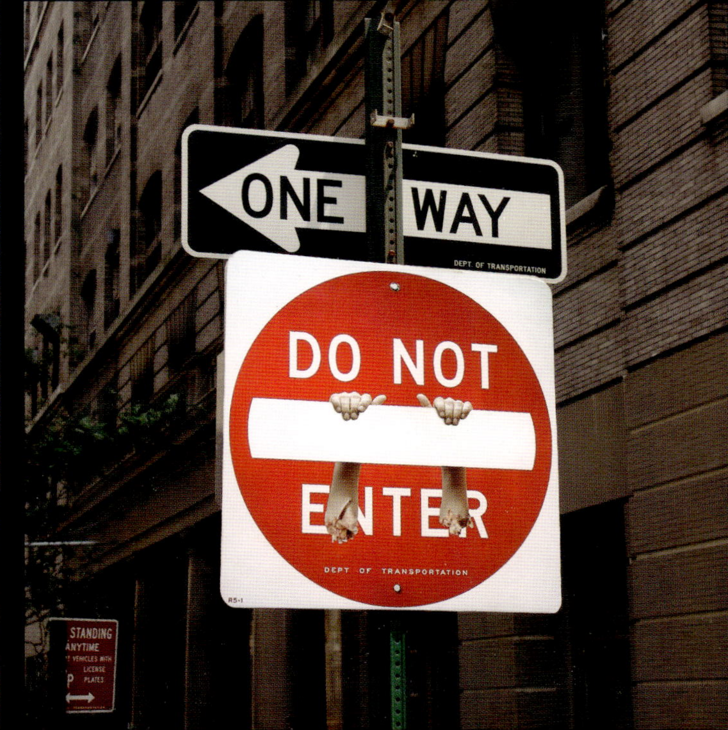


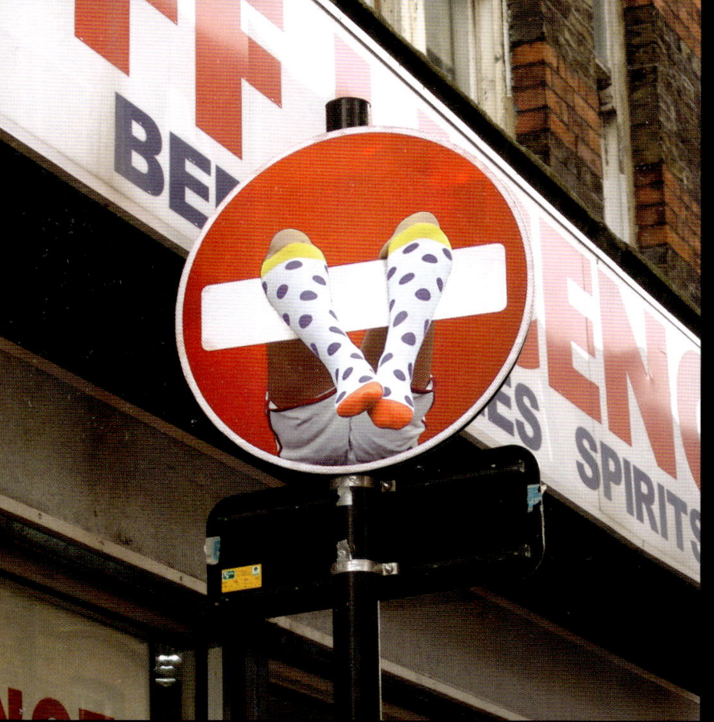


What's the difference
between zero tolerance
and intolerance?

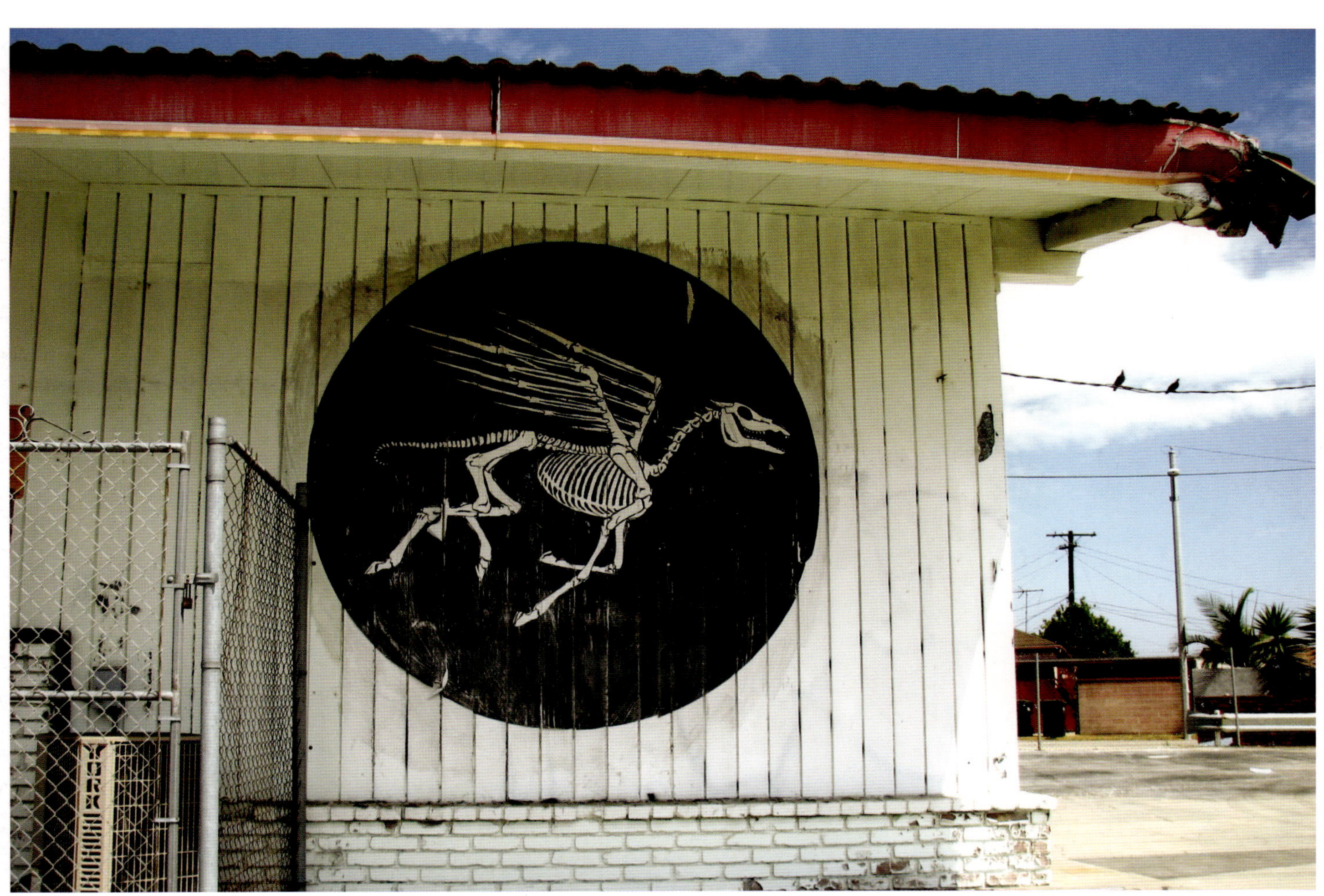

YORK

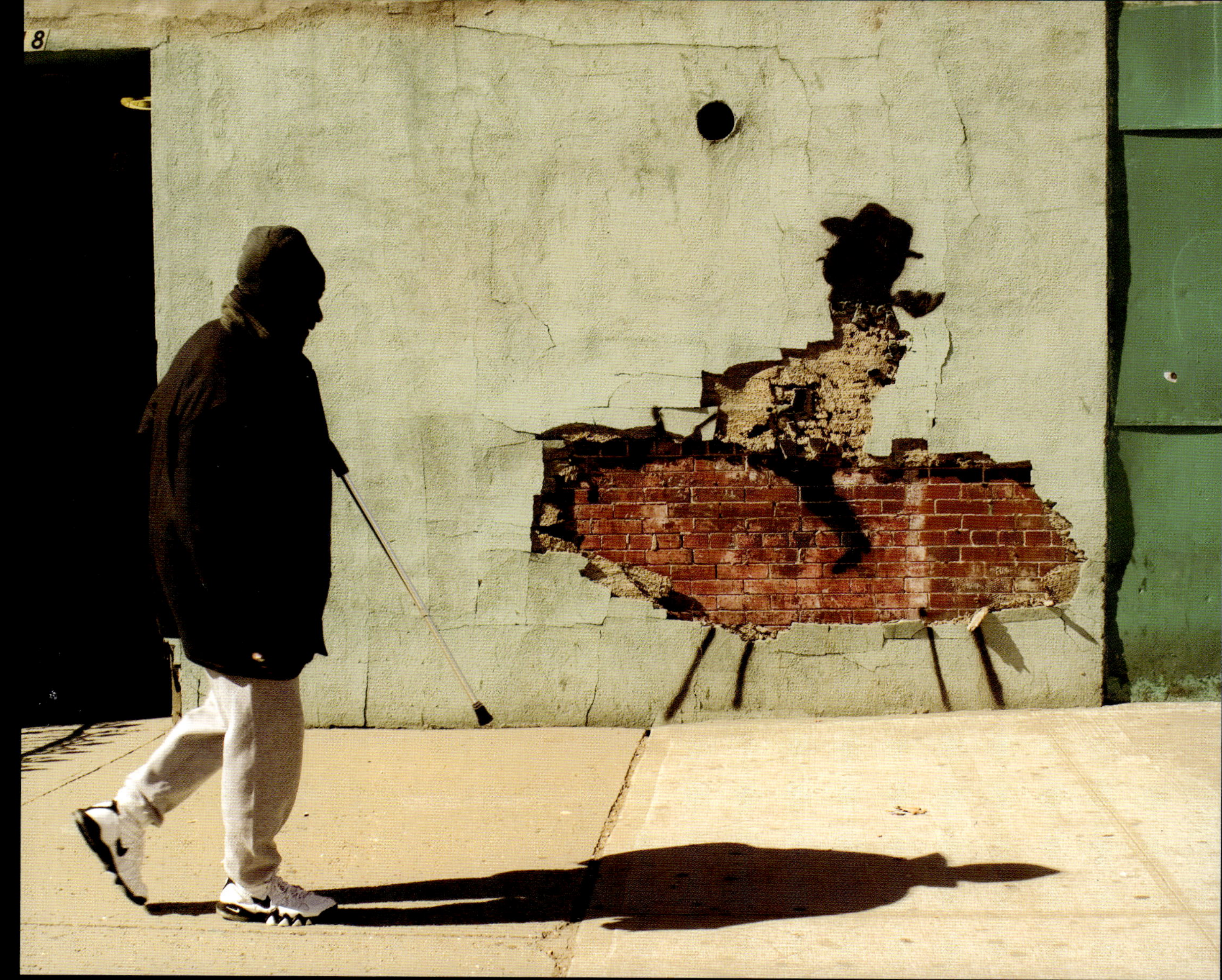

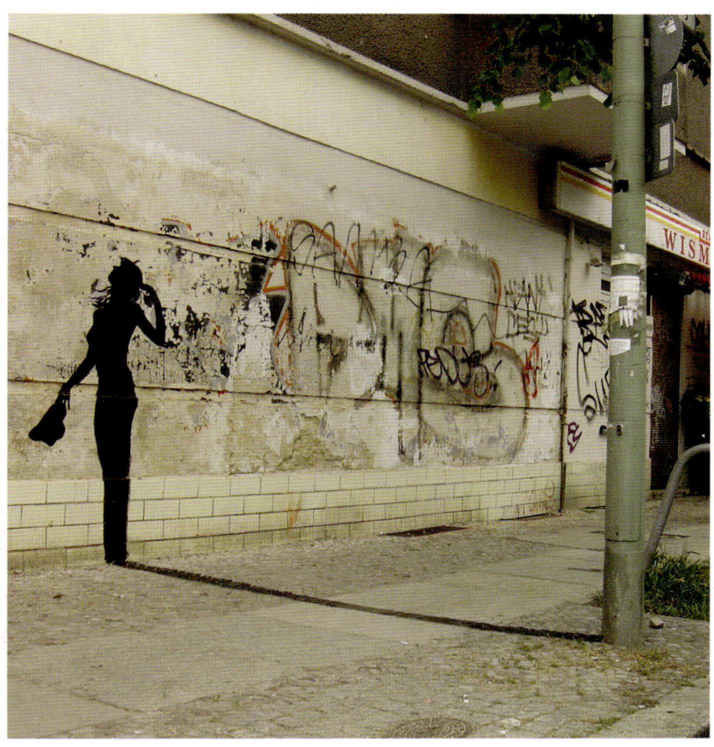
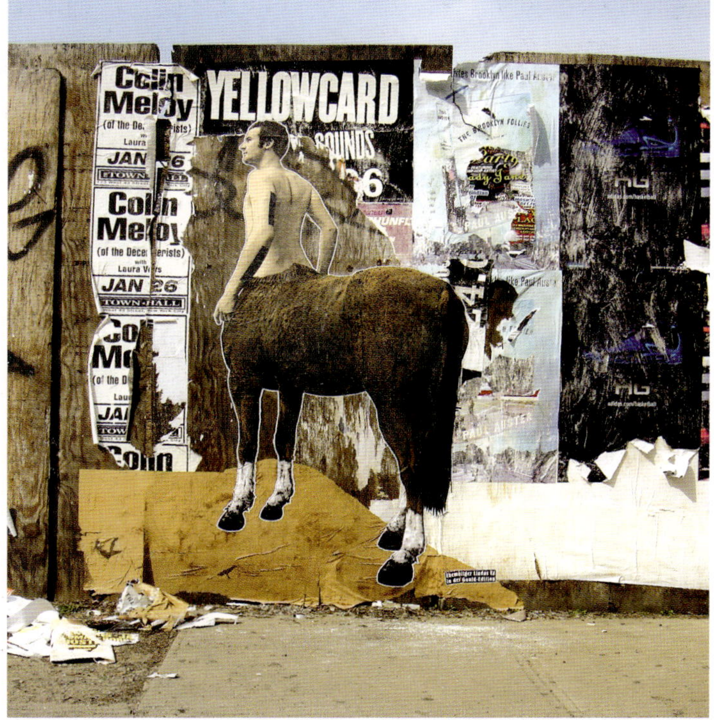

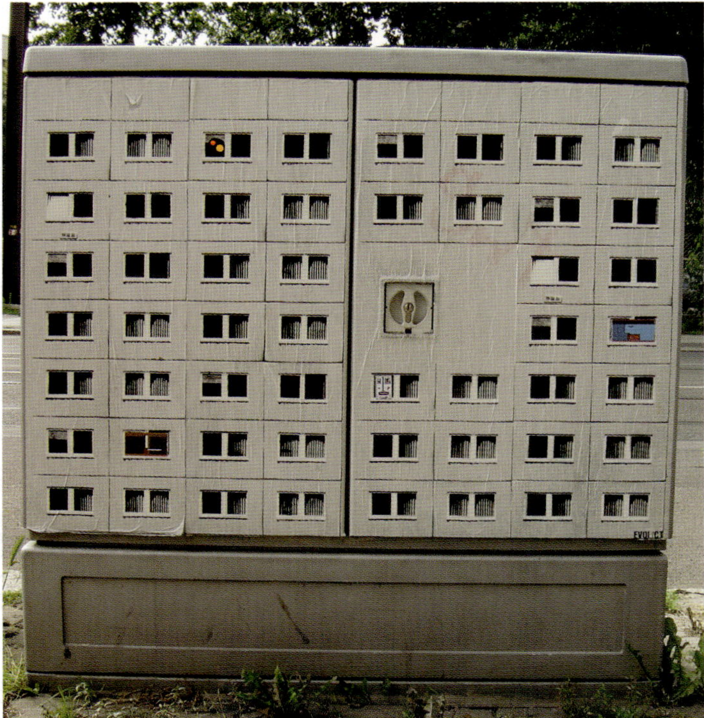
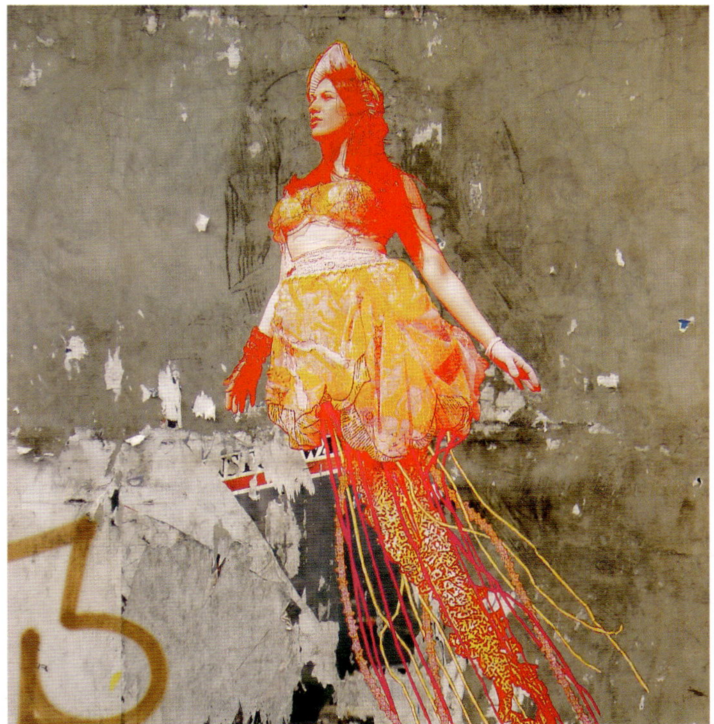

Clockwise: VARIOUS, Berlin 2006. GOULD, New York 2006. GOULD, Basel 2008. EVOL, Berlin 2004. All Photos: Antonia Schulz

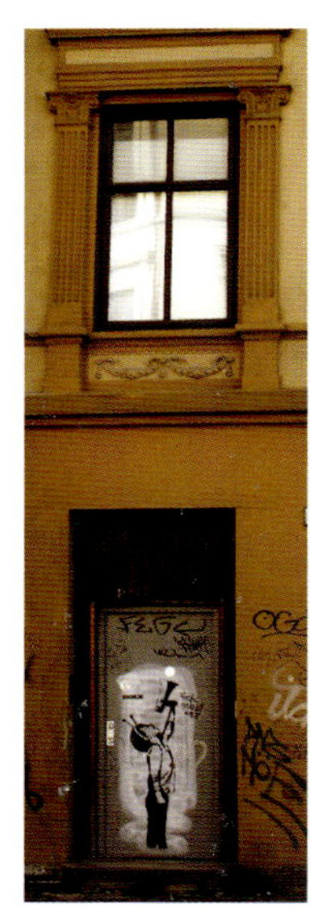

# You Can Try This At Home!

It's relatively safe. It's easy. You don't have to worry about pleasing a client or target audience. You get to experience the empowerment of being a cultural producer and the thrill of being an outlaw. You have moments and experiences that you would never otherwise have had. It grants you direct access to an audience without forcing you to package yourself as a product or prostrate yourself before the emperors of art and entertainment to beg for your fifteen minutes. It's fun! It's exciting. Do it! Do it tonight!

(Disclaimer – We Are not Speaking of Graffiti Here. What We Are Speaking About is A Secret. Shh.)

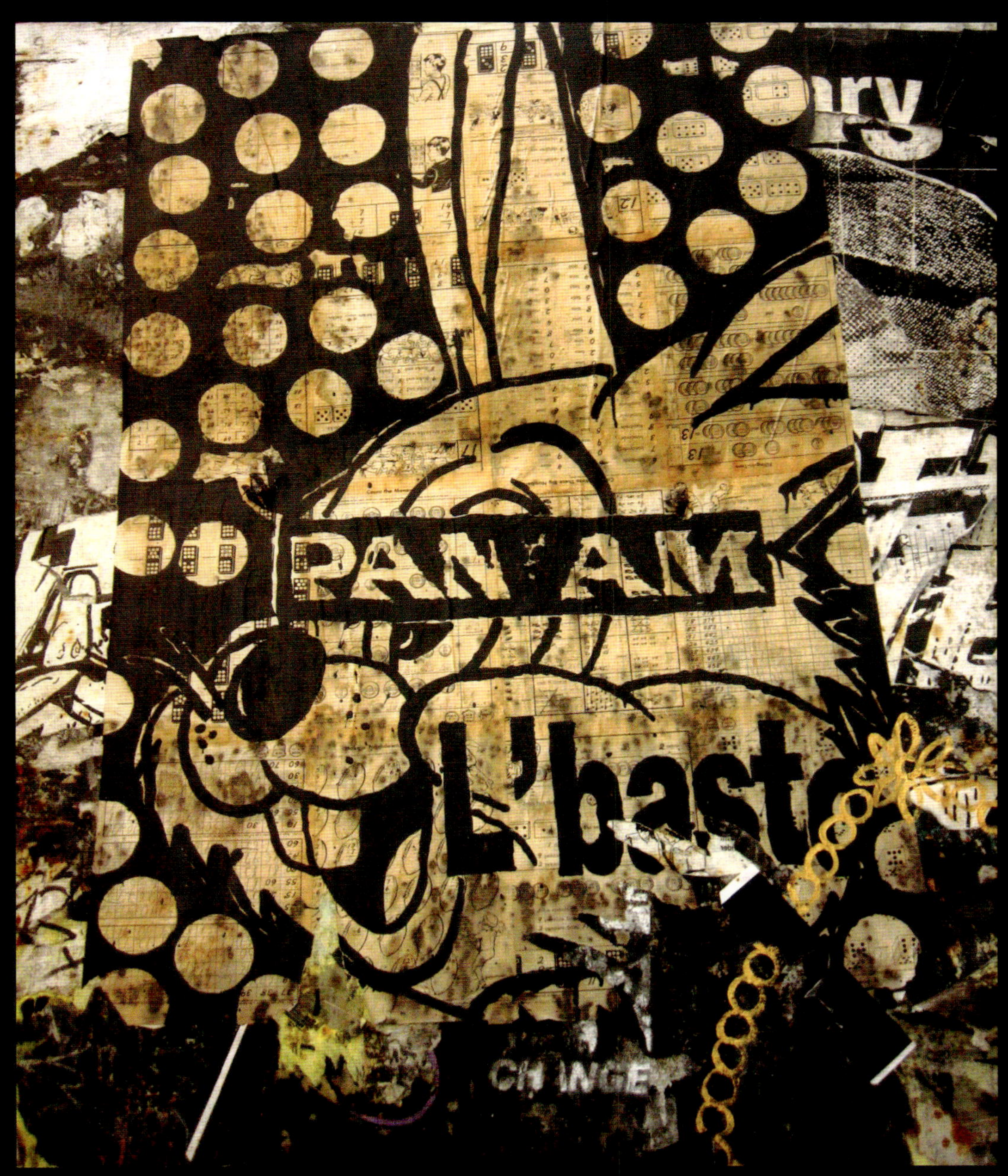
PAN AM
L'bast
CH NGE

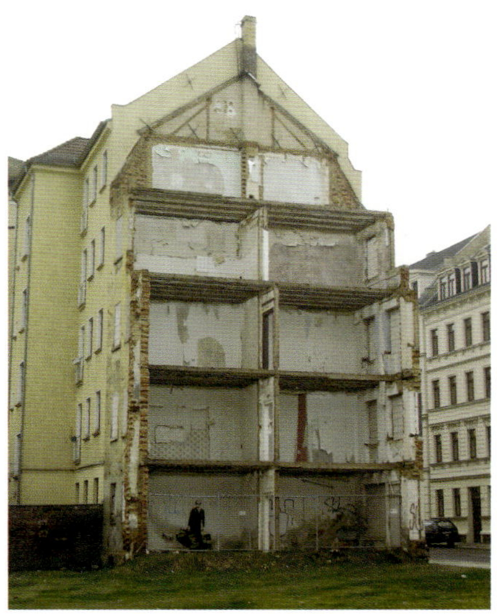



this masterpiece will self-destruct in...5...4...3...2...1

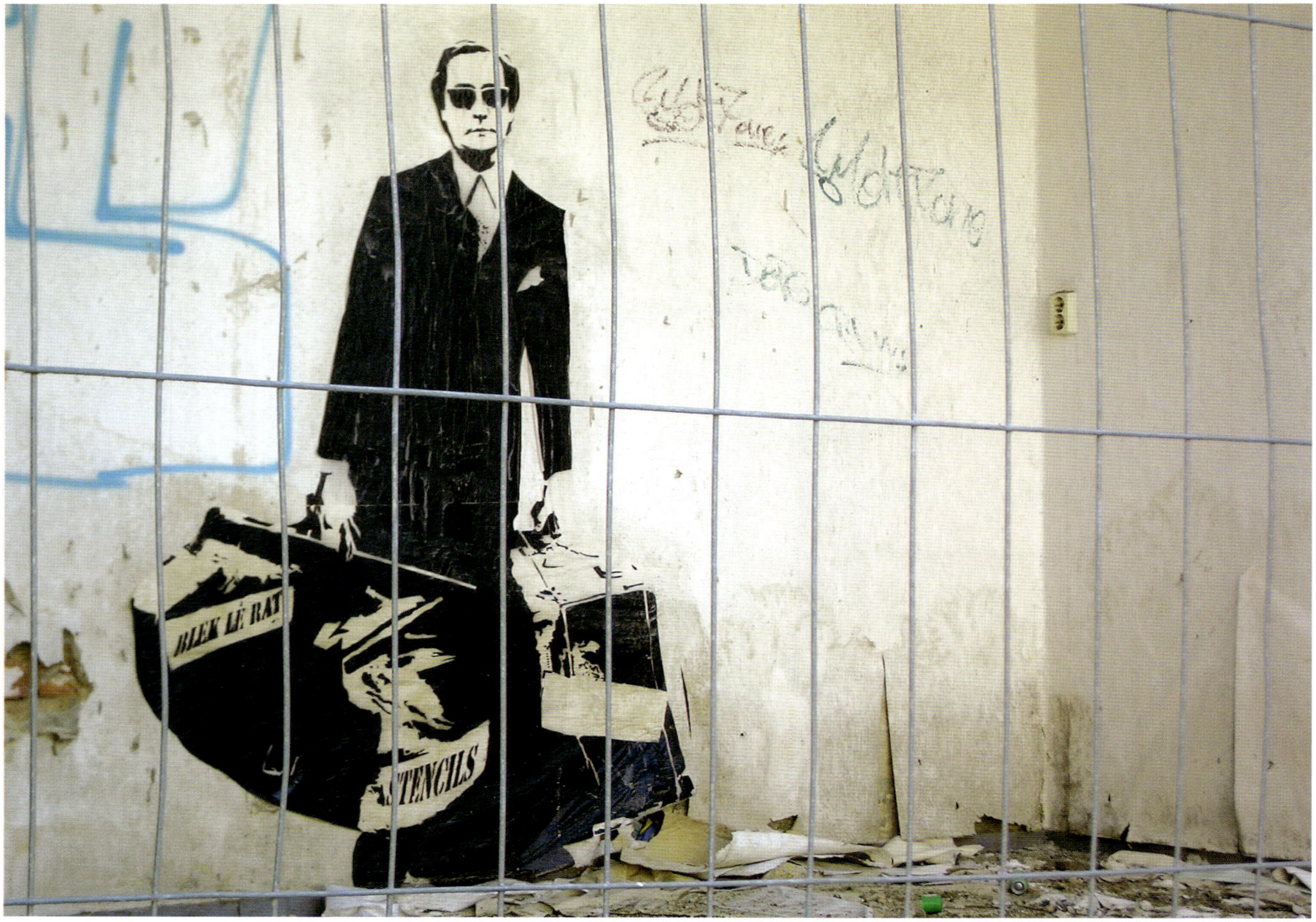

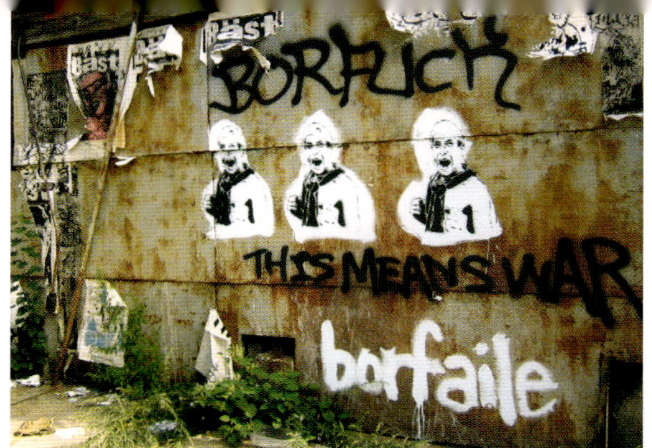
BORFUCK
THIS MEANS WAR
borfaile

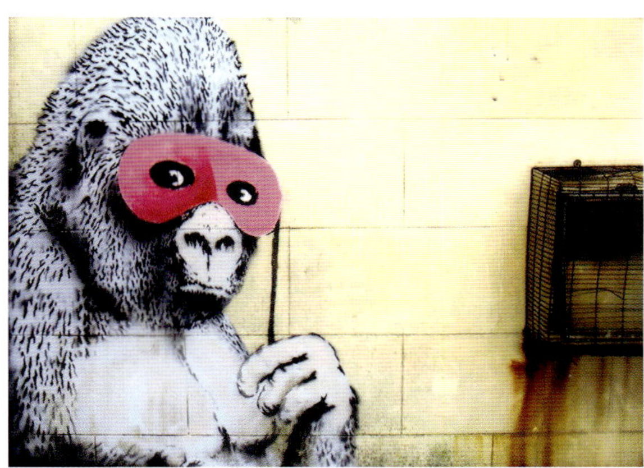

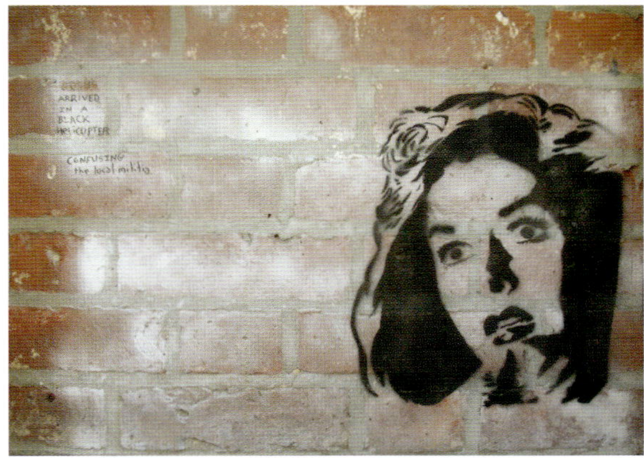
ARRIVED
IN A
BLACK
HELICOPTER

CONFUSING
the local militia

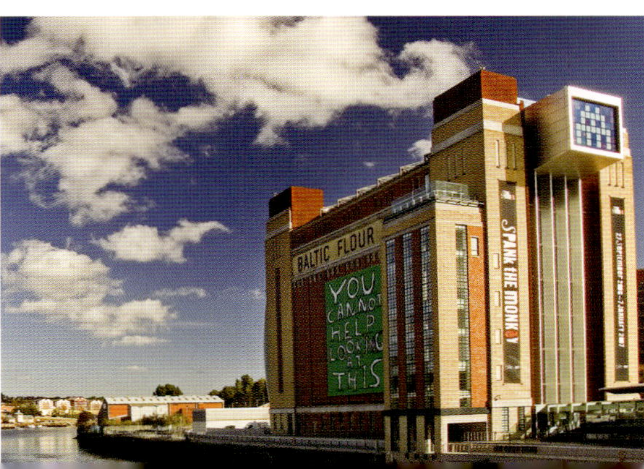
BALTIC FLOUR
SPANK THE MONKEY
YOU
CANNOT
HELP
LOOKING
AT
THIS

This one guy fitted up this paint dispenser to his car and just drove all the way up and down the country painting a rainbow in the middle of the road. They never got him. He's still out there now howling at the night. They say he's working on a crop duster plane.

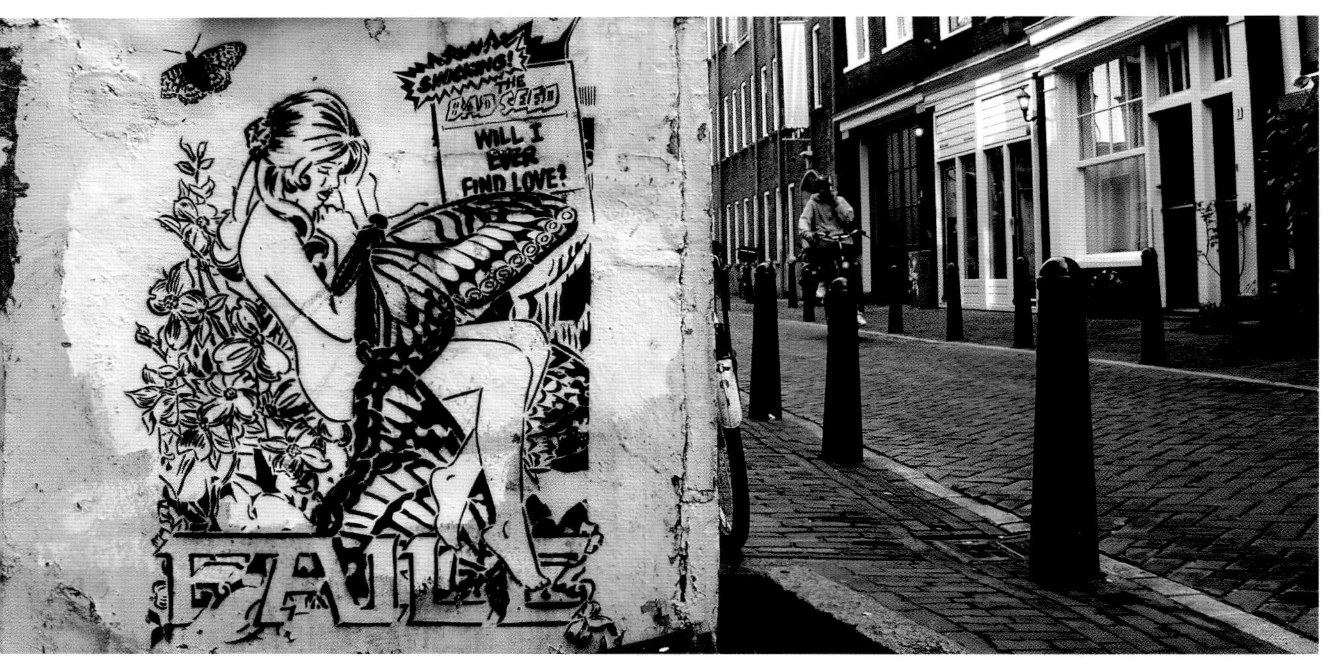

It's official. Street art is now flavour of the month for the bleeding edge man about town. Tens of thousands of kids queuing round the block for the latest release like it was the second coming of Pokemon. A marketing man's dream or just the law of supply and demand?

Will it all end in tears? Pensions stored away in the form of A3 pieces of deckled edged paper, signed from an edition of only 500?

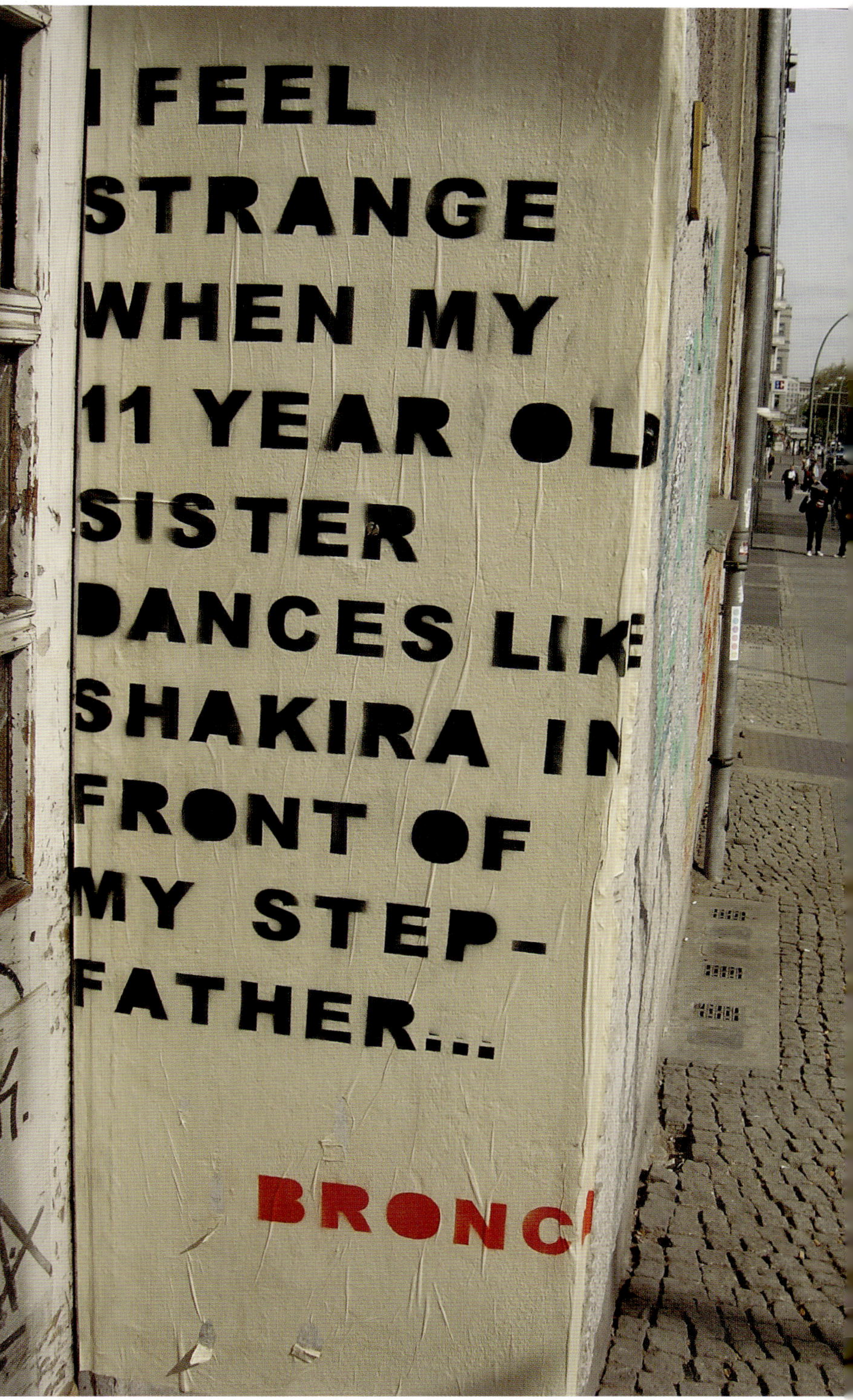


Artist: BRONCO, Berlin 2007; Photo: Antonia Schulz

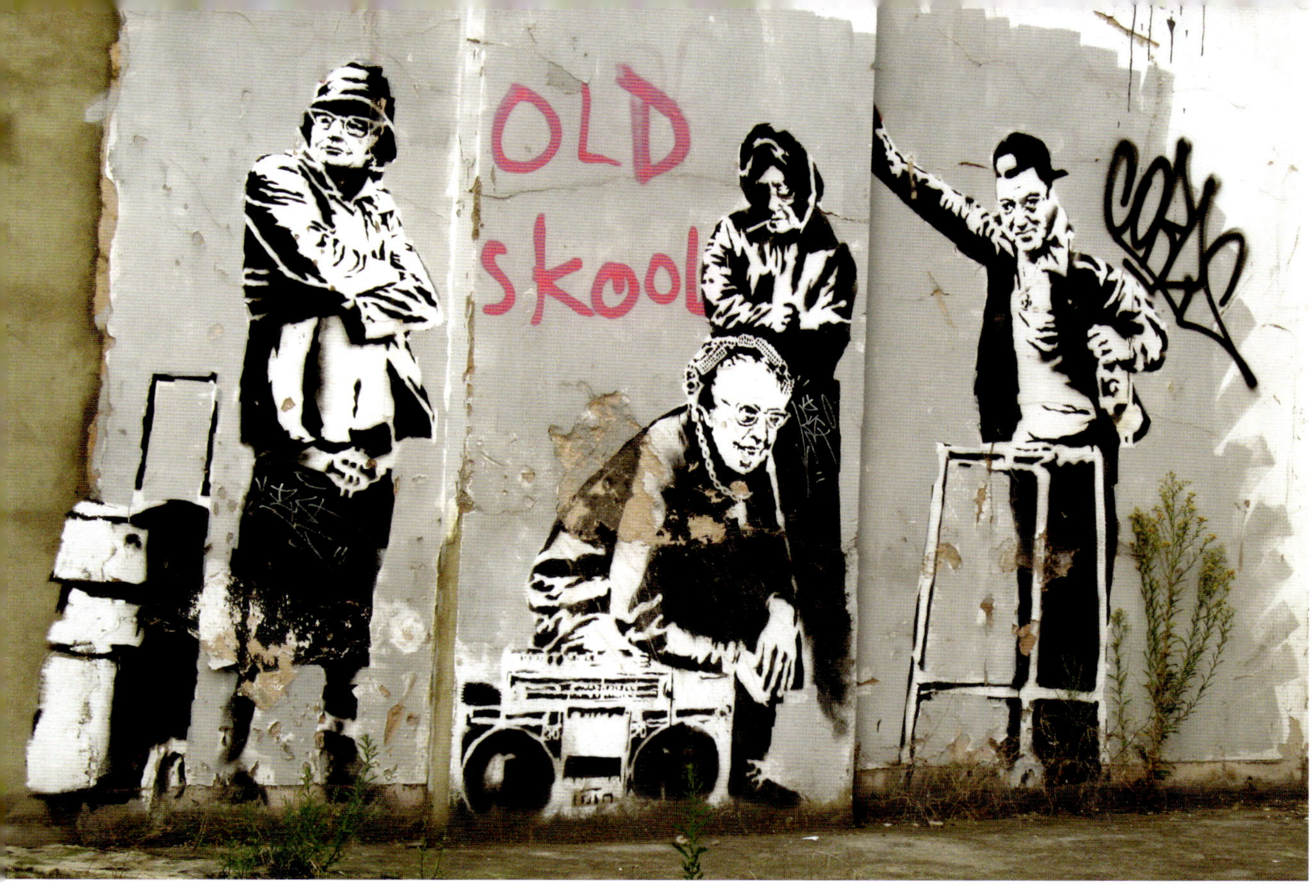

# End of Days

How long before graffiti disappears completely? Legions of guys just following all the graff artists around the globe chipping their shit off the wall and sticking it on eBay before the paint even dries? You'll just be seeing these chipped off bits of wall and saying "Sweet that was a Banksy." This is not actually happening. It could though. It sounds logical.

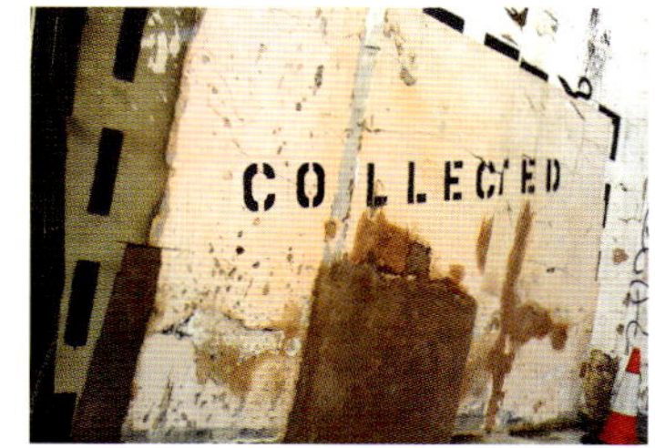

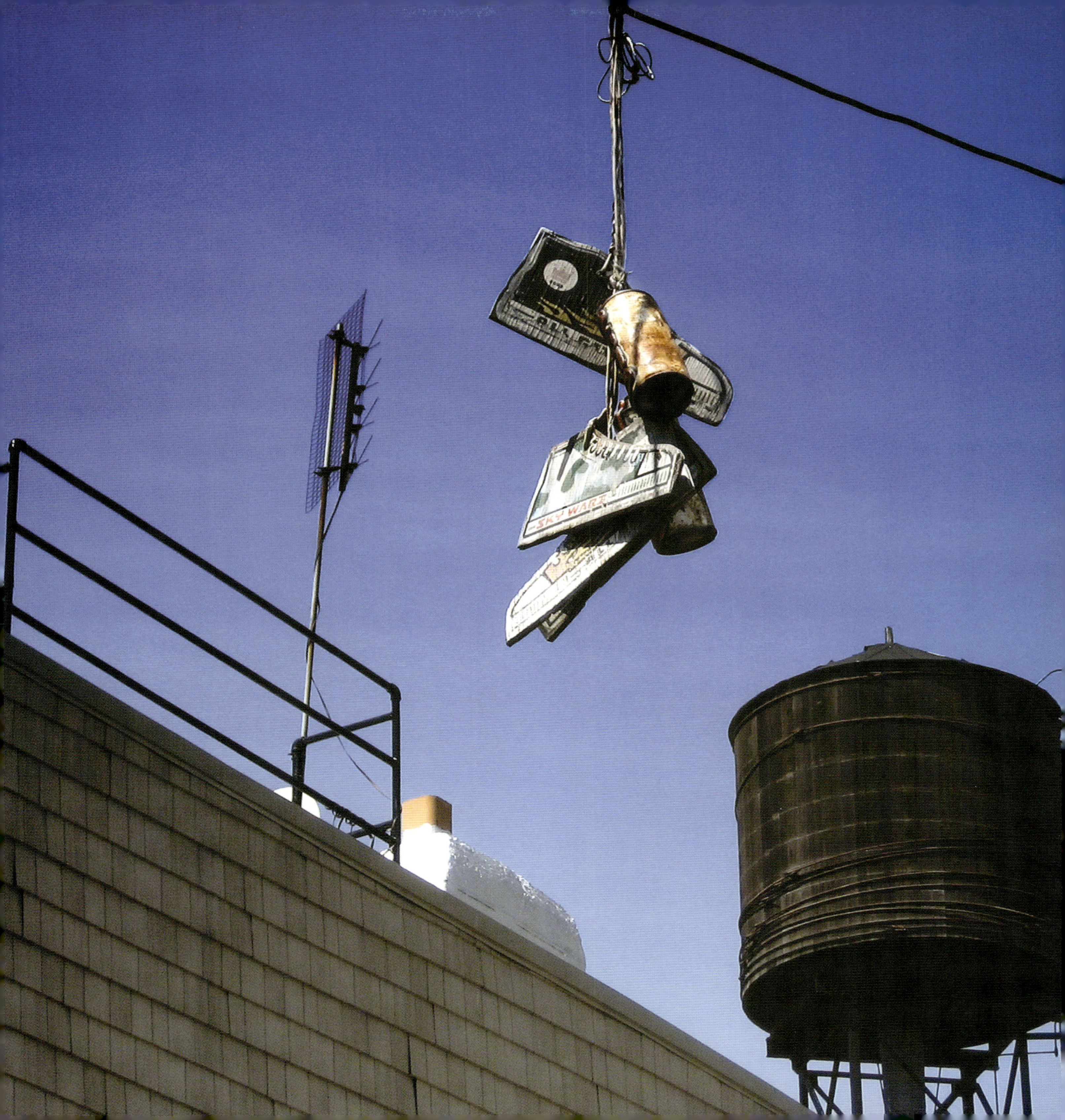

SKY WARS

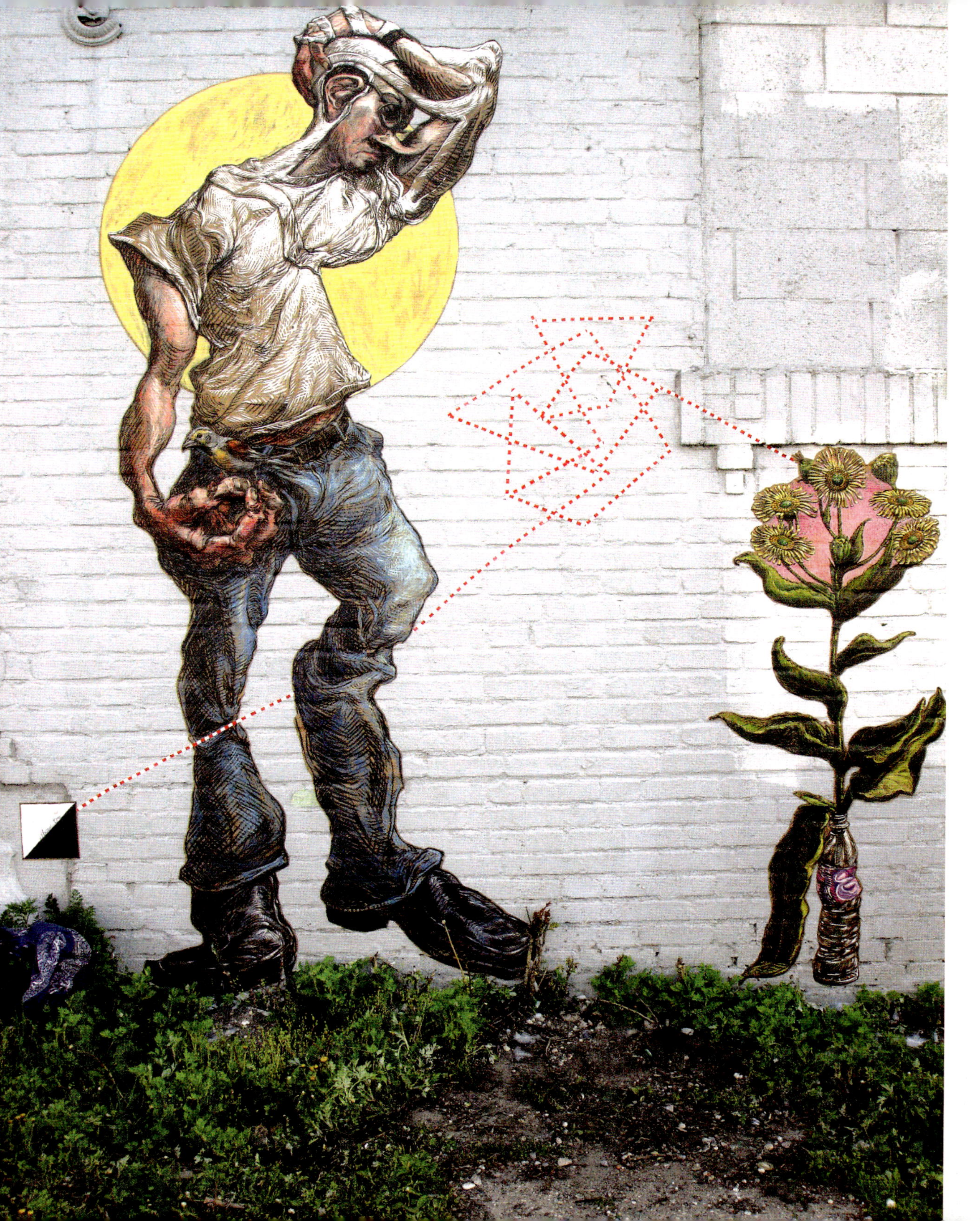

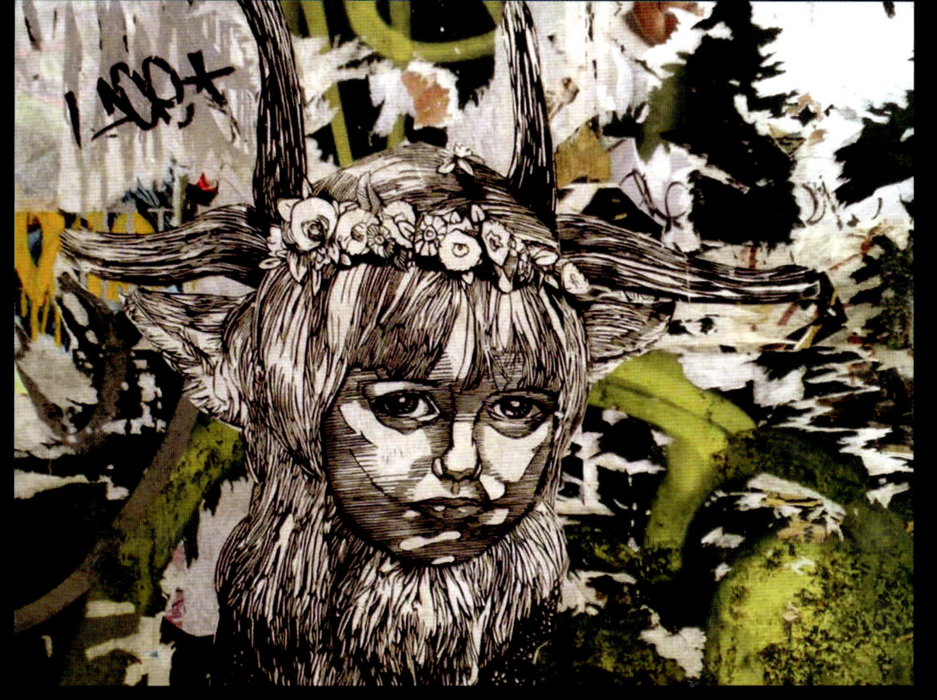


to the trained eye, museum pieces lurk everywhere

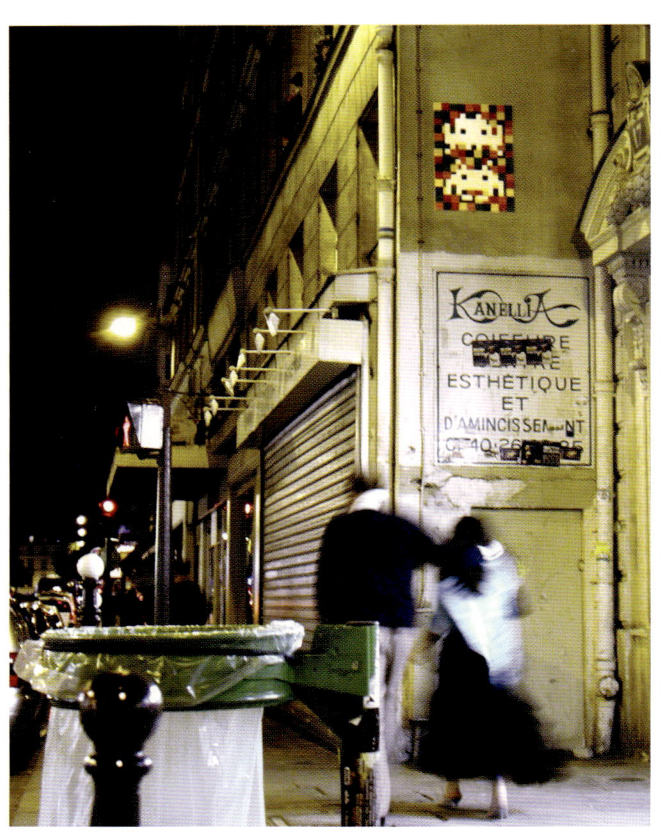


KANELLIA
COIFFURE
ESTHÉTIQUE
ET
D'AMINCISSEMENT

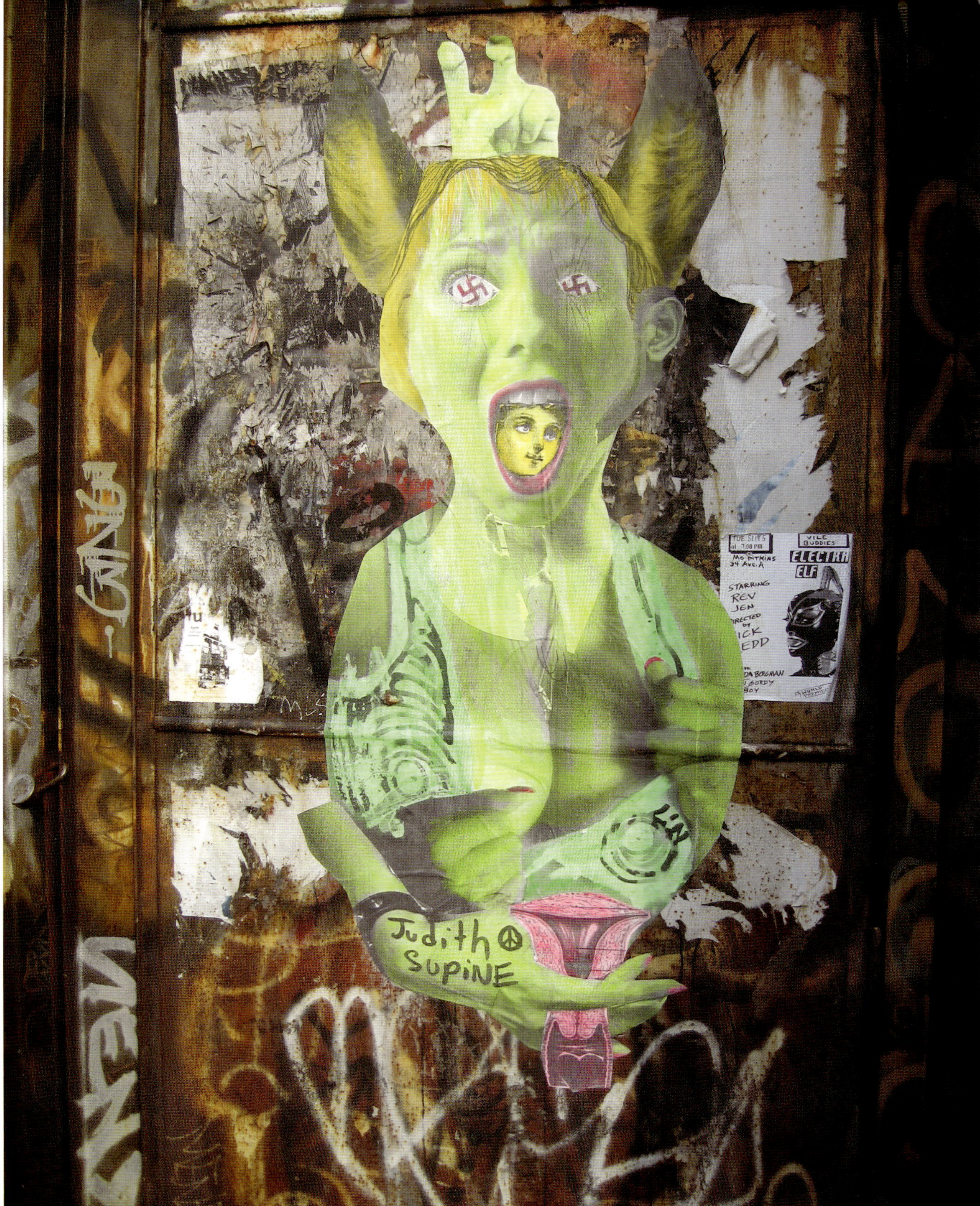
Judith
Supine

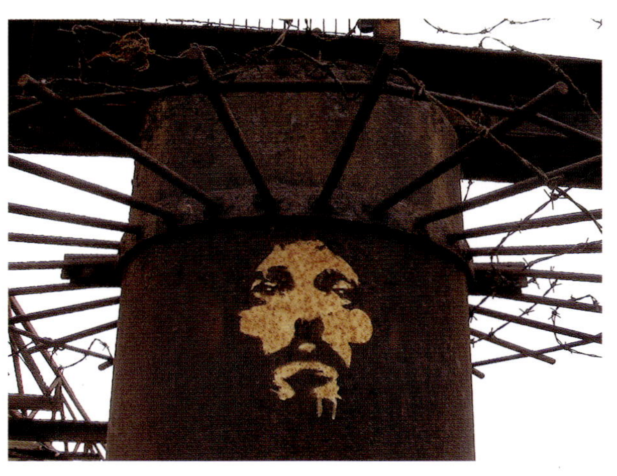

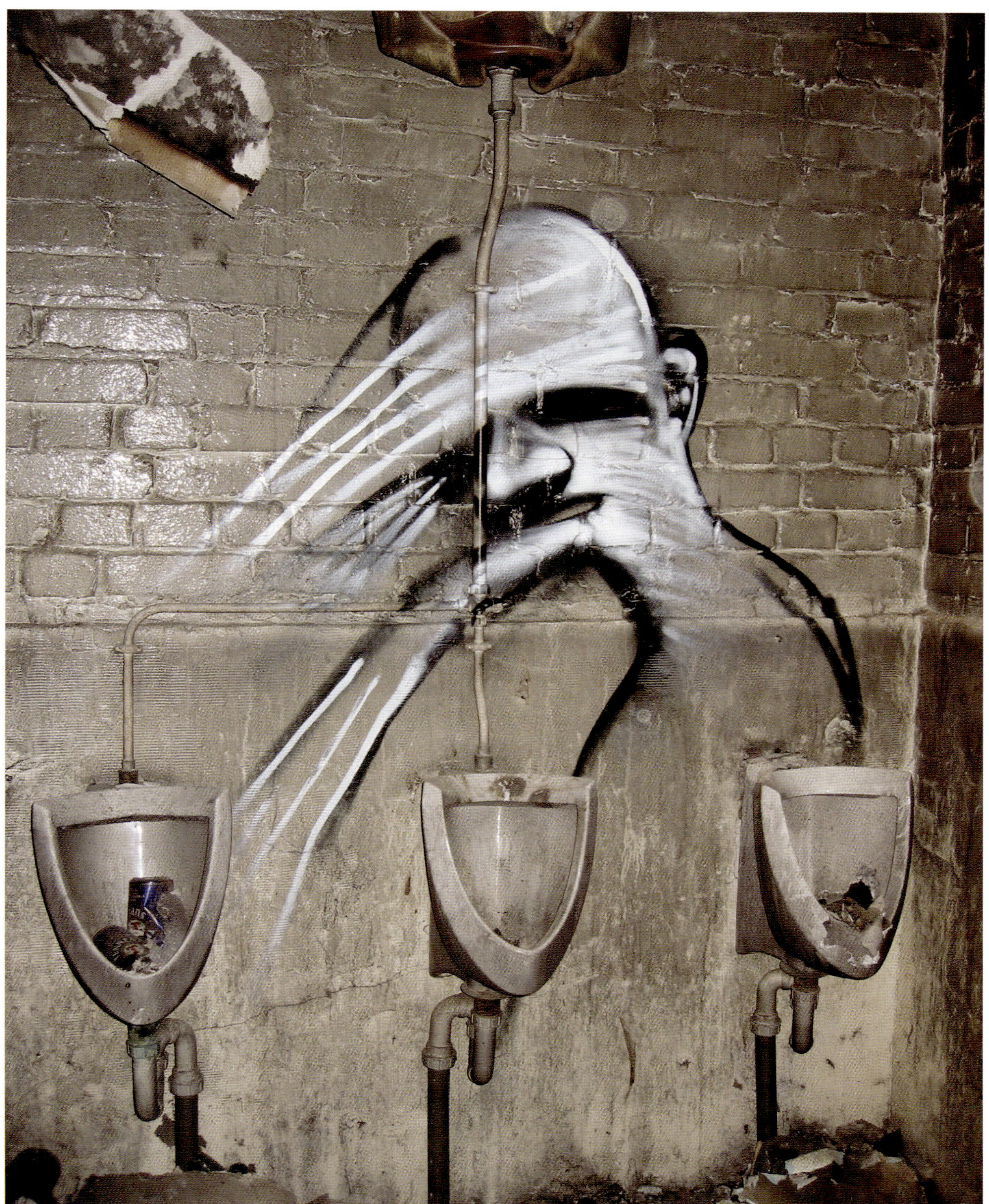

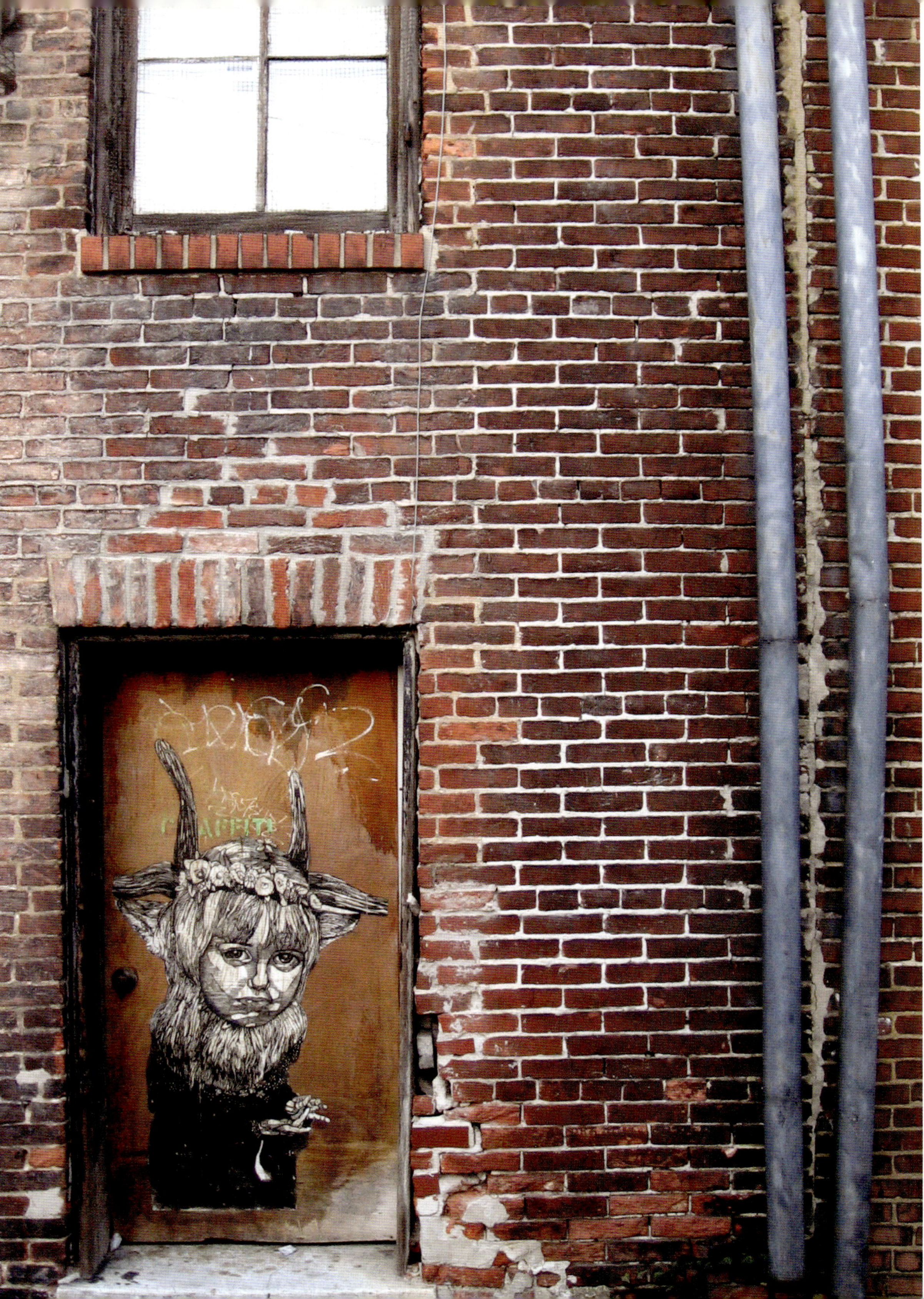

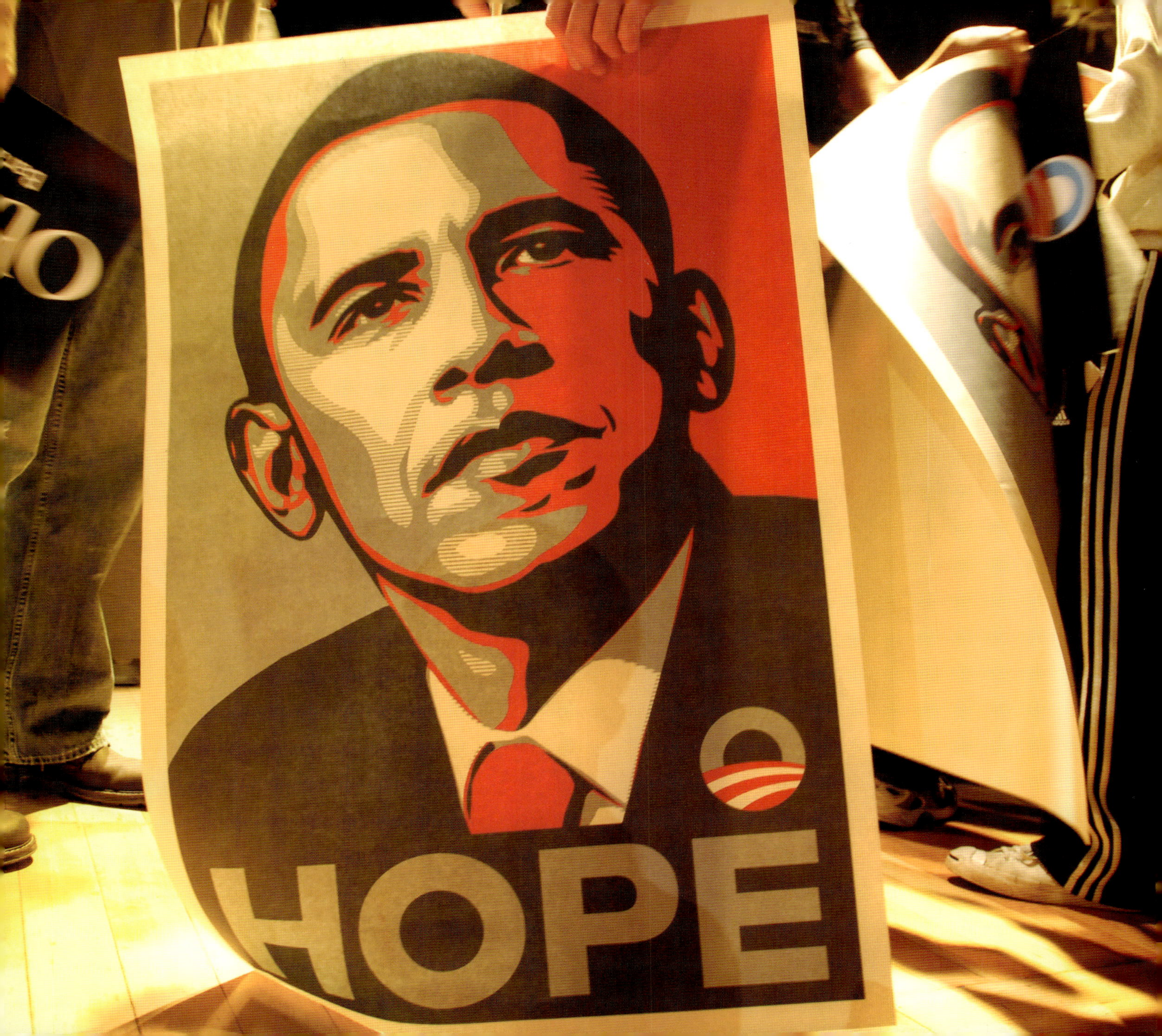
HOPE

# High coup

The thing about the built environments that we live in is this. We didn't build them. All the ideas that went into creating the plans and the buildings and the streets come from elsewhere. We were not at the planning meetings. How could we have been?

**Nobody really figured out that the city would become an environment in and of itself.** It just grew that way, and the field of architecture, for all its grand designs was always, really, just running to catch up with urban overpopulation. Those visionaries who tried to make our environment a thing where a whole life could be lived, they were undermined by conditions and circumstance, well that is to say – they were undermined by profit margins.

For these reasons the city came to remain an ugly environment (it always was) in spite of attempts to humanise it after the Second World War. So why not re-paint it? Why not let the people decorate their own living space? Well the simple answer is, because it does not belong to them. Apart from council property that is, in theory, communally owned such as the road itself or the street lamps.

(Well not all of it. Sometimes the bus shelters are paid for and built by private companies in exchange for the ad space. This even leads to shelters being built on dead bus routes).

The more complex answer is that no single rogue street artist can represent the whole community without some process of group decision making to determine what is welcome and what is not. This leads us to the horrendous question of government.

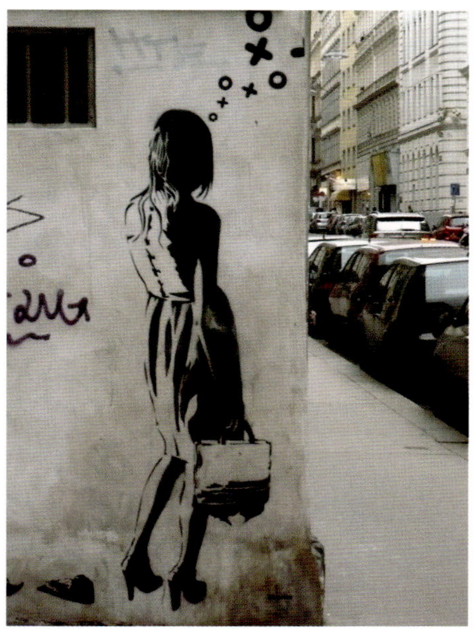

Who are the council? Have you ever seen these people? What do they actually do? Well the council are for one thing, the people who sell all the wall space to advertisers ensuring that you cannot turn your head a centimetre without being reminded that your life is not as good as it could be with product X on your side. They are also the people who whitewash over staggering works of street art and awful teenage scrawls without making any aesthetic differentiation between the two.

Truth about graffiti is that the people do make a choice. It is naturally democratic. If it ain't right it disappears. If people love it, it stays there. (If only as much could be said for the local government.) This is no romantic notion. We tested it. We put a haiku poem on an envelope label sticker and stuck it on the wall at platform eleven Clapham Junction. It went like this:

**Eyes out of window,**
**Revolution today,**
**Takes form of light rain.**

The station staff ripped down all the stickers advertising club nights and left the poem. It was there for four months. No word of a lie.

**Test it yourself.**

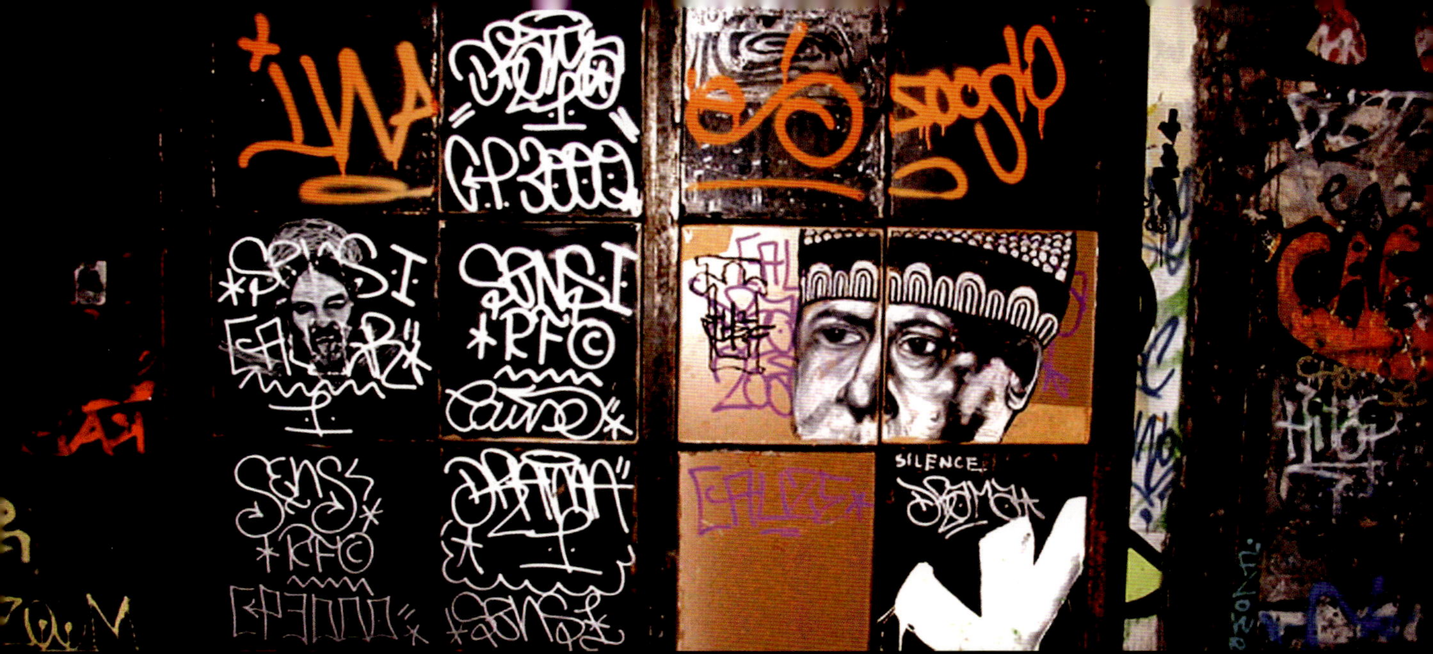

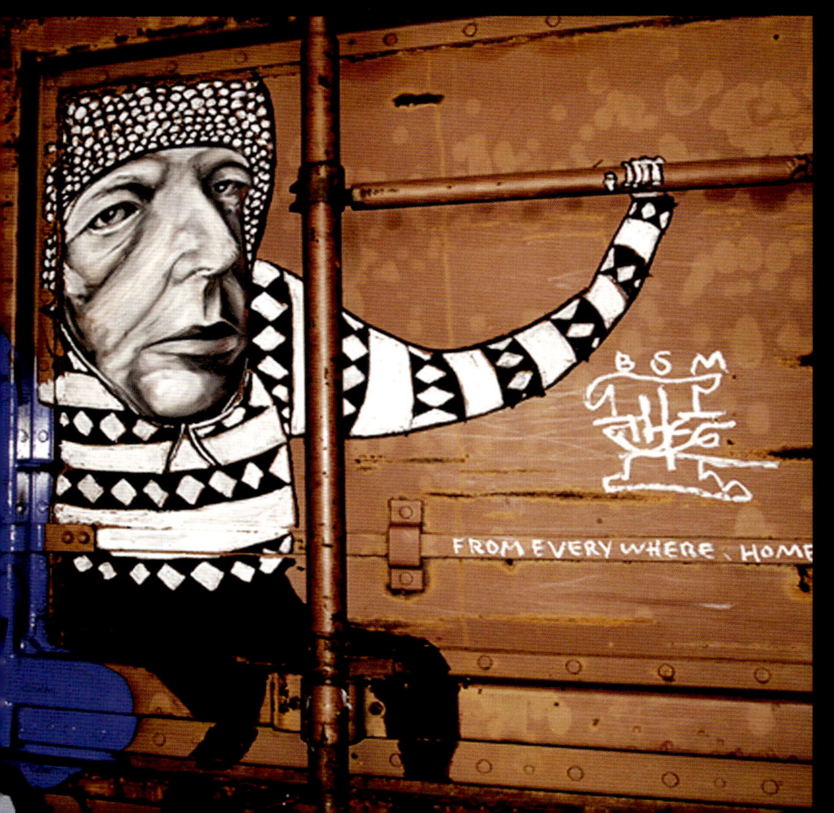
BSM
FROM EVERY WHERE, HOME
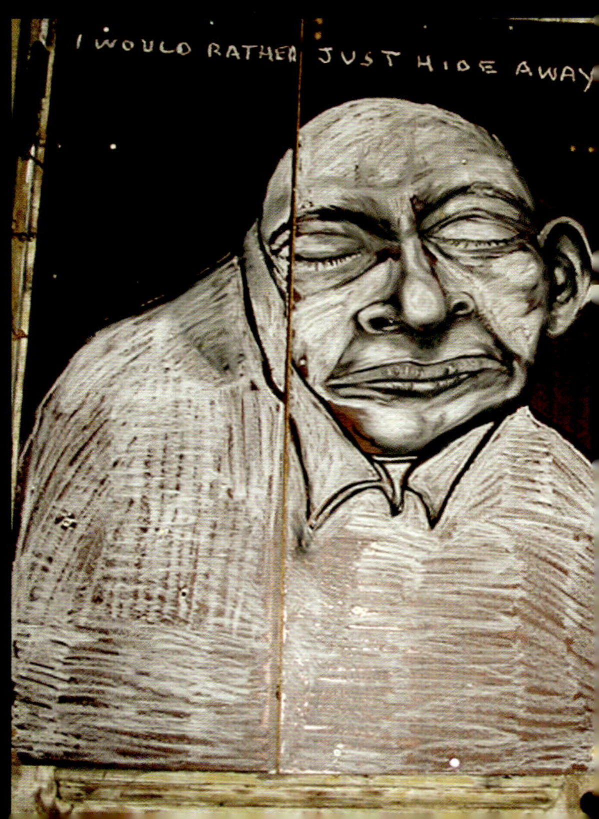
I WOULD RATHER JUST HIDE AWAY

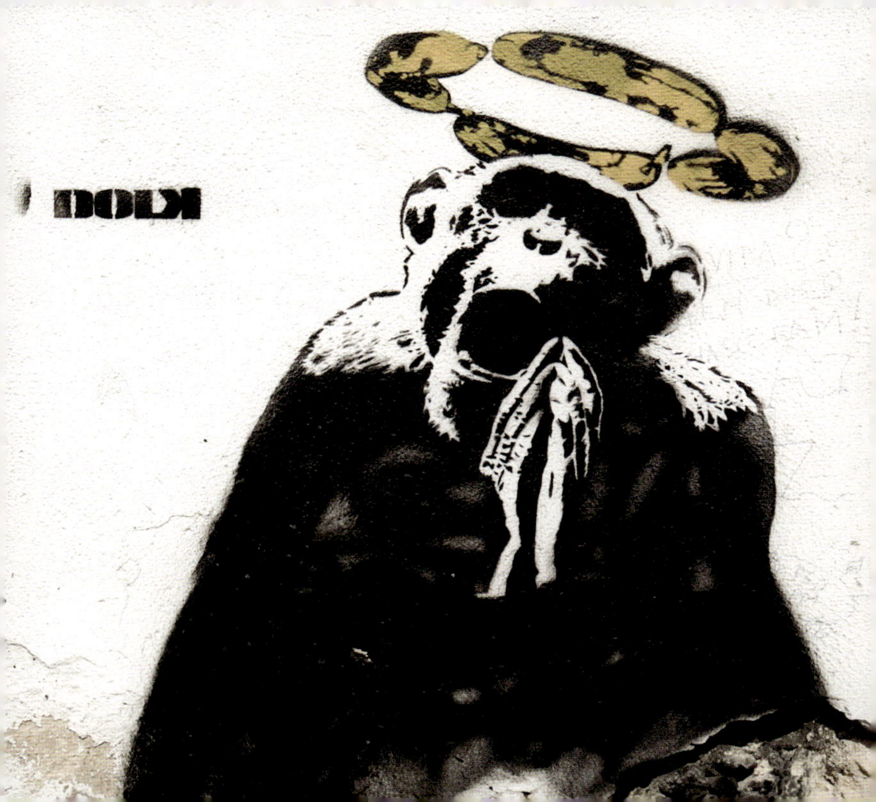
DOLK

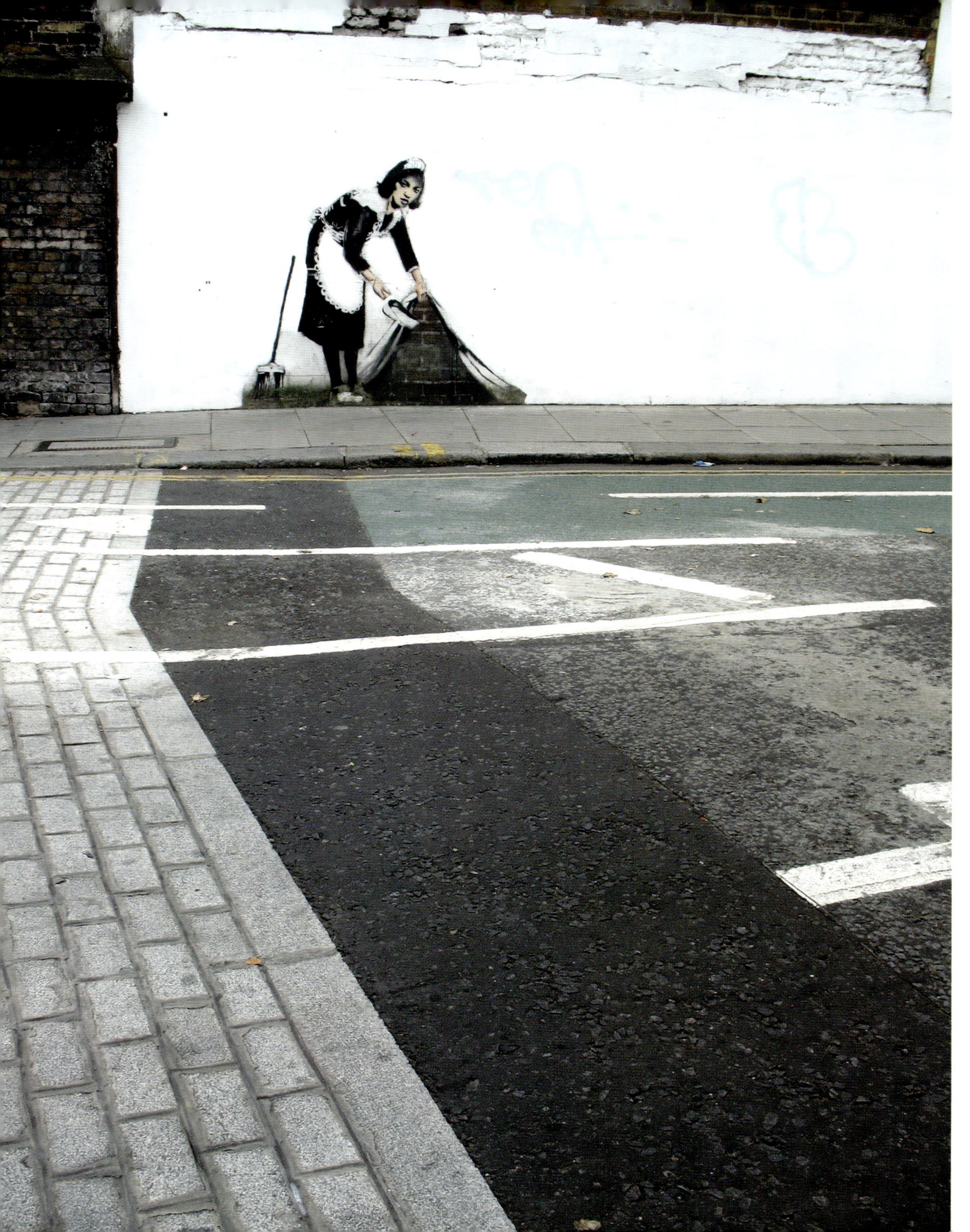

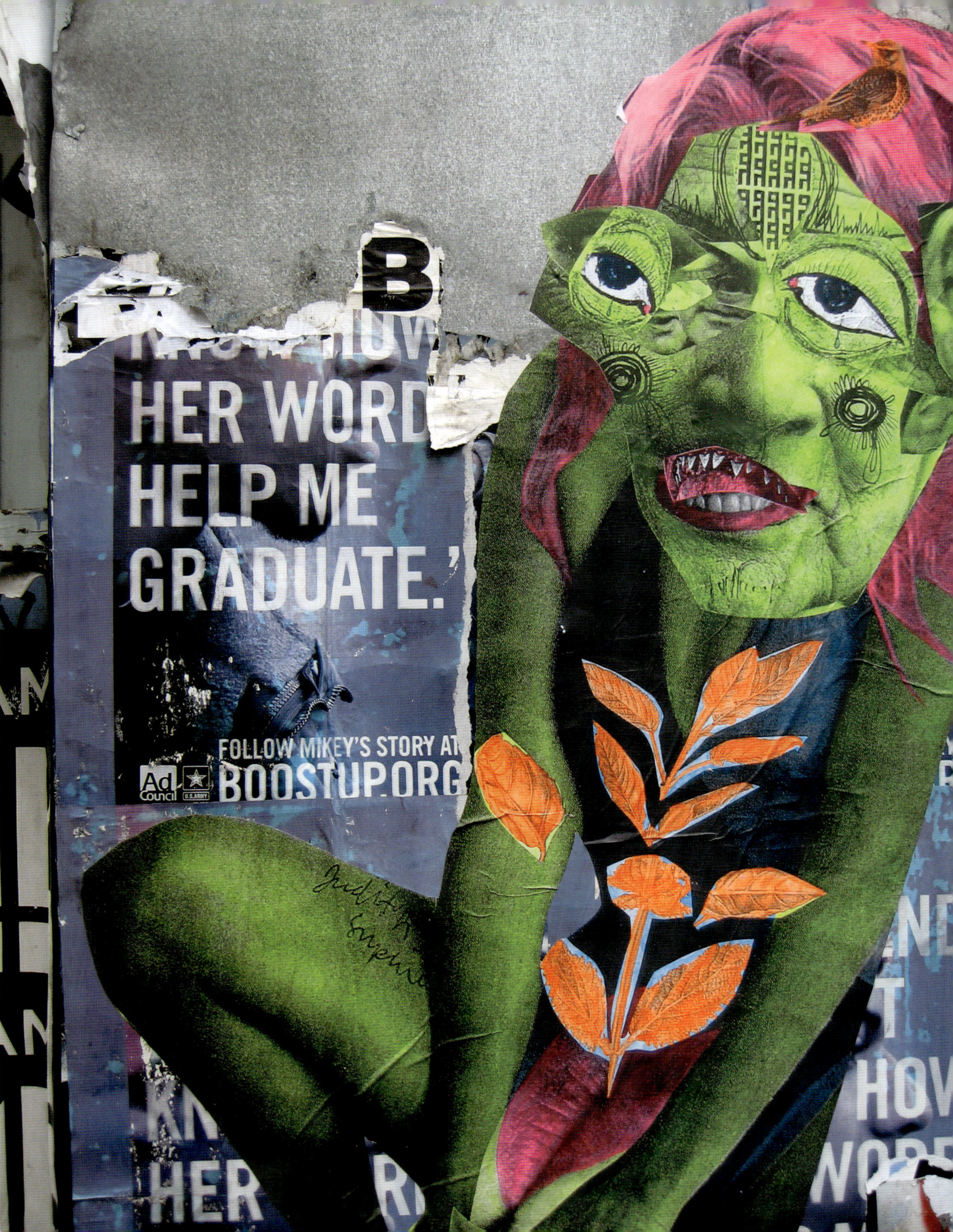
B
HER WORD
HELP ME
GRADUATE.'
FOLLOW MIKEY'S STORY AT
BOOSTUP.ORG
Ad Council
HER

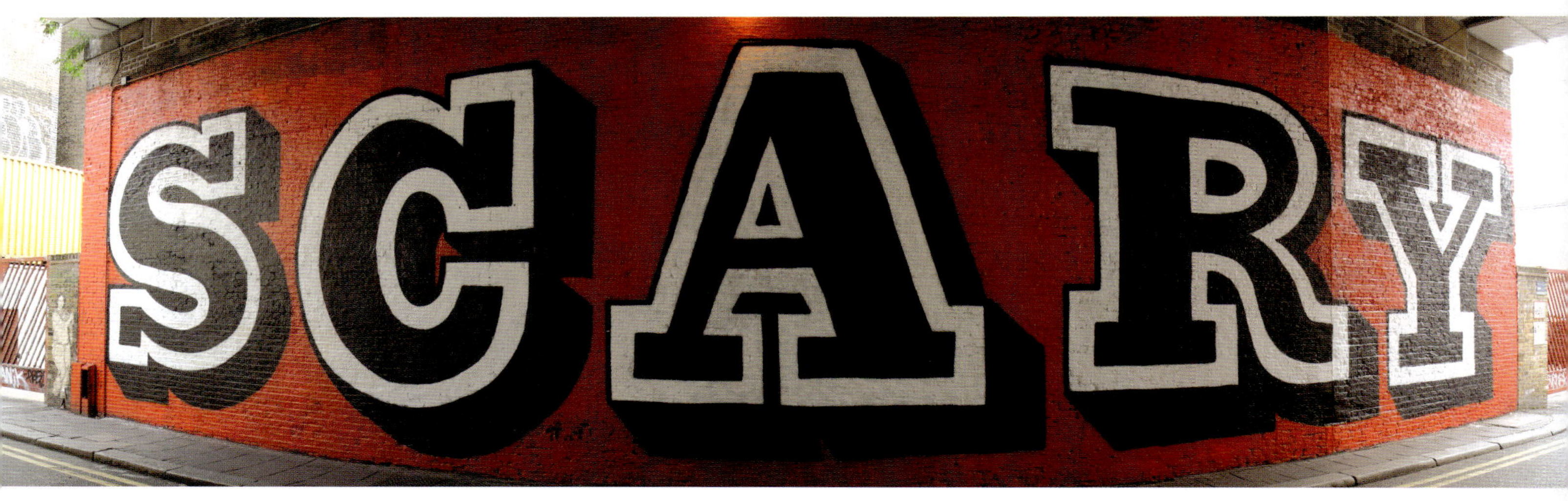

SCARY

"This is absolutely the most fascinating time we could possibly have hoped to be alive. So whatever you do don't be bored."

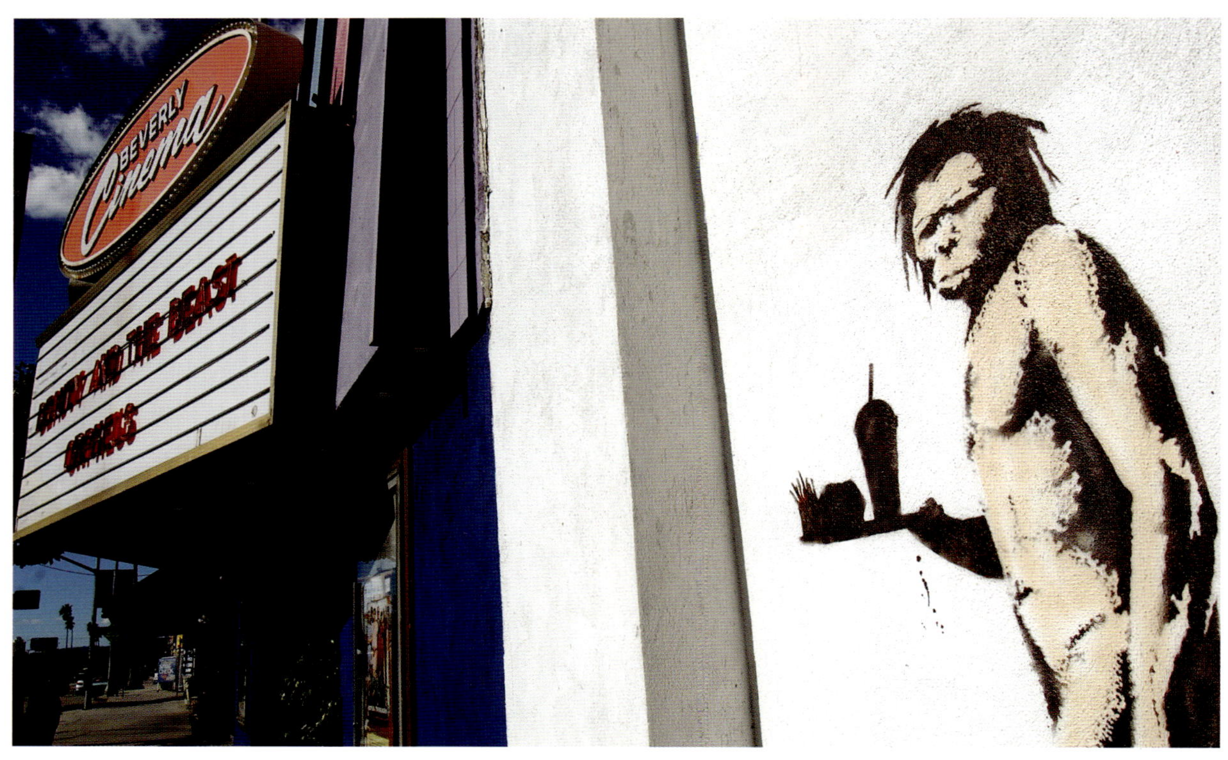


The city is more vivid when you speak to it.

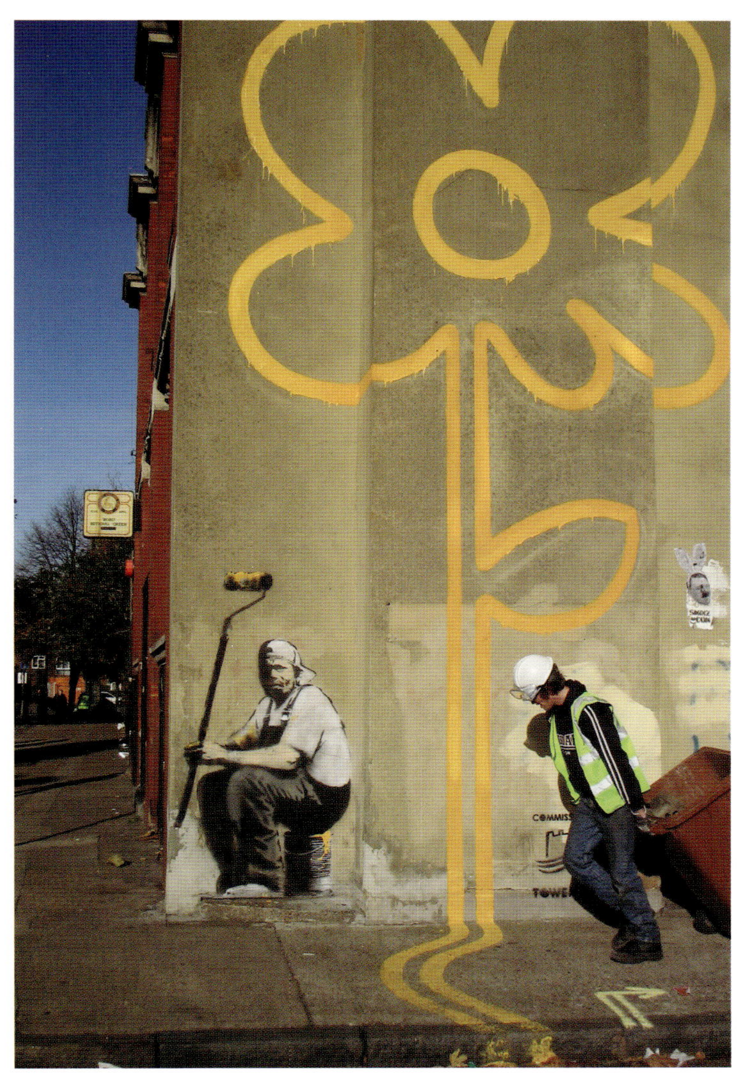

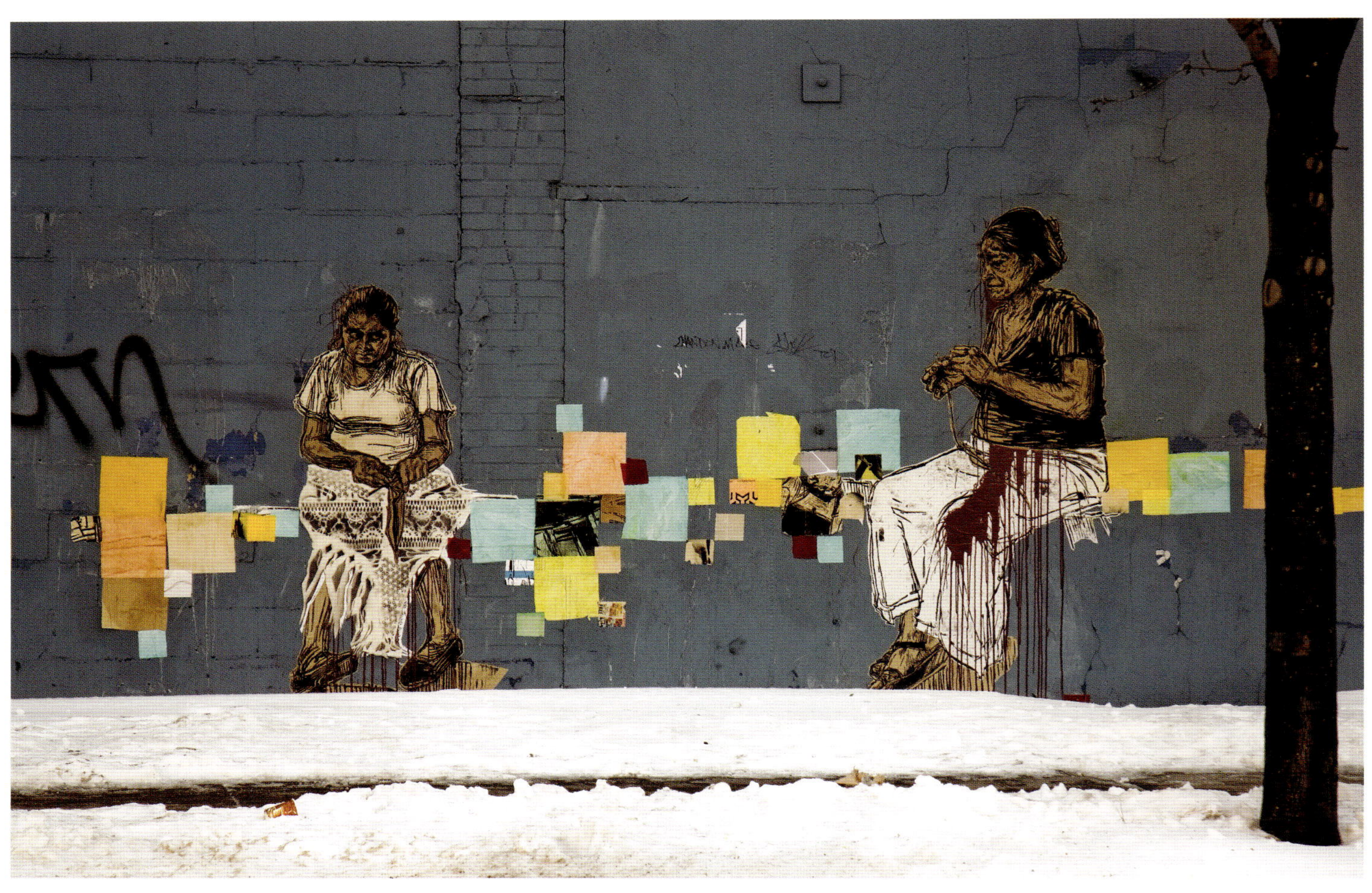

Avant-Garde: Advance scouts for capital

Several students from an inner city primary school were arrested yesterday in connection with a series of vandalism cases. The local community was shocked to discover that a gang of five and six year olds were being held for questioning. Local police stood by the arrests and highlighted the strong evidence against the youths. The graffiti in question consisted largely of pictures of a house with mummy and daddy and a dog outside of it and a large sun depicted with rays coming from it. Materials used were water based glue, dried pasta, glitter and some pipe cleaners. Police suspect that a stylised image of the sun with a smiley face may well be the gang insignia. The investigation continues.

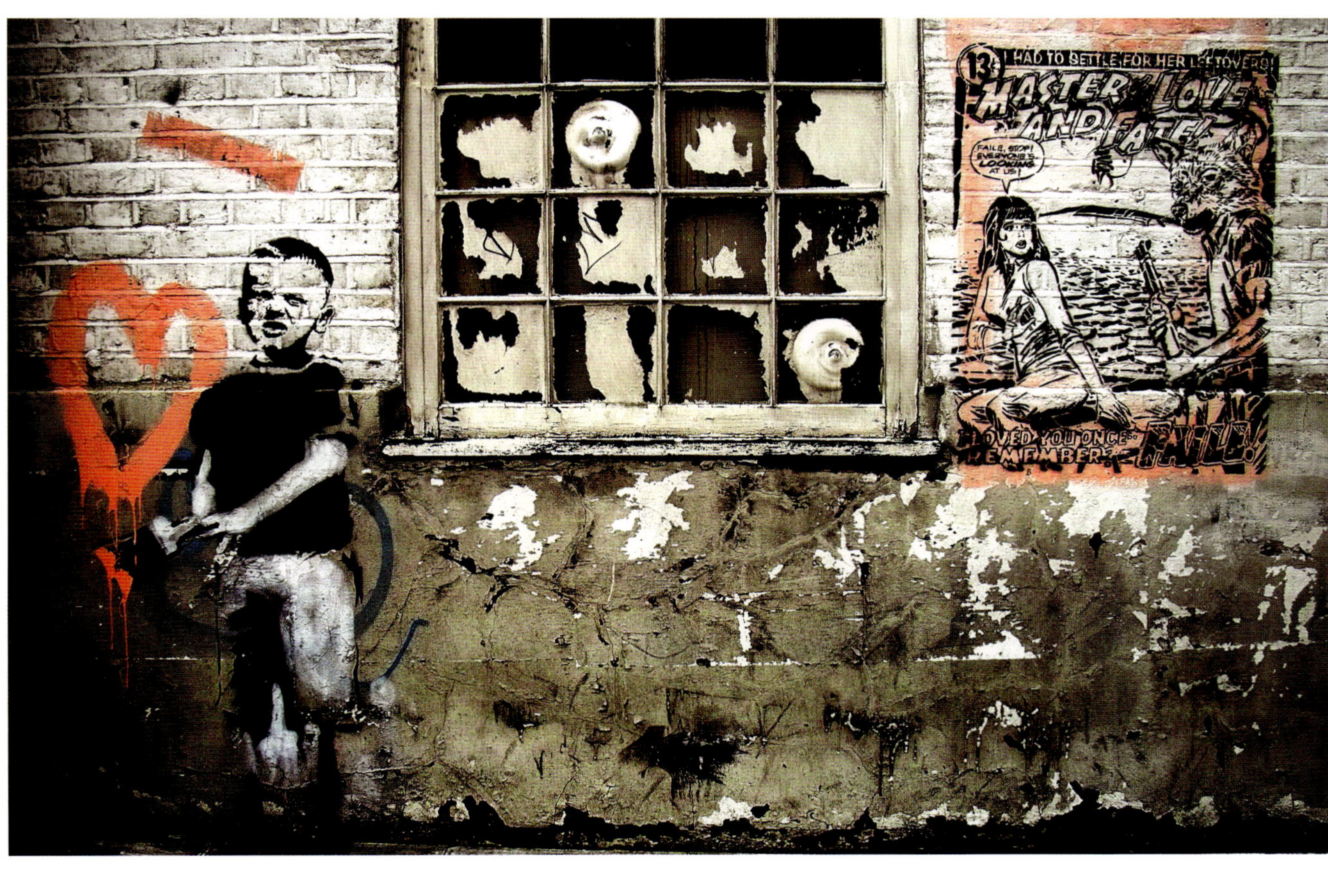

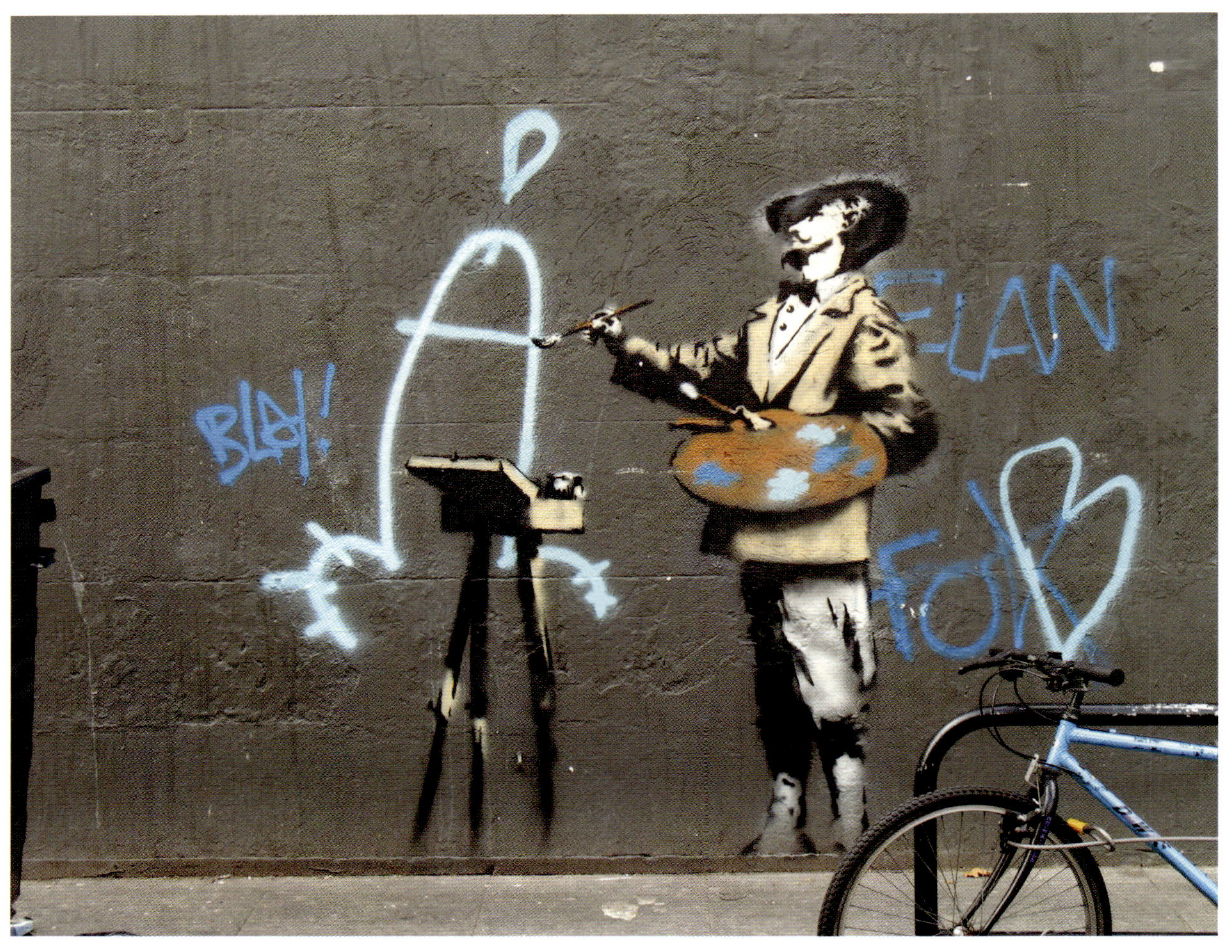

If you were lying in the gutter dying, one can of spray paint in your hand, watching your own blood spill out on to the road. If you had one last chance to paint the piece that let god know just exactly what you think of this little life of his; what would you paint? Because that's the kind of graffiti that saves people.

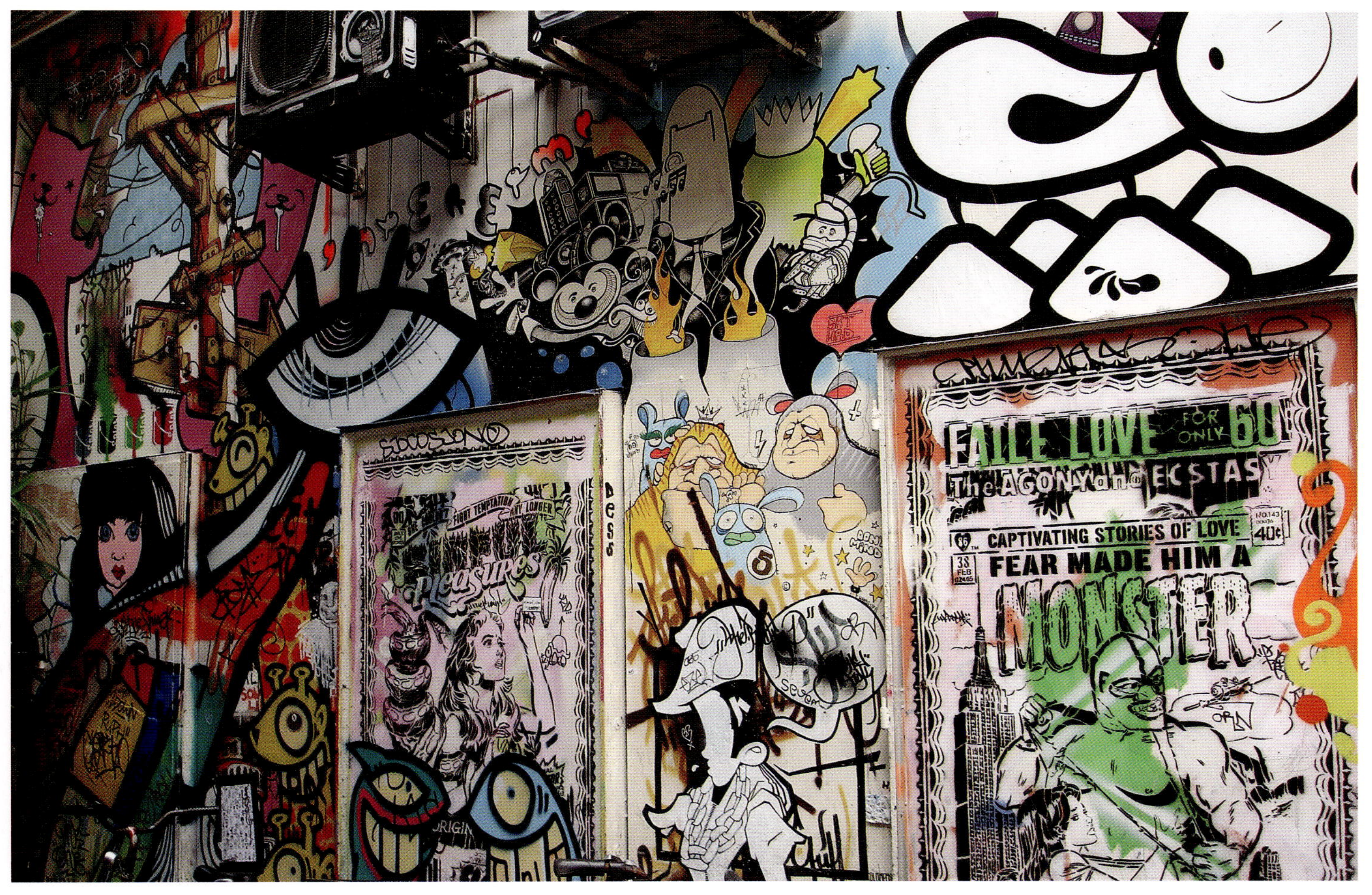

## If I shit on a plate is that art?

I could do that. My five year old daughter could do that. My senile great grandmother could have done that. My dog could do that. My 17 year old toothless mangy old cat could do that. A dying beetle could do that. A swarm of malignant hornets could have done that in a passing indignant rage. A 1982 home computer attached to a rabid monkey holding a bunch of rusty keys could do that. A feeling of uncertainty, engendered by a bruised sky on a long walk home, after one has received news of the return of a long departed friend from a distant foreign war could have done that. I could have done it. Actually, hang on, I think that was me. Yeah sorry, that is one of mine.

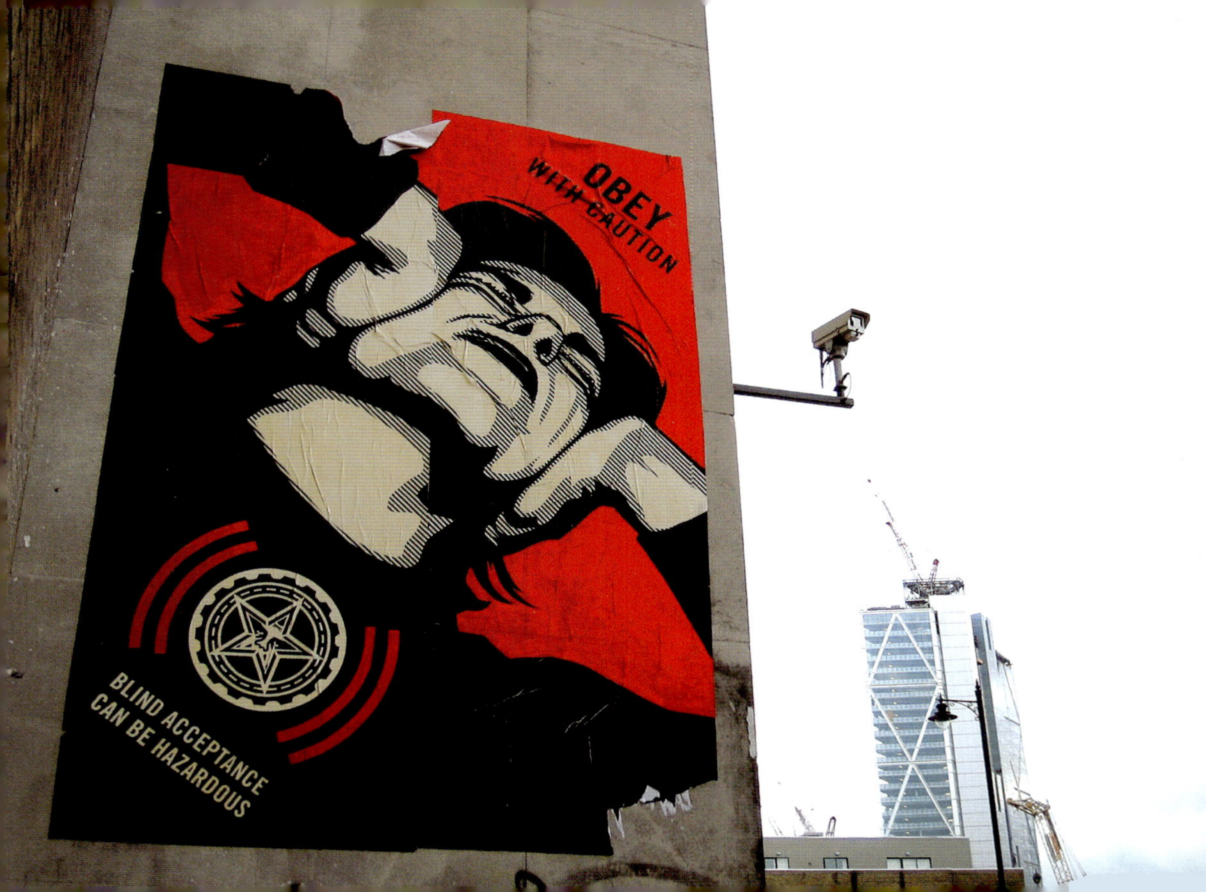

OBEY
WITH CAUTION
BLIND ACCEPTANCE
CAN BE HAZARDOUS

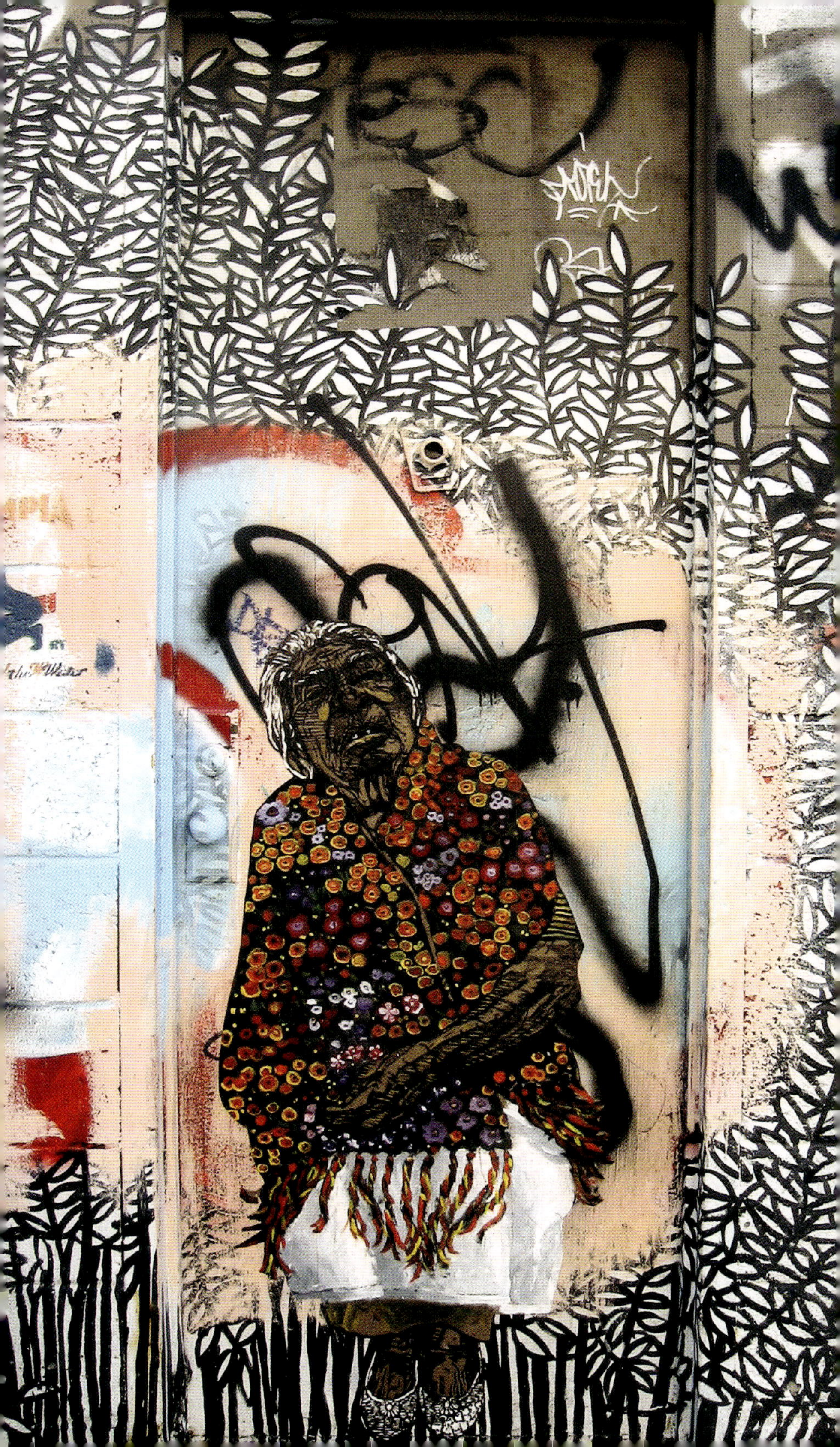

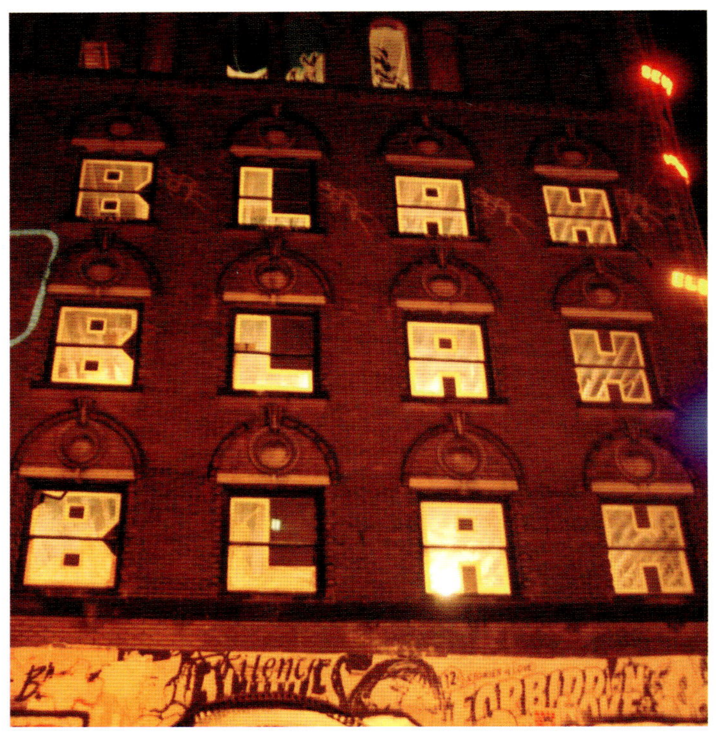

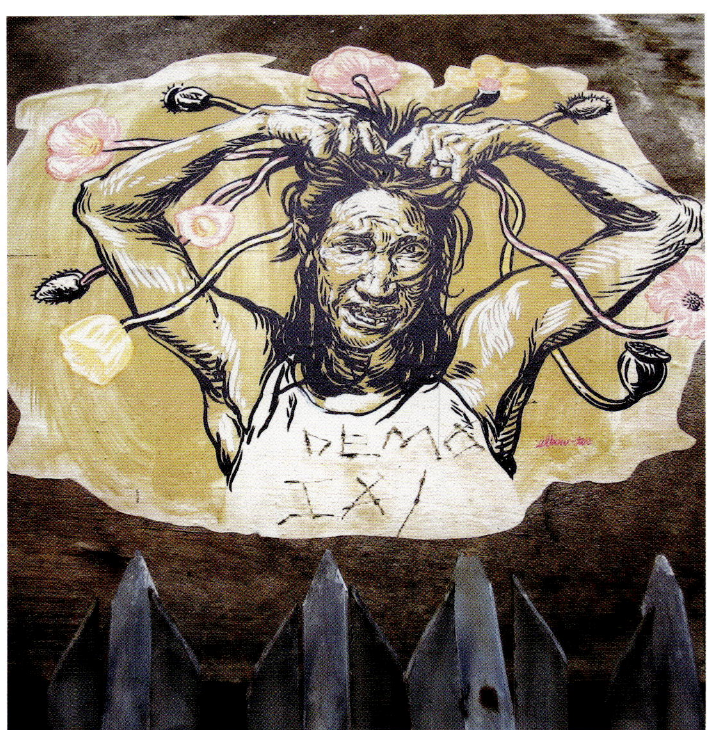

You get the feeling that taggers are like over enthusiastic fans that can't really play the sport. Someone scratching DAVO into a bus window with his keys is like that kid next door learning to play violin. It's not very good.

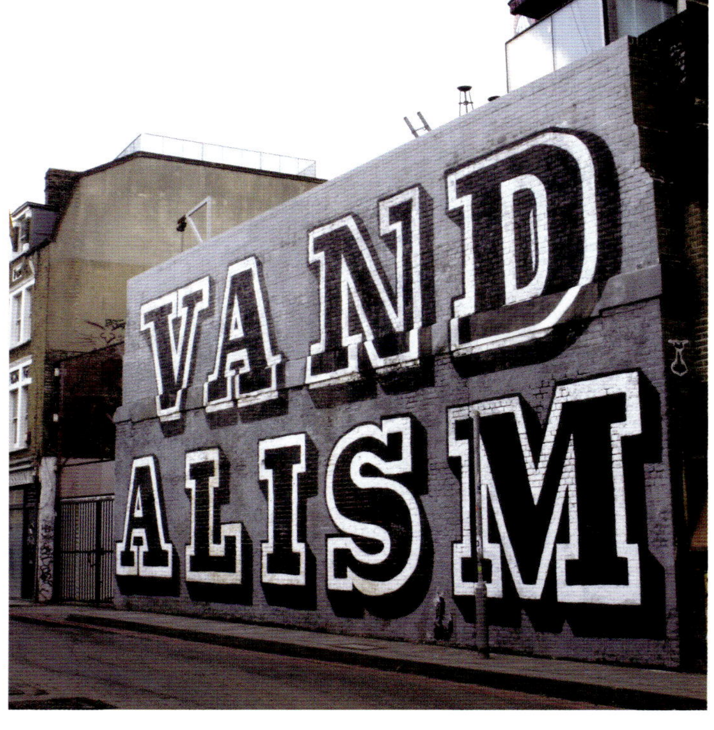

# Your Life Is Meaningless

Ever notice that your life is like a tale told by an idiot full of sound and fury, signifying nothing? Well I had the same problem until I discovered graffiti art. I liked it so much I bought the rights to it. Within ten days my life was filled with a deep sense of purpose and spiritual depth. You too can easily access these feelings with my special package. I'm so confident you'll love it I'm offering the trial version absolutely free for 28 days. If you don't like it you can send it back at any time! Don't take my word for it. Just listen to some of my satisfied customers!

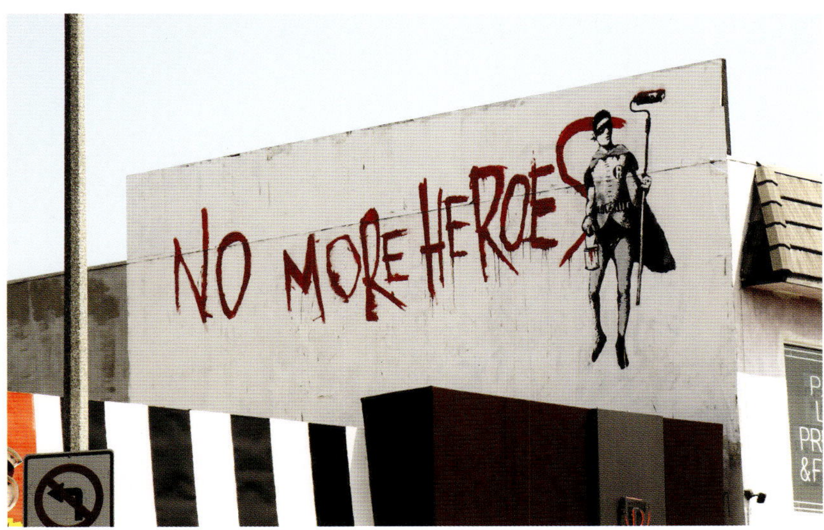

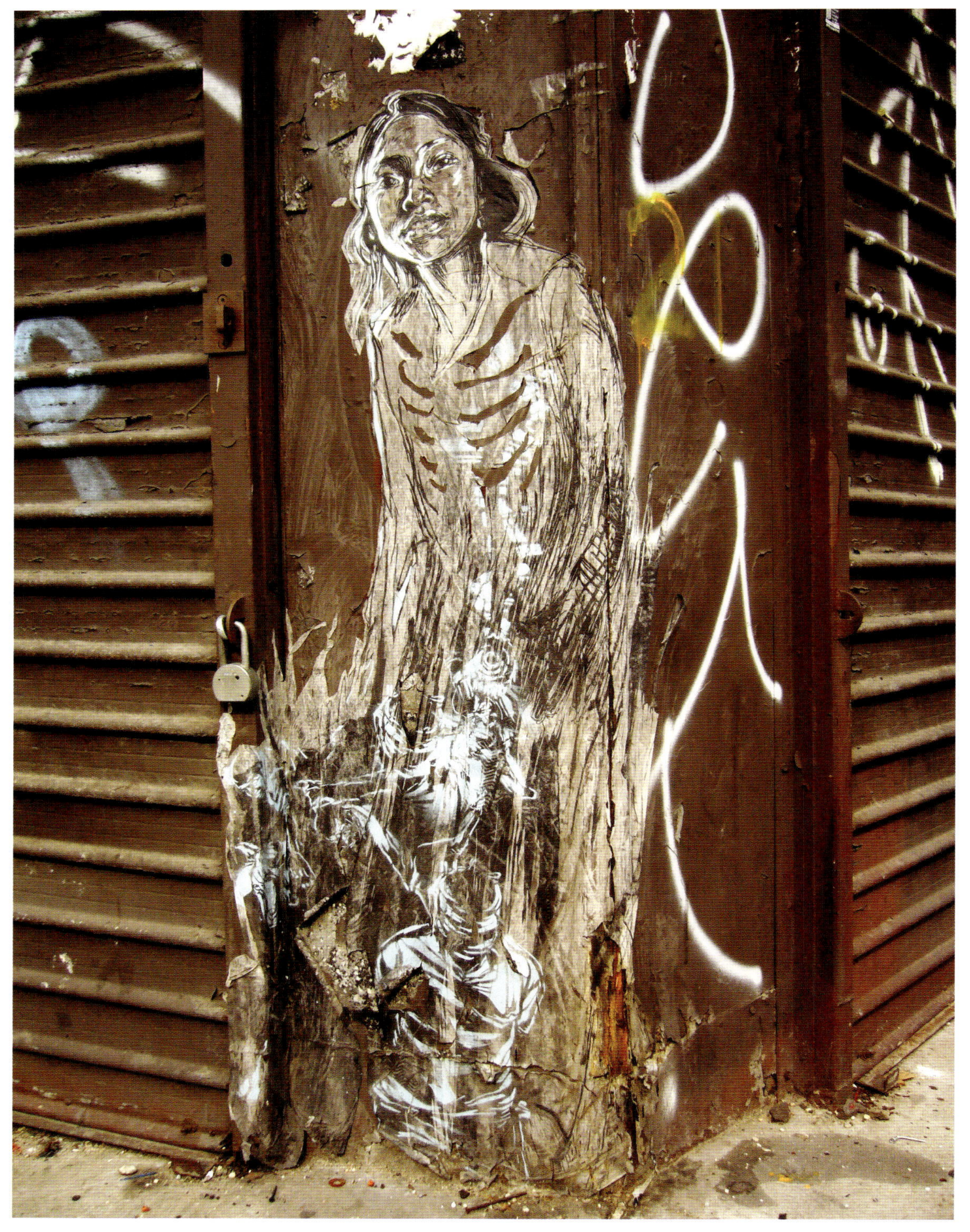

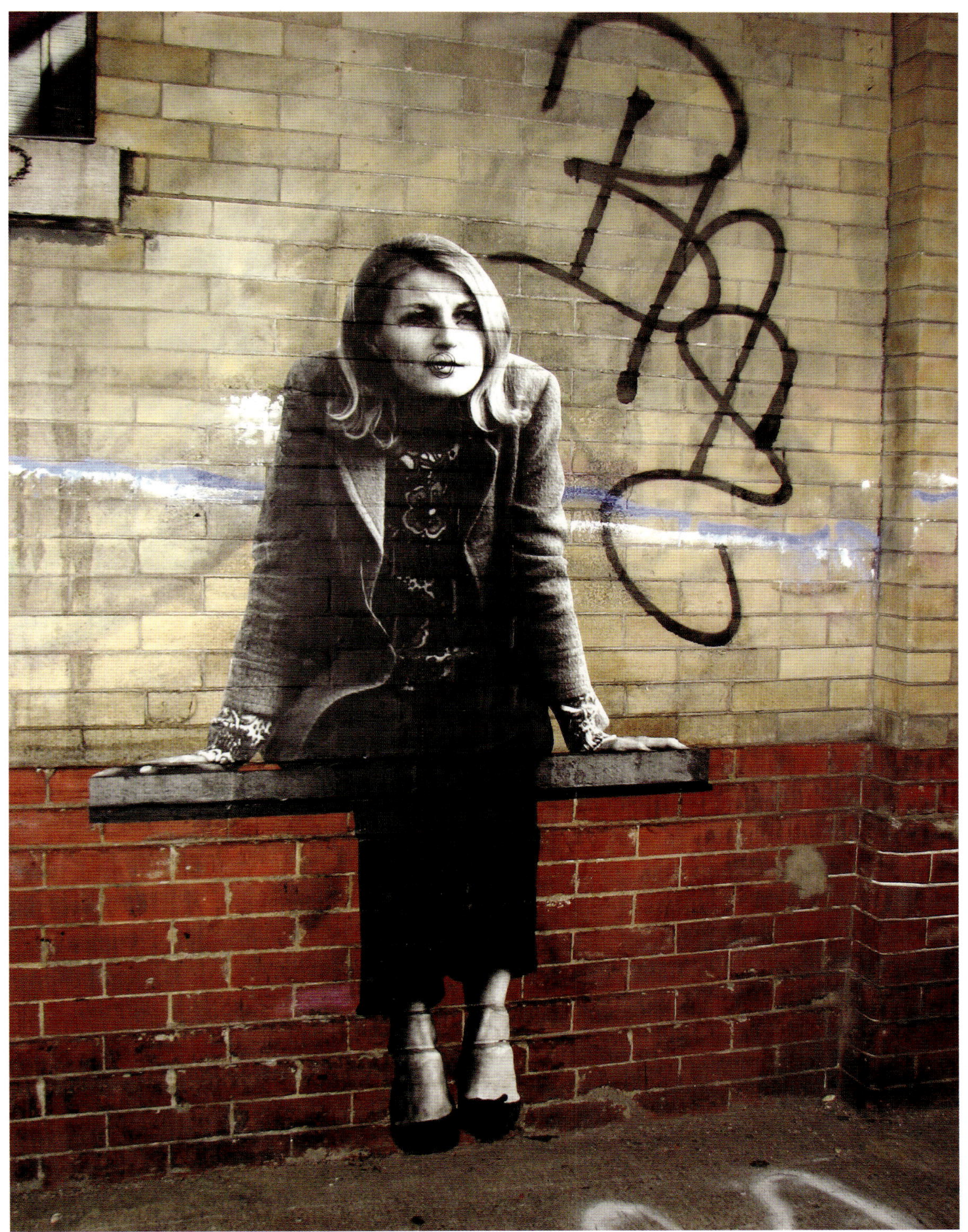

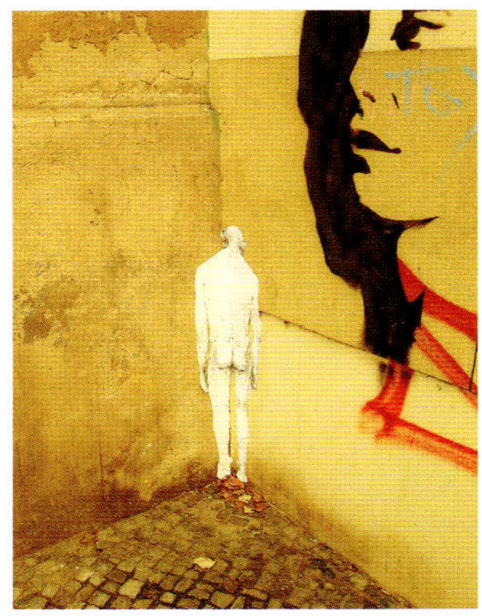

# Many Voices

I'm at work right and the banter is wearing thin, so I says i'm writing this thing about graffiti and this seven foot tall Aussie she says 'What that stupid primitive urge to go and deface every available flat surface you see?' The lady on my left chimes in 'Well some of it can be quite beautiful.' Another lad pipes up about tagging, he leaps up as if to tag the office wall. 'What's tagging?' comes another. Well, says I, it's writing your name in a squiggly way everywhere. It's just barking your own name over and over like a moron. Like if you did that at a party, it would perhaps be poorly received. Except maybe if it was some truly raw kind of affair.

I could say some academic business about how tagging expresses the desire of the oppressed individual to make mark on the landscape of the mono culture which oppresses her. But sod it, if tagging is territorial then it's just a reflection of the logic of power itself. The gangsta is not a rebel, just a less successful form of government. The true rebel opposes the core idea of power, not it's most recent manifestation.

As the conversation draws on I fade back a little into the distance and just listen. The babble of voices is a good sound. It sounds like culture. I think of sitting at the Metro station Placa Espanya, bored to tears, irritated with having to wait 4 minutes. Then the train rolls in and the whole thing is covered in huge great works of art. Small transcendent moment. If you are listening to one voice then you are listening to the language of power. If you are listening to many voices…

## Childish Vandalism

Psychologists argue that child development works in several stages of obsession. These stages can broadly be defined as: Oral, anal, homo-sexual, hetero-sexual, writing accusations of homosexuality about your mates on textbooks with a biro, tagging, raving, getting a job in a call centre.

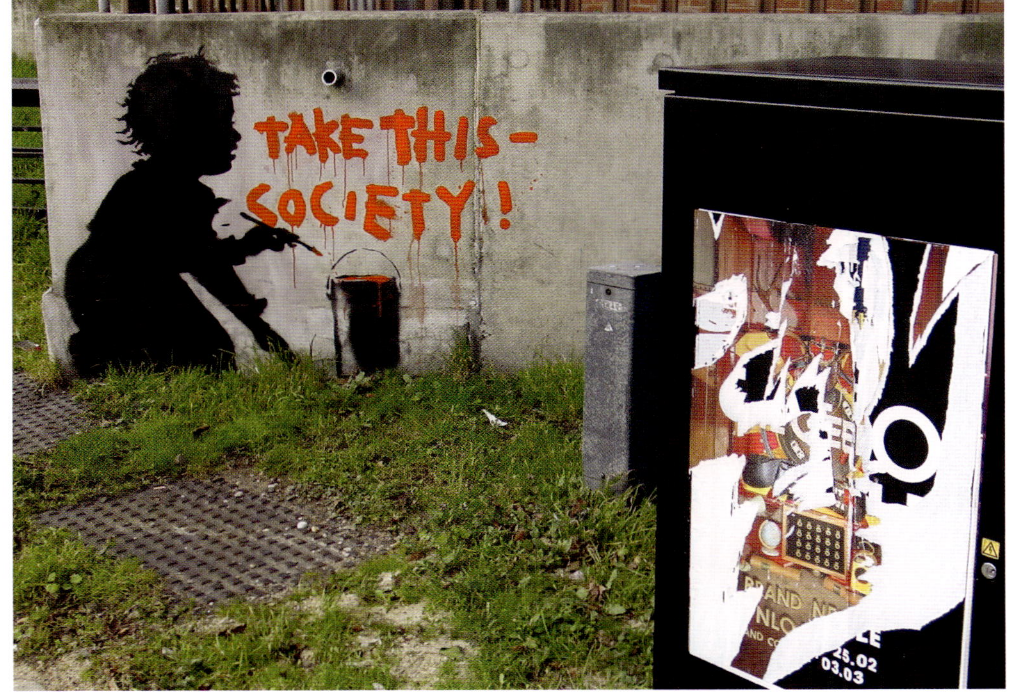

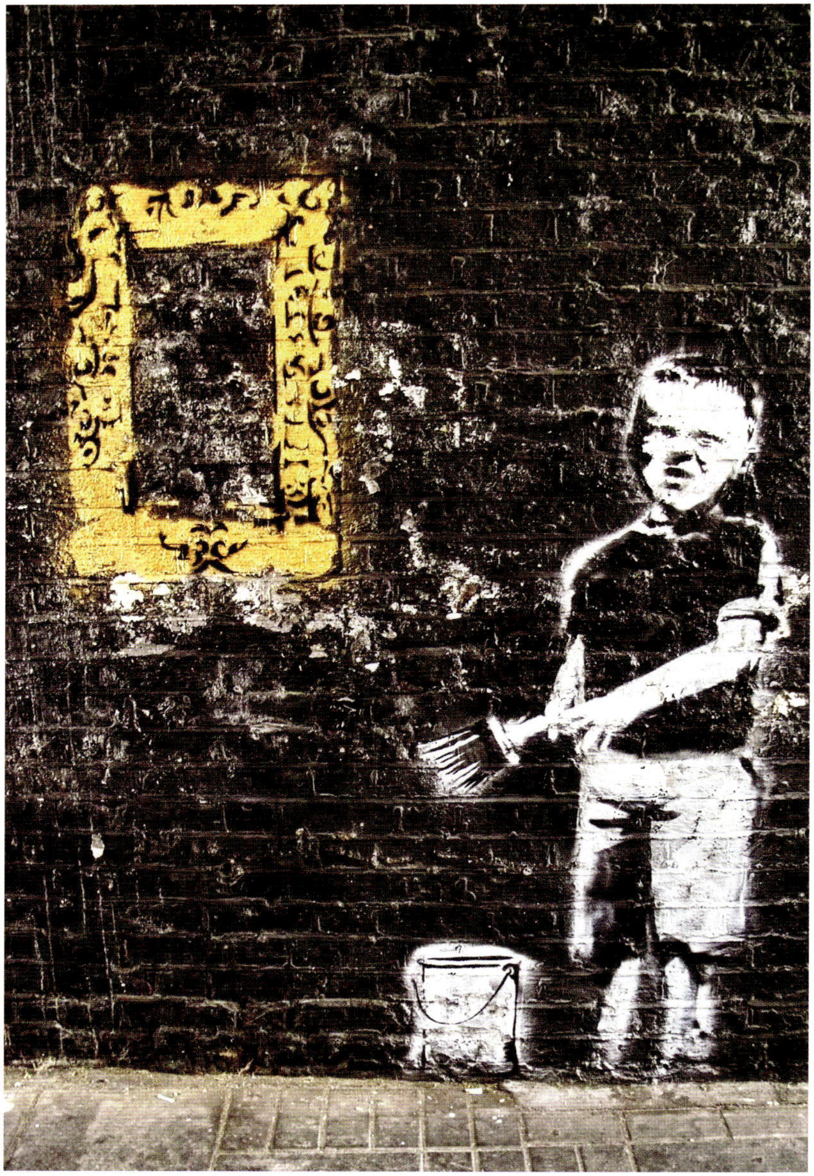

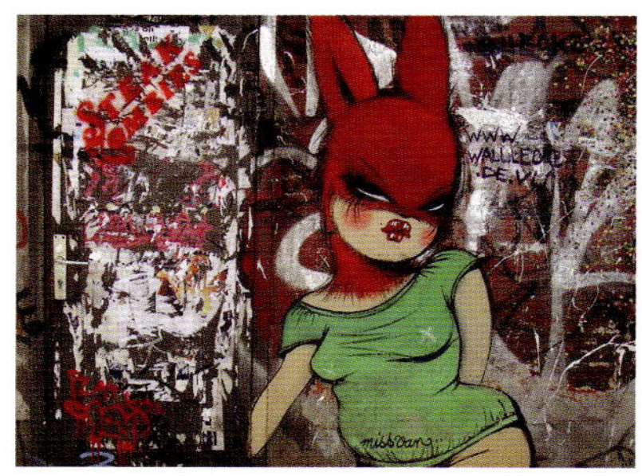

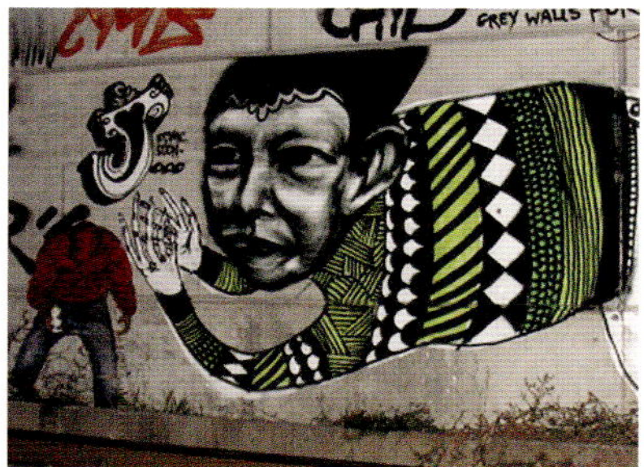

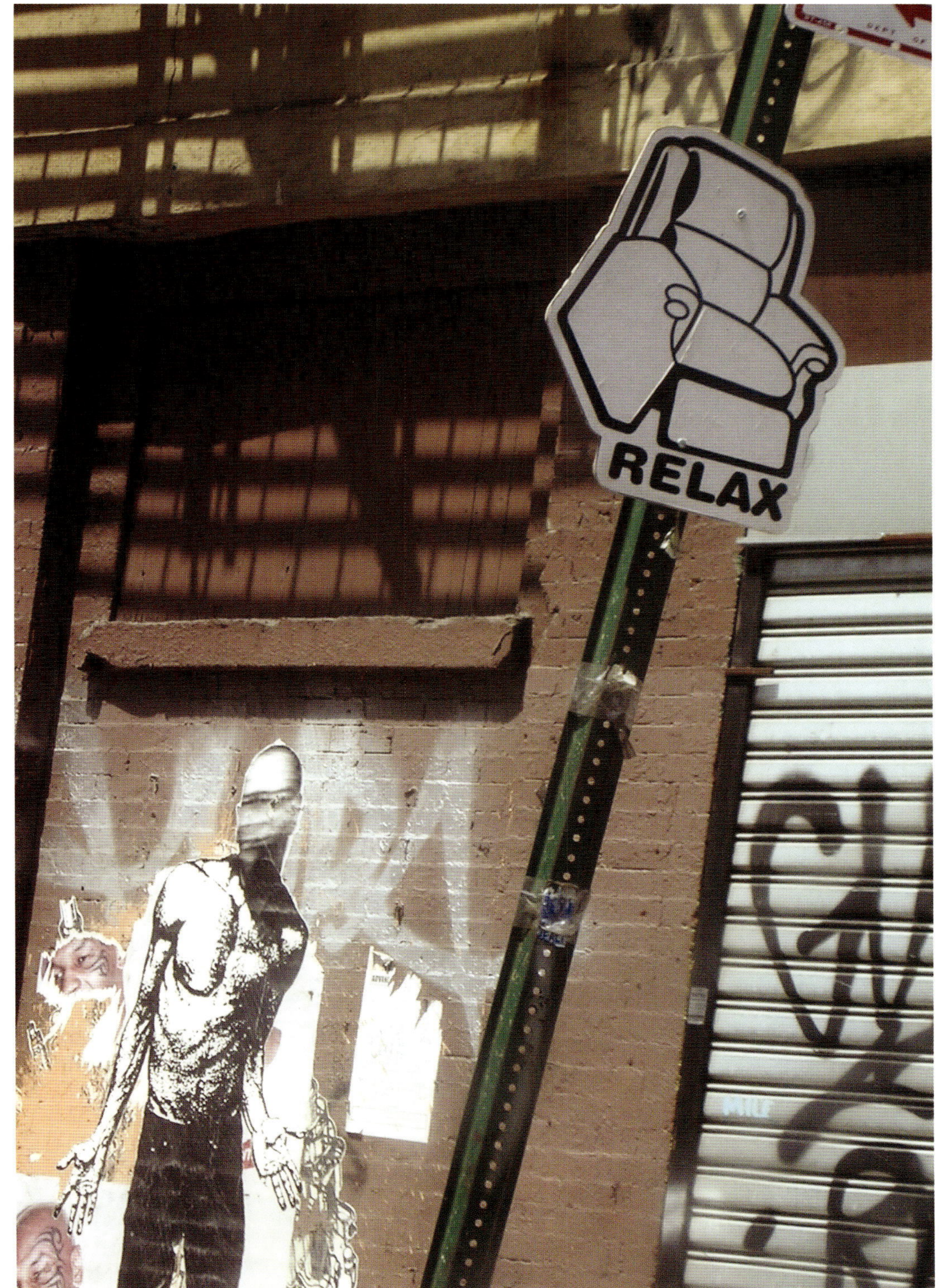
RELAX

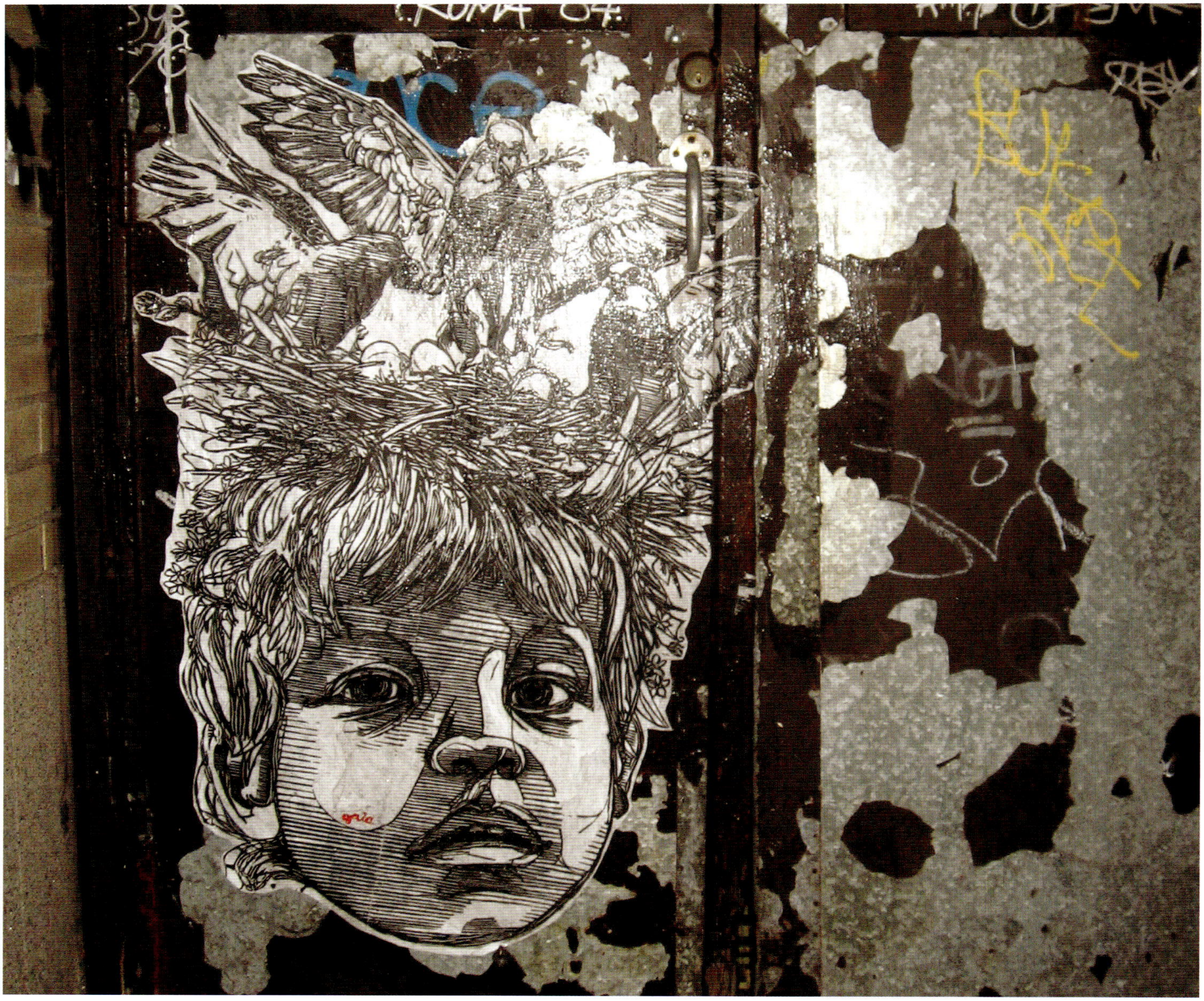

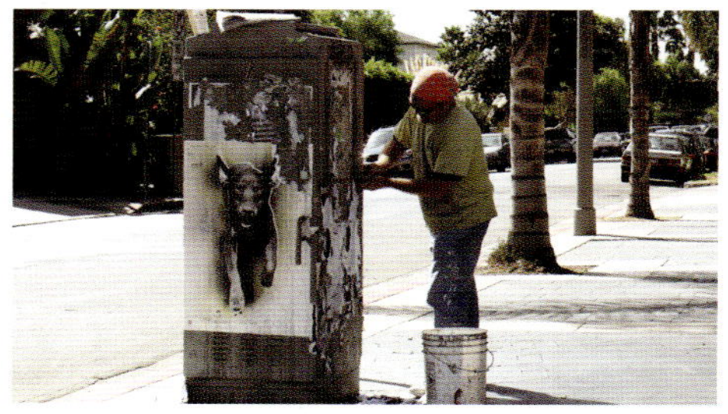
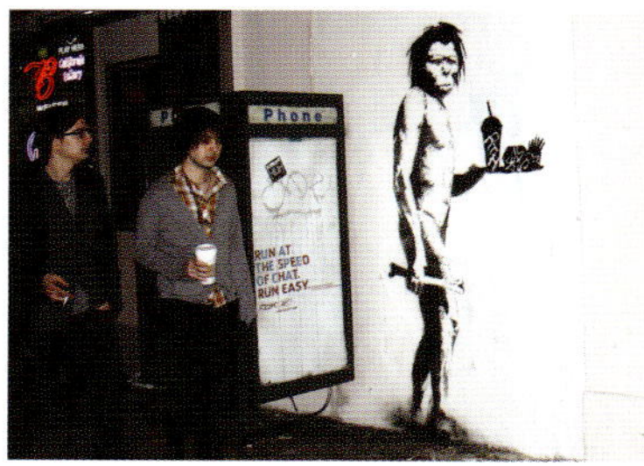
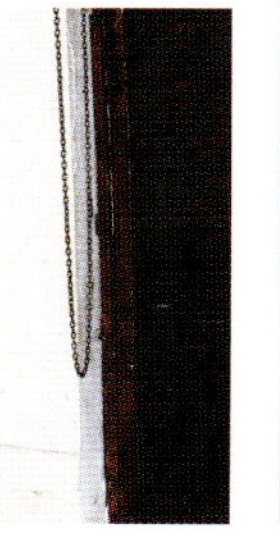
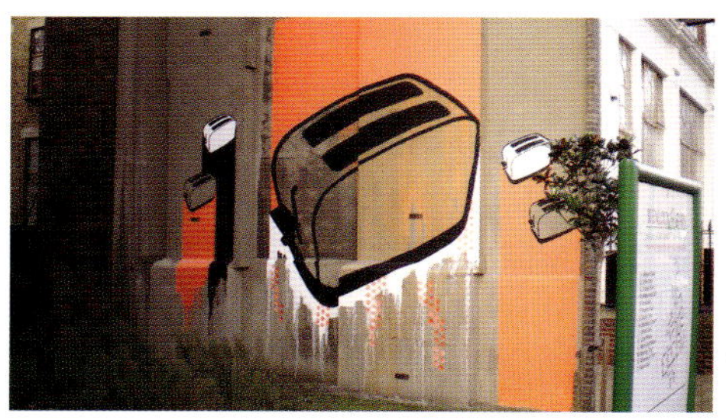

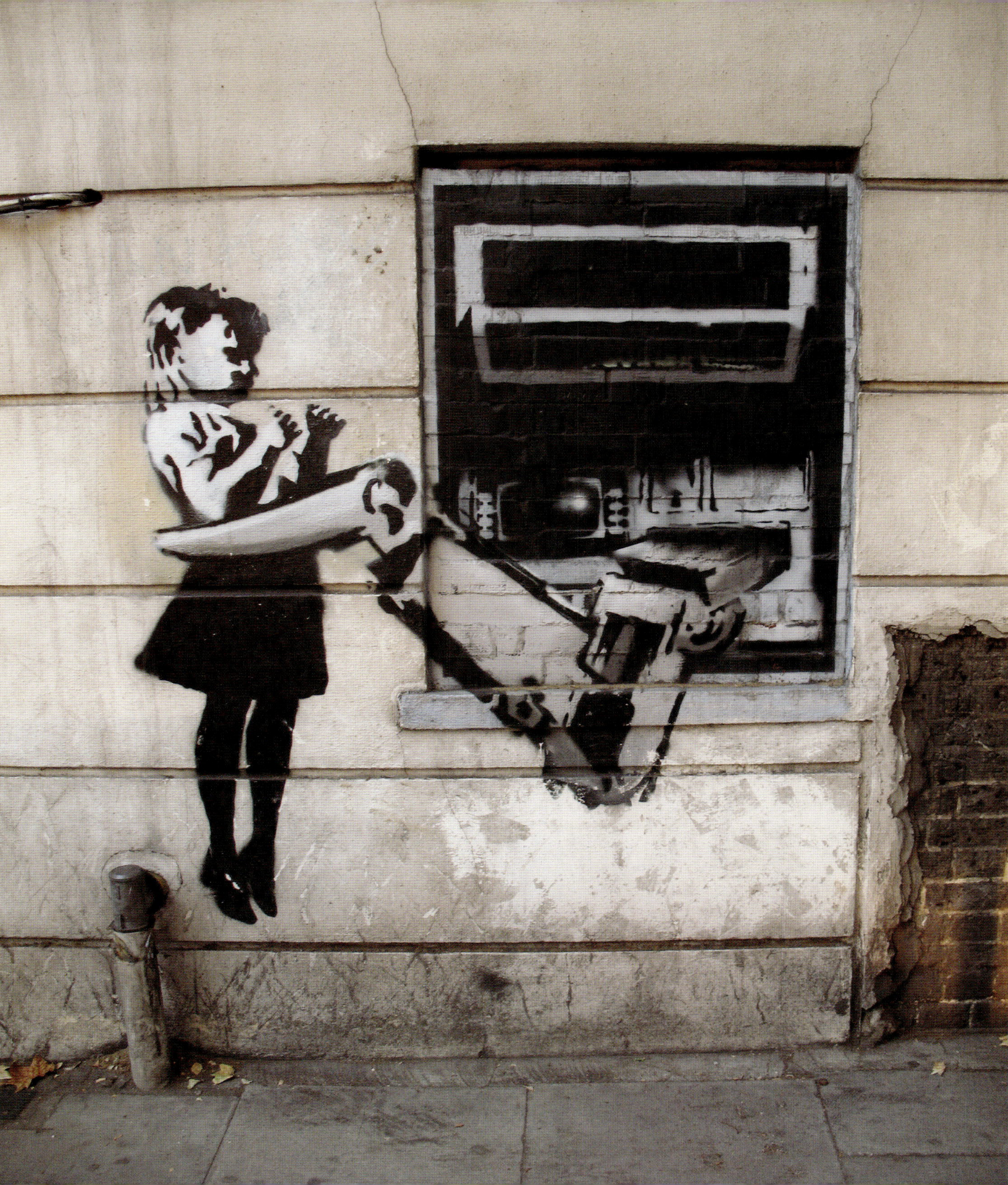

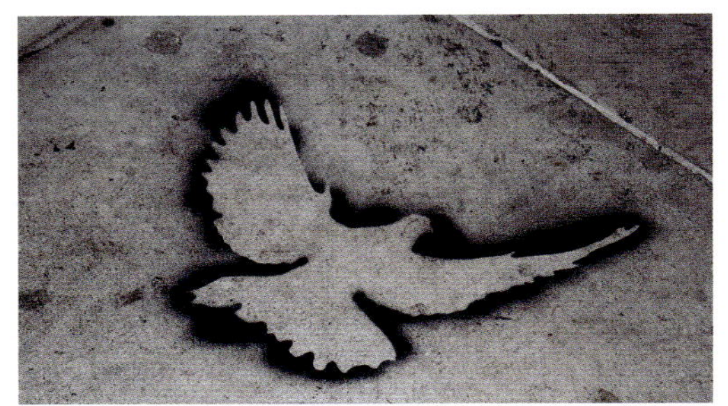

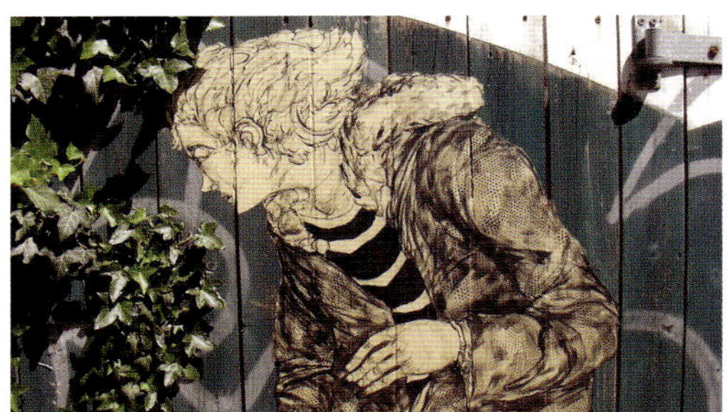

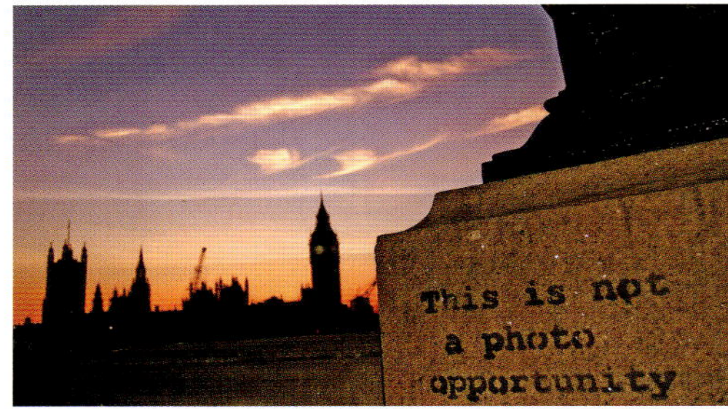
This is not
a photo
opportunity

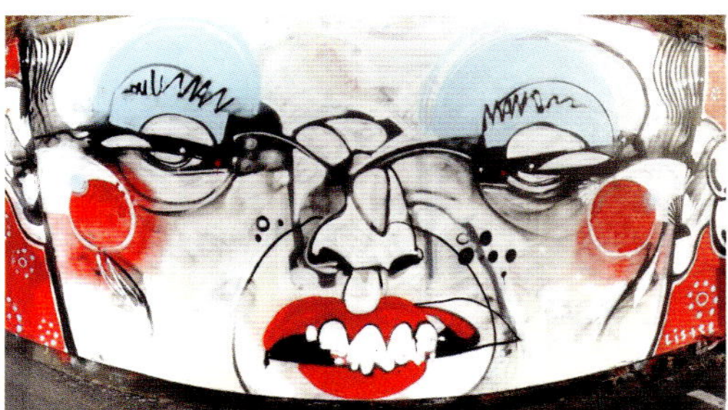

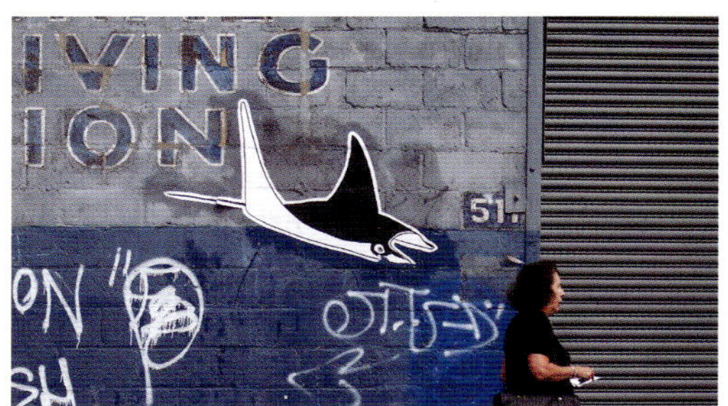
IVING
ION
51

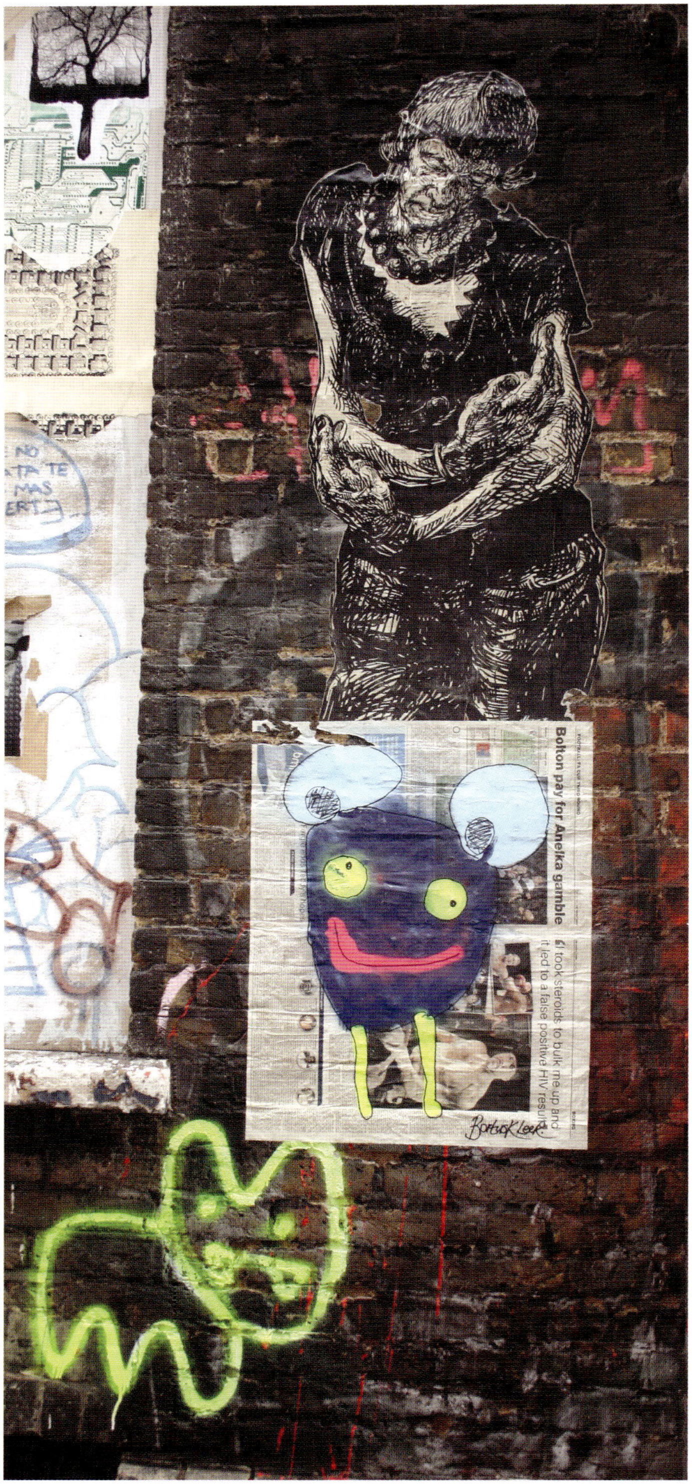

# Keyword Rich Content

Are you wasting valuable graffiti time wondering how to optimise the number of hits your street art generates? Are you only getting a trickle of people looking at your work before the council scrub it off? Why not relax and let the experts optimise your street content with our extensive knowledge of keywords that get people to read your paint. We offer packages to suit all urban painters and you won't believe the results. Did you know that the phrase 'fuckbadger' gets 20% more hits than 'Cacknipple'? Well now you do. Discover All this and more at www.fuckbadger.com.

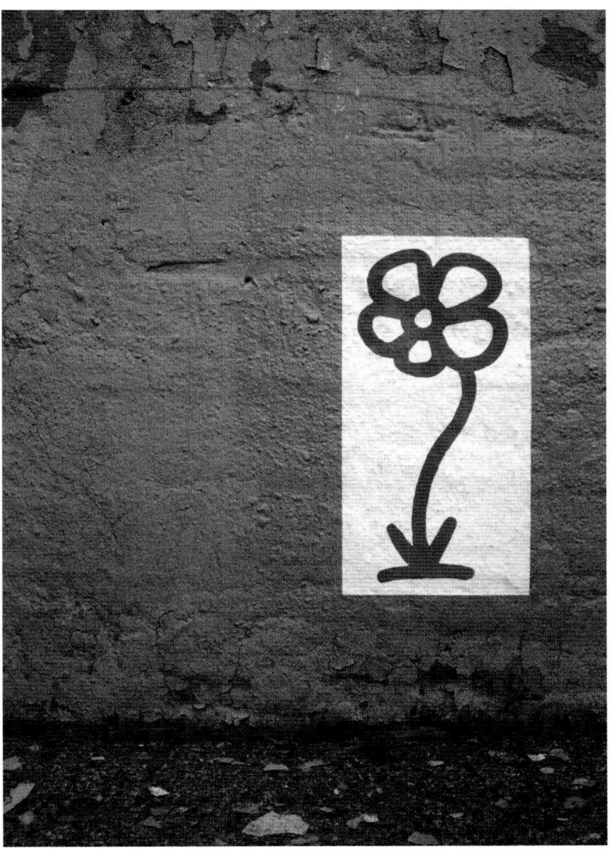

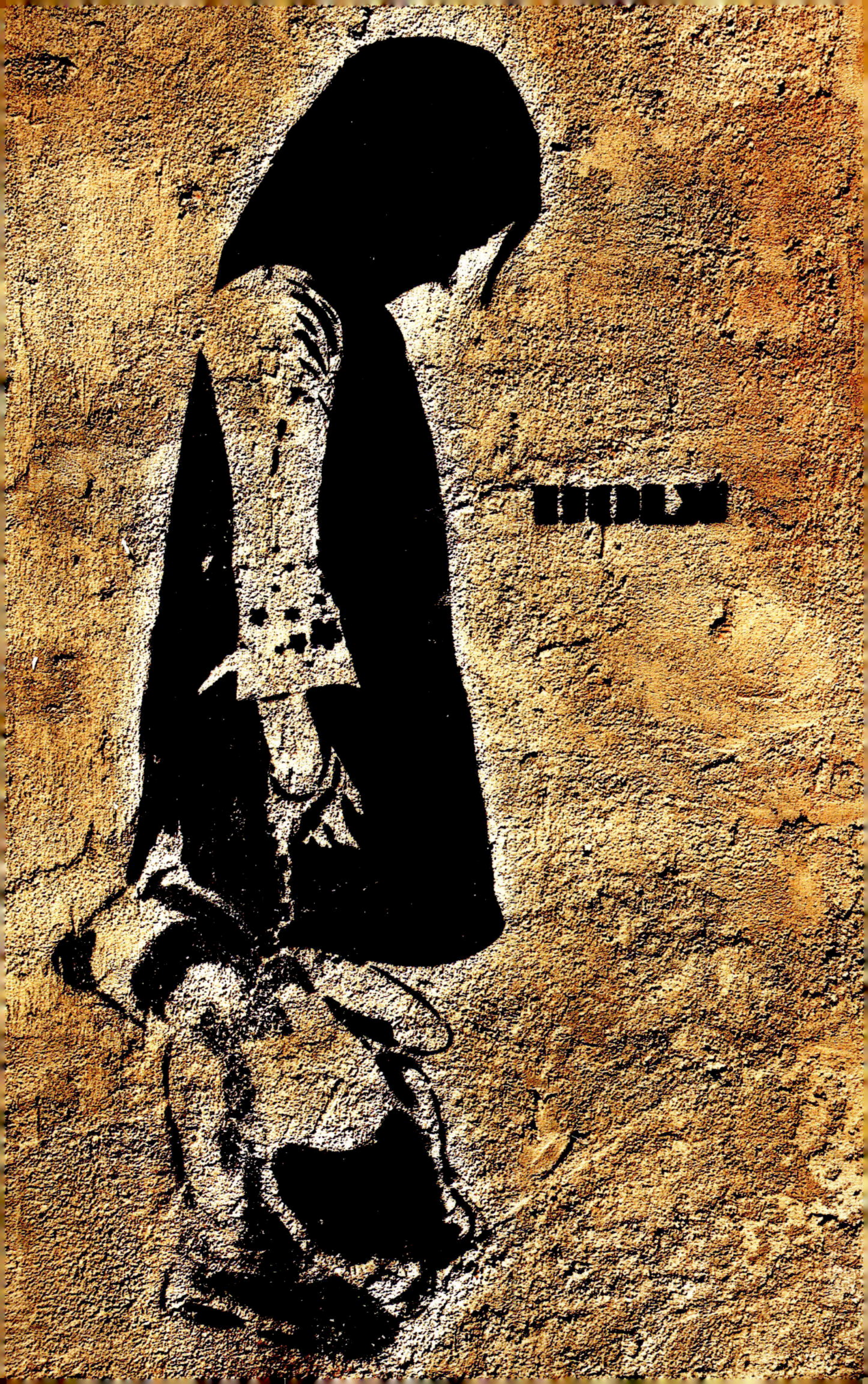

# Womb Envy

Dudes are out there painting walls in the night just wishing they could make babies grow inside them. Believe. Wake up one morning some guy has painted a fifty foot high foetus on the side of your maisonette. Can happen. Ask your Grandma about it.

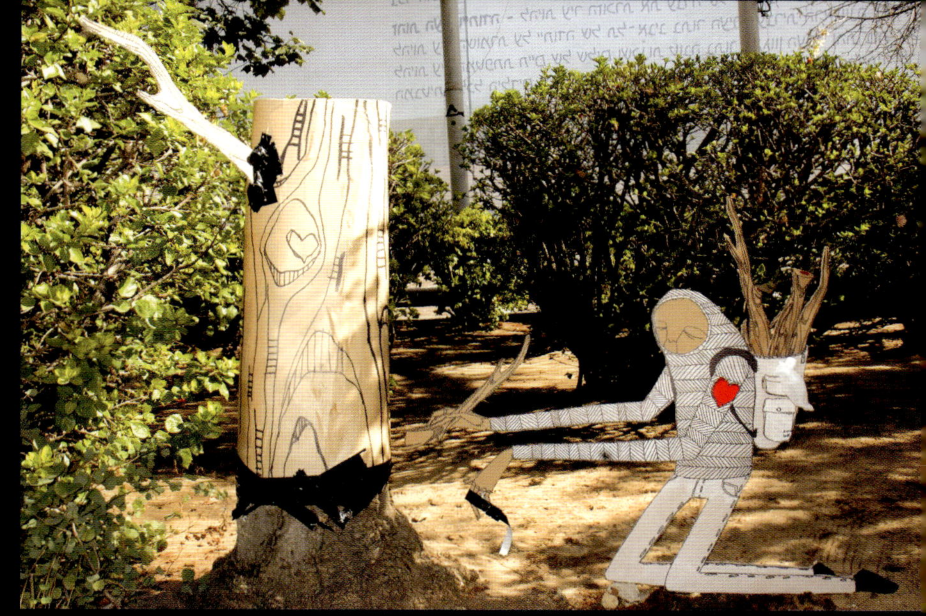

## Fictional Graffiti Hero no 5 - Little Benny Spelk

People often talk about the ethics of graff and whether or not it is a right or moral thing to do. Well I don't think the issue is clear cut. There was this incident in 1976 where a gang of buildings actually captured a Graffiti artist. Several bungalows in Stoke Newington held this kid up behind an industrial estate for like four hours. In the end police negotiators talked them down. One of the buildings was shot by a police marksman as he was running away. Poor kid was actually writing a poem for his girl. It was a real ethical mess. One of the bungalows later turned out to be into shed porn anyway. Who was in the right? You tell me.

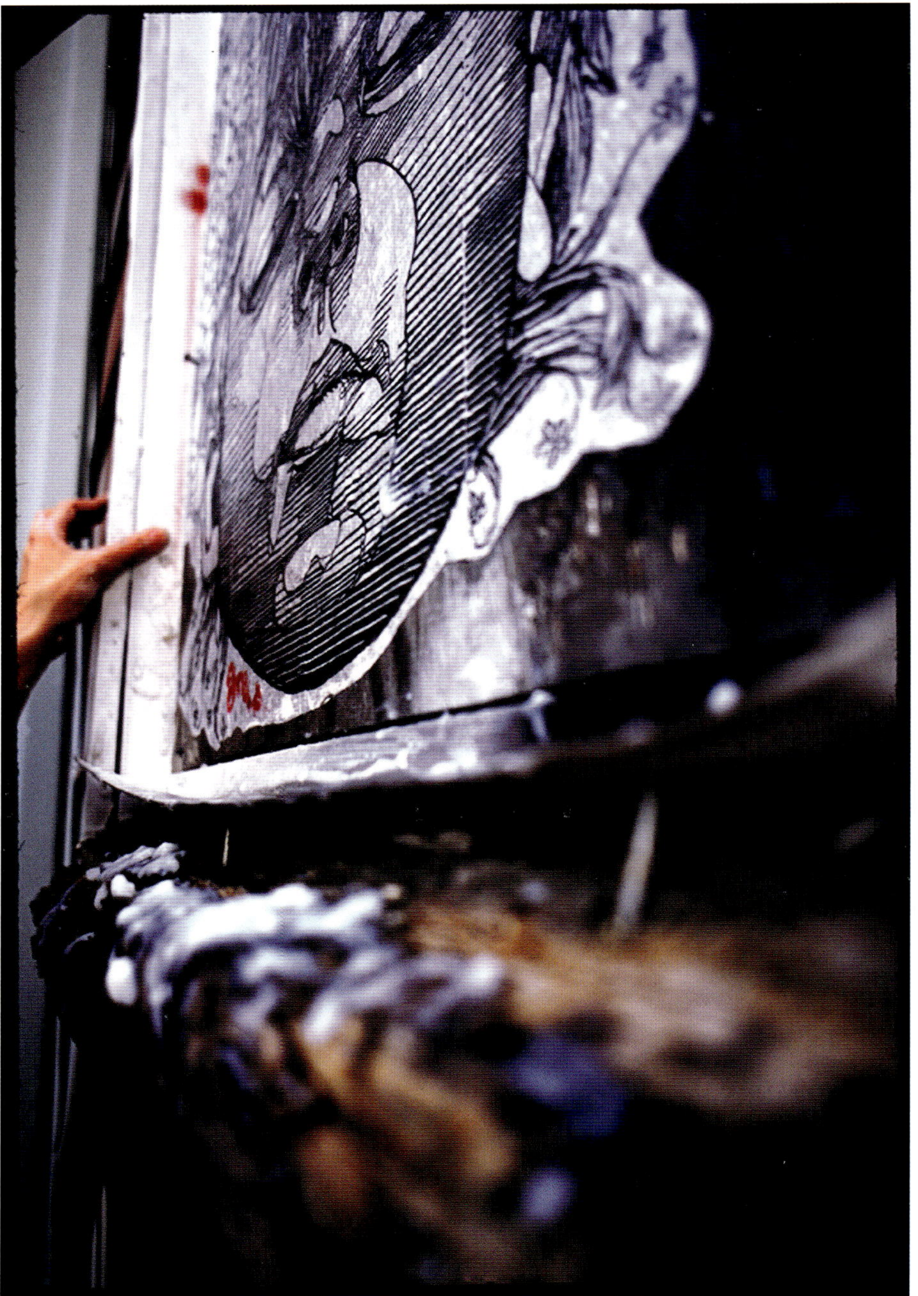

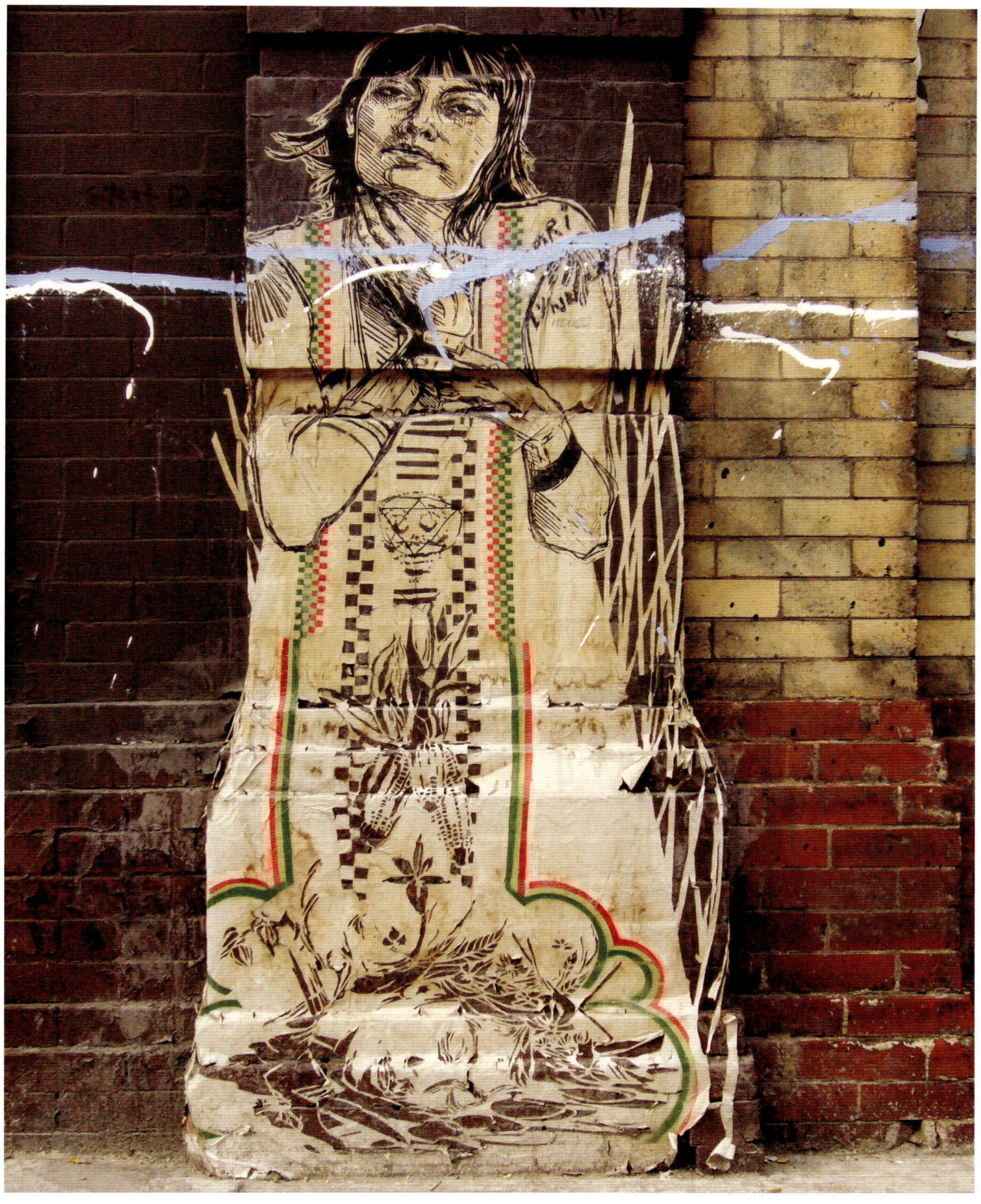

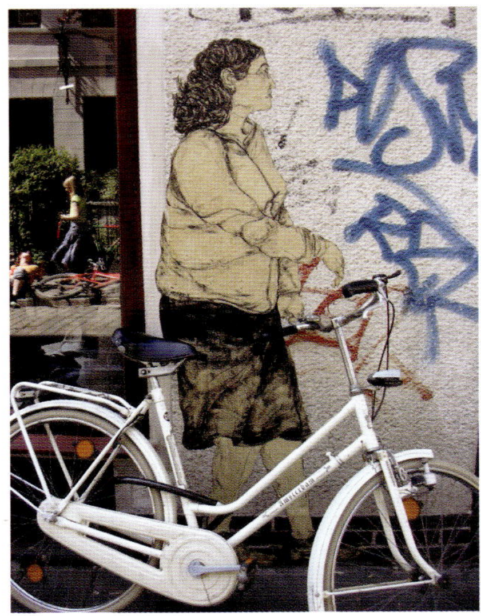

The argument goes that graffiti creates a sense of danger or lawlessness in an area that in turn intimidates the locals and creates an atmosphere wherein petty crime is tolerated. In a zone where people are scared to criticise each other larger acts of crime become easier to do, such as peddling drugs or occasional beatings. This is the theory of zero tolerance. Discuss.

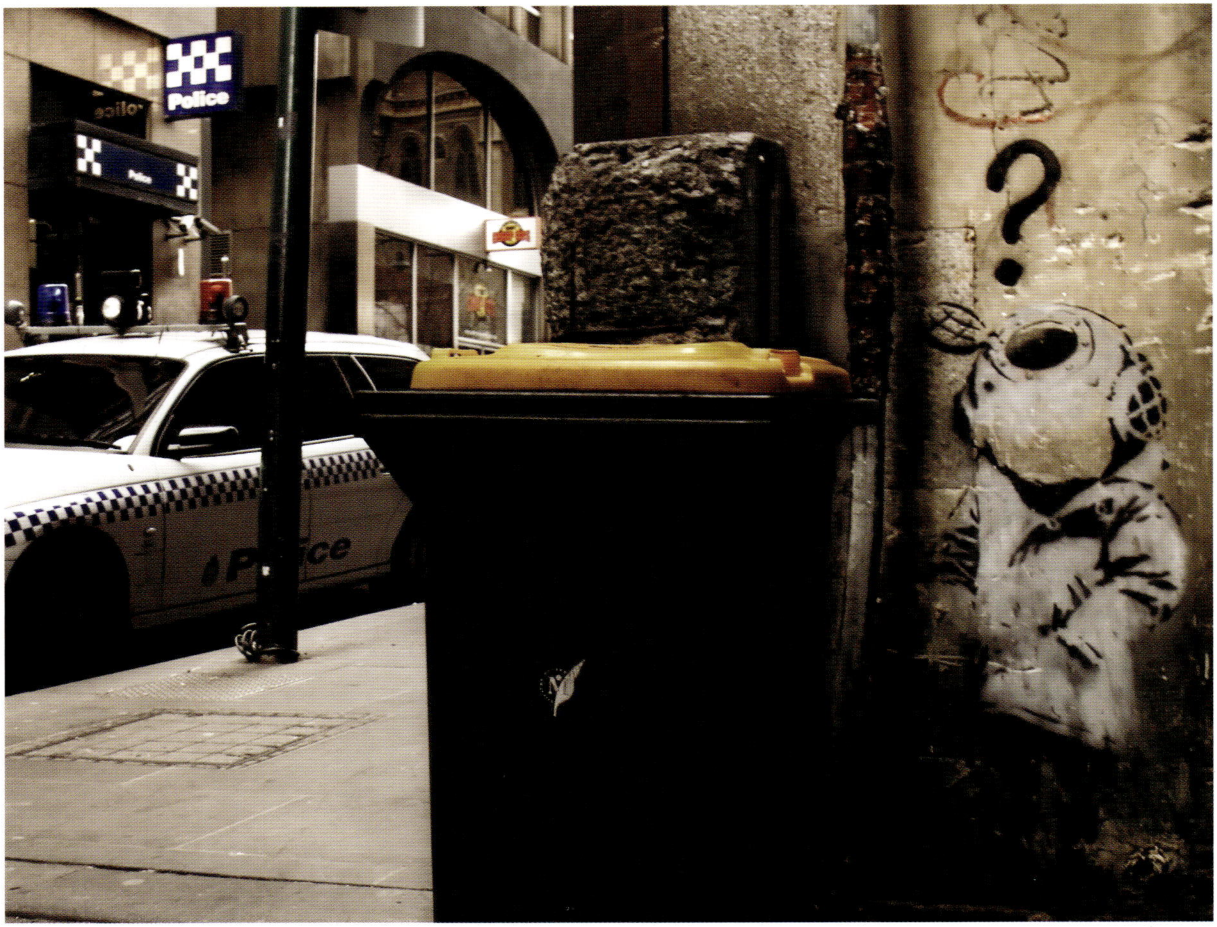

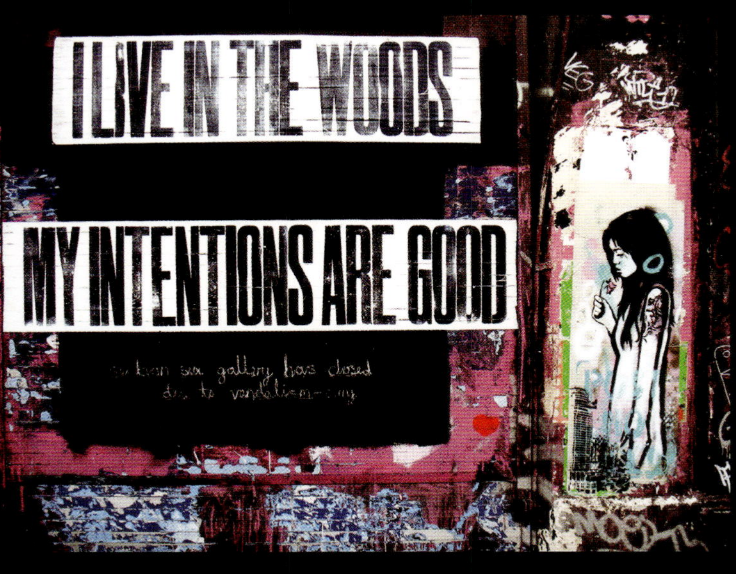



the hacienda must be rebuilt!

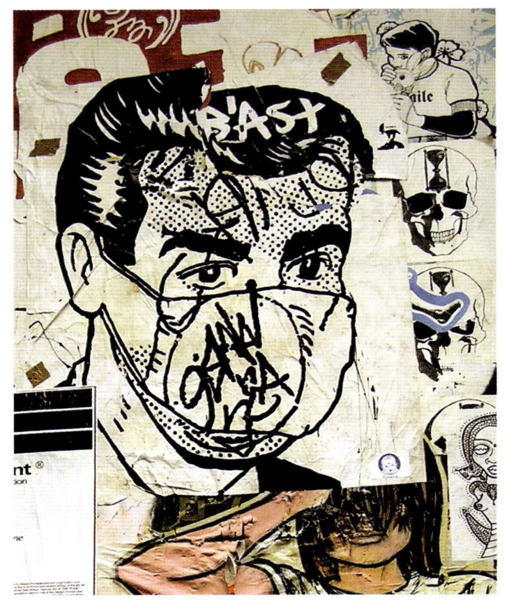
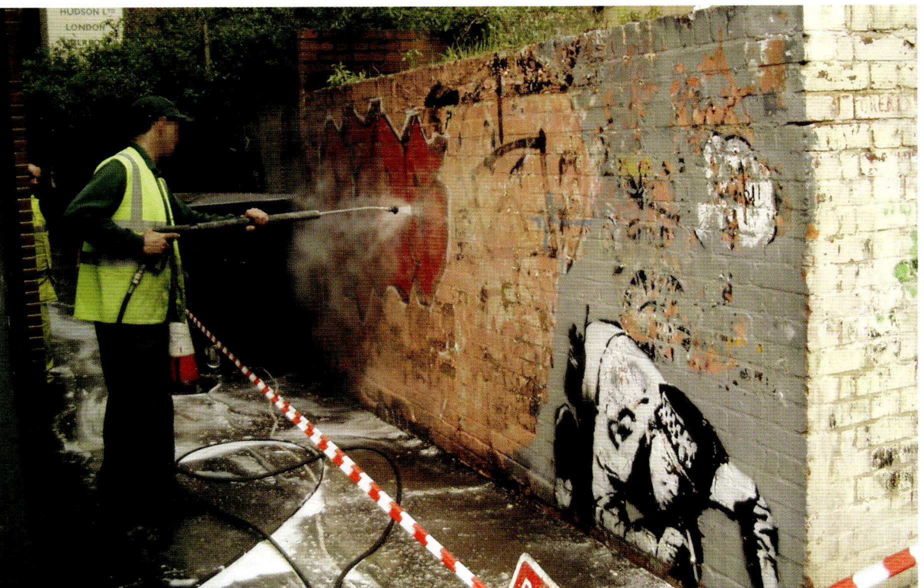

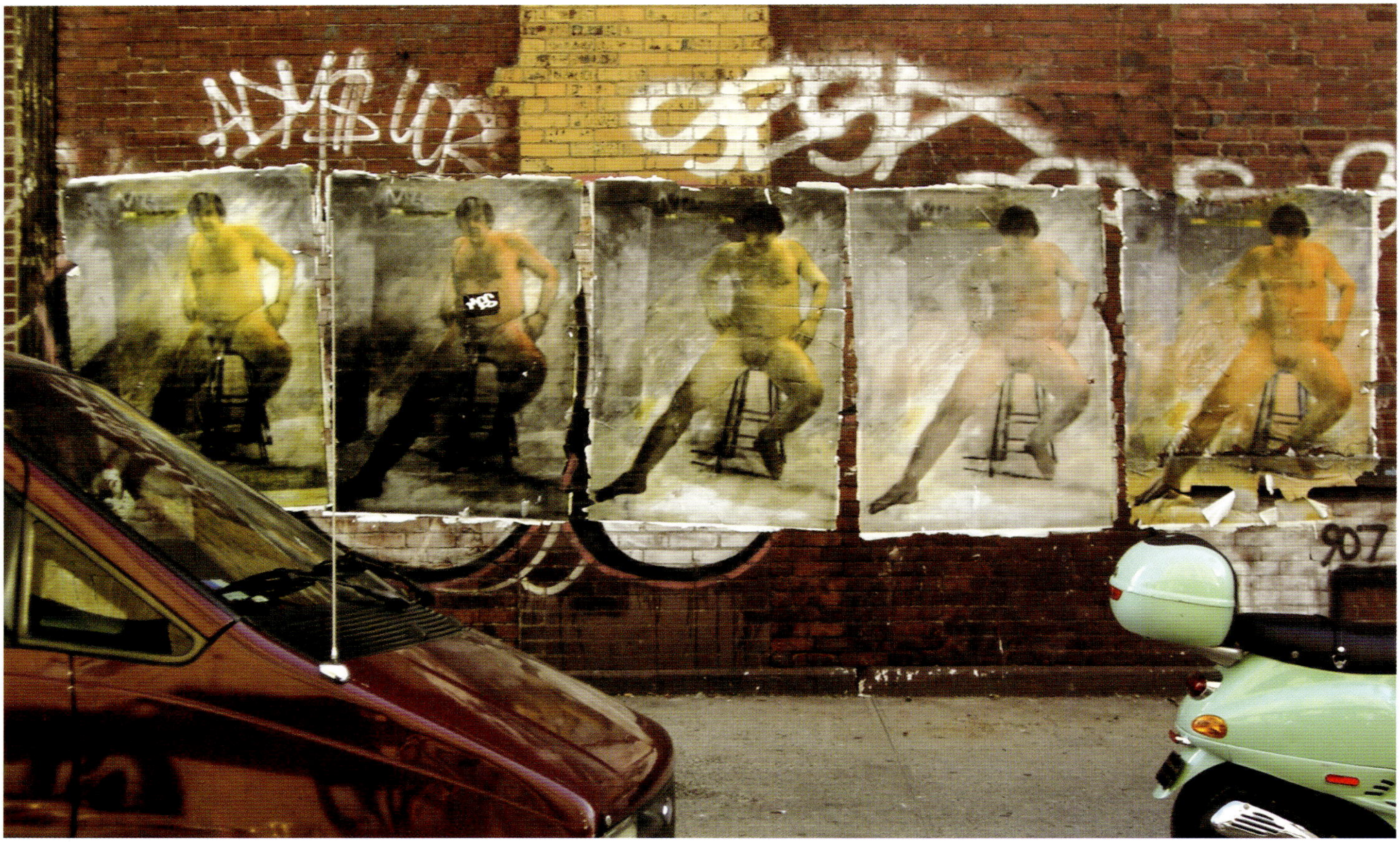

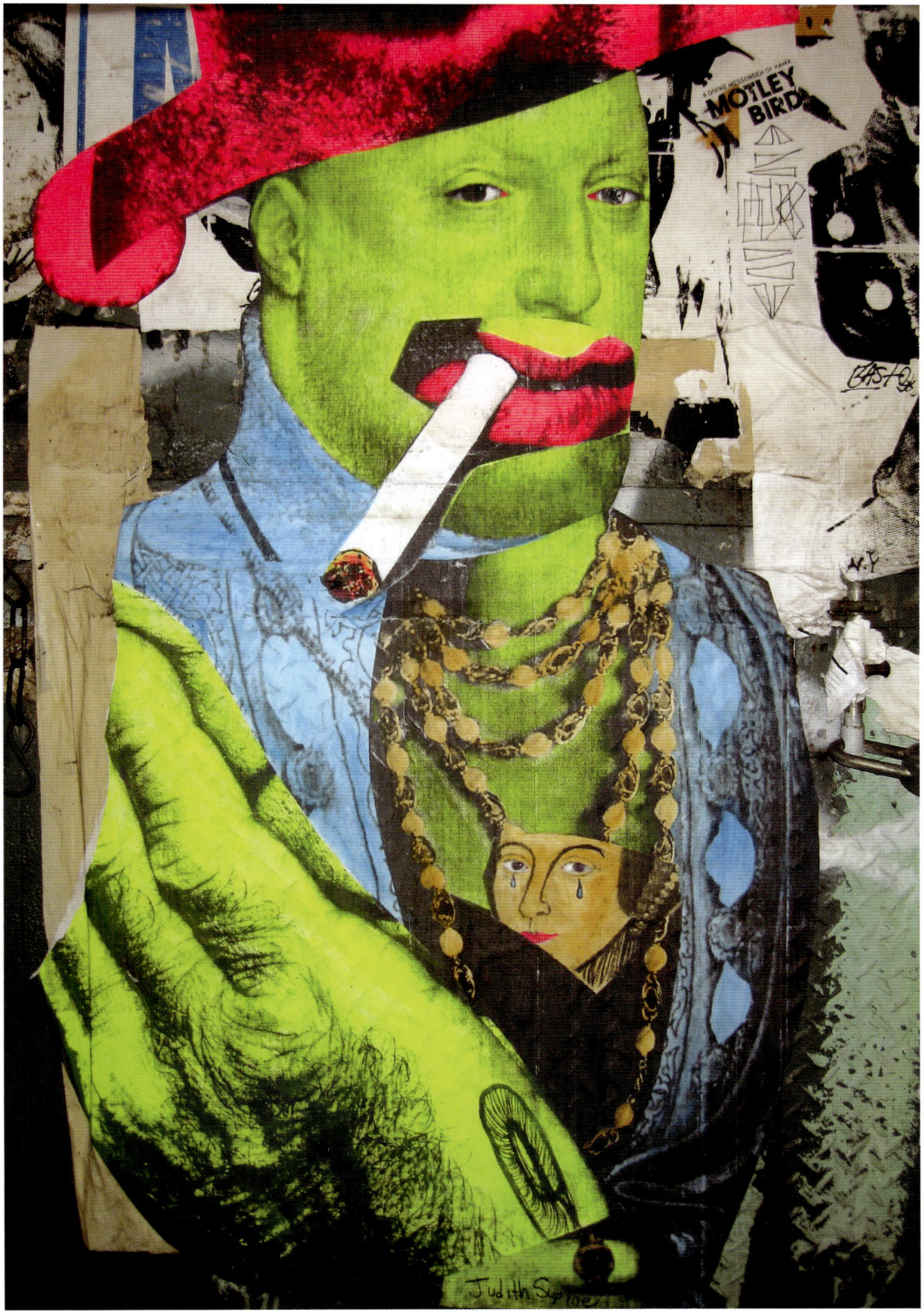

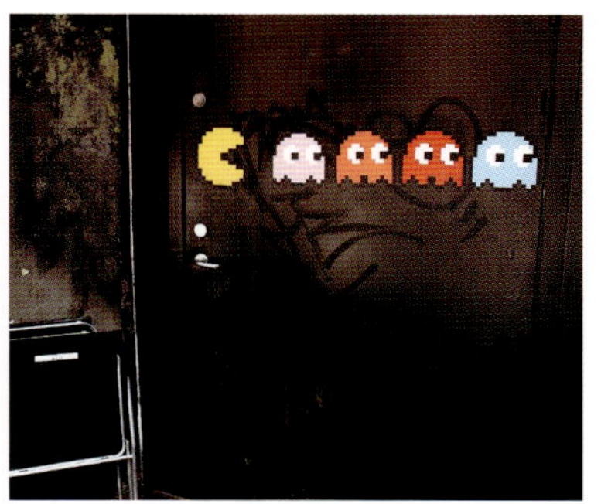
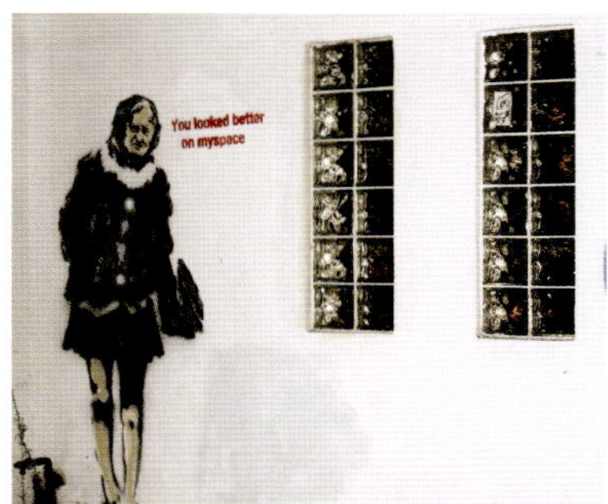
You looked better
on myspace
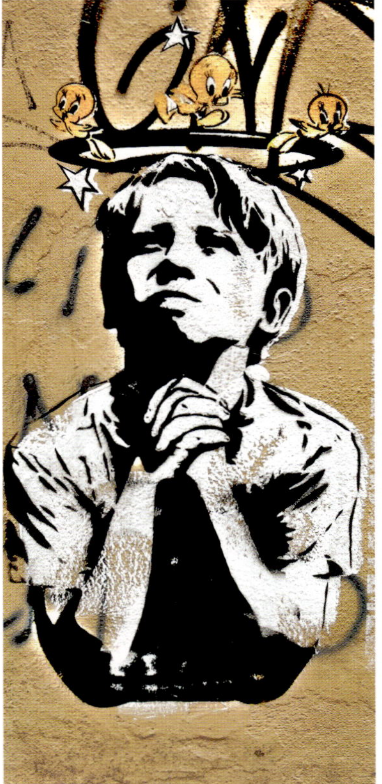

Oh little town of Bethlehem how still we see thee lie…

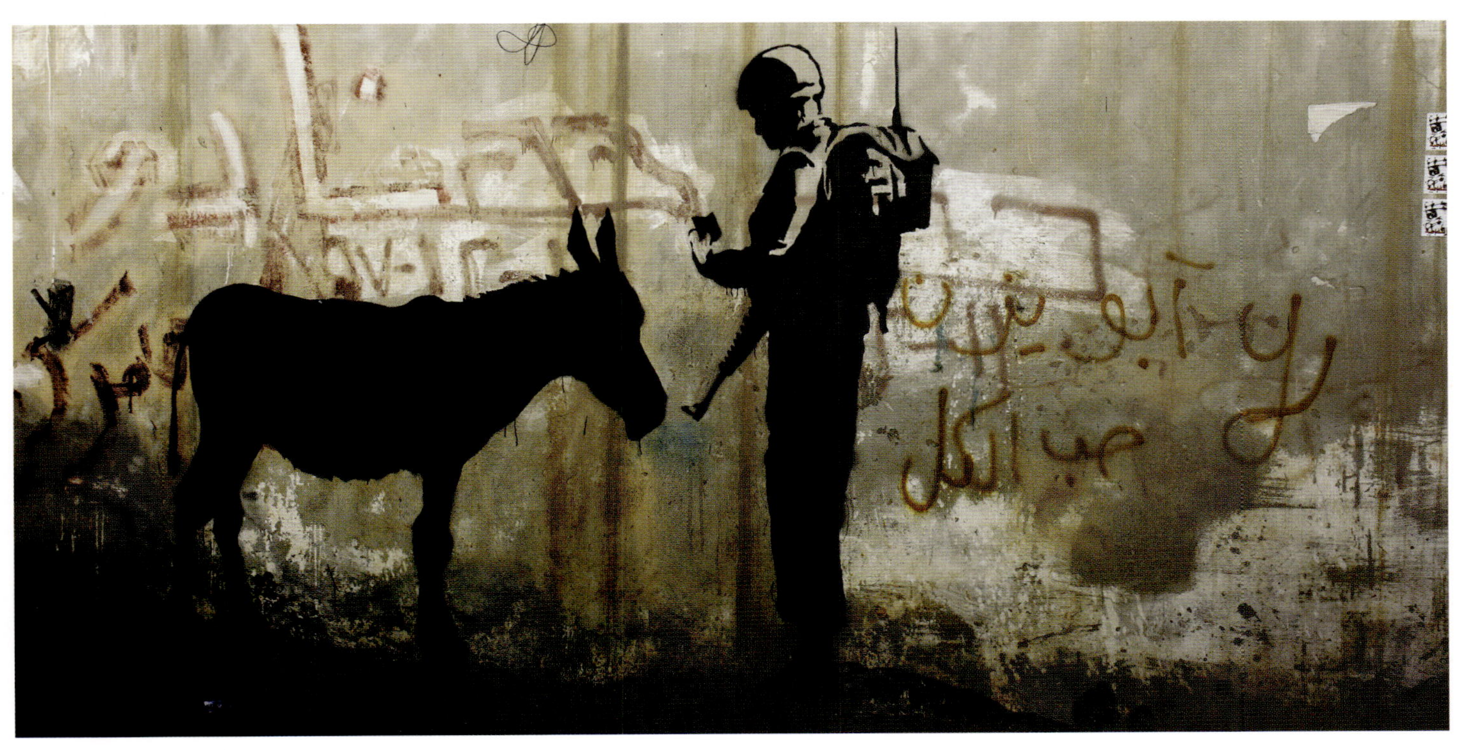
يا أبو شنب
حب الكل

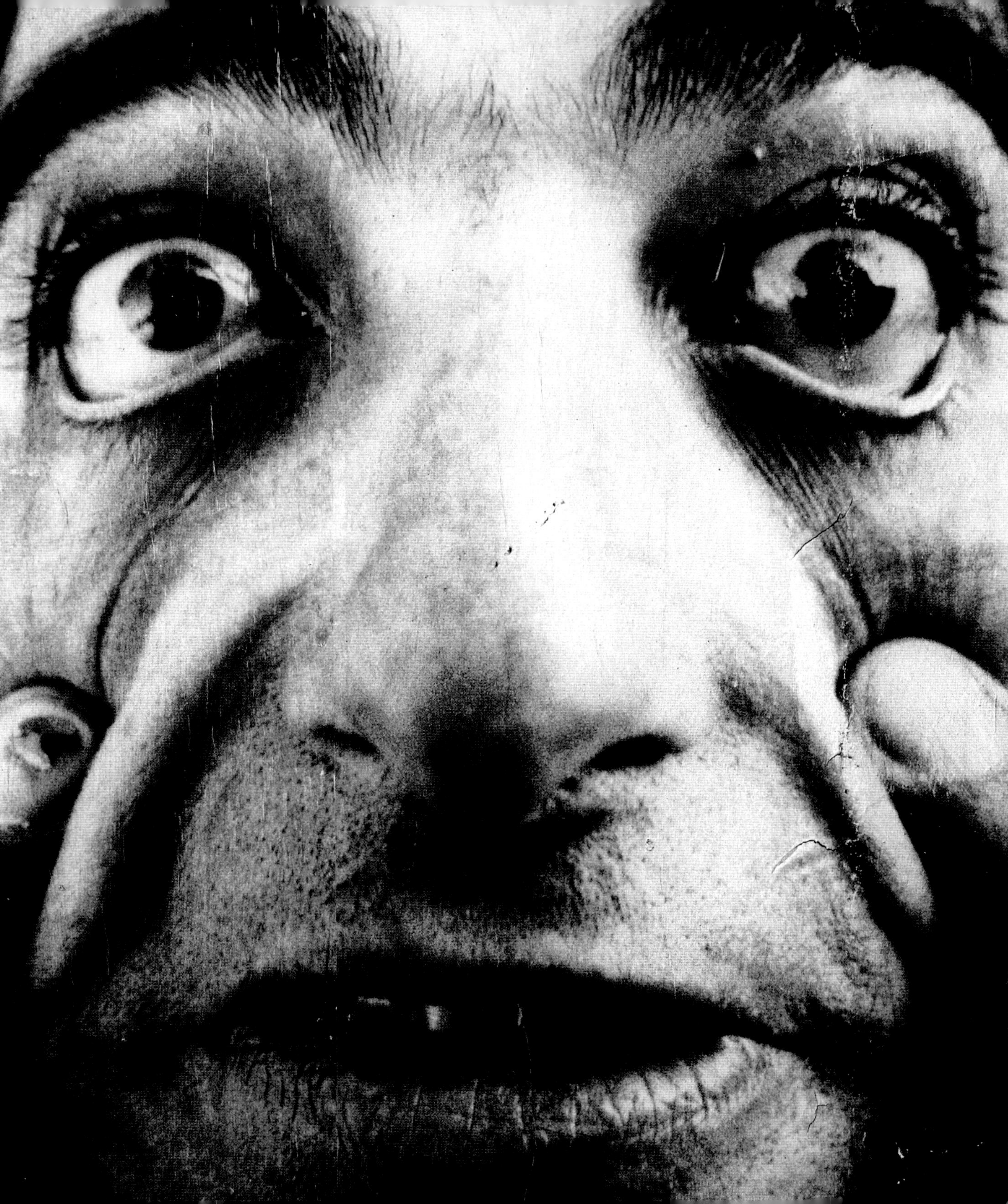

IN THE LAST DAYS OF THE YEAR 2007 ANNO DOMINI IN THE TOWN WHERE OUR LORD (Depending on who you are) JESUS CHRIST WAS BORN AS A MORTAL MAN (Depending on what you believe.) A SEMI-ANONYMOUS STREET ARTIST AND HIS MATES LO DID COME AND BRING WITH THEM PICTURES WHAT THEY HAD MADE TO SELL FOR A CAUSE IN A LITTLE SHOP KNOWN AS A 'GALLERY' AND ALSO TO PAINT ON A WALL WHICH IS PROBABLY ILLEGAL BUT IT DOESN'T LOOK VERY NICE ANYWAY BECAUSE IT IS A MILITARY WALL SET THERE BY THE GOVERNMENT OF ISRAEL FOR REASONS WE ARE SIMPLY TOO LAZY TO GO IN TO HERE, BUT ULTIMATELY BECAUSE THEY ARE HAVING AN EXTENDED ARGUMENT KNOWN AS 'A WAR' WITH PALESTINE WHICH LOOKS TO THE PASSING MONKEY MORE LIKE 'AN OCCUPATION' BUT WHAT THE sod DO WE KNOW? WELL I MAY NOT KNOW MUCH ABOUT ART…

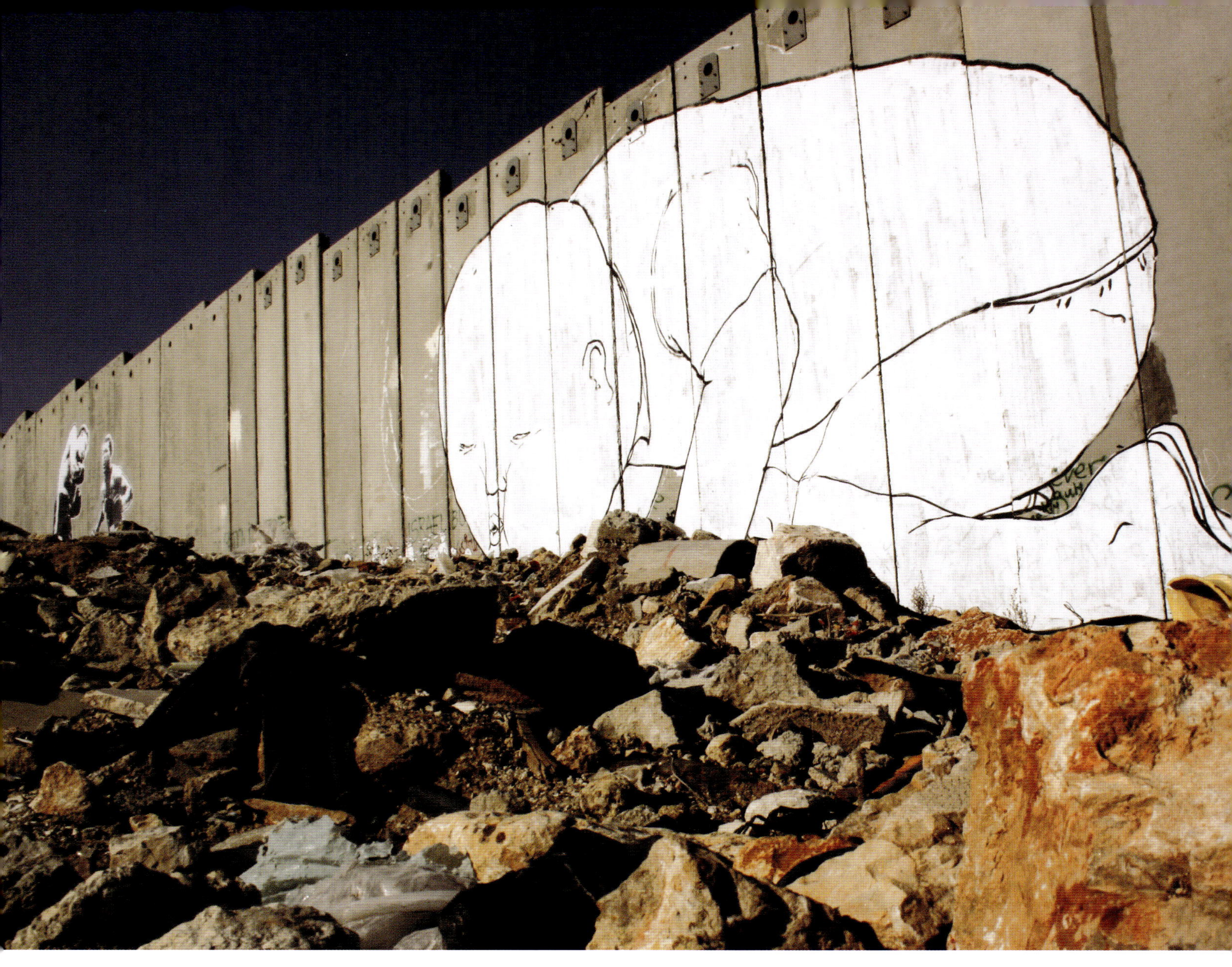

Monkey see...

# Free
# Palestine?

Eyes glaze over rapidly. The truth is that we are always forgetting that other people, beyond our tribal boundaries, are actually as real as we are. No amount of beard stroking or political debate can make us empathise with the strange aliens that throng the world beyond. Sometimes we catch a glimpse of other realities than our own, but if we are ten percent angel we are ninety percent monkey. If we accept this then at least we are working at ground zero. This is the perspective that gets you into situations like spray painting a military patrolled security wall in Palestine. The monkey idiot with a glimmer of consciousness goes where the wise man cannot.

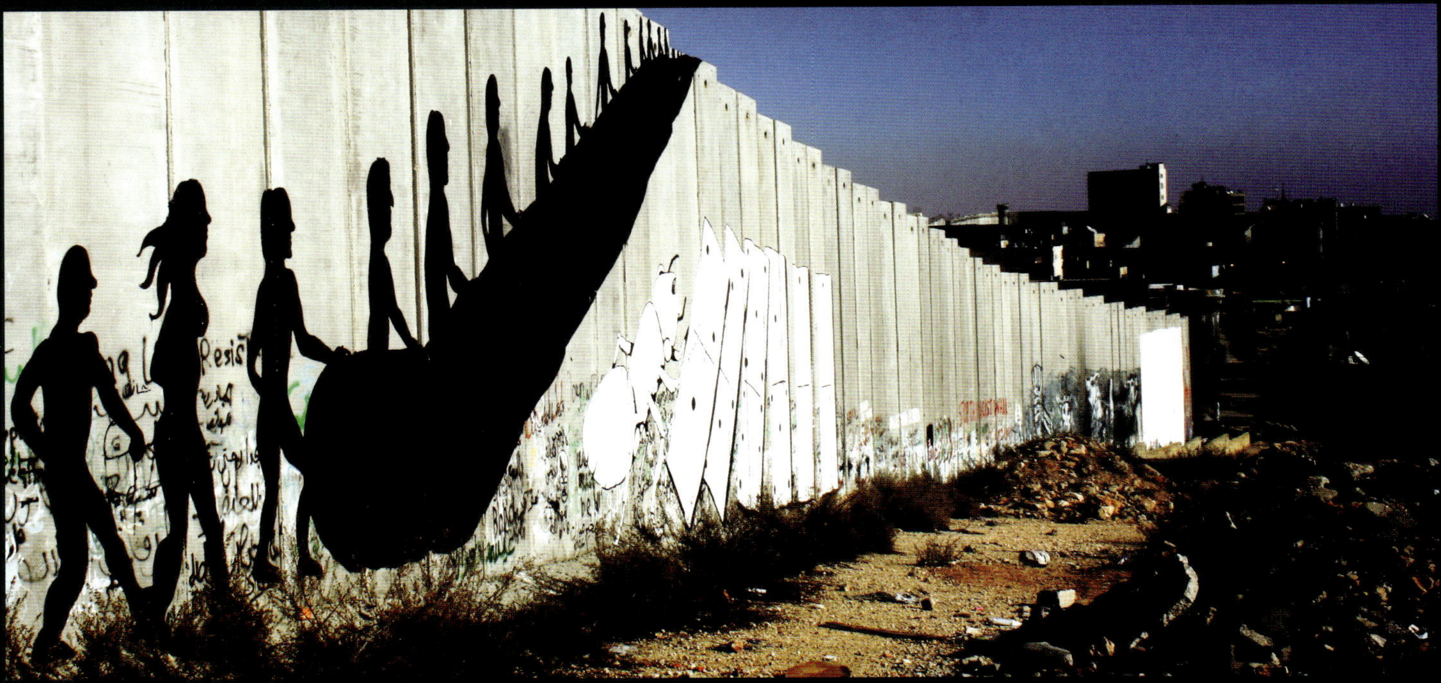

Welcome to the neighbourhood.

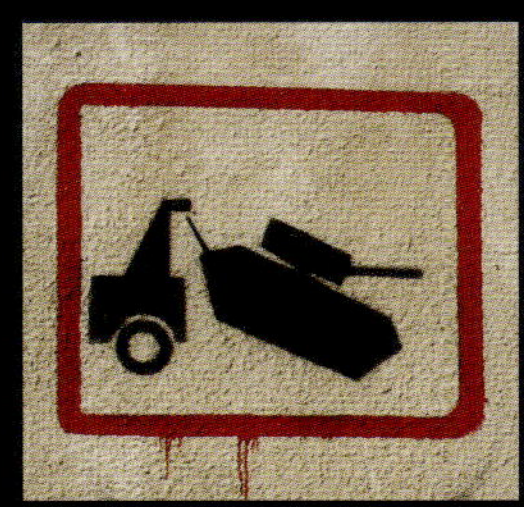

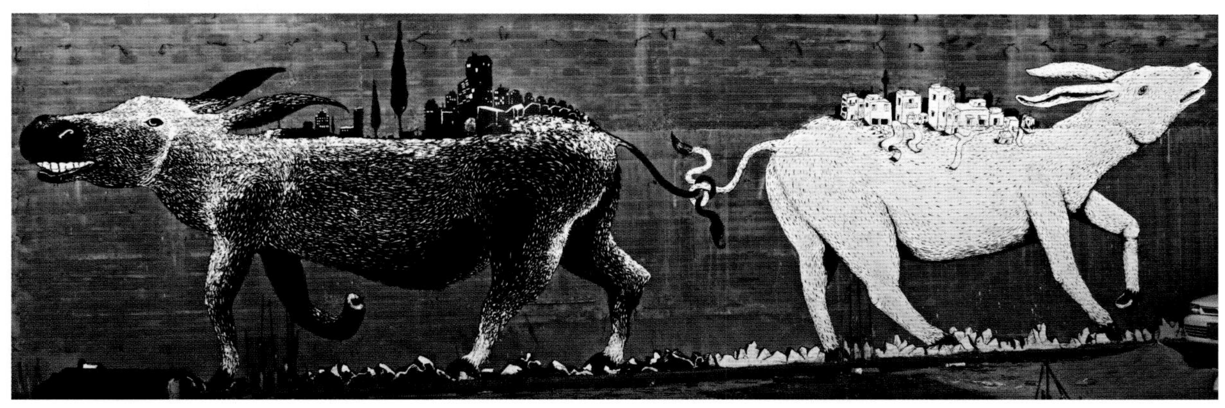

## Graffiti Aid

One muses upon charitable actions and sees only images of Bob Geldof and Terry Wogan. One slips into a milieu of images of earnest telethons featuring Gyles Brandreth in a knitted tank-top. All engagement with the great and noble problems of our time require one only to phone in with a credit card number. As if we could fit in solving the questions of poverty and oppression between two shifts at the office and a trip to Ikea! How unutterably fucking dull! Where is the engagement? Where is real life? Even a small adventure of some kind is better than this. Any intervention in the world around you is worth more than a disengaged and passive 'act' of charity.

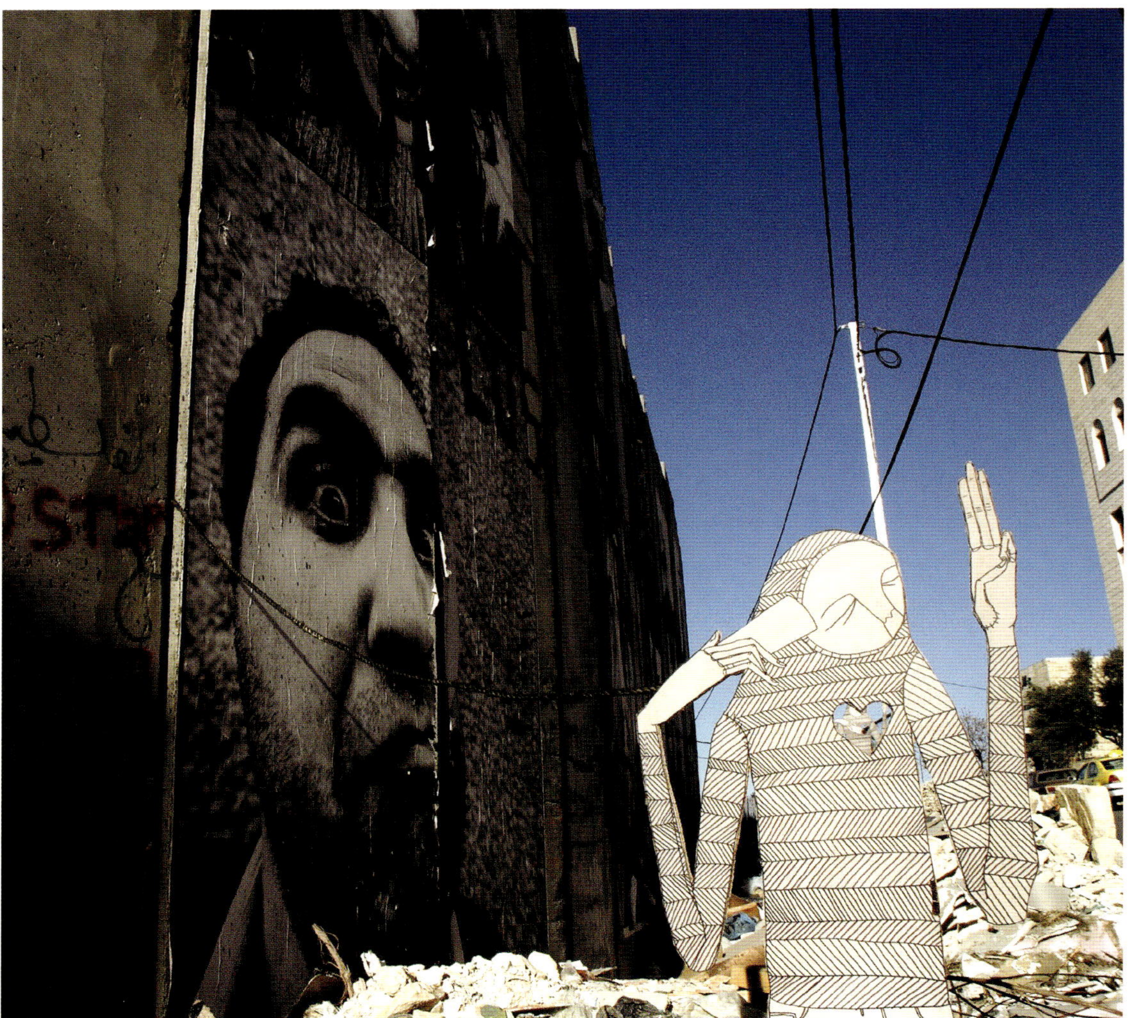

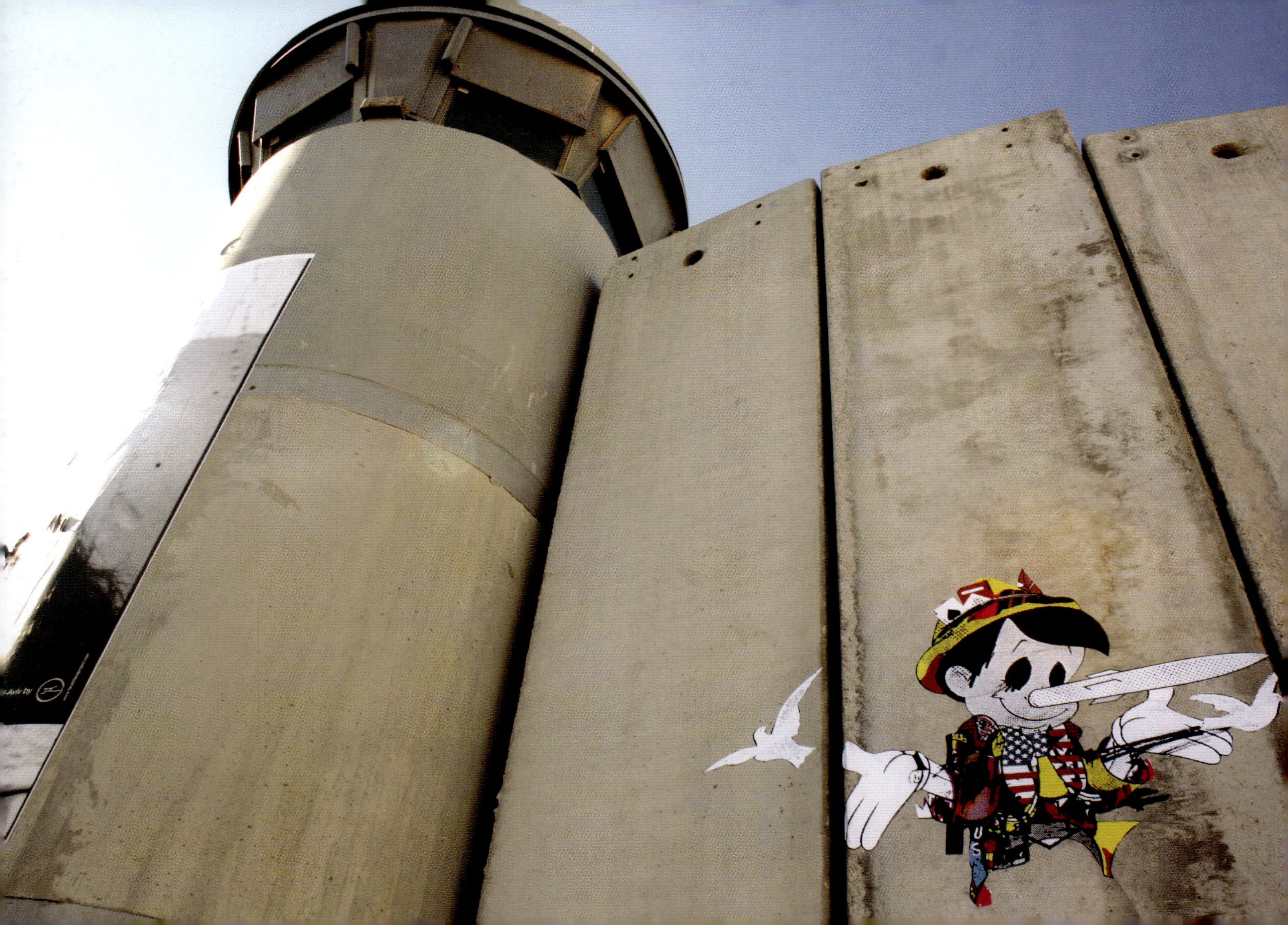

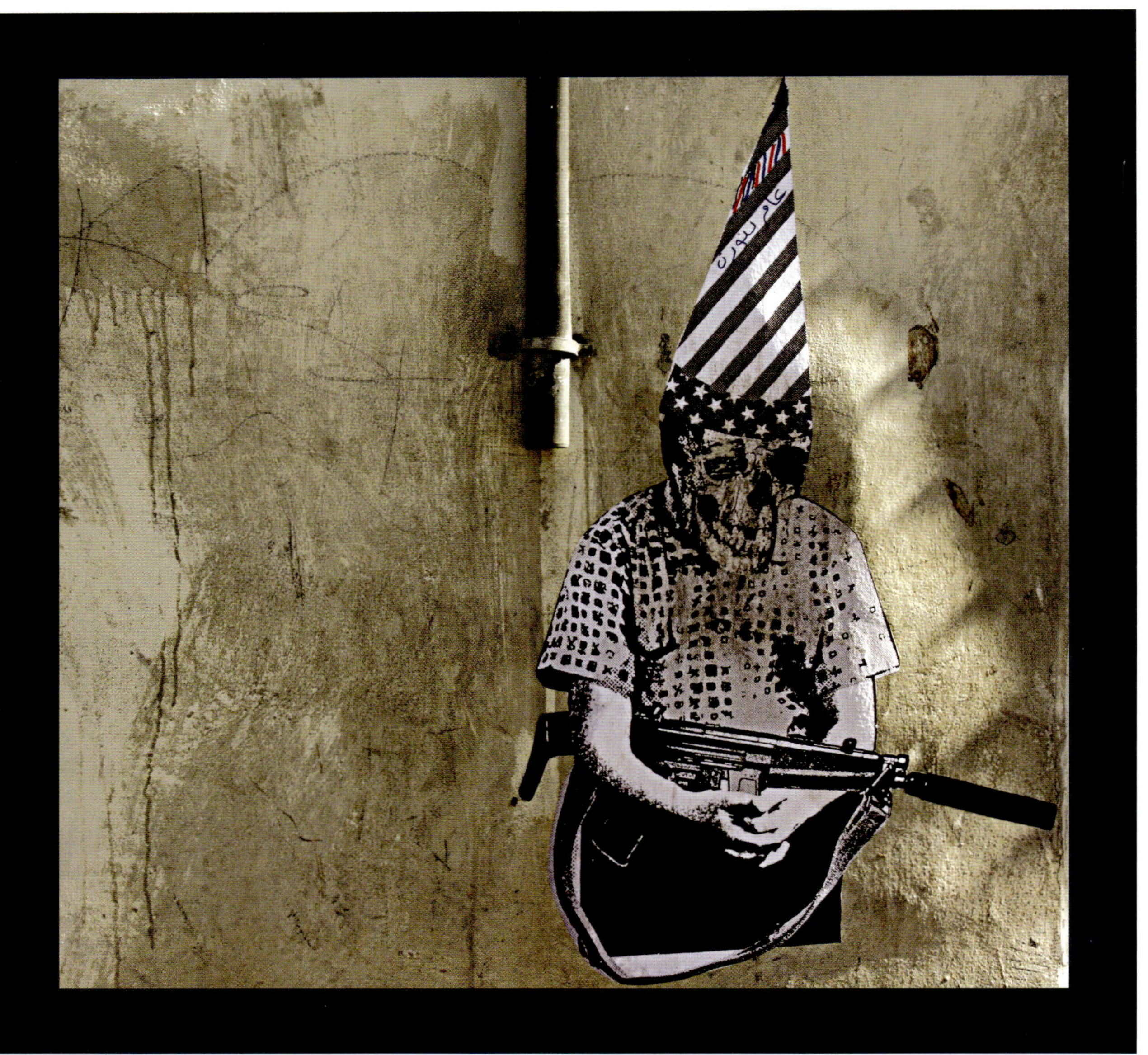

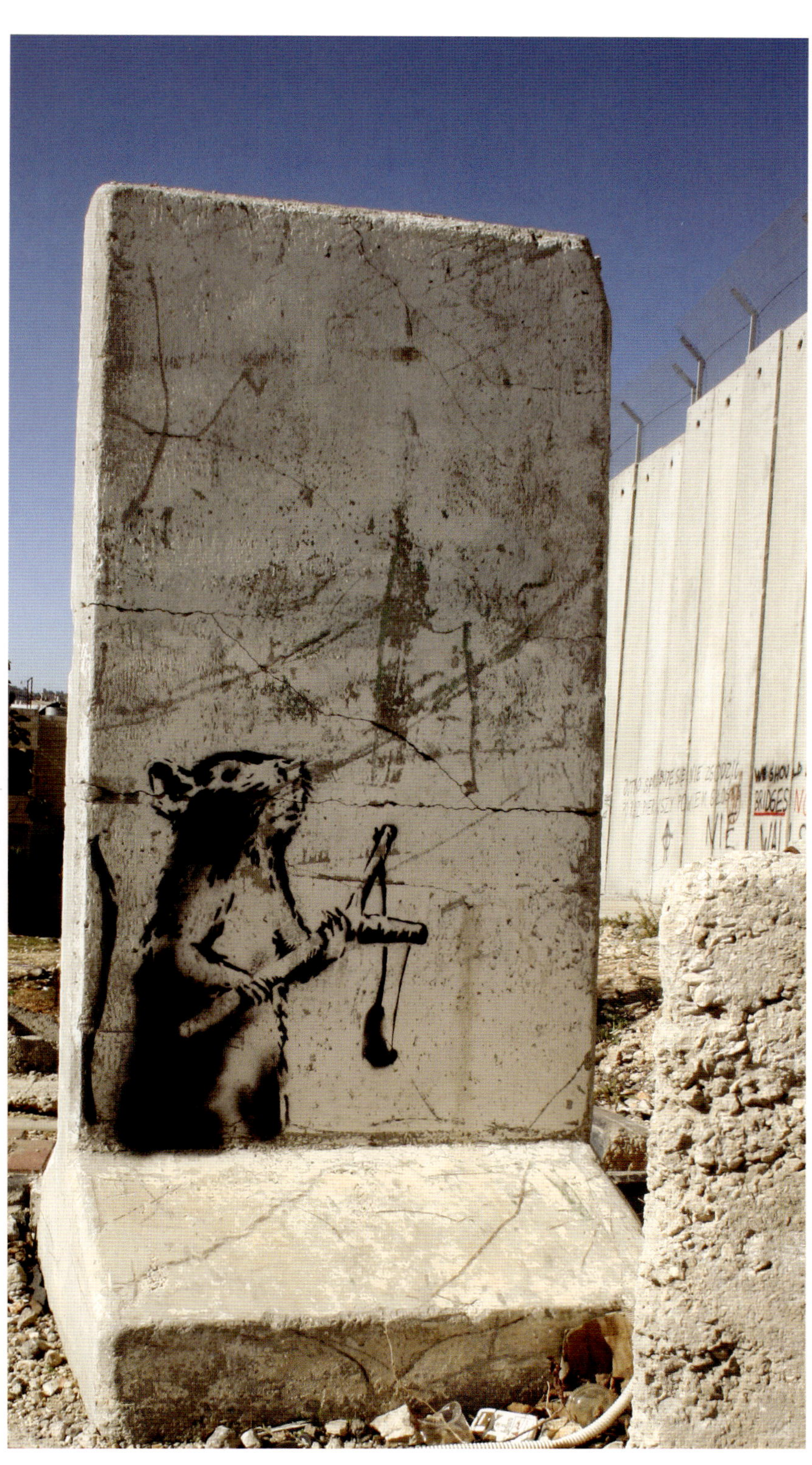

# Here Lie Dragons

Maybe the strongest thing about Santa's Ghetto is simply that it was in Bethlehem. It is as if our map of the world still features 'Here be Dragons' scrawled over places like Gaza. A bunch of skinny artists go over and the bubble is burst. They have spray-painted 'Didn't see any Dragons. There's a great big bloody wall mind' over the top.

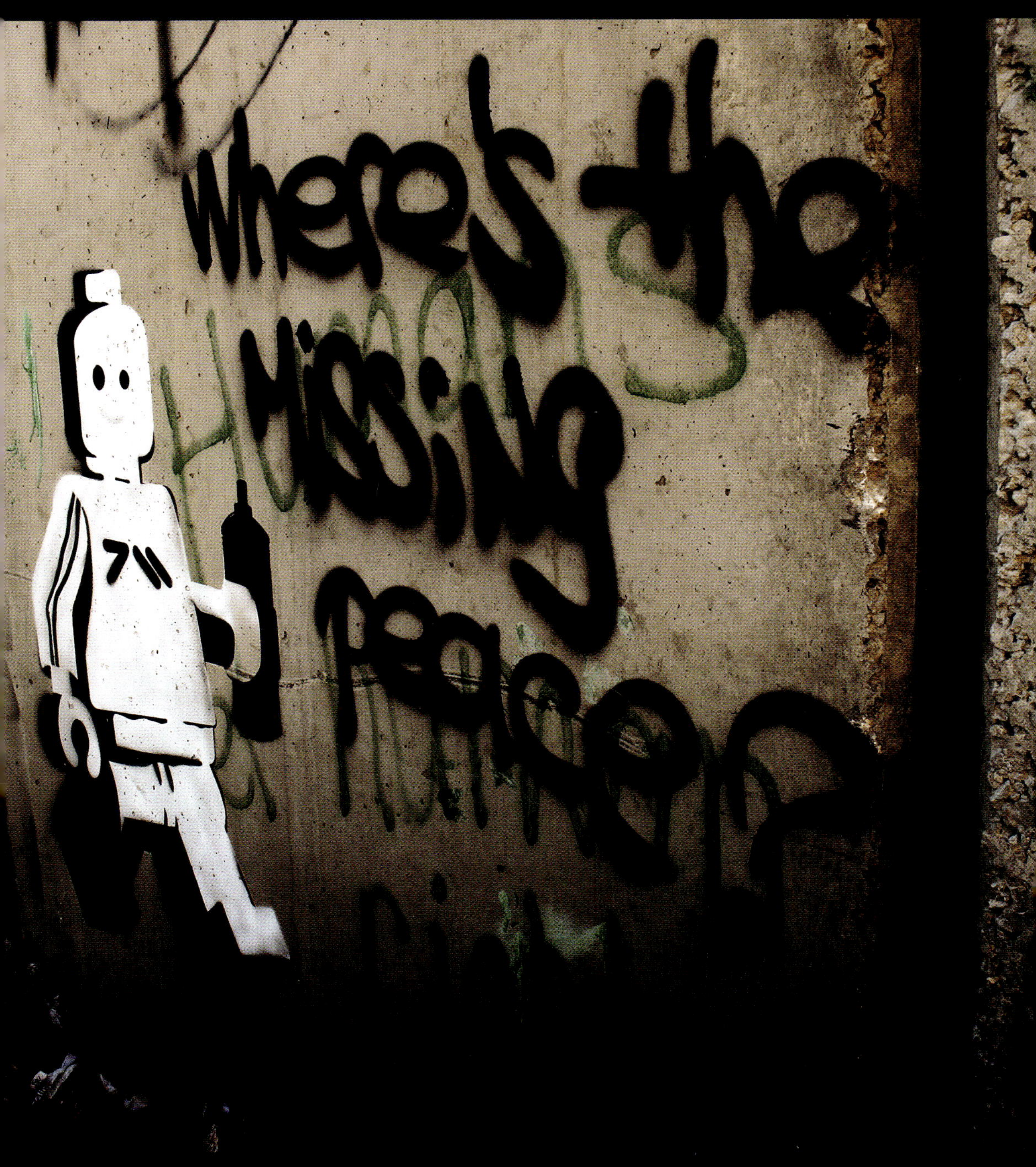


above thy deep and dreamless sleep . . .

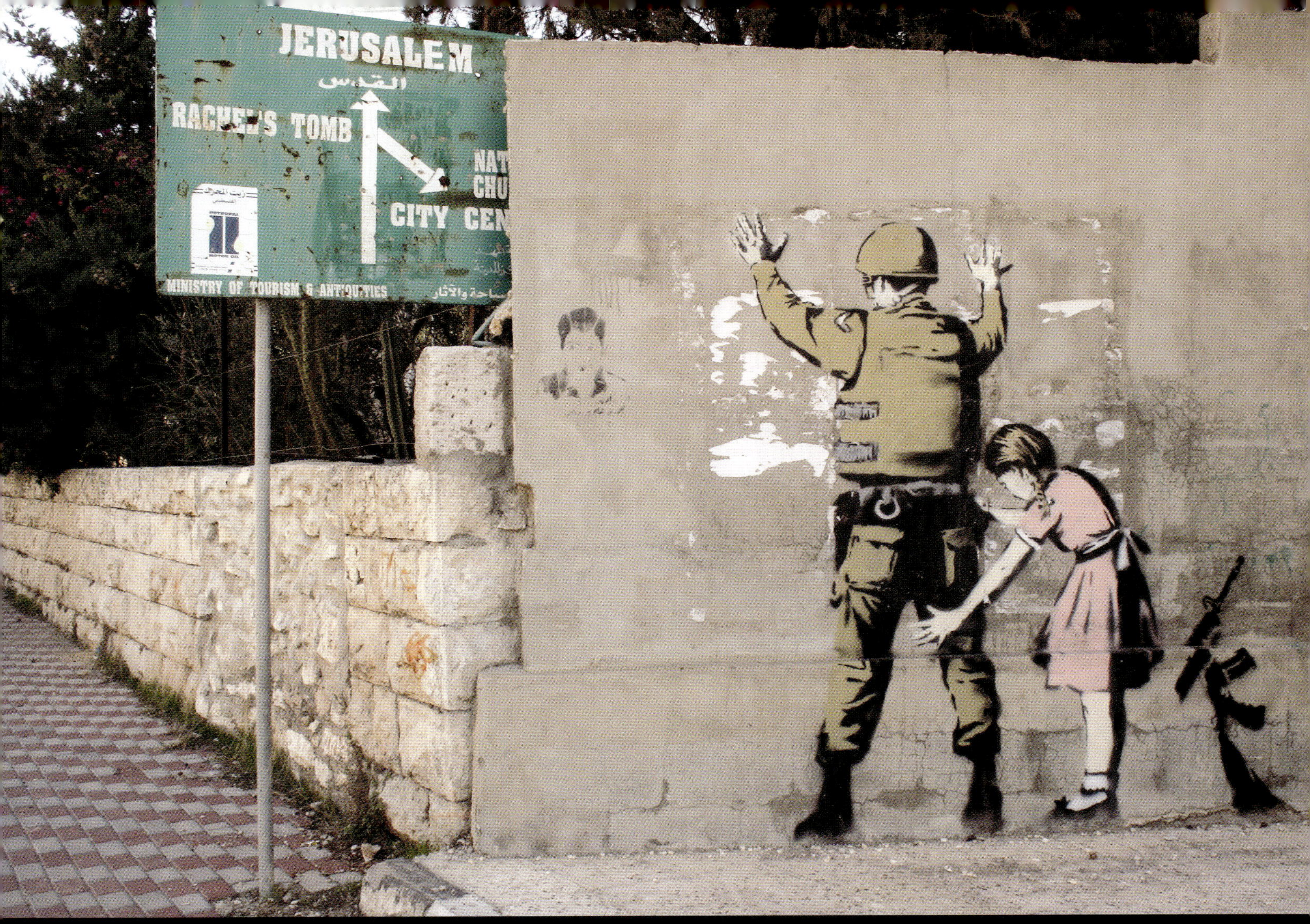


The nativity scene is built all over the world every year with all manner of variations. Some feature a fat man from a cola advert sitting in a sleigh on the roof. Some feature a small boy having a poo in the corner of the stable. Many of them feature a chubby pink Caucasian baby born in the middle-east 2000 years ago and most likely fated to a life of terrible sun-burn. And people think art is obscure?

than the little town that really exists. We need to poke something with a stick these days to see if it is real or not. Street Art is as good a way as any to bite a coin to see if it is made of gold. Coins are generally not made of gold anymore. Pinch yourself now because you may be dreaming. Look at your hands to control the dream.

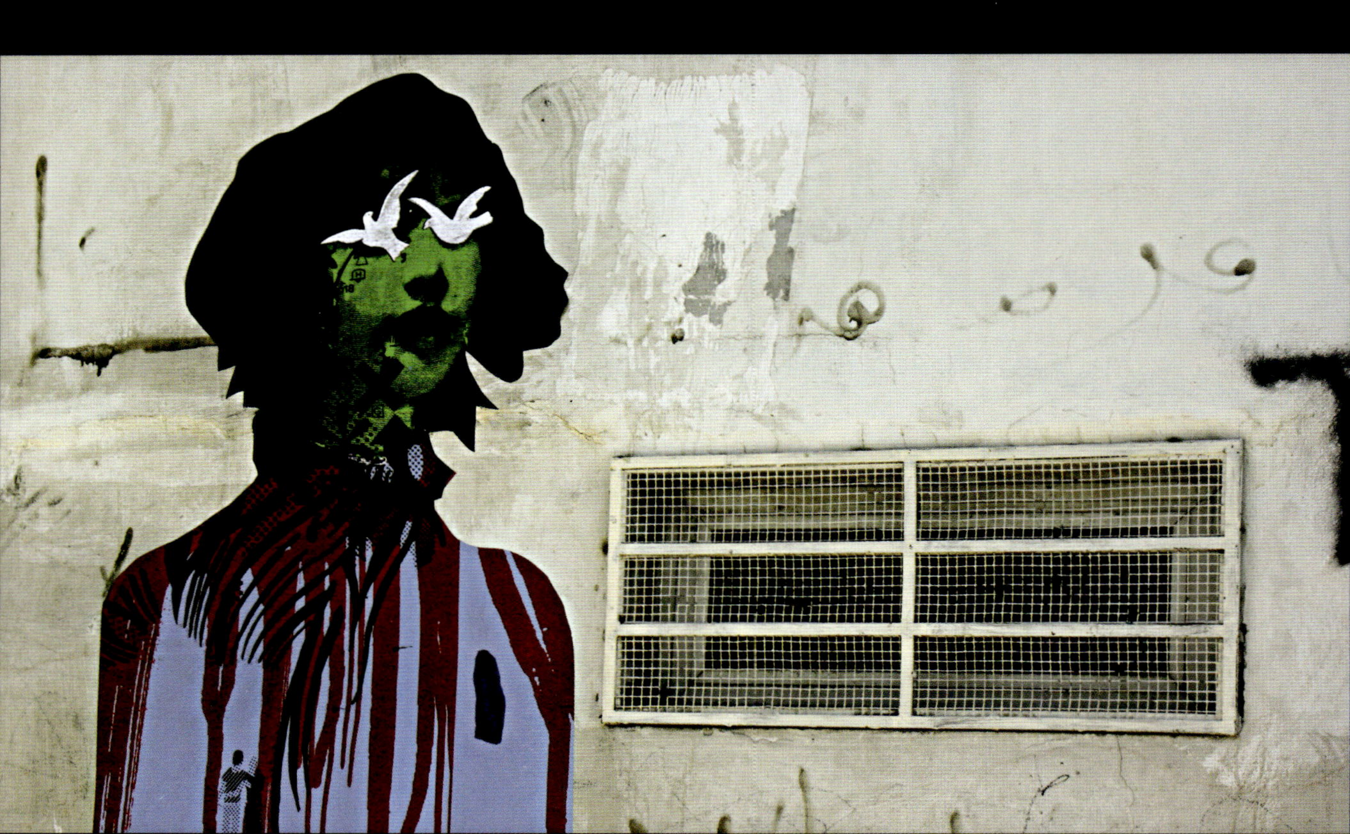

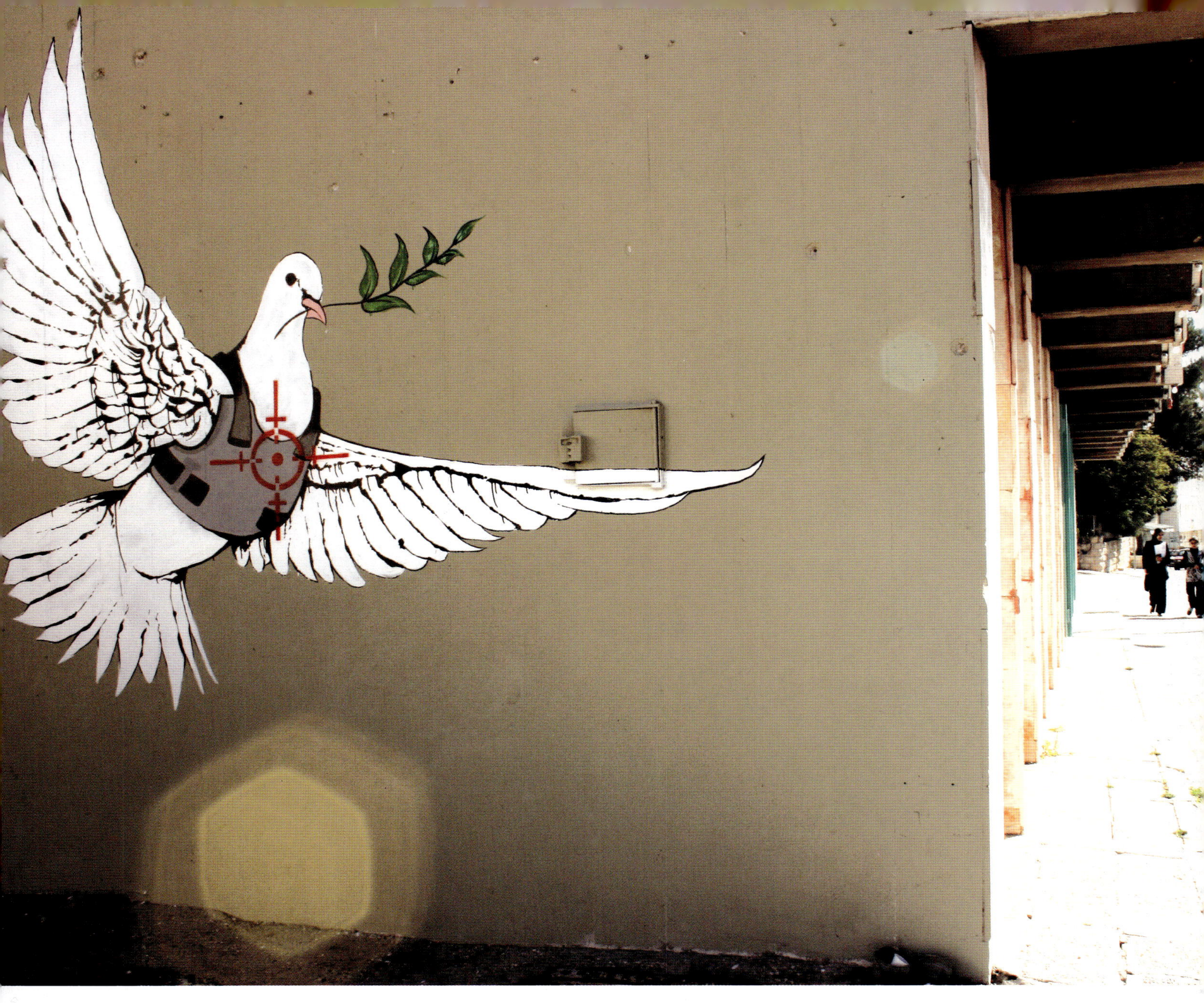

all we are saying is give peace a chance . . .

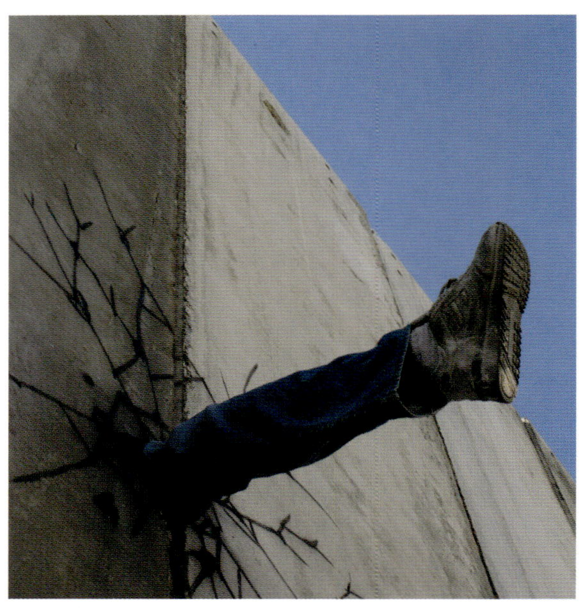

They seem to be obsessed with illusions, tricks and games. They paint fake windows opening up onto illusory scenes. Like the leg that sticks through the wall. When you catch a glimpse it throws your perception. It is a little stumble off the train tracks of everyday thought. It opens up the world a little. It reminds you to switch your mind on and question the messages you are fed. It reminds you that a wall is not just a wall, it is somebody else's opinion and you do not have to accept it.

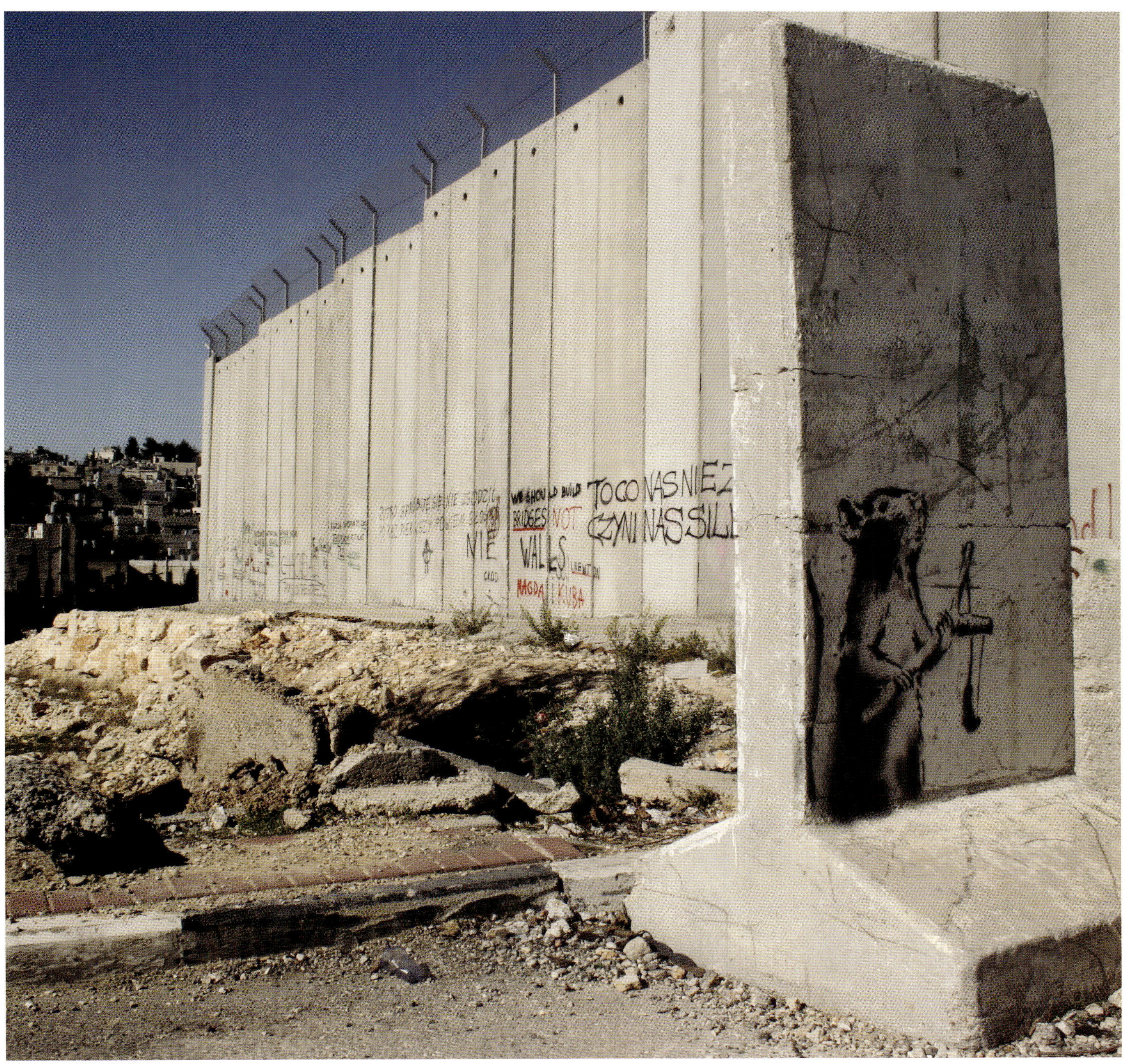

WE SHOULD BUILD
BRIDGES NOT
WALLS
TO CO NAS NIE
CZYNI NAS SILE

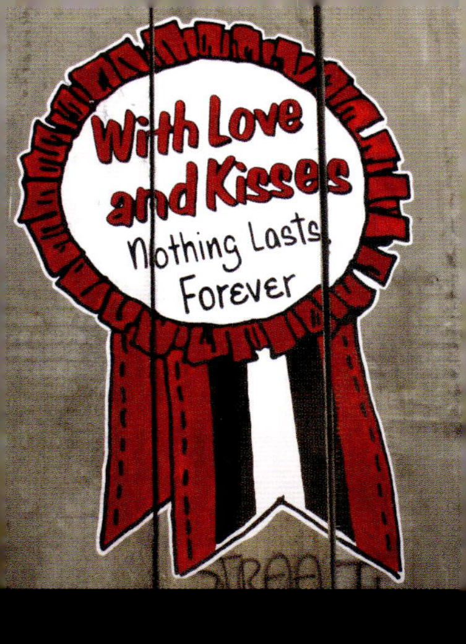


. . . a wall is not just a wall, it is
somebody else's opinion and
you do not have to accept it.

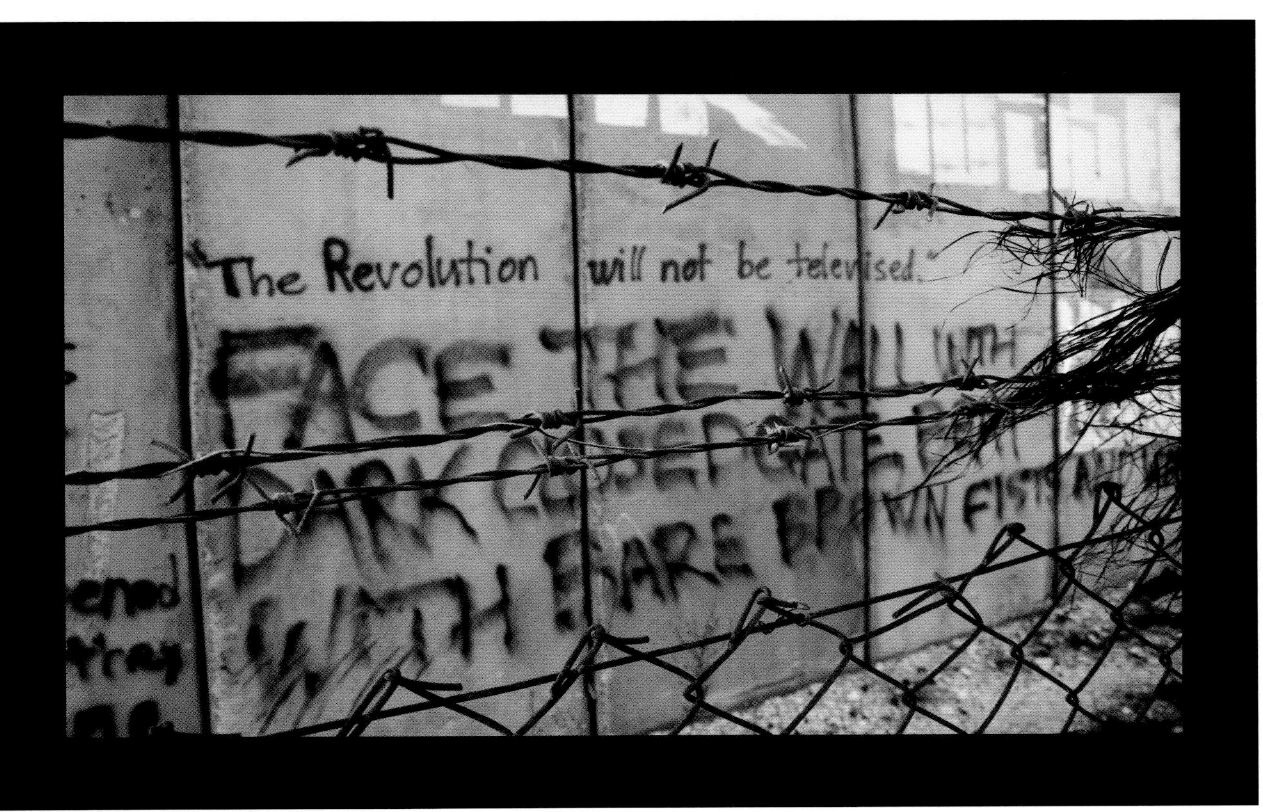

"The Revolution will not be televised."
FACE THE WALL WITH
DARK CLOSED GATES
WITH BARE BROWN FISTS

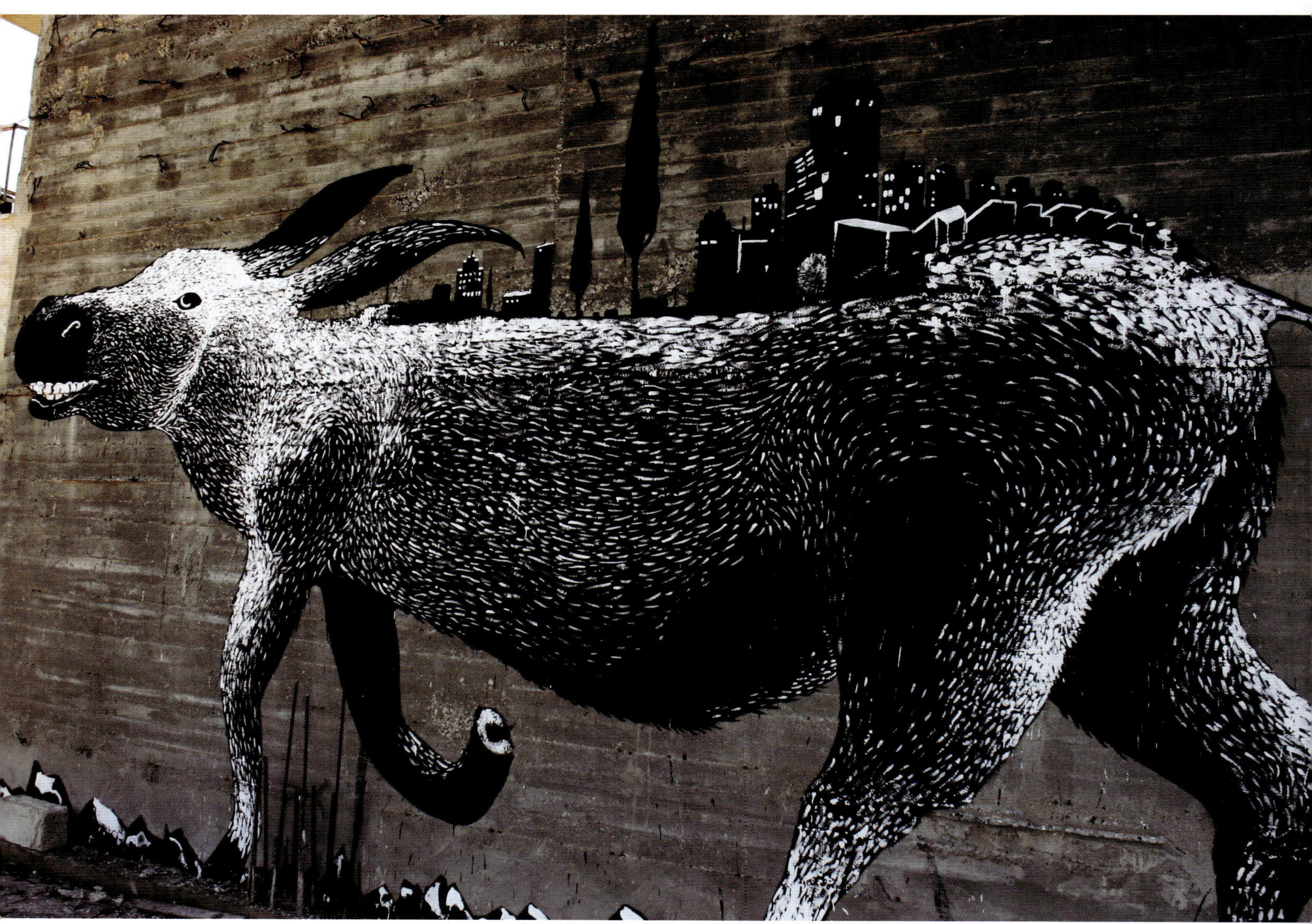

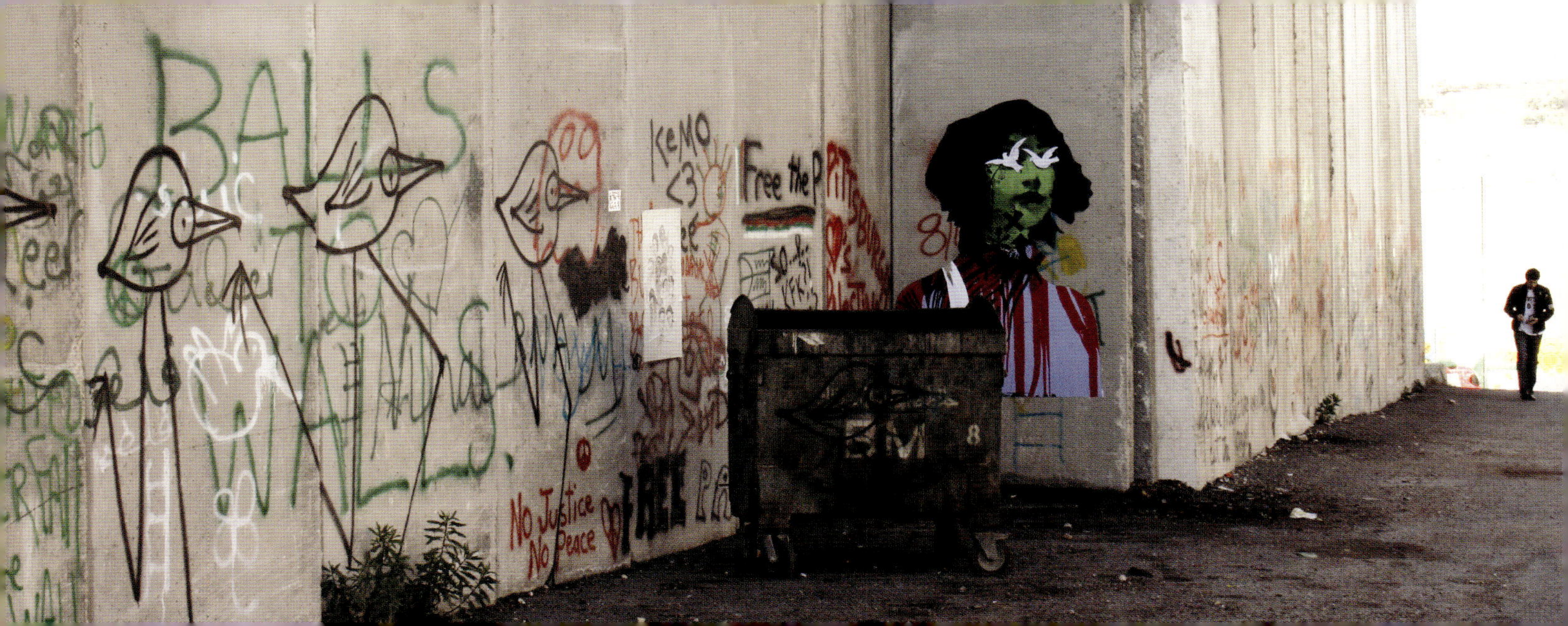
BALLS
IceMO <3
Free the P
No Justice
No Peace
BM  8

now put down the book...

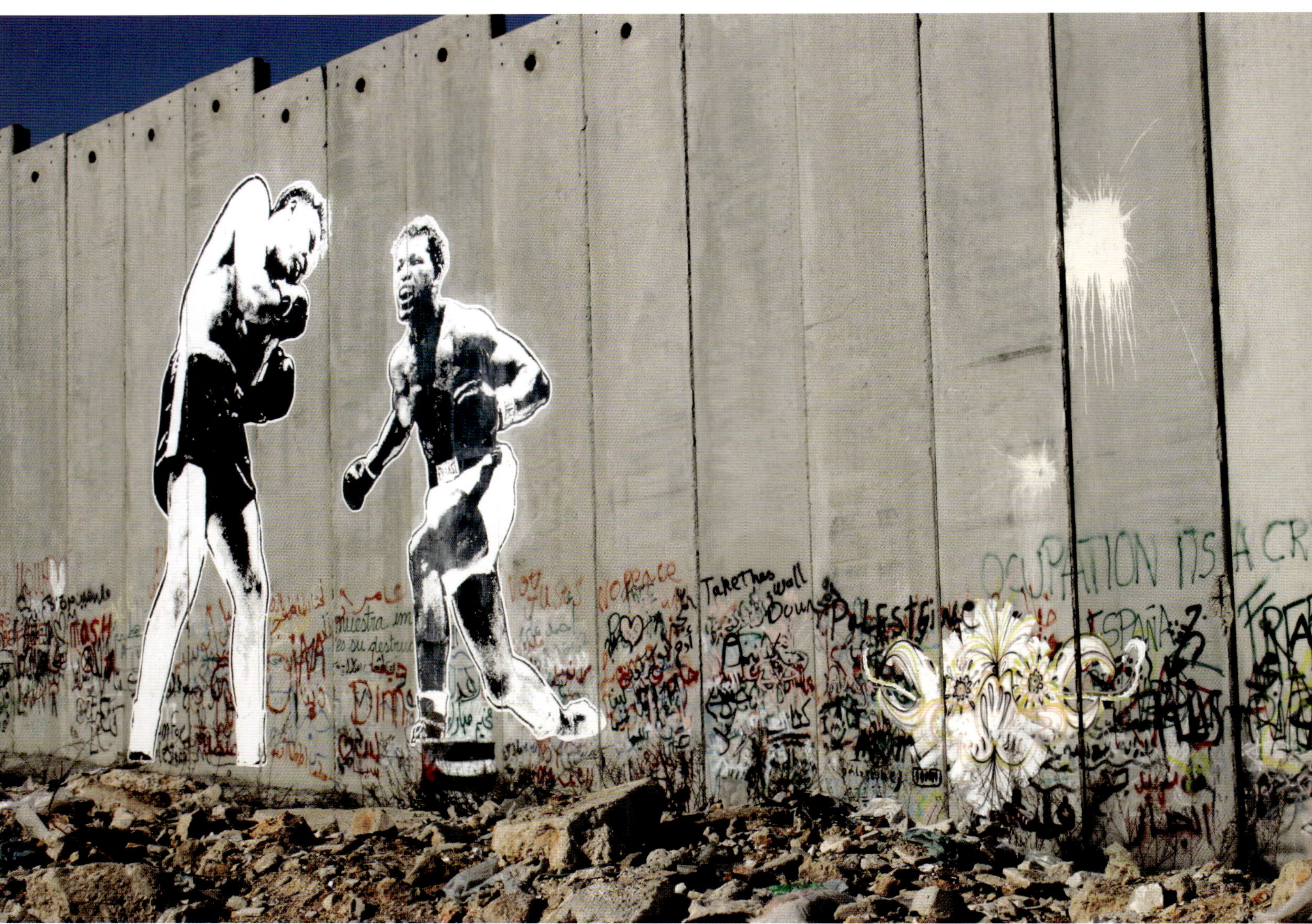

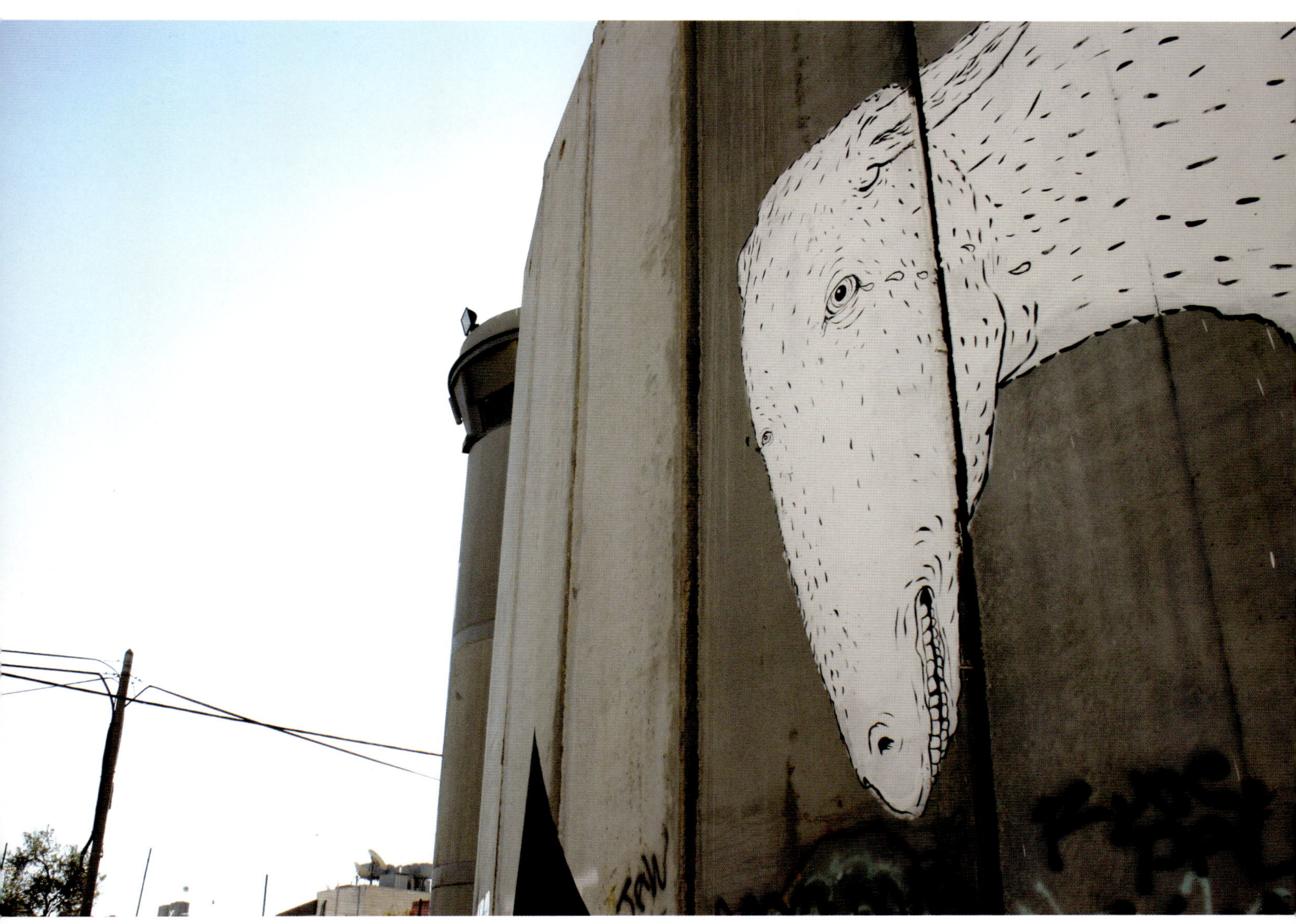

...and go google the Israel / Palestine thing

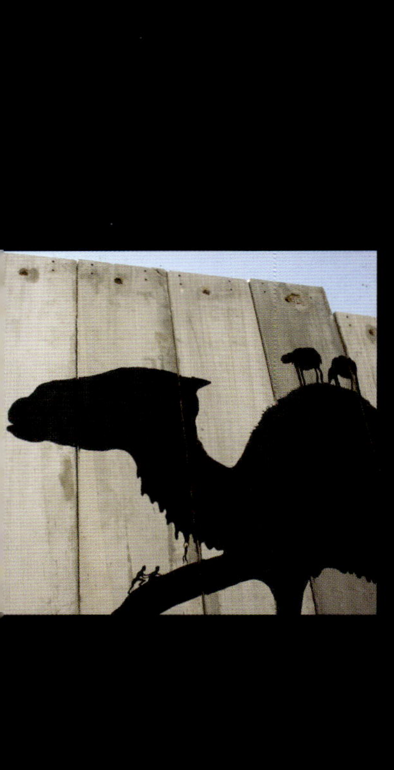

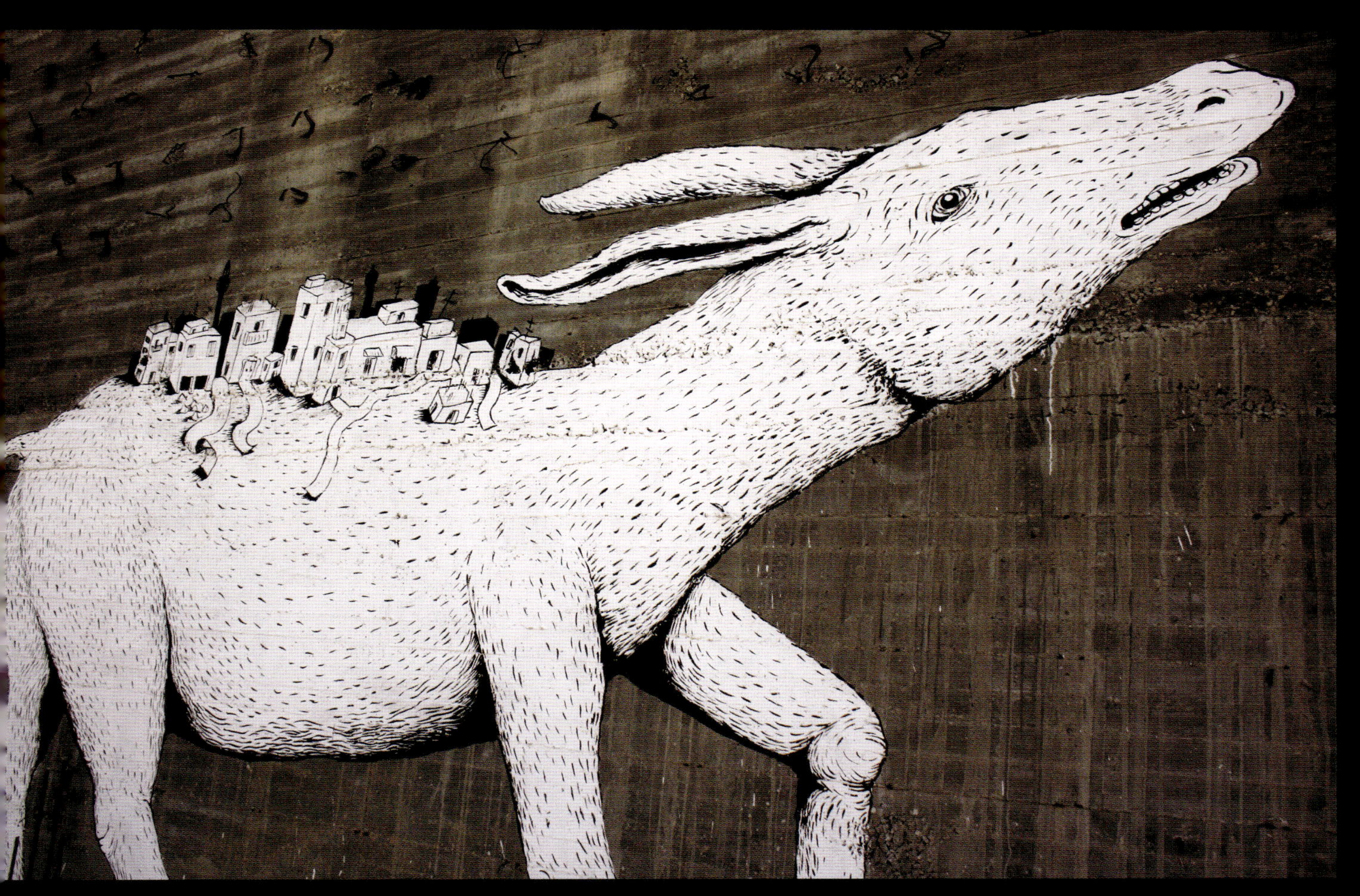

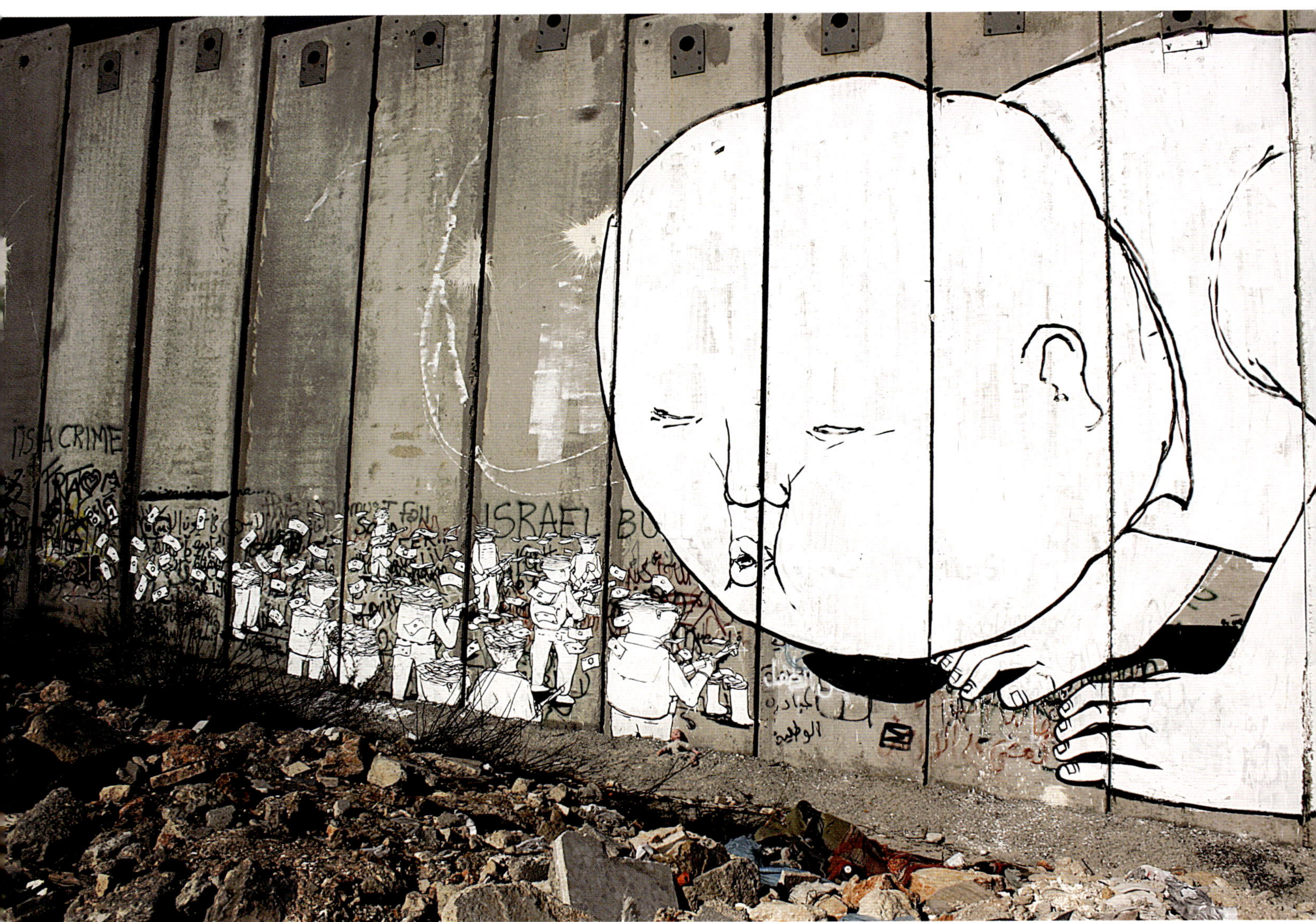

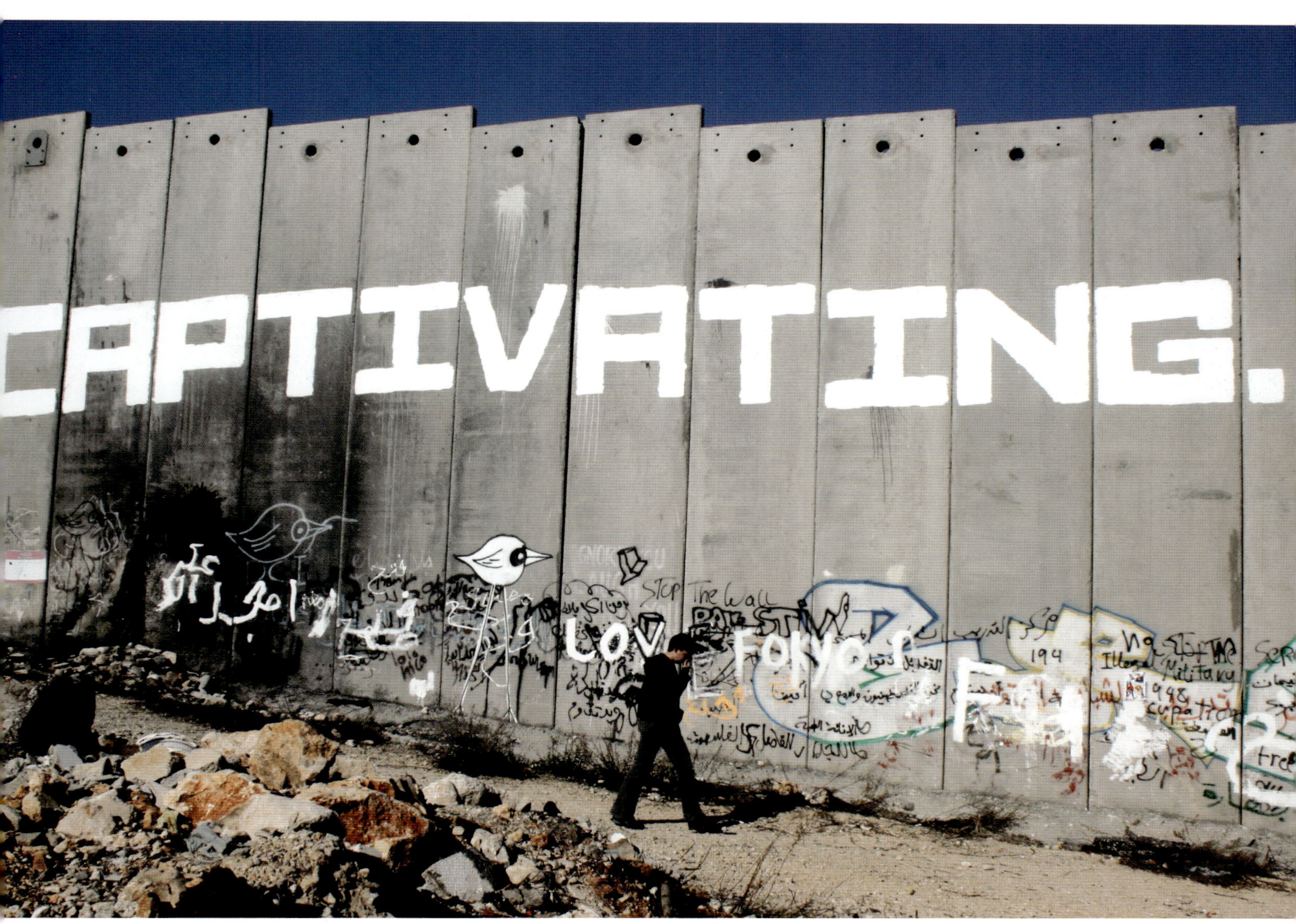

CAPTIVATING.

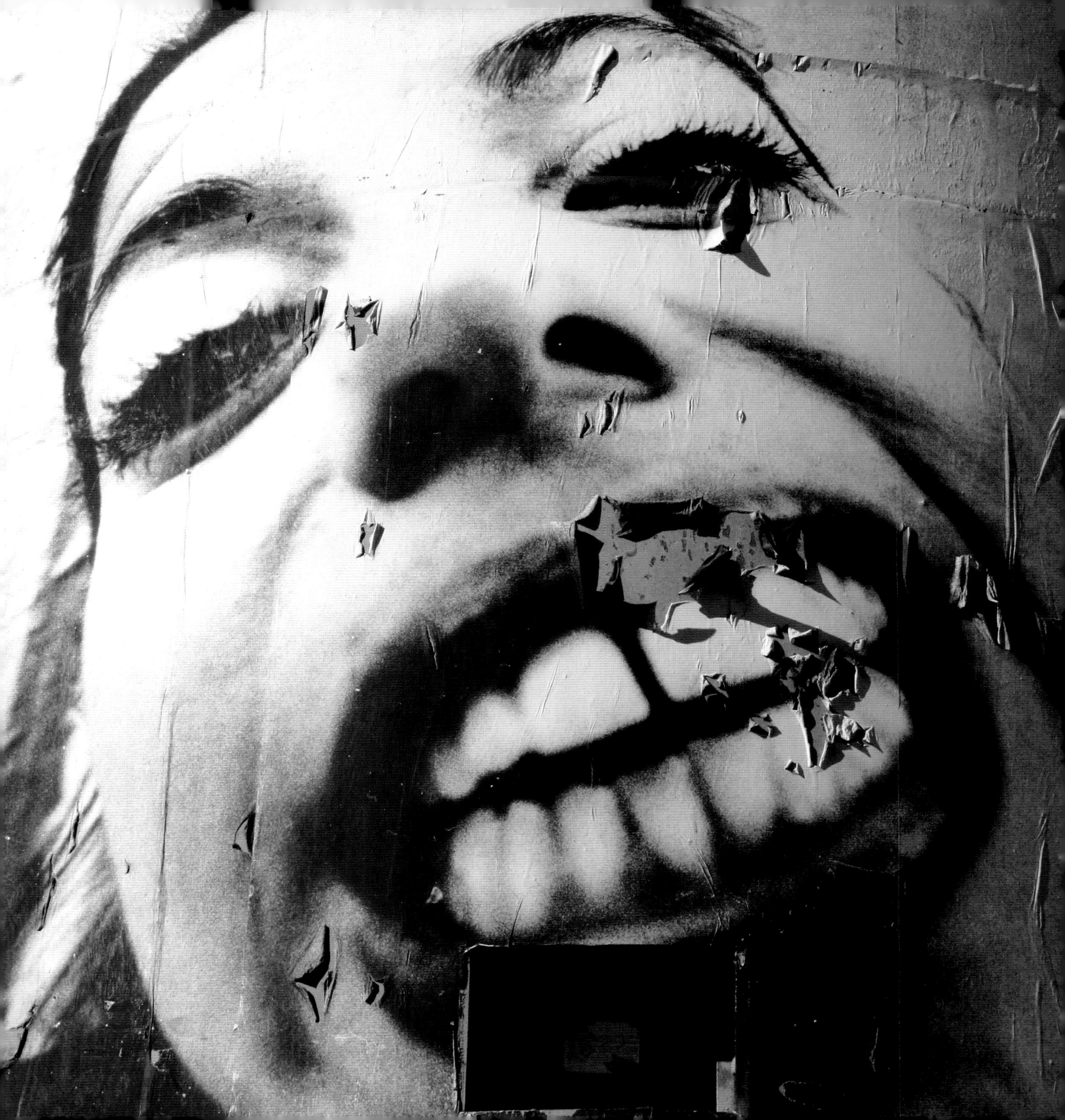

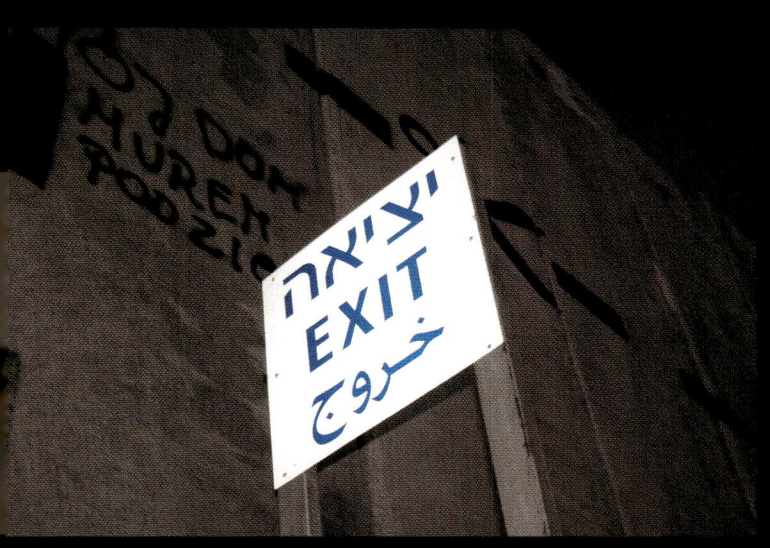
יציאה
EXIT
خروج

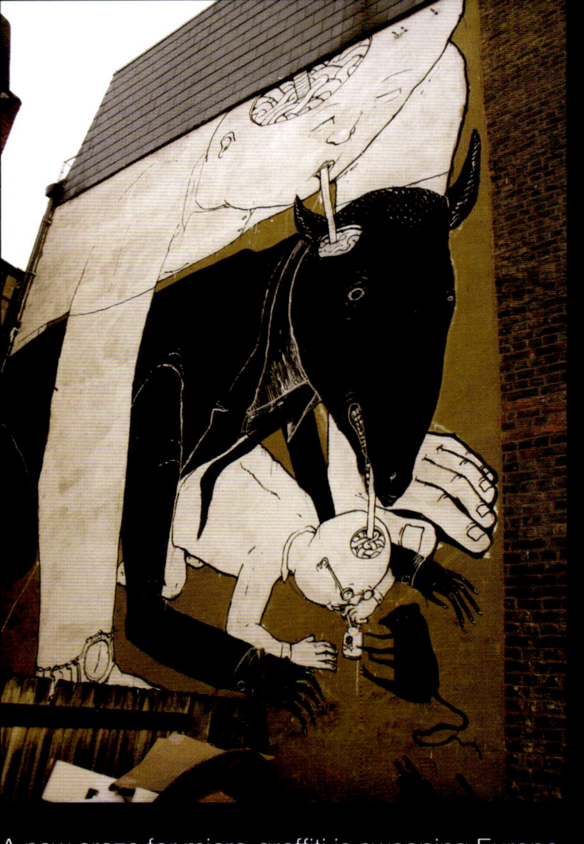

A new craze for micro-graffiti is sweeping Europe. Its chief proponents NAZEL and STRAWBERRY FACE have gathered a cult following of sorts in the wake of thousands of acts of mini art vandalism. The two are seemingly locked in competition to create the smallest graffiti yet. NAZEL is currently in the lead with a minuscule picture of the Queen of Spain vomiting onto a chisel said to be located on the wing of an aeroplane near the science museum of Berlin. German Police are said to be utterly confounded by their inability to actually locate the work. A spokesperson for Europol said "This must be stopped. If these youths start messing around with atoms they could end up splitting one and we all know what happens then. Kaboom."

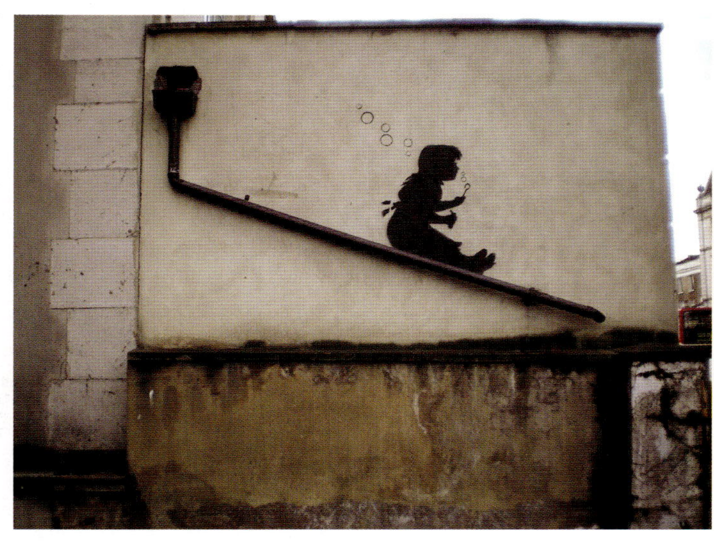
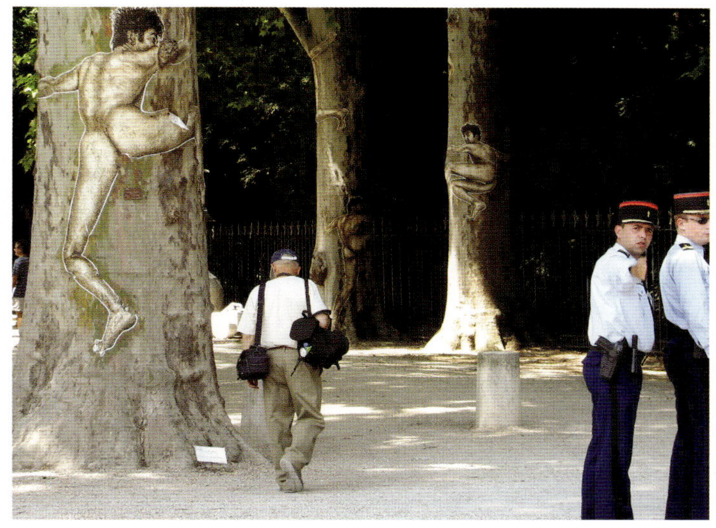
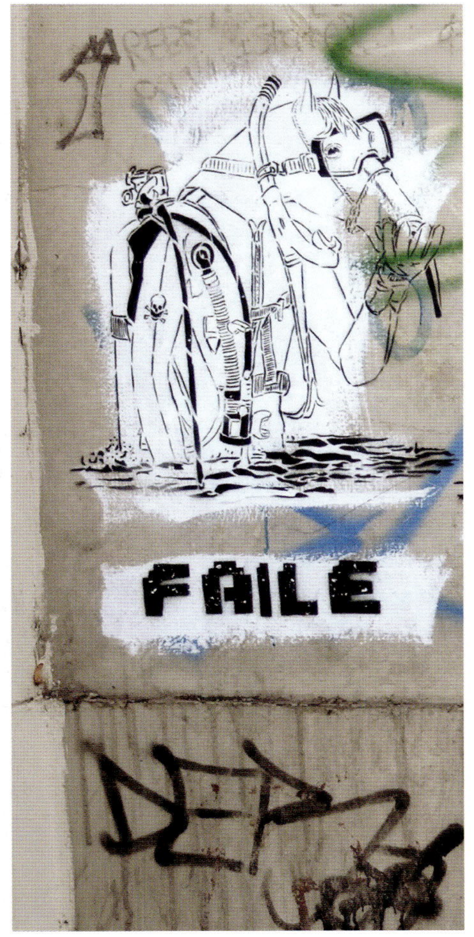
FAILE
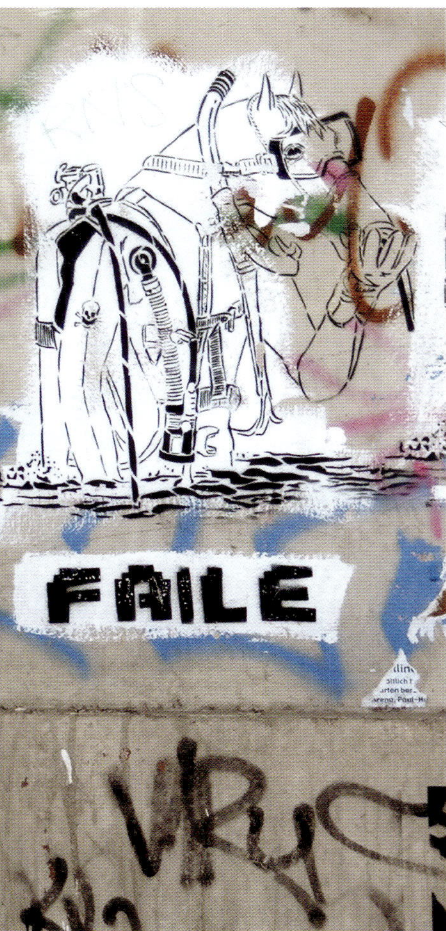
FAILE
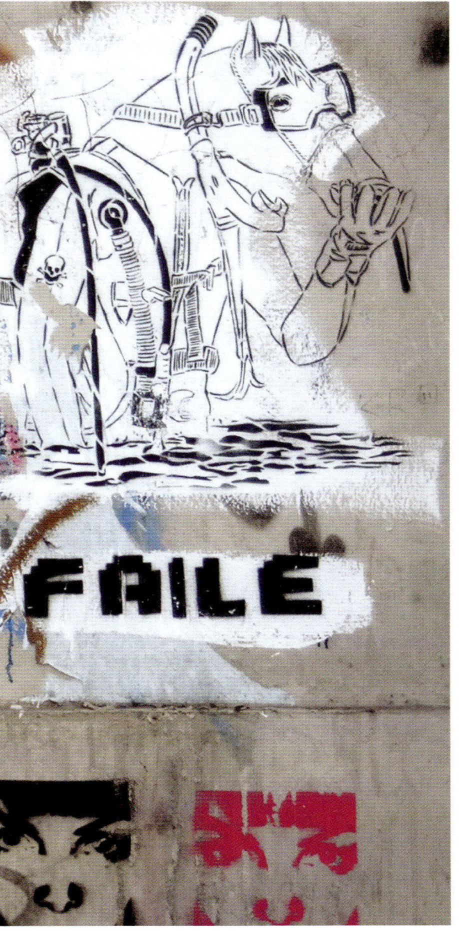
FAILE

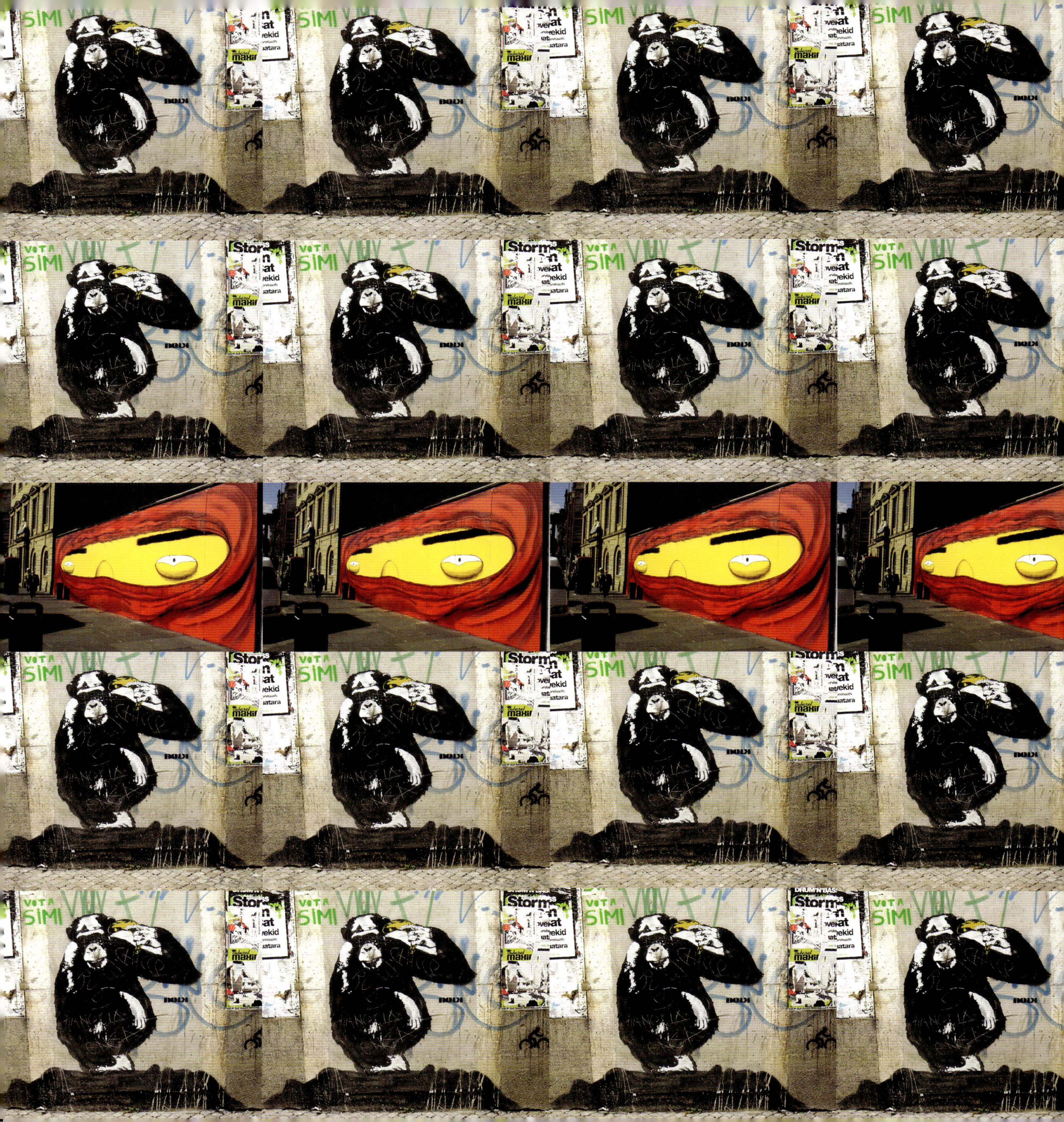

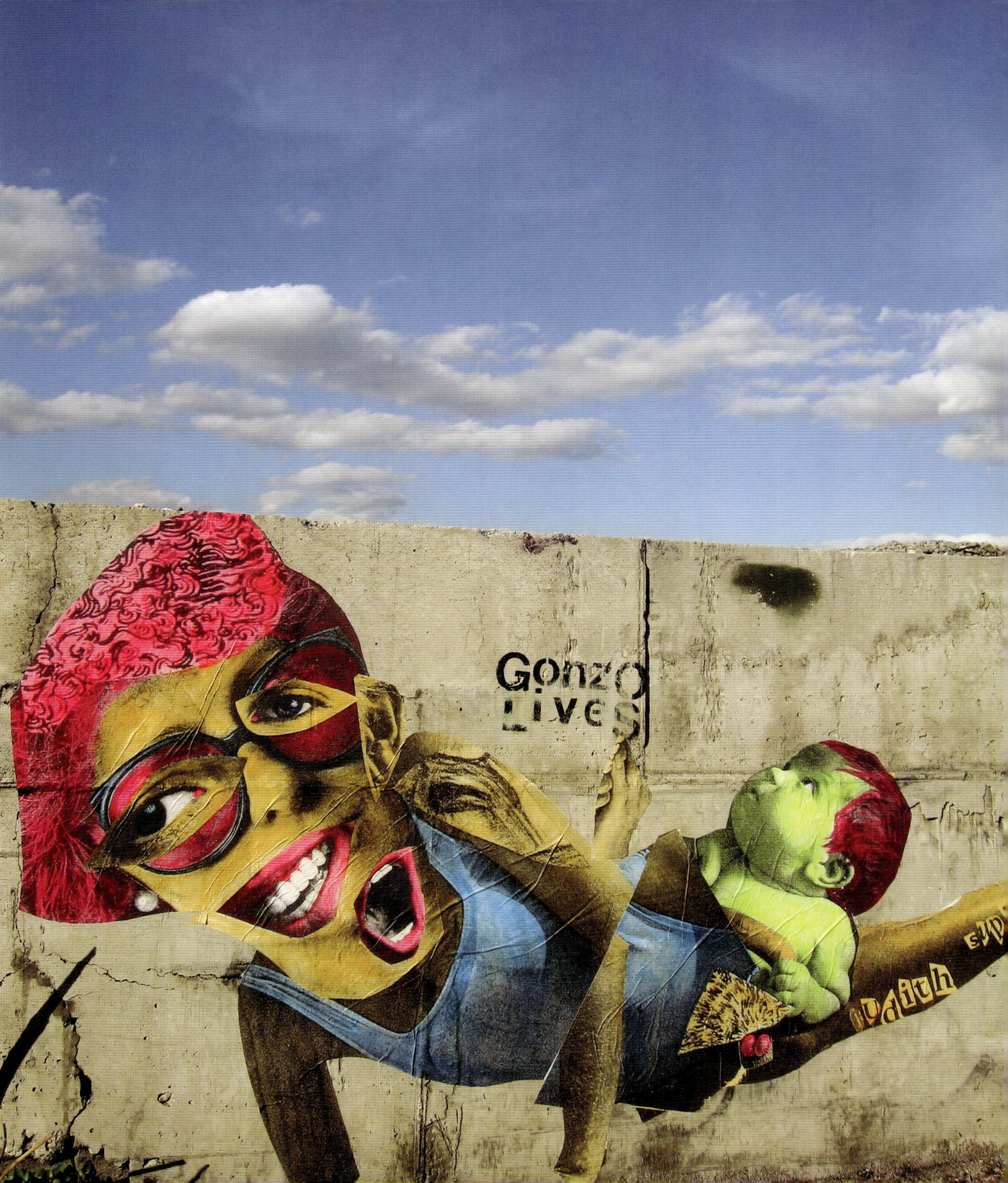

Gonzo
LIVES

Turning>
Ourselves
>Inside
<Out

…we turn ourselves inside out. The world is harsh and cold and dark so we dig into the ground and huddle under the earth. We make the cellar and the foundations where our feet take root and send that old black magic up the legs and into them lustful organs. The cellar be the place where it all begins and the monsters in us lurk down there but also our roots.

Then we build up the ground floor where lies the middle realm where the ordinary doings of the daily life are lived. Right in the centre we put the fire to keep away the wolves and burn up the meat and bake the bread, then we have the living room where we put the TV and do the ironing, and we have the porch and the front door which is basically our face. And the kitchen is the stomach where the fuel is burned to warm the limbs and head, and the living room is the heart where we meet the people that we love enough to let in and interact with them.

We move up to the head, upstairs to the bedrooms and bathrooms where we dream and think and wash off the dust of the days thinkings and play all manner of games some sexual and some not. It is up there in the tree tops we keep the chiddlers safe from the sabre tooth tigers on the jungle floor below. Up again to the attic, where the junk lies piled up with the old dusty bones, reminding us that we will die one day and be in someone else's attic, a ghost and nothing more…

…so the house is the body and the body is the house. And the city is the body too. The roads and train tracks are its arteries. The institutions are its organs. And the digital world is its nervous system. The world we built is the body inside-out. So when we paint a wall we paint ourselves, both our skin and our insides too. And soon when we paint we will be dripping fluorescent inks into the speedways of our nerves. The process continues, and will continue until we can find a way to make the soul visible. Perhaps when the genome is mapped, we will paint the soul with flesh, reverse it all and turn the body back the right way in, then there'll be nothing left but humans huddled in the earth finally healed of their alienation…

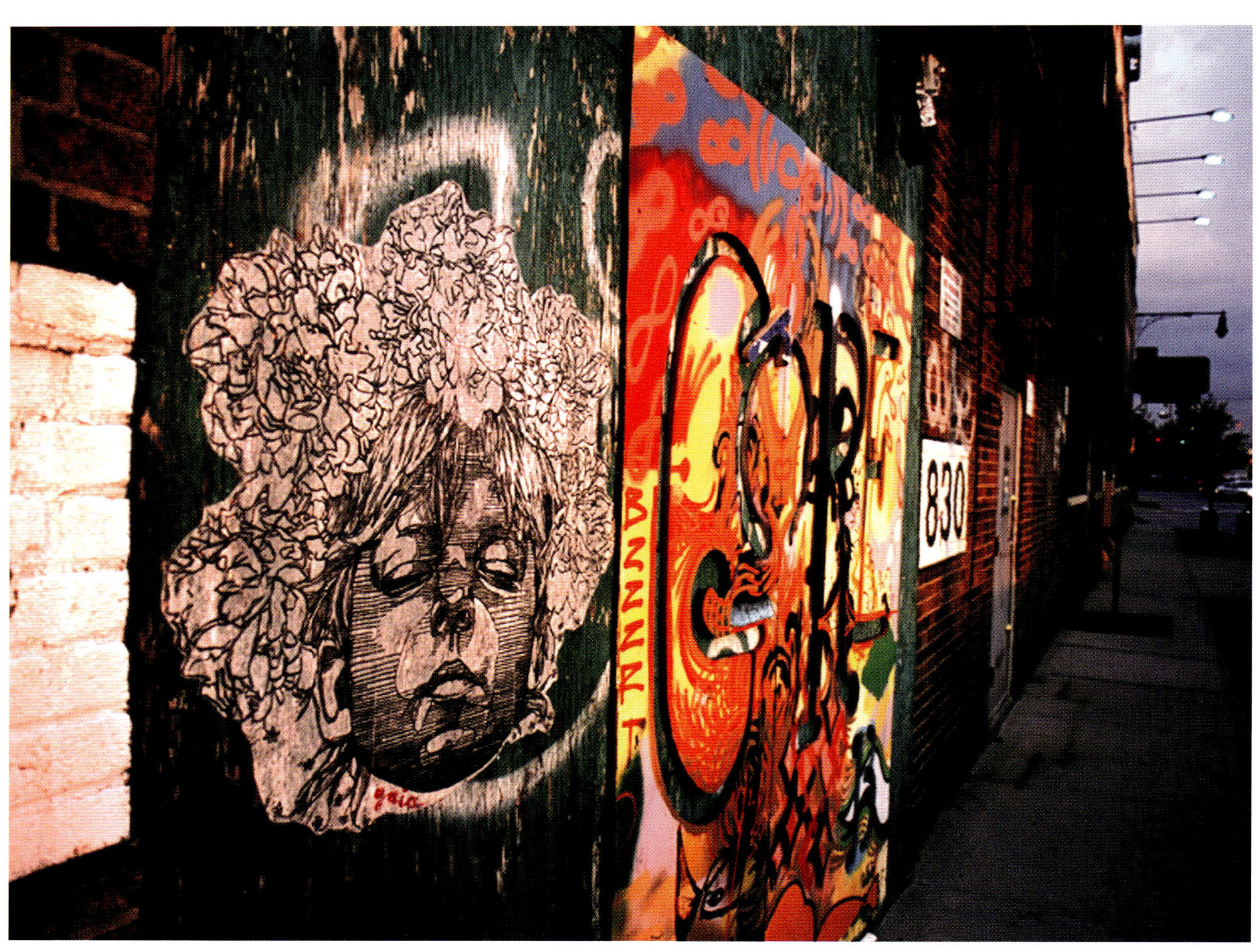


830

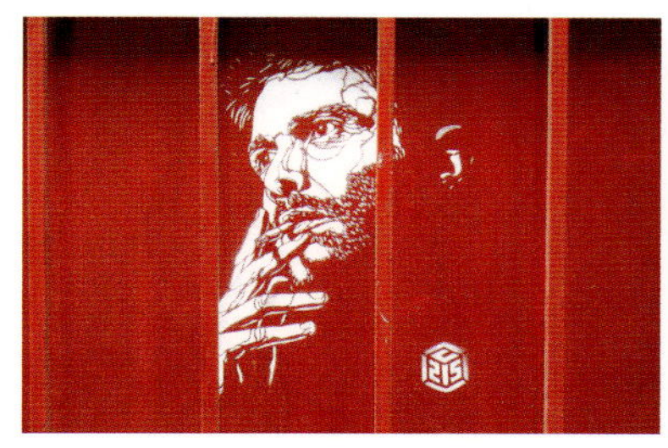

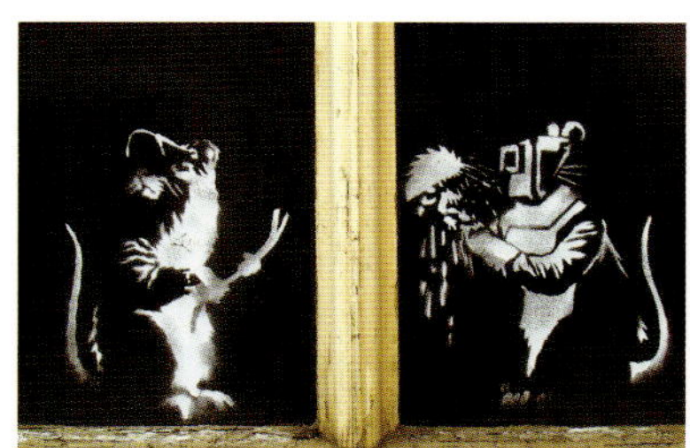

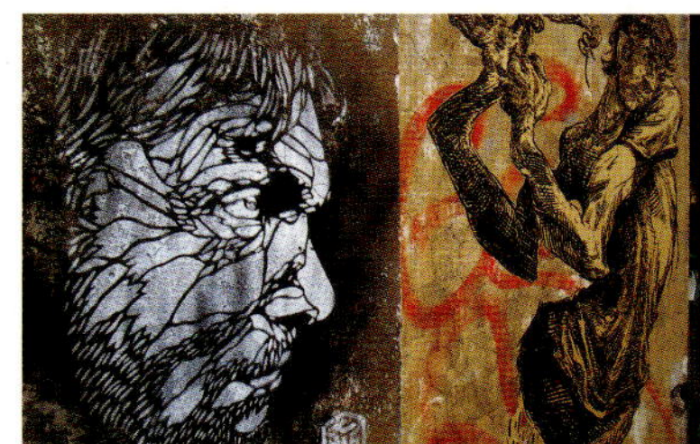

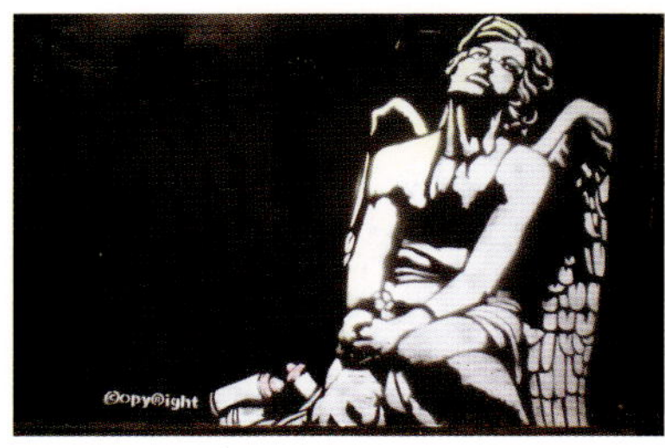

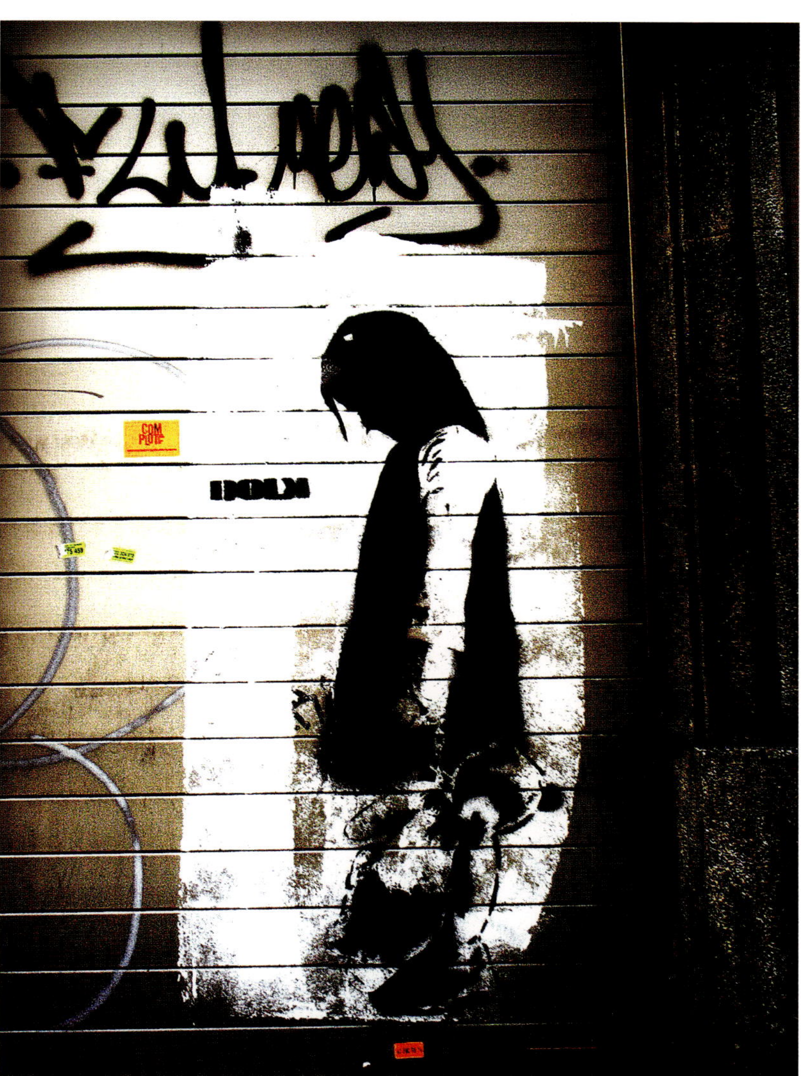

# Nuart

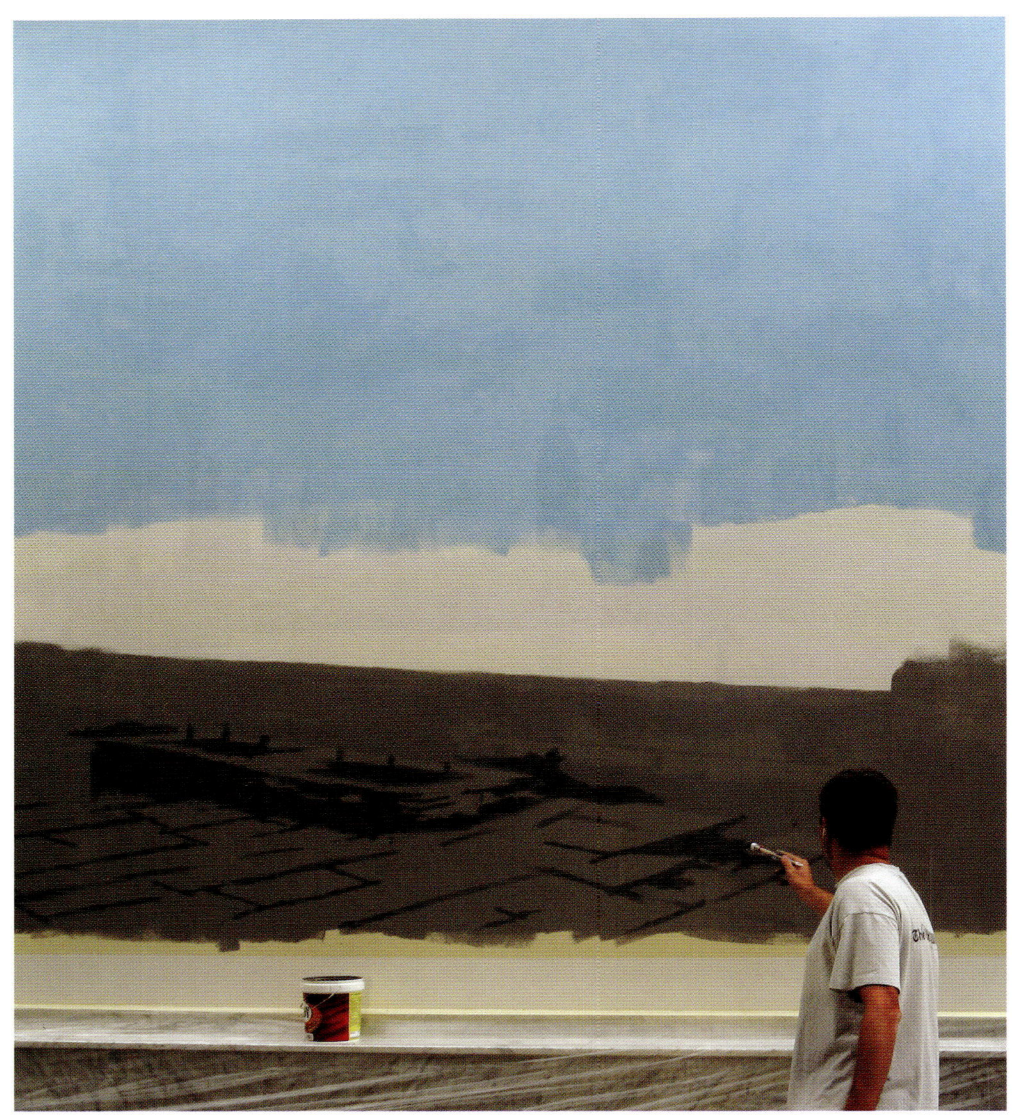

Rewind to 2007: Street art moves into the museum. The Nu Collective and C6 from Stavanger in Norway jointly hosted their first annual indoor street art show at the ROGALAND KUNSTMUSEUM. Stars of the scene included D-Face, Nick Walker, MIR and Graffiti Research Lab. Of course it didn't just stay in the museum.

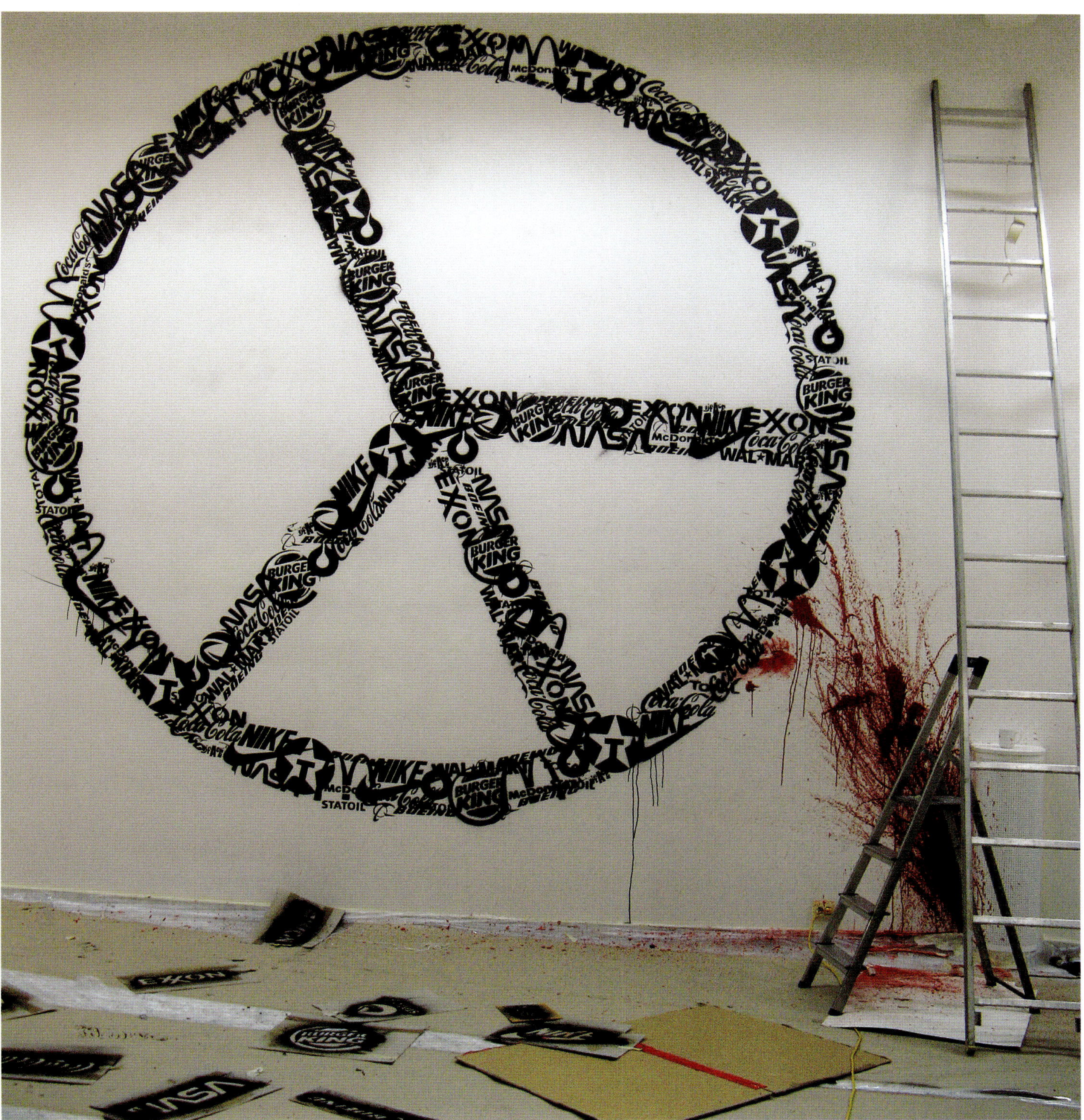

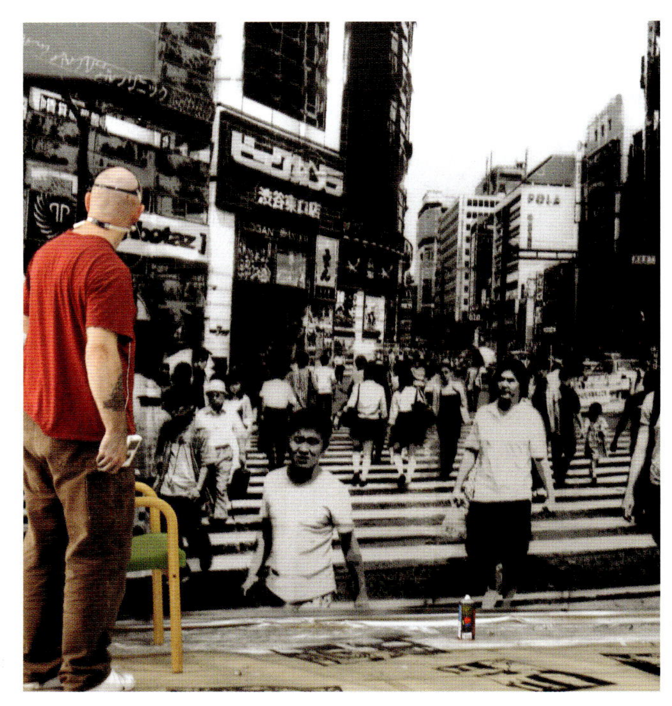

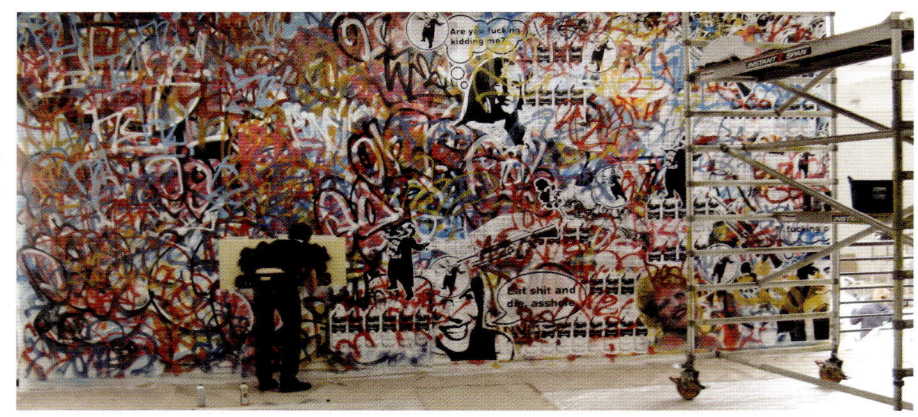
Are you fucking kidding me
eat shit and die, asshole

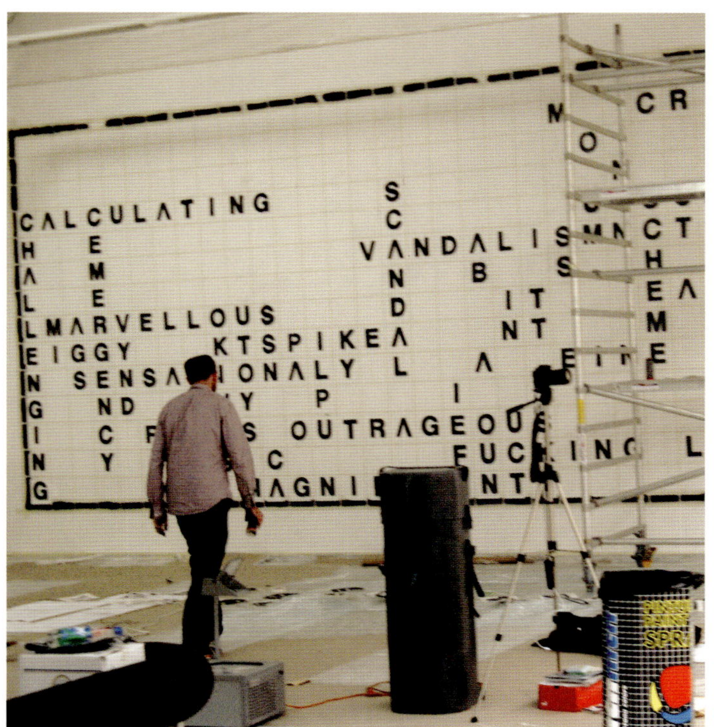


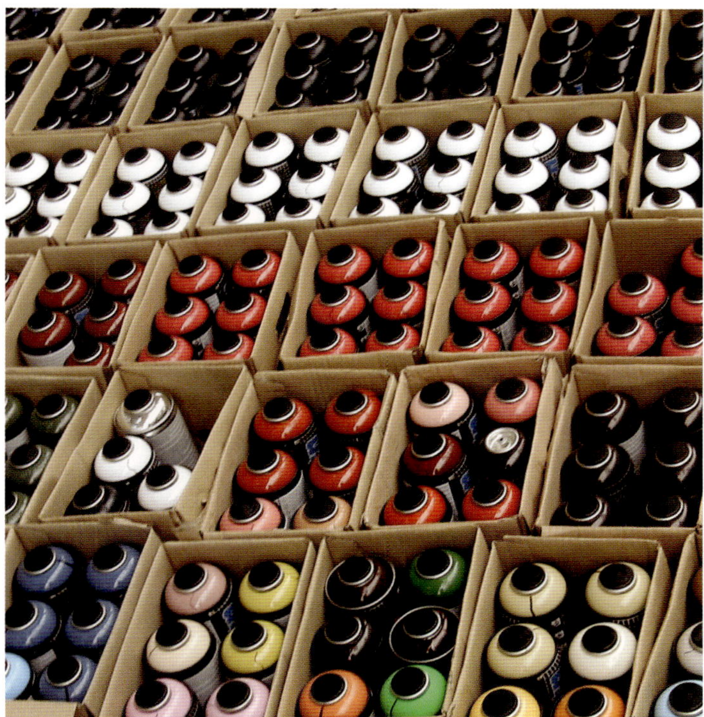

"Contemporary public art practice has become an audience less affair with application based works directed purely at those that fund them, while the artists and funding bodies are locked in dialogues of mutual gratification the public are the ultimate losers."

*C6 Press Release*

Exactly. And NuArt mashes up new art in all its forms not just the painting on walls. Electronic music, VJ shows and multi-media 'stuff' are all thrown in together. This is underground culture at its best, a great big enthusiastic clash of ideas. Check it out. Now.

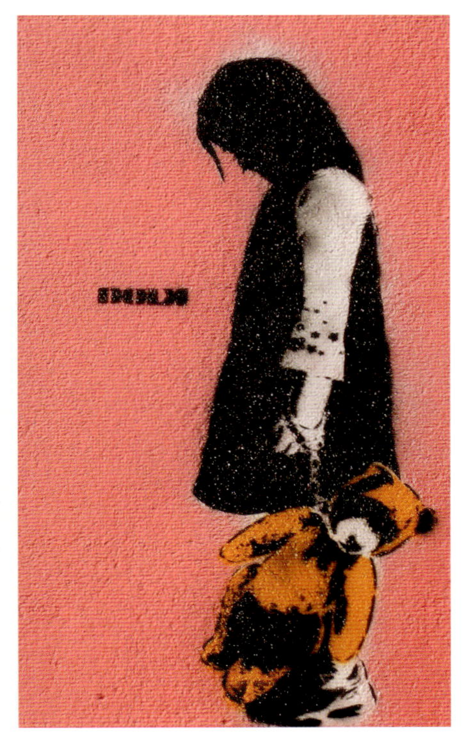

We painted the hunt and the animals, we painted the gods and their symbols, we painted the sun and the world of the dead. We painted our faces and bodies and the walls of our temples and then we started painting new pictures called hieroglyphs, letters and words and numbers. We painted the glorious kings and their families and their various deeds and we painted the old myths. After many years we painted just stuff that we saw around us like nature and towns and pictures of anyone who could afford to pay. Finally when the world turned upside down and the war and fury ripped us all apart we rebelled and painted twisted abstract images of many kinds, we painted the fractured dreams and nightmares of our time all in a desperate search to find out why we had all gone mad. That's more or less what we continue to paint now.

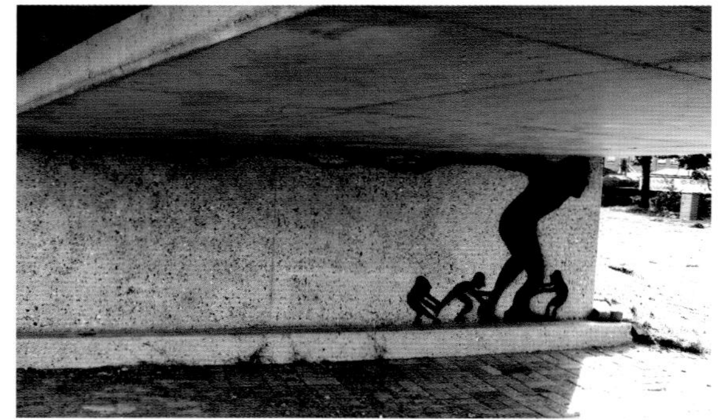

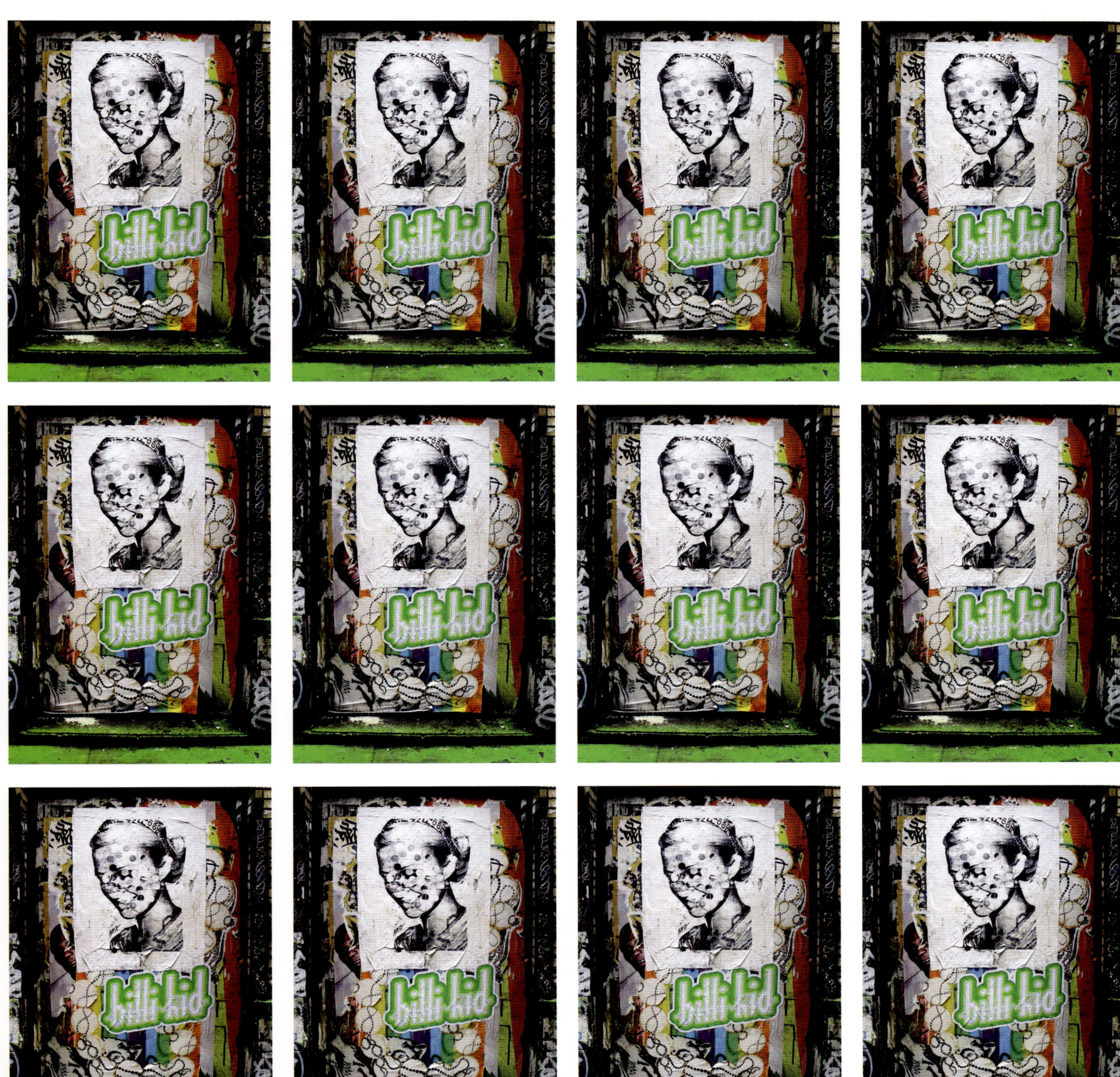

Borf is not caught. Borf is many. Borf is none. Borf is waiting for you in your car. Borf is in your pockets. Borf is running through your veins. Borf is naive. Borf is good for your liver. Borf is controlling your thoughts. Borf is everywhere. Borf is the war on boredom. Borf annihilates. Borf hates school. Borf is a four letter word for joy. Borf is quickly losing patience. Borf yells in the library. Borf eats pieces of shit like you for breakfast. Borf is digging a hole to China. Borf is bad at graffiti. Borf is ephemeral. Borf is invincible. Borf. Borf ruins everything. Borf runs near the swimming pool. Borf keeps it real. Borf writes you love letters. Ol' Dirty Bastard is Borf. Borf knows everything. Borf is in the water. Borf doesn't sleep. Borf systematically attacks the infrastructure of the totality. Borf is a foulmouth. Borf eats your homework. Borf brings you home for dinner. Borf is the dirt under your fingernails. Borf is the song that never ends. Borf gets down. Borf gets up. Borf is your baby. Borf is neither. Borf is good for your heart, the more you eat the more you. Borf is. Borf knows. Borf destroys. Borf is immortal. Borf pulls fire alarms. Borf scuffs the gym floor. Borf is looking through your mom's purse. Borf is M. Borf is the size of Alaska. Borf likes pizza. Borf is in general. Borf is X. Borf ain't nothin' to sod with. Borf runs it. Borf has reflexes like a cat. Borf is immortal. Borf sticks gum under the desk. Borf is omnipotent. Borf is flawed. Borf is winning.

©Borf

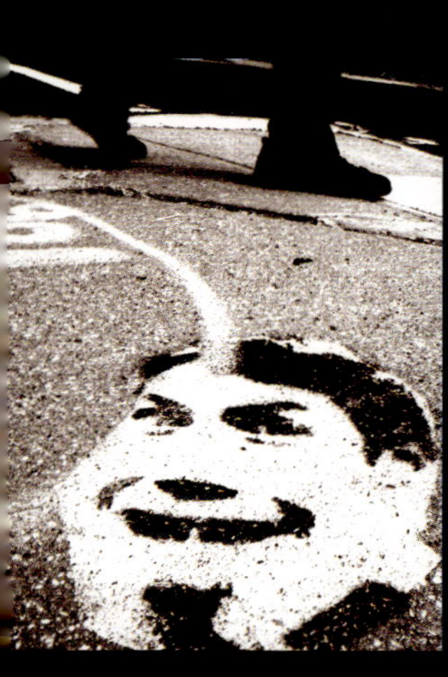

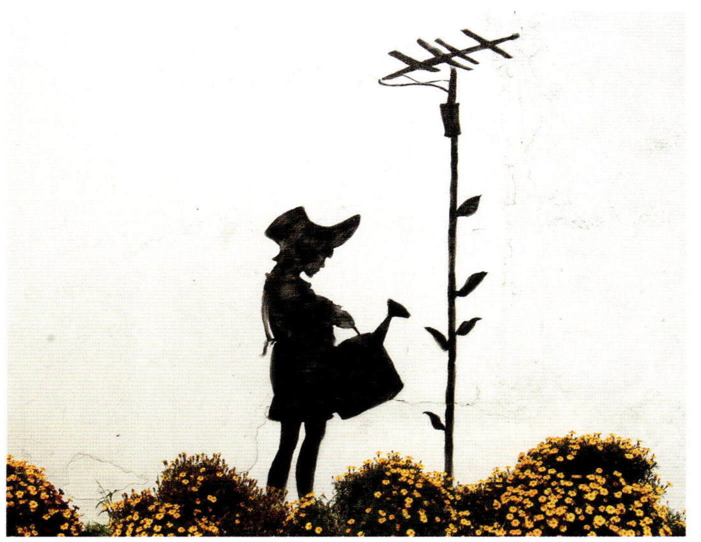
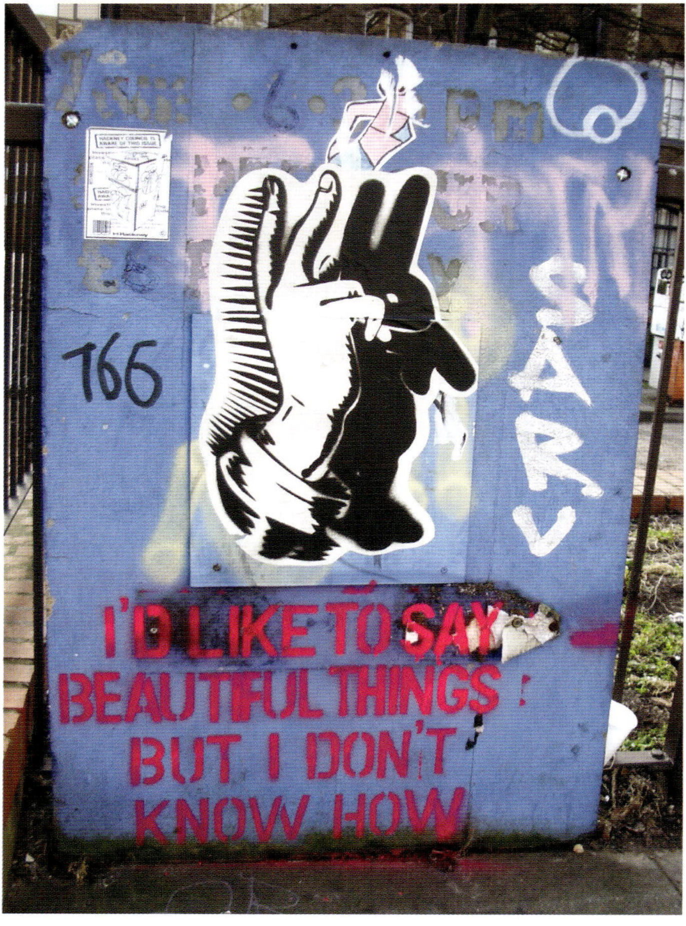
T66
SARI
I'D LIKE TO SAY
BEAUTIFUL THINGS :
BUT I DON'T
KNOW HOW

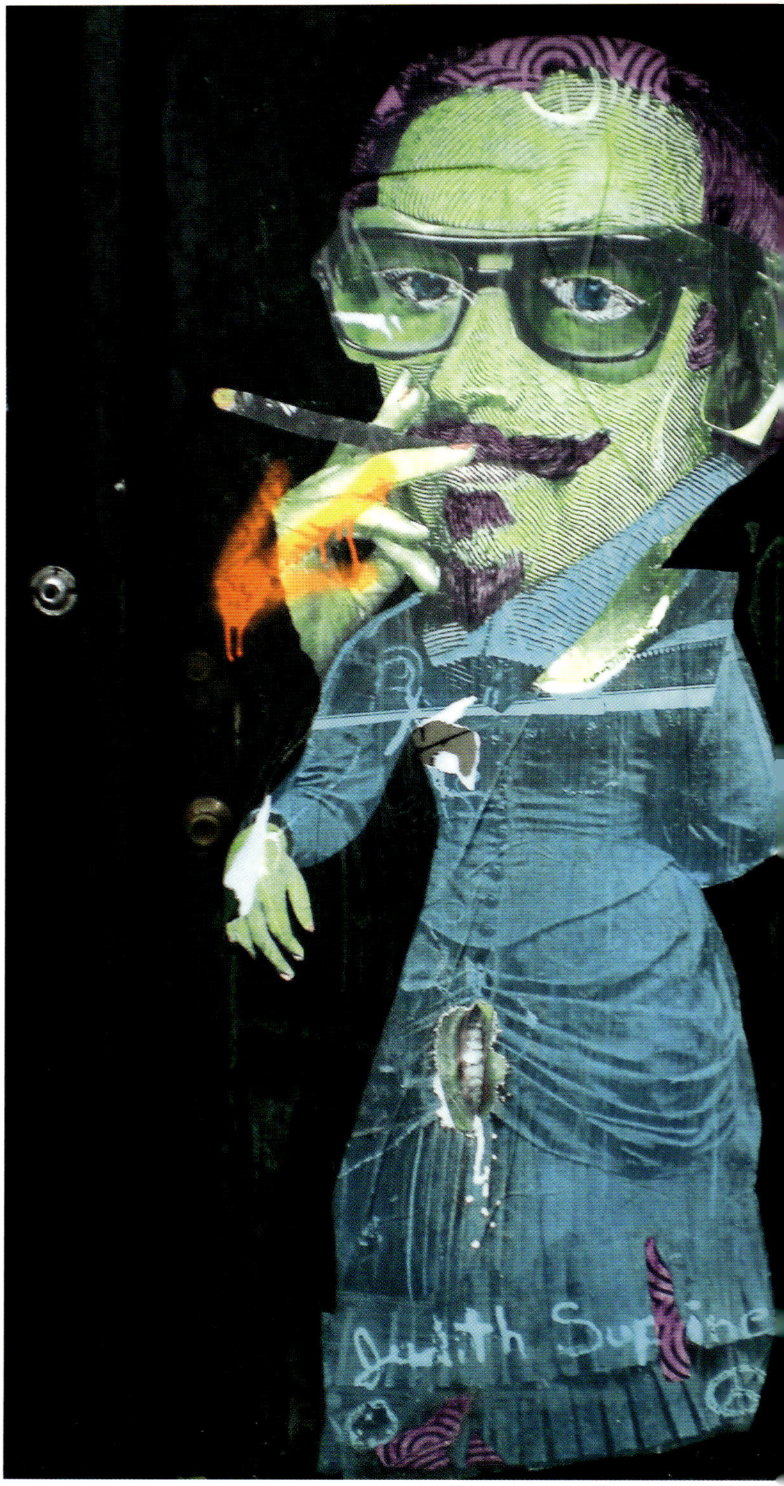

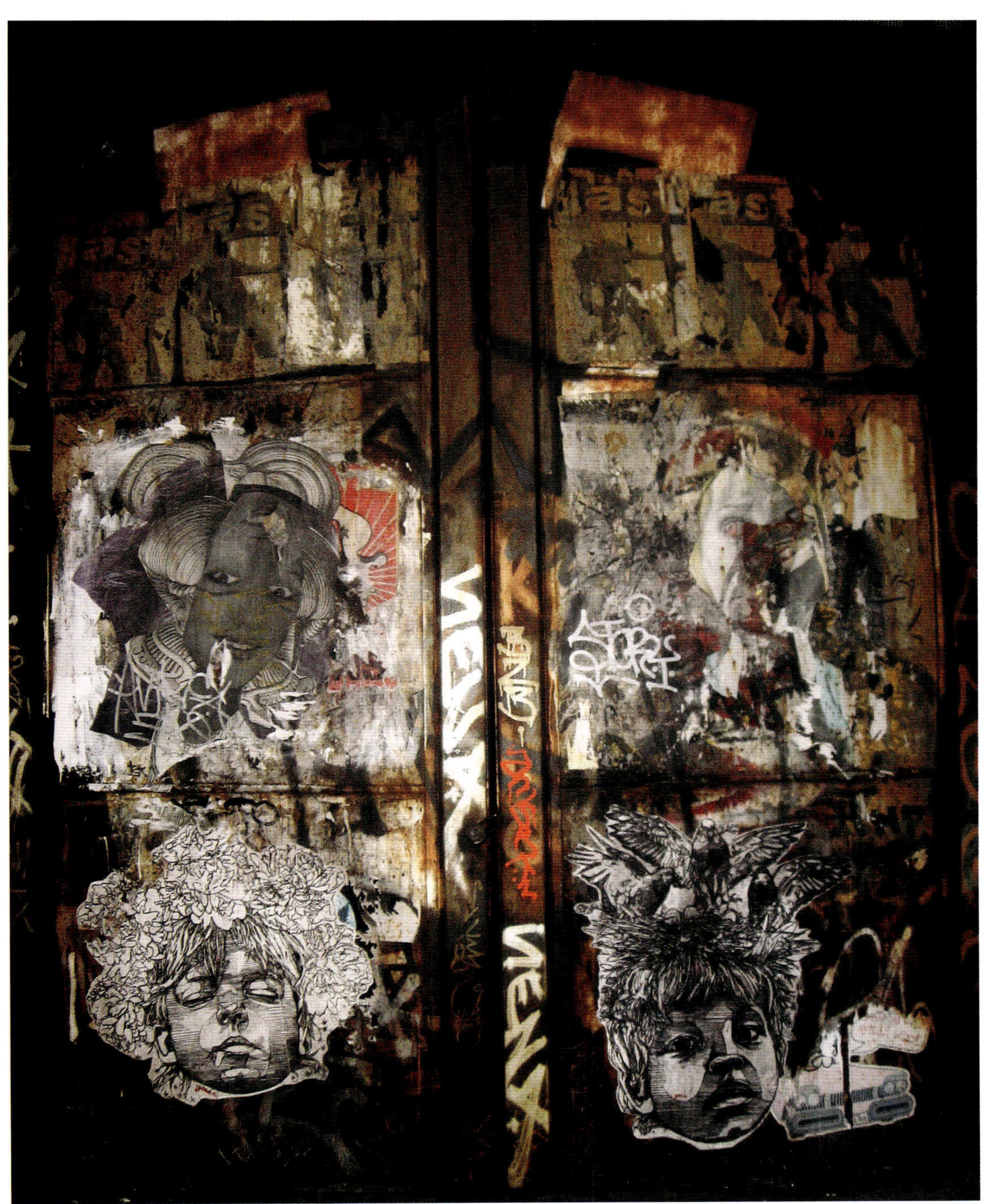

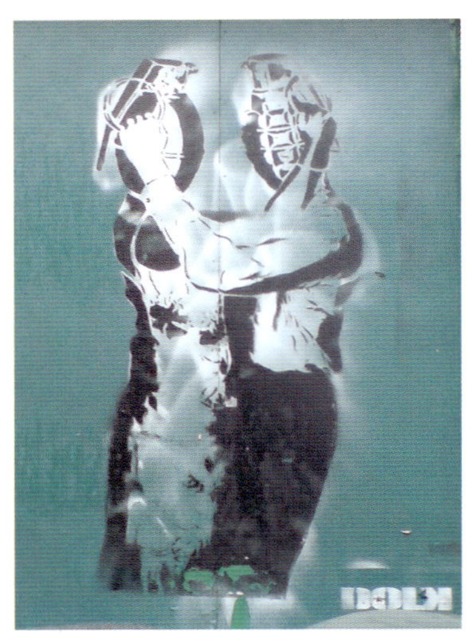
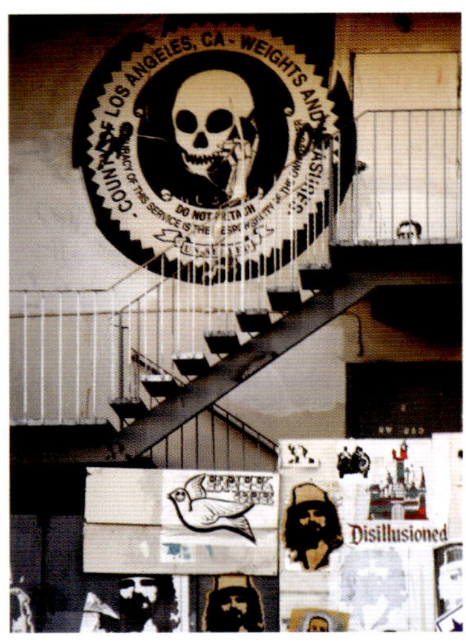

COUNTY OF LOS ANGELES, CA - WEIGHTS AND
Disillusioned

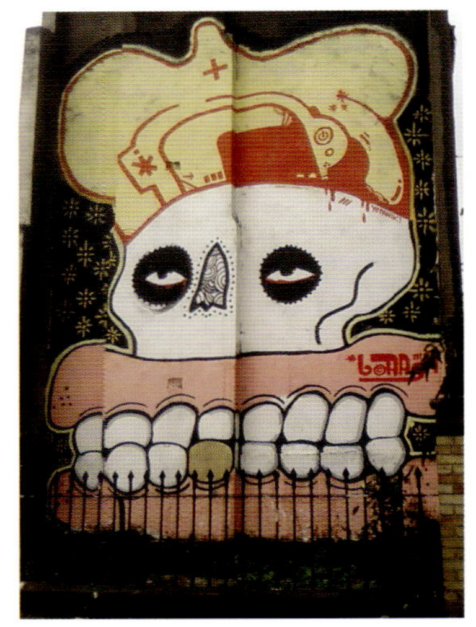
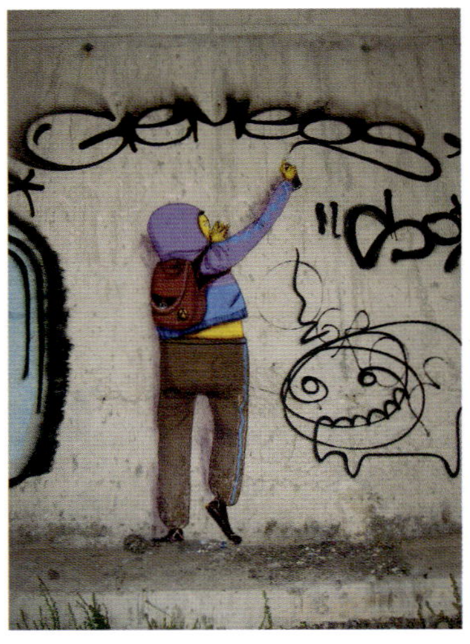

GENEOS

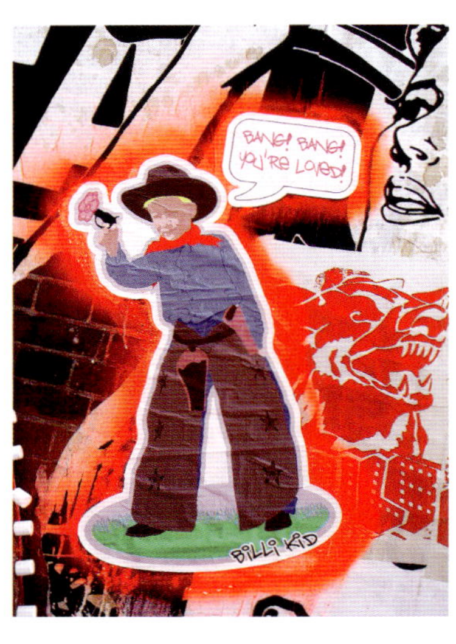

BANG! BANG!
YOU'RE LOVED!
BILLI KID

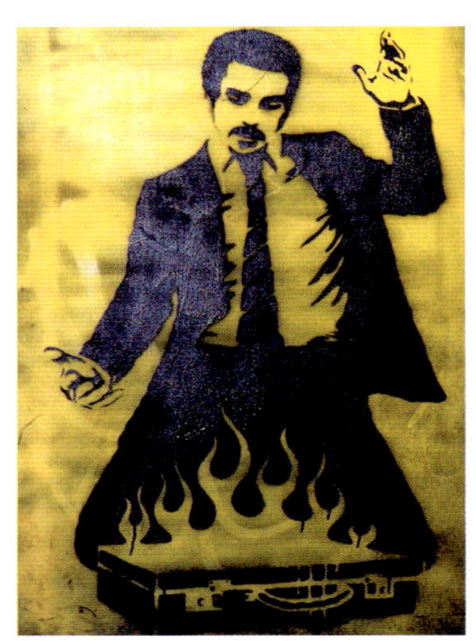
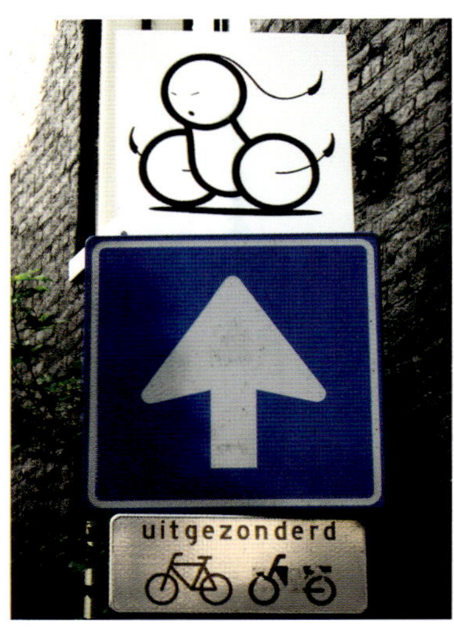

uitgezonderd

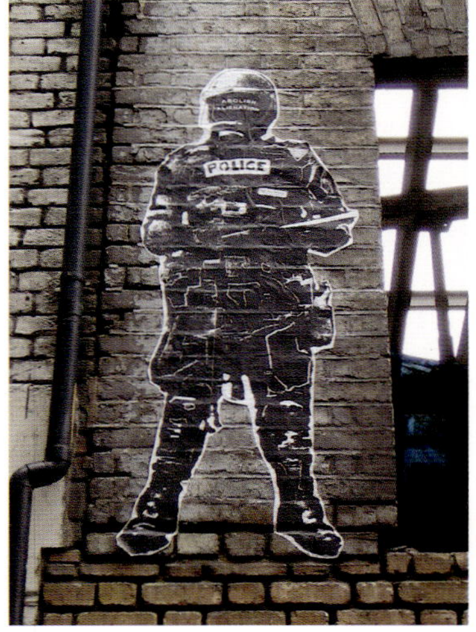

POLICE

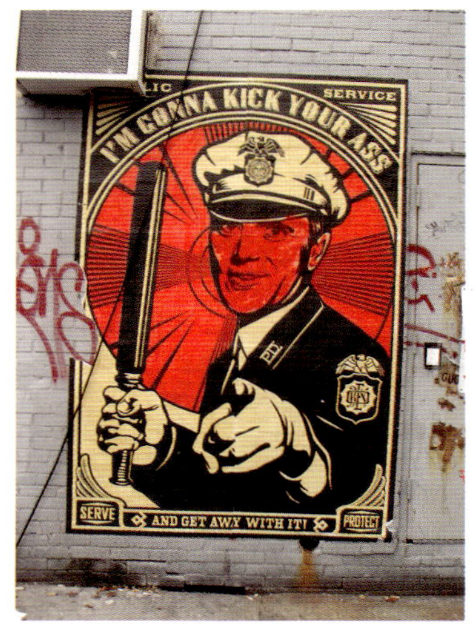

PUBLIC
SERVICE
I'M GONNA KICK YOUR ASS
SERVE
AND GET AWAY WITH IT!
PROTECT

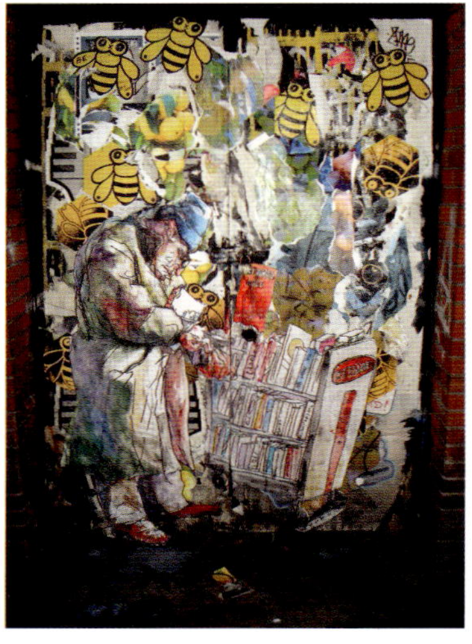
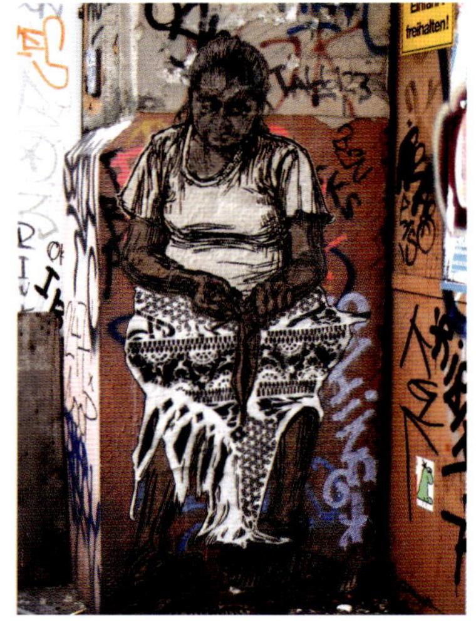
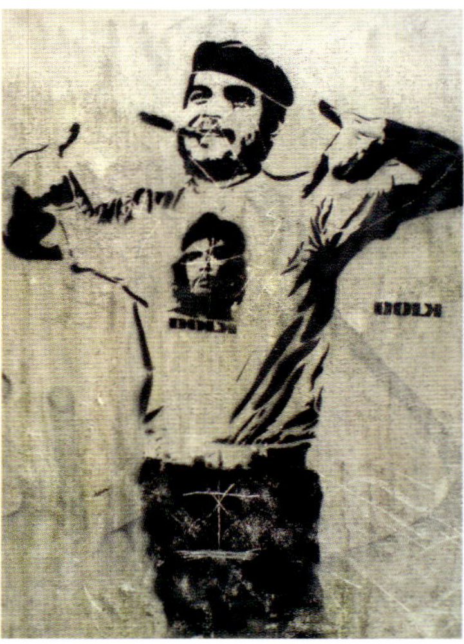

DOLK
DOLK

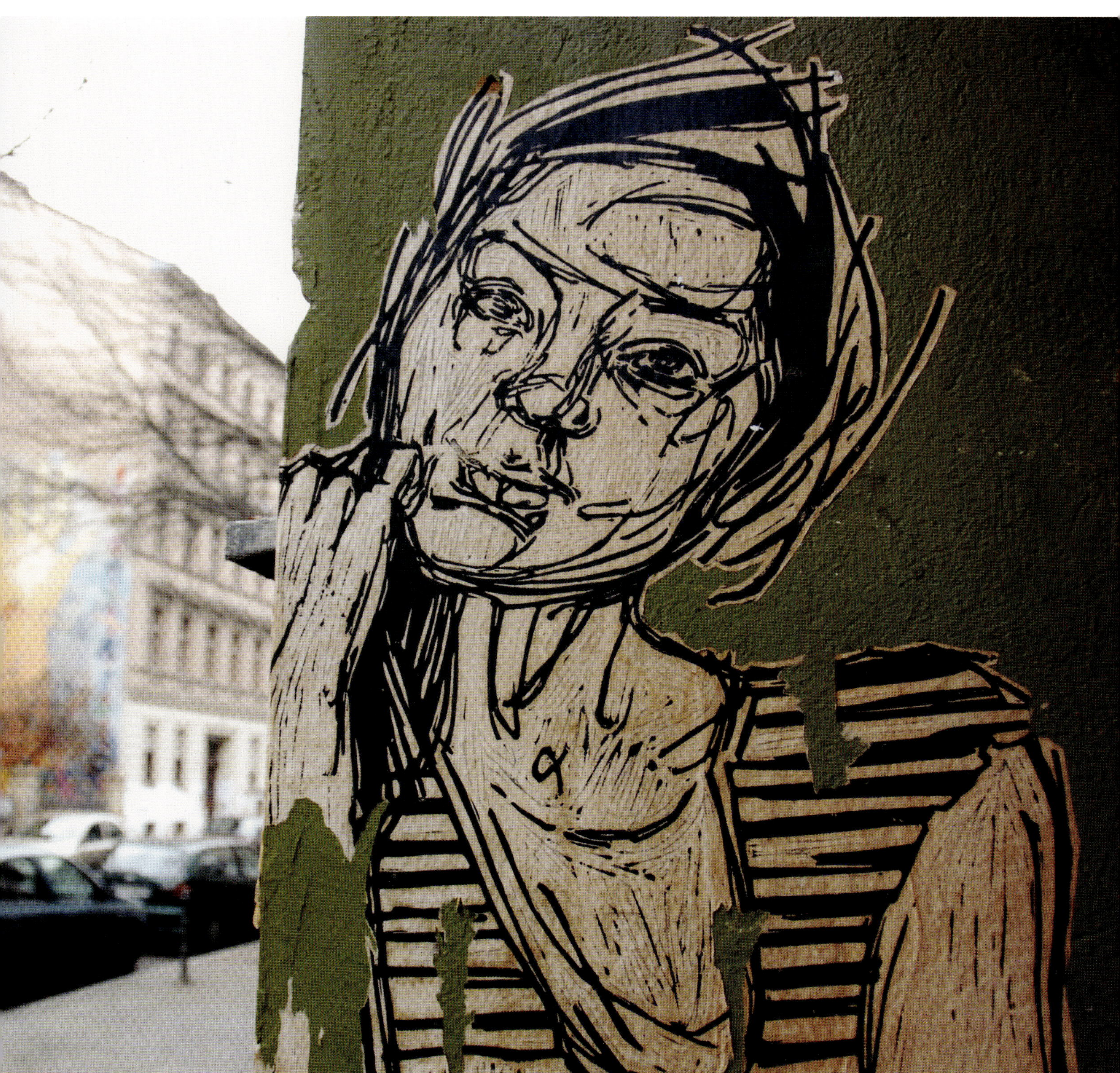

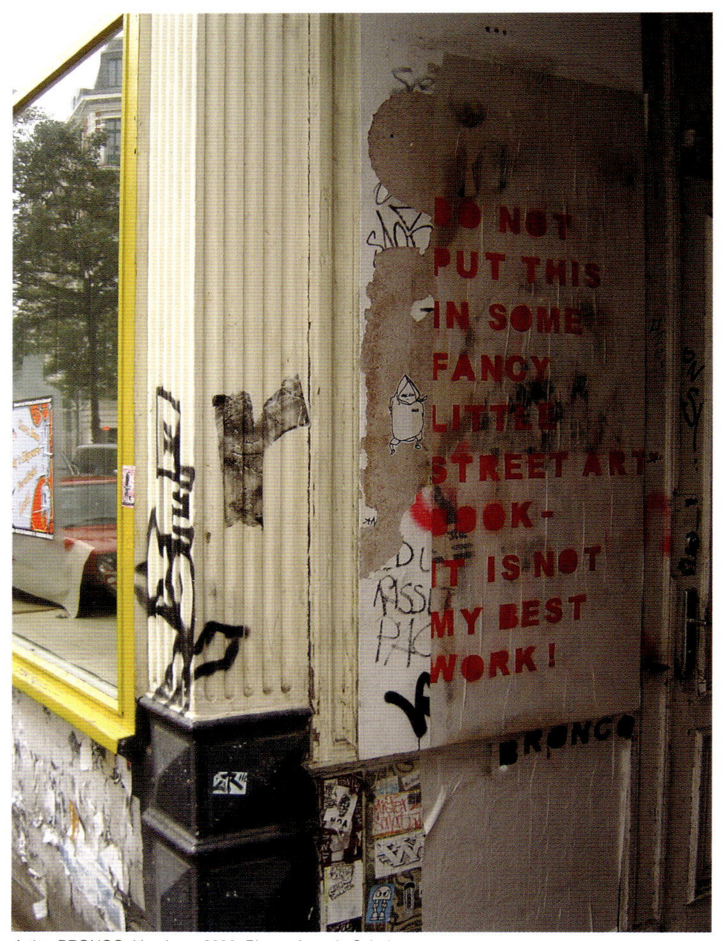


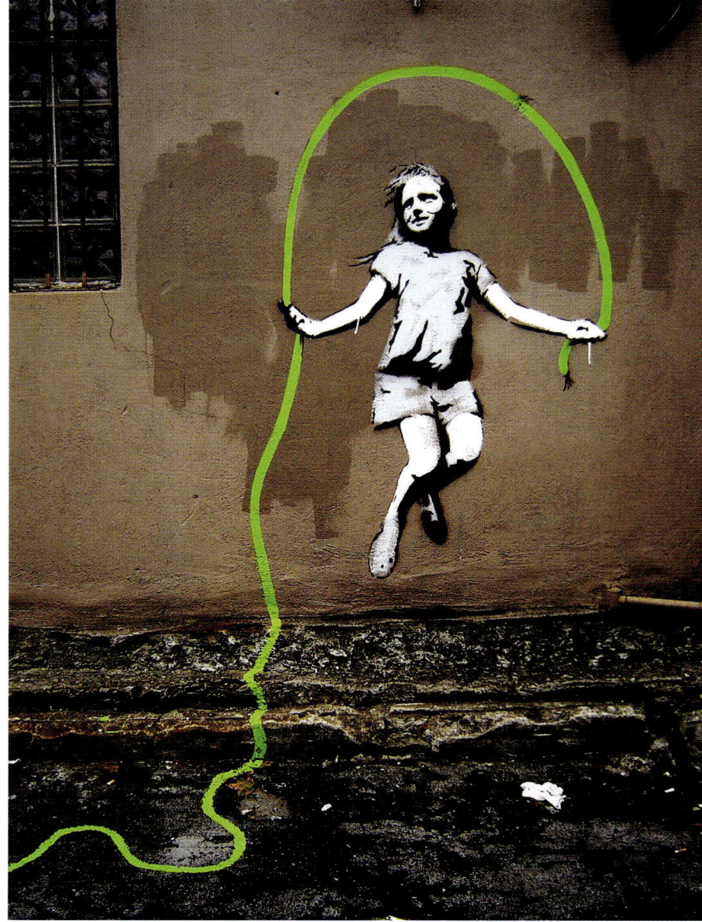

Artist: BRONCO, Hamburg 2006; Photo: Antonia Schulz

Artist: Banksy. Photo: P. Villerius

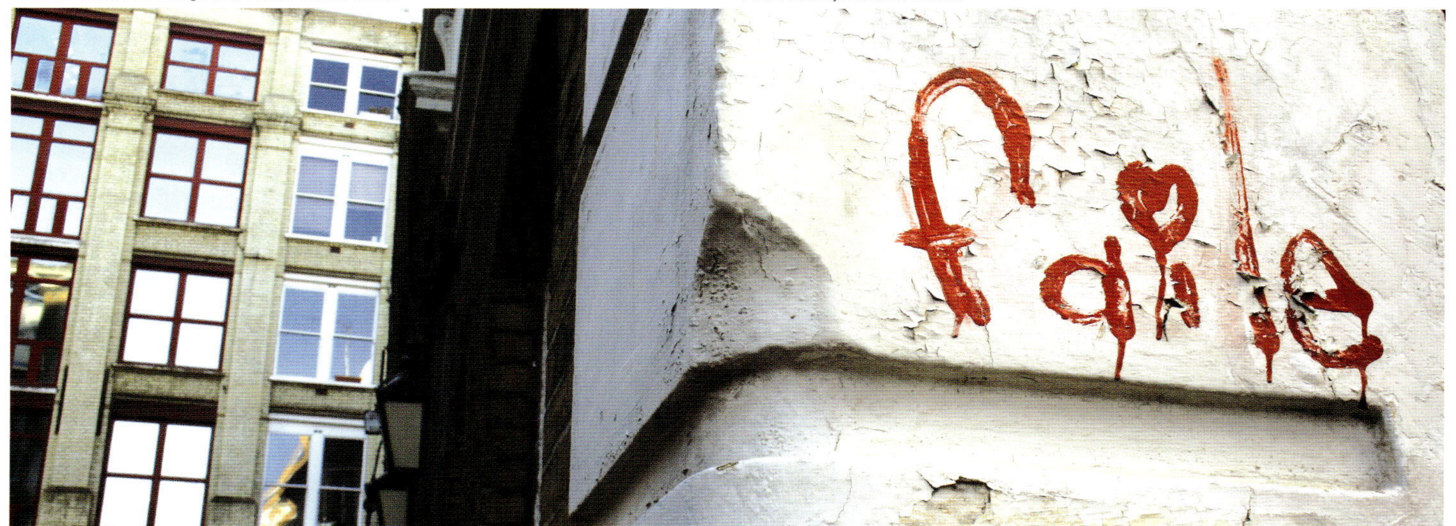

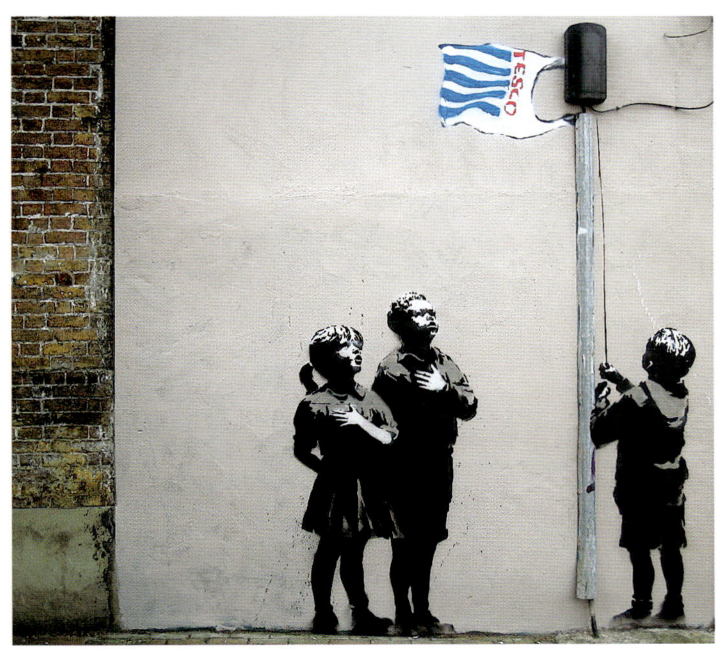
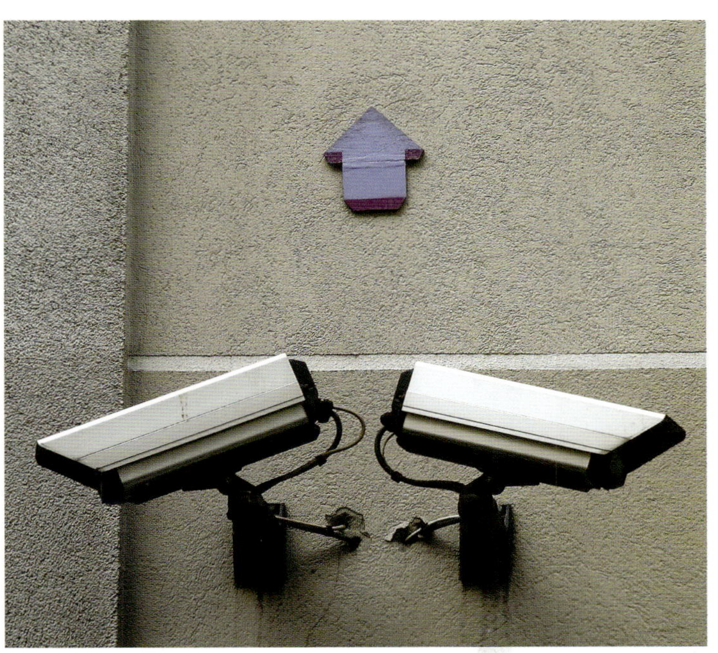

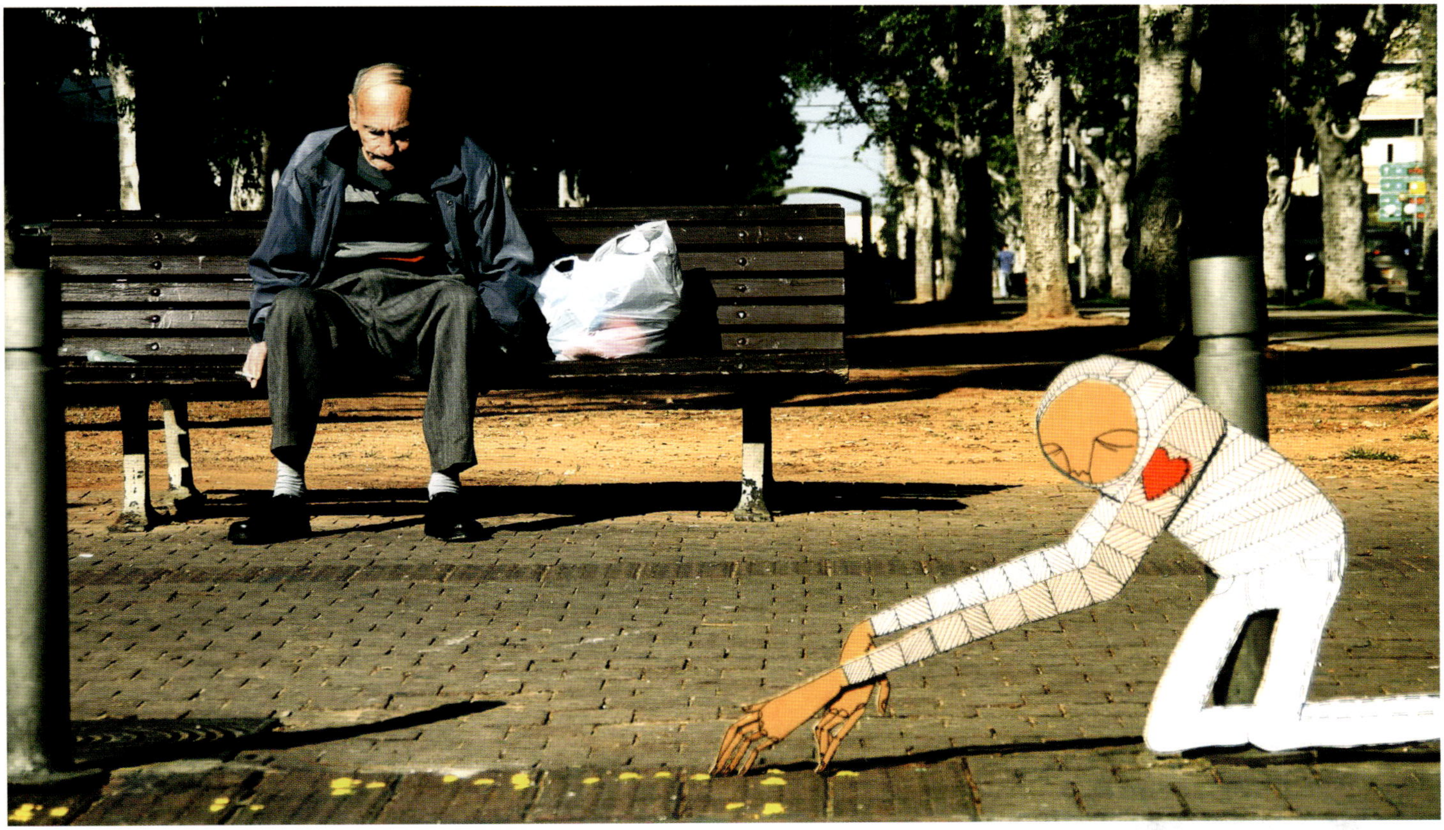

# 'Brain-Storming' – A Fancy Name for Talking Without Thinking

Moments from the movies mix up with our lives. Scripted conversations feed conversations inspire scripts etc ad infinitum. We talk naturally about characters who are real people who are pretending to be naturally talking. Time is mixed up.

So much of what we see (re: art or commercial creative activity) is pre-meditated. When something is said it was decided that it was going to be said sometimes years before you hear it. When you experience a moment in a movie or commercial, what you are seeing is long passed. It's like looking at a star. It may be long dead by the time the light hit your eyes.

At least with street art there is a sense of the immediate. Woman has idea, makes stencil, hits spot. The idea is alive and kicking when you catch it. Or it is at least fresh dead.

You don't spend months researching what you are going to say when you are talking to someone. You don't worry about individual arm movements when you are dancing. You don't care about the theoretical implications of post-modern thought when you are high on the moment, spraying paint on a wall, sticking it to the man.

(On the other hand, if you never think about what you're saying, you end up saying things that you've heard other people say without wondering whether or not they are true for you. If you completely stop thinking and just let loose and speak out from the heart without using real words its called 'skat' and it can be quite good in the right moment. Another variation is 'speaking in tongues' which looks exciting but wouldn't sound good on your stereo.)

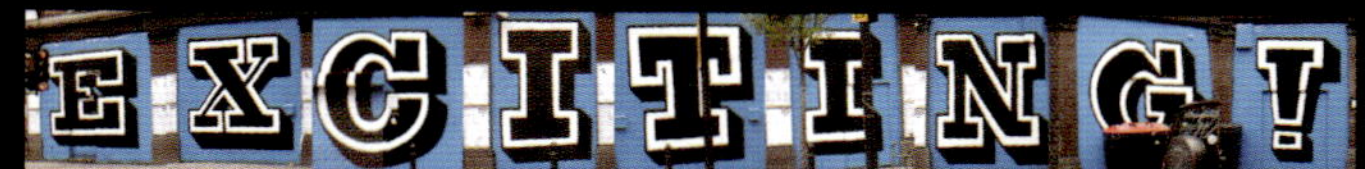


## Why do people paint on walls? Why do they paint what they paint?

Someone opens up their mouth to say something direct and it vanishes into a landscape of louder images. Of that variant of graffiti that we call advertising we will see vast numbers of pictures and symbols every day. All these images are brewed and concocted over months and sometimes years by teams of 'experts'. Money you would not believe, thousands of hours of research and development go into these seemingly effortless ideas. Against this backdrop we are startled and confused by he who posts a picture of a cartoon Viking 20 foot high on a wall. No slogan and no brand? What is he not selling?

Remember that most artists are employed in advertising. Never forget that. Everyone sitting in a think tank, brainstorming up a campaign is essentially an artist. We all gotta make rent. The effect of this is to make it appear that brightness, creativity and ideas are a commodity outside of the reach of ordinary schmucks. Of course the real truth is that everyone is an artist. Individual genius is a big fucking lie. You express only a fragment of the flow of ideas when you produce a piece. We are all part of the flow of ideas. It is us. No piece of work has ever had just one author.

## How would we talk to each other if no-one cared what we might or might not buy?

The cat and mouse game plays out like this…

I don't make art for the man in the
street. I've met the man in the street
and he's a cunt

(Actually this was what we think Tony Wilson said Sid Vicious said and is not a direct quote but hey ho, when asked to choose between history and legend...)

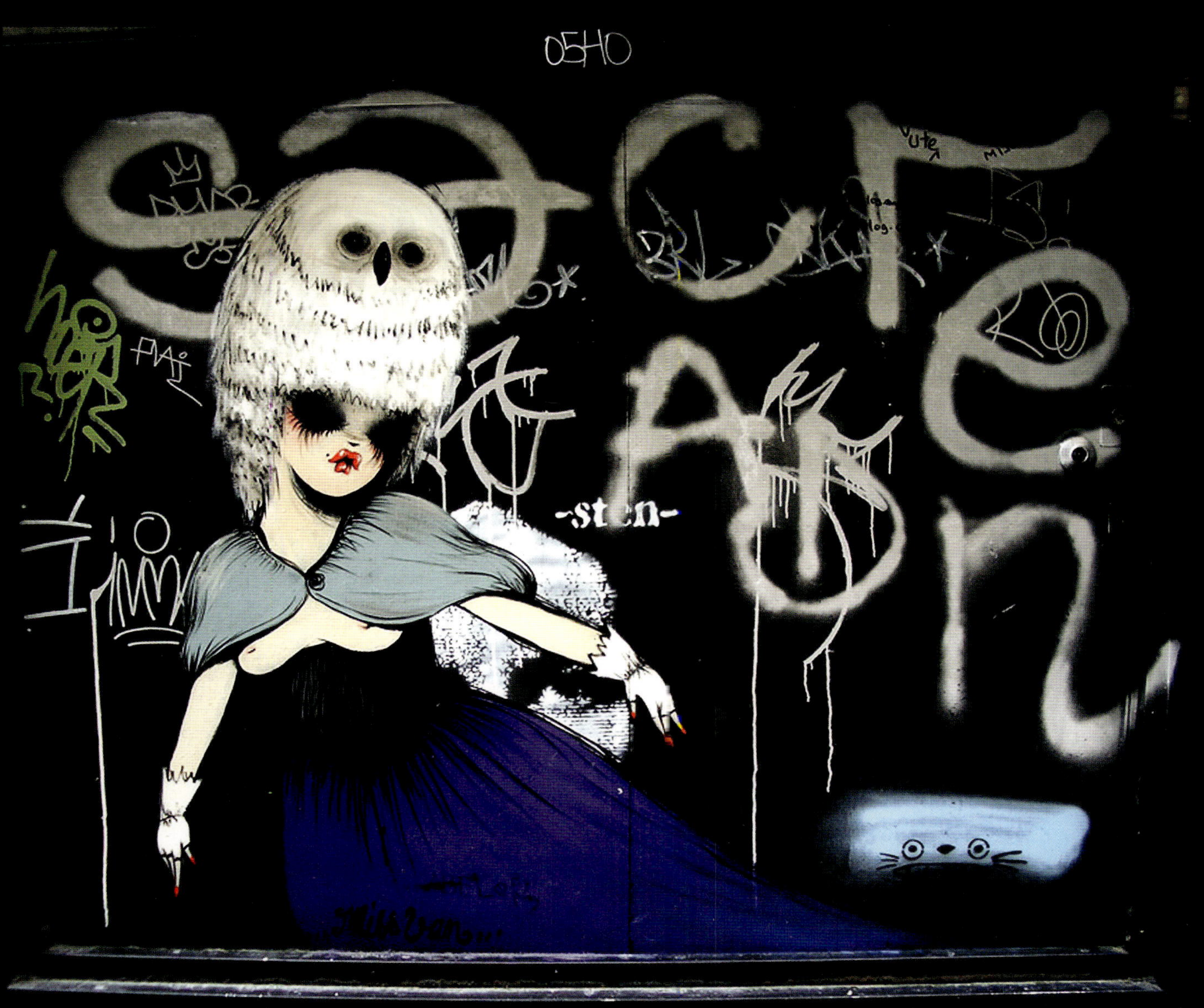

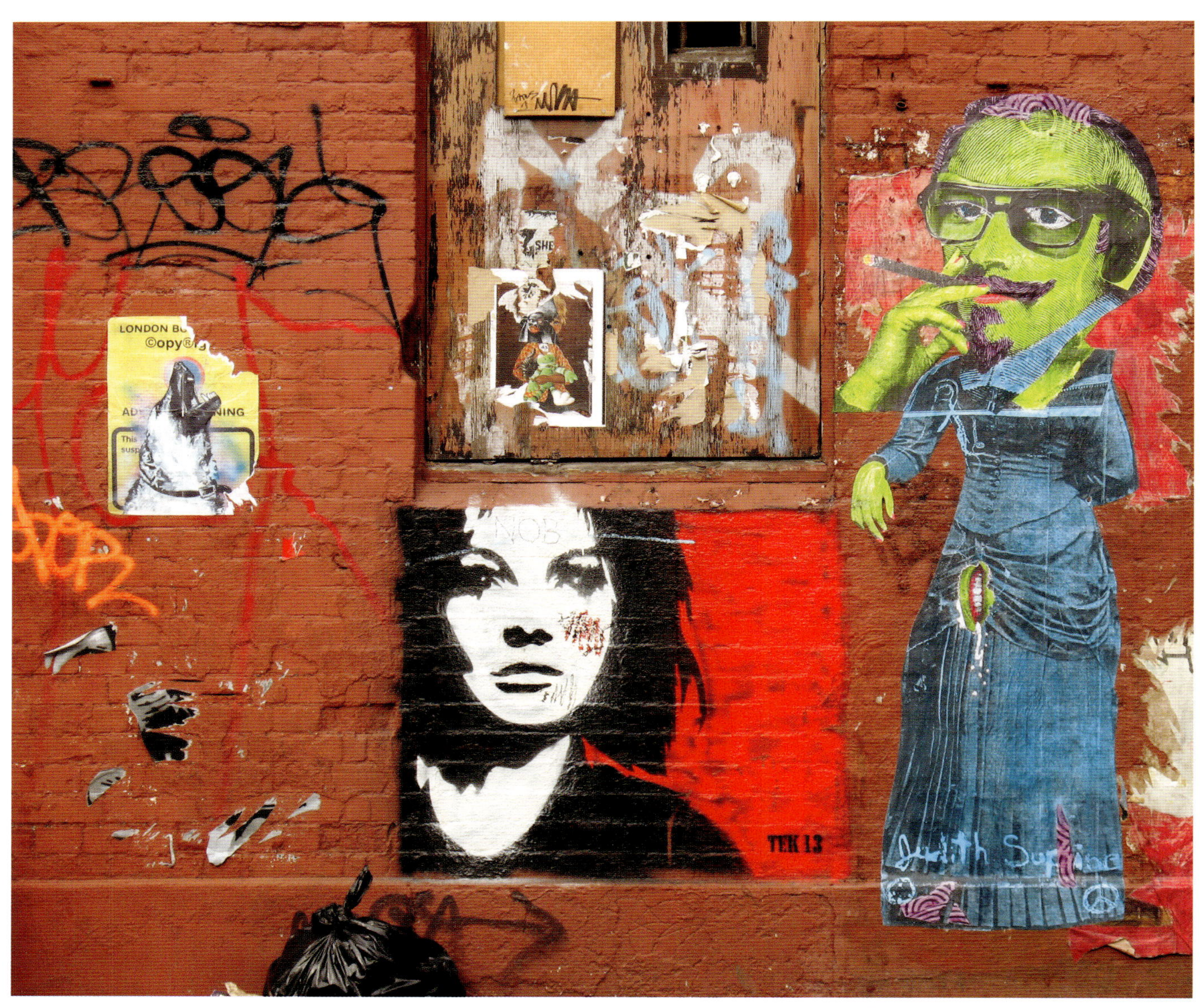

LONDON B
©opyR
This
susp
TEK 13
Judith Supine

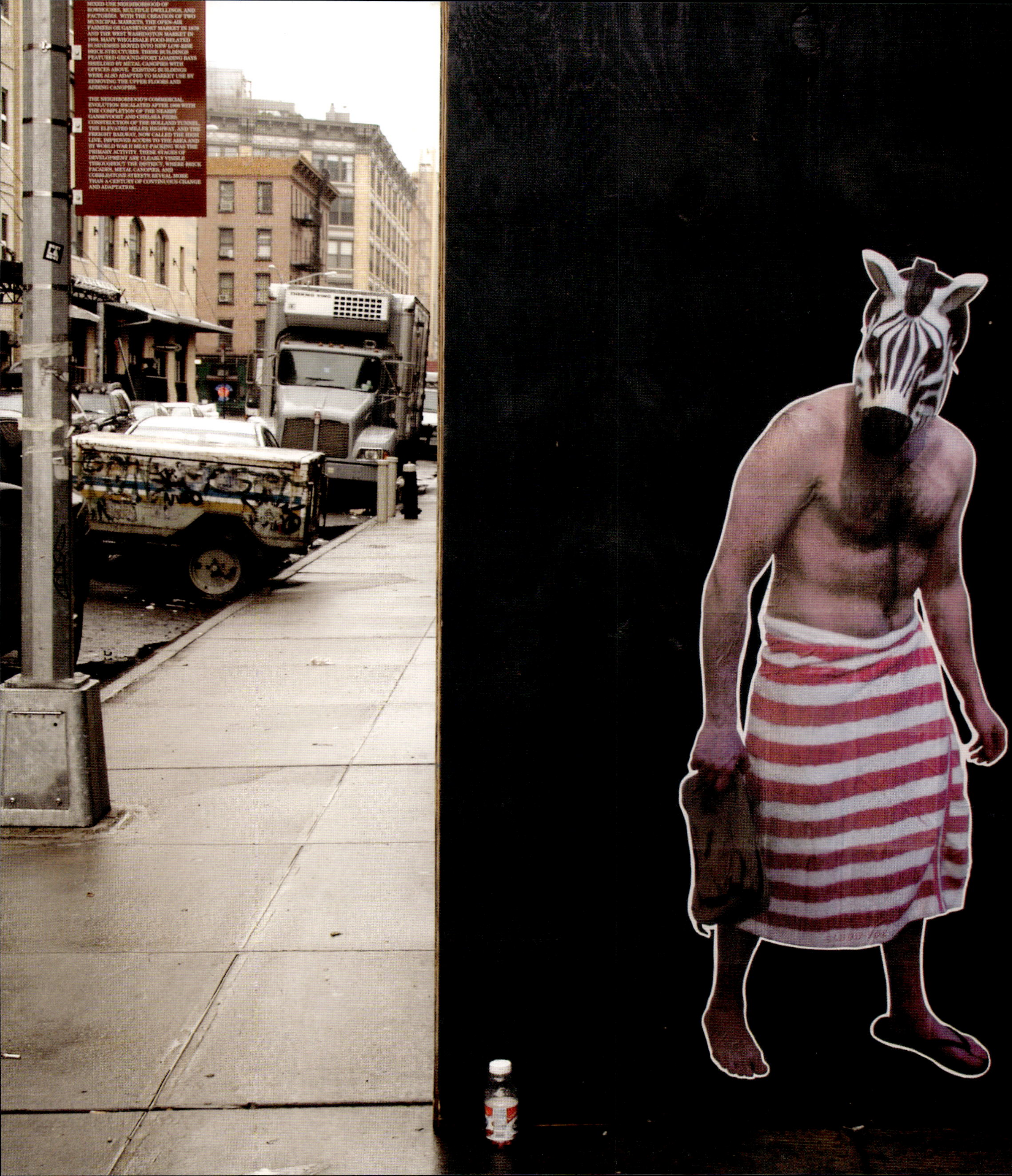
MIXED-USE NEIGHBORHOOD OF
ROWHOUSES, MULTIPLE DWELLINGS, AND
FACTORIES. WITH THE CREATION OF TWO
MUNICIPAL MARKETS, THE OPEN-AIR
FARMERS OR GANSEVOORT MARKET IN 1879
AND THE WEST WASHINGTON MARKET IN
1888, MANY WHOLESALE FOOD-RELATED
BUSINESSES MOVED INTO NEW LOW-RISE
BRICK STRUCTURES. THESE BUILDINGS
FEATURED GROUND-STORY LOADING BAYS
SHIELDED BY METAL CANOPIES WITH
OFFICES ABOVE. EXISTING BUILDINGS
WERE ALSO ADAPTED TO MARKET USE BY
REMOVING THE UPPER FLOORS AND
ADDING CANOPIES.

THE NEIGHBORHOOD'S COMMERCIAL
EVOLUTION ESCALATED AFTER 1900 WITH
THE COMPLETION OF THE NEARBY
GANSEVOORT AND CHELSEA PIERS,
CONSTRUCTION OF THE HOLLAND TUNNEL,
THE ELEVATED MILLER HIGHWAY, AND THE
FREIGHT RAILWAY, NOW CALLED THE HIGH
LINE. IMPROVED ACCESS TO THE AREA AND
BY WORLD WAR II MEAT-PACKING WAS THE
PRIMARY ACTIVITY. THESE STAGES OF
DEVELOPMENT ARE CLEARLY VISIBLE
THROUGHOUT THE DISTRICT, WHERE BRICK
FACADES, METAL CANOPIES, AND
COBBLESTONE STREETS REVEAL MORE
THAN A CENTURY OF CONTINUOUS CHANGE
AND ADAPTATION.

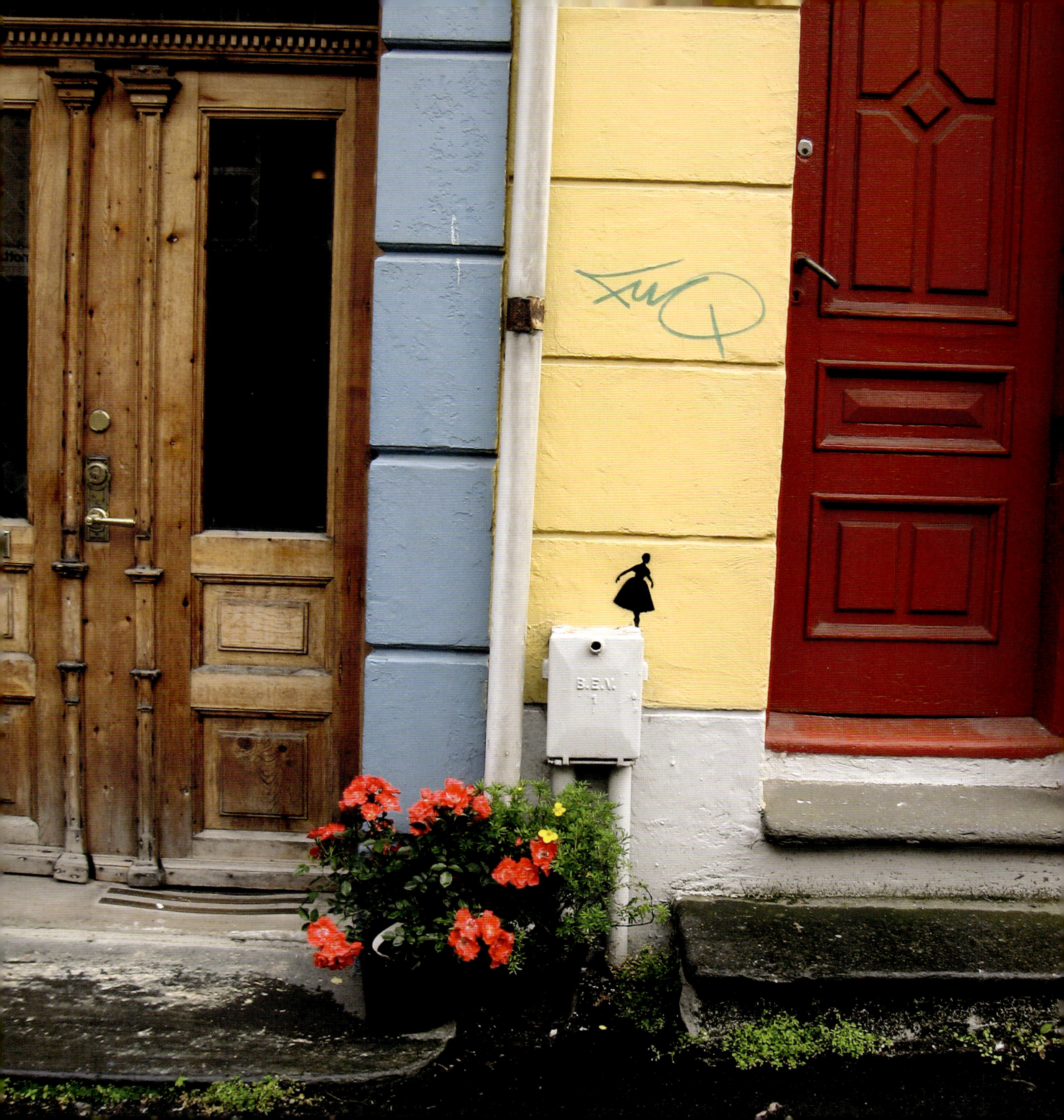

481
OLDER BROTHER

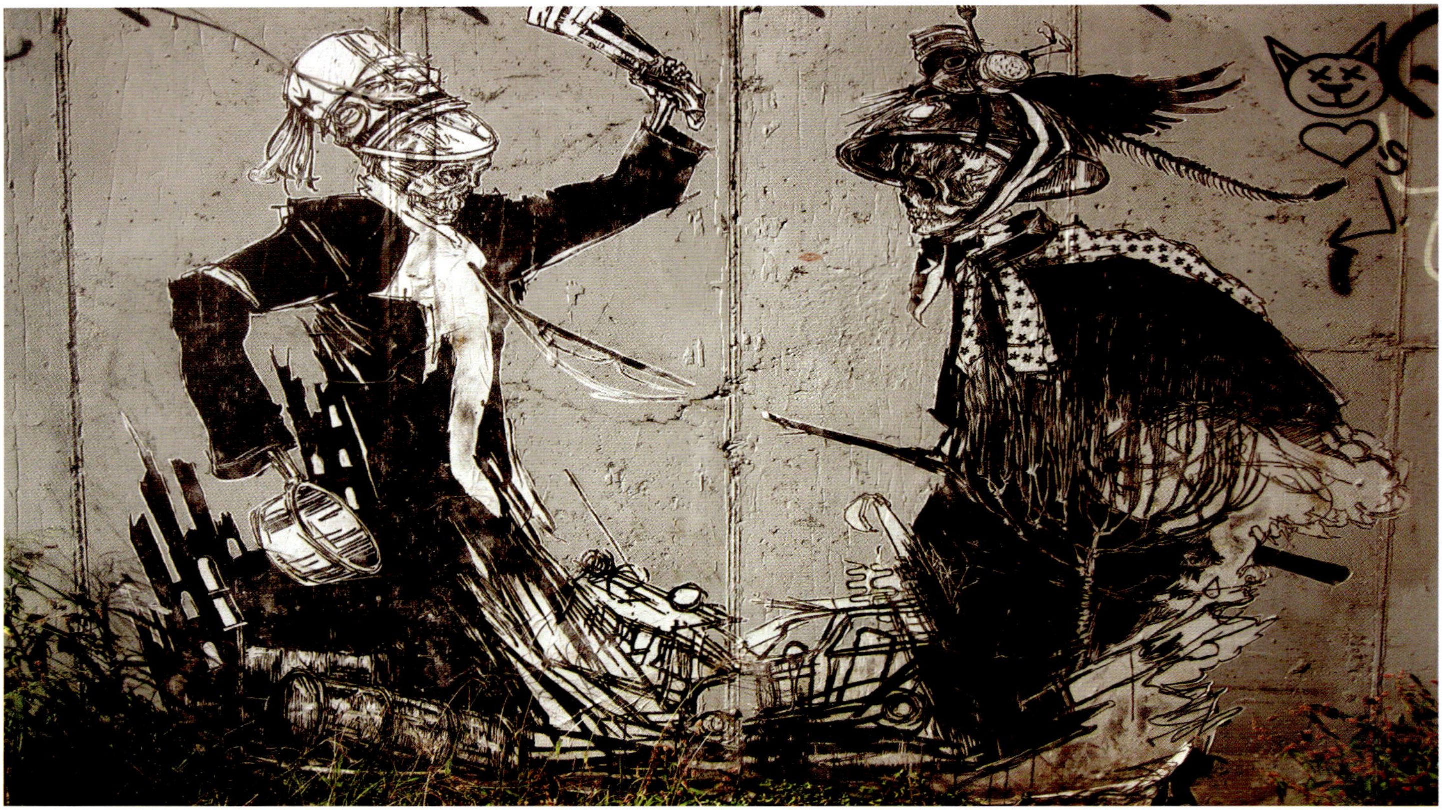

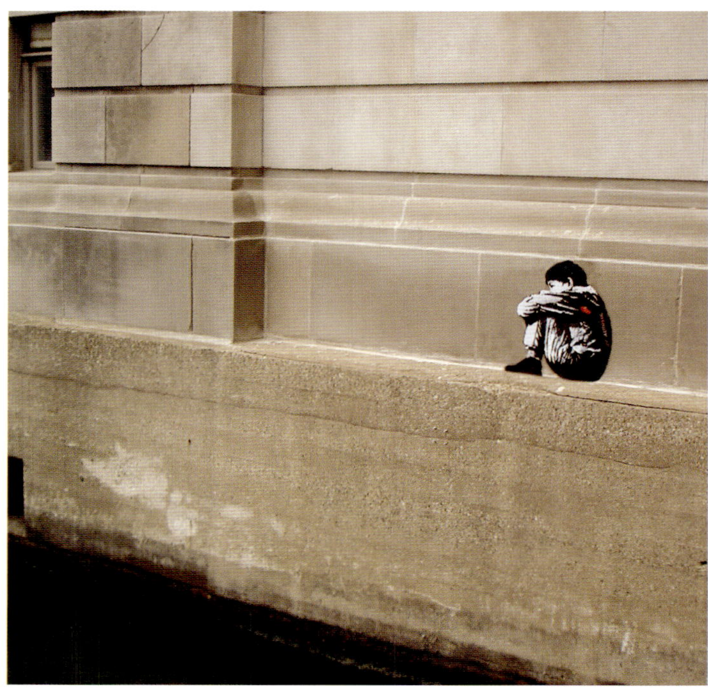

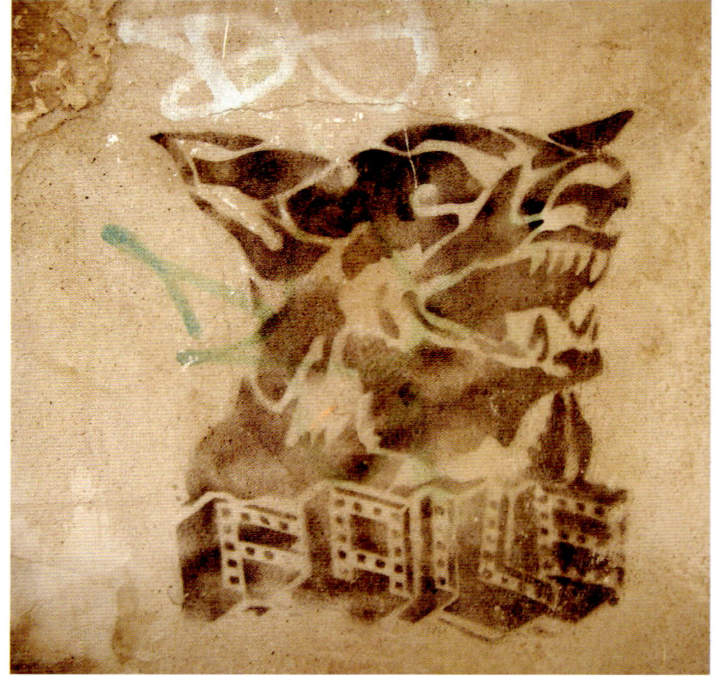

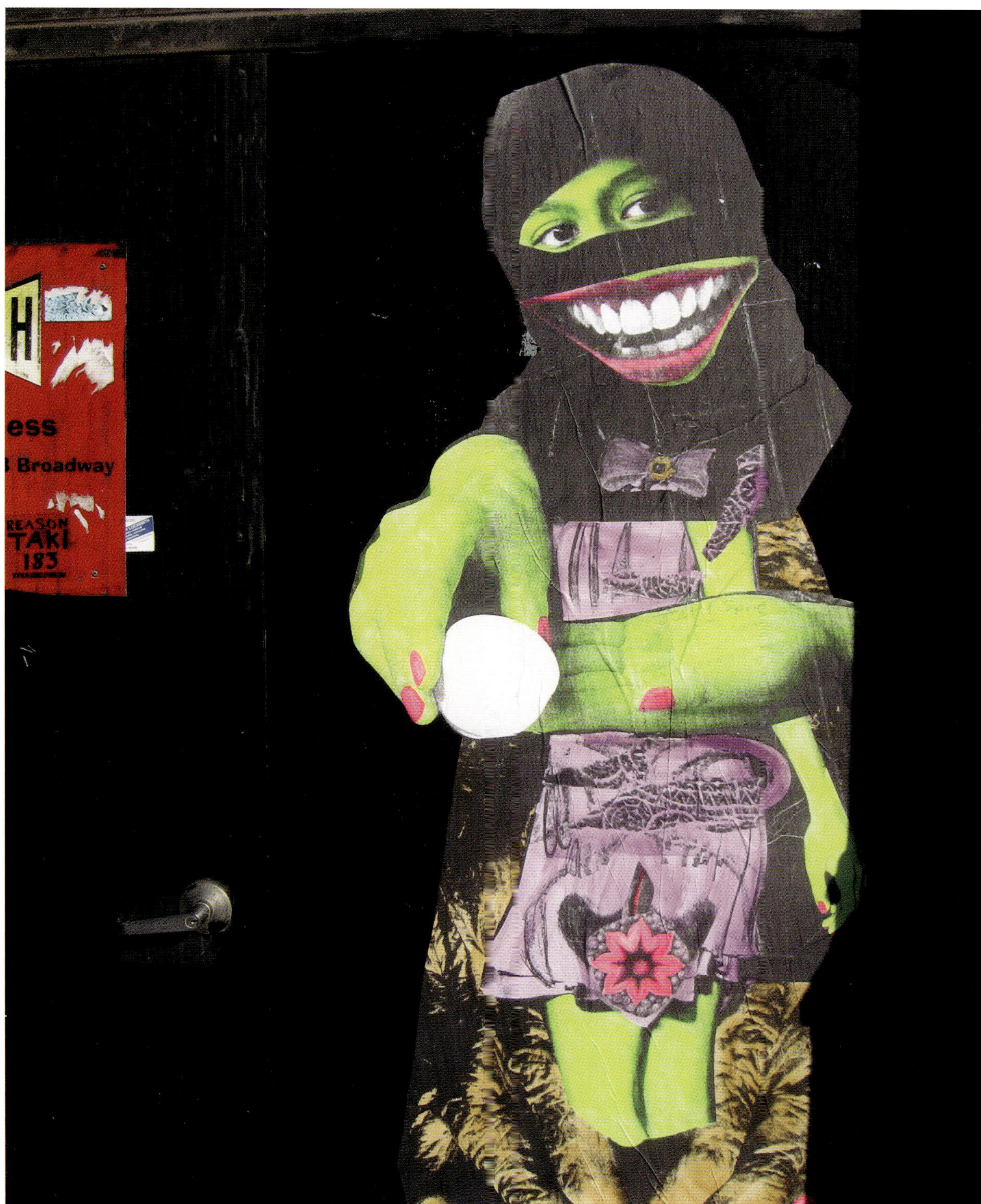
H
ess
Broadway
REASON
TAKI
183

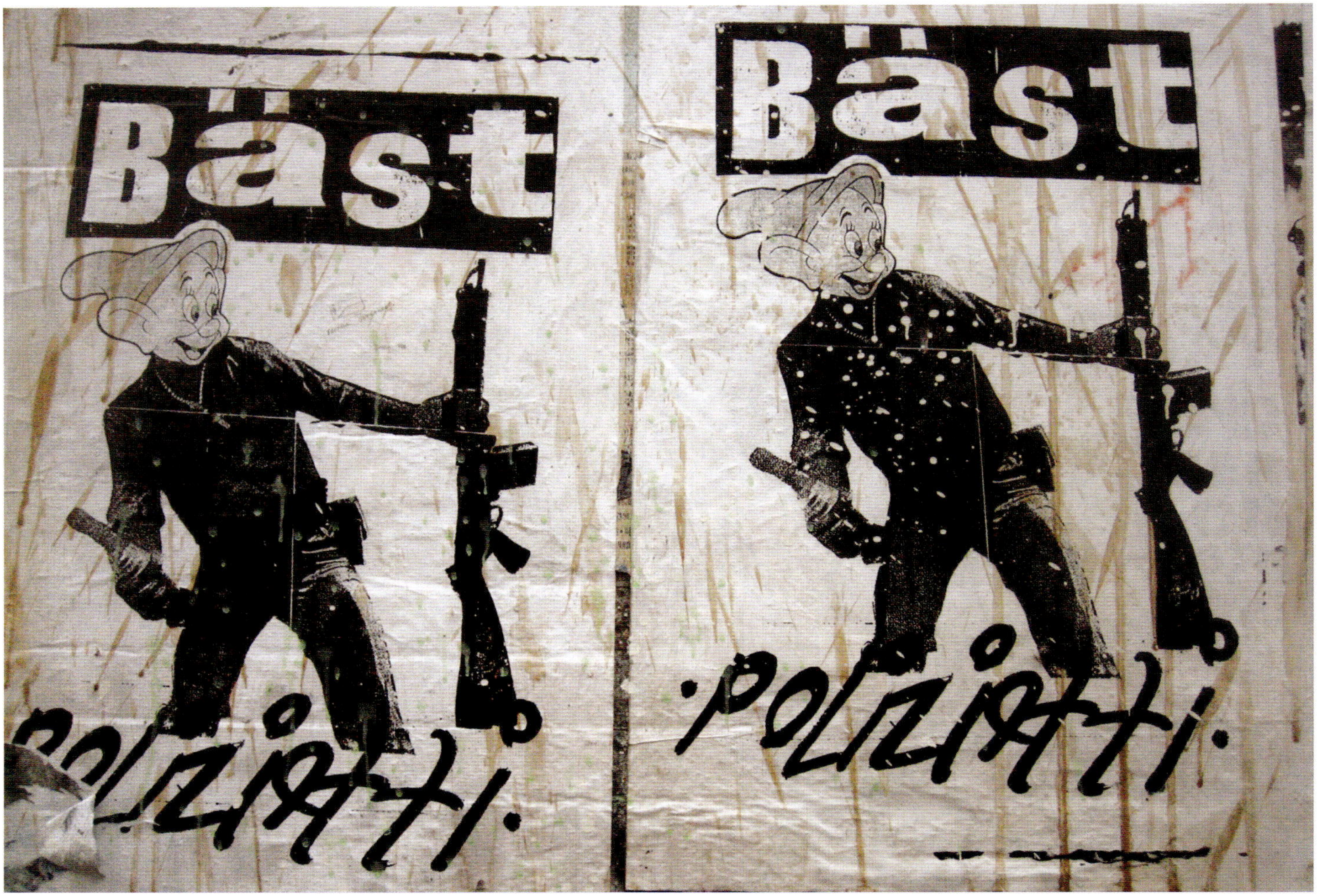

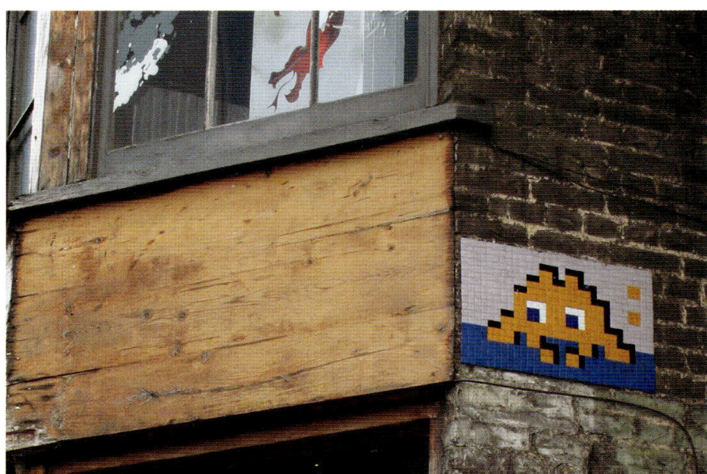

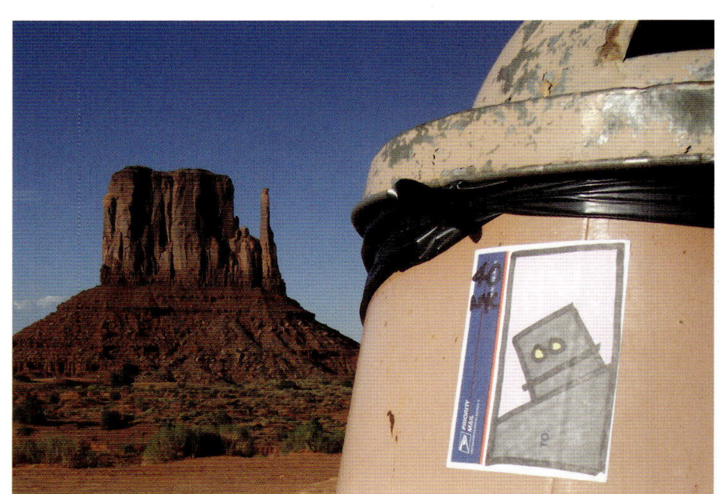

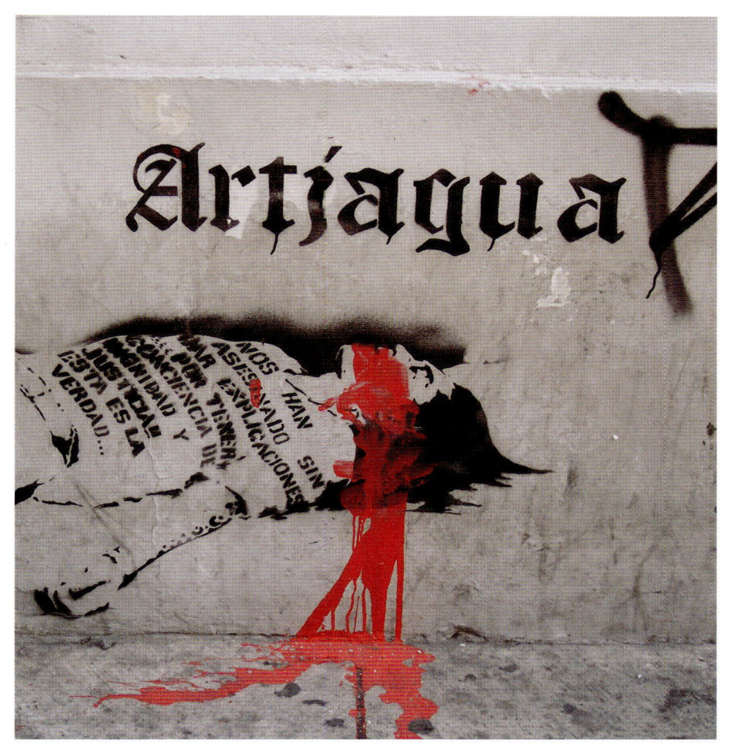
Artjagua

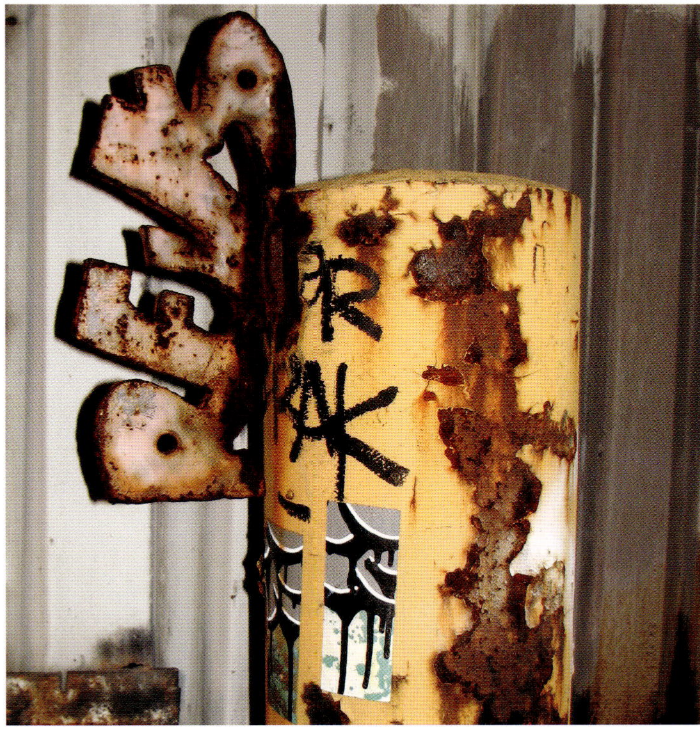

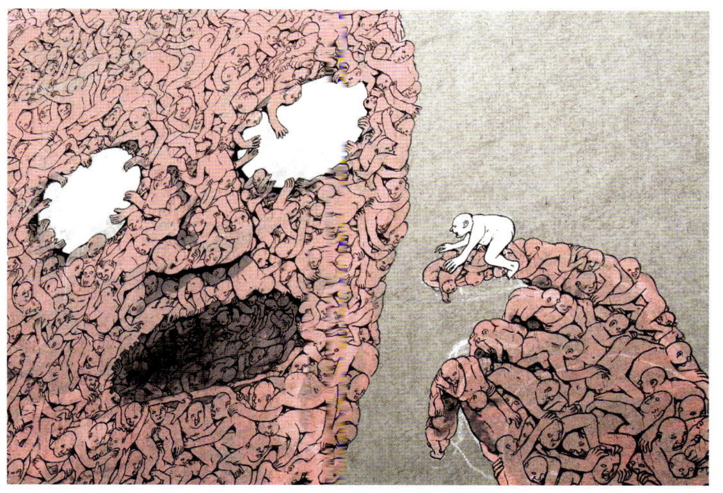

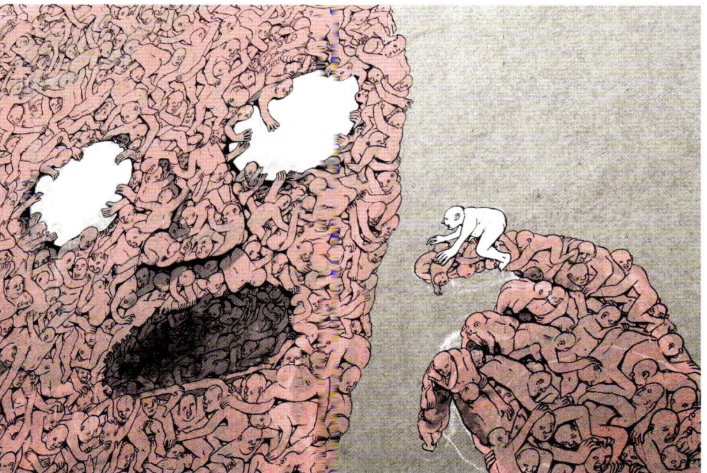

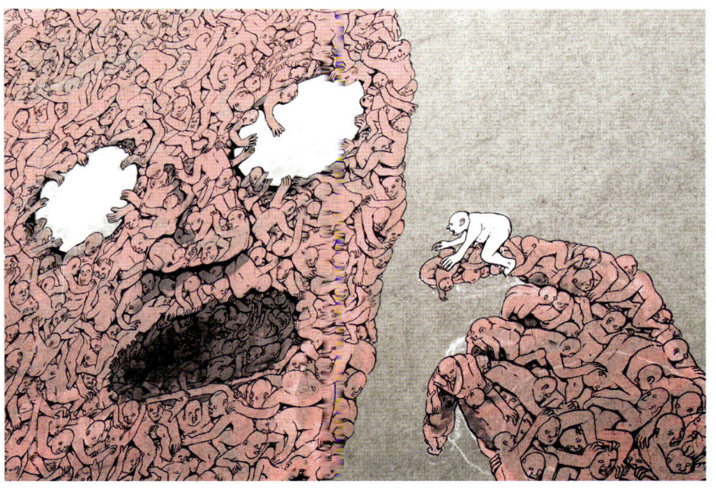

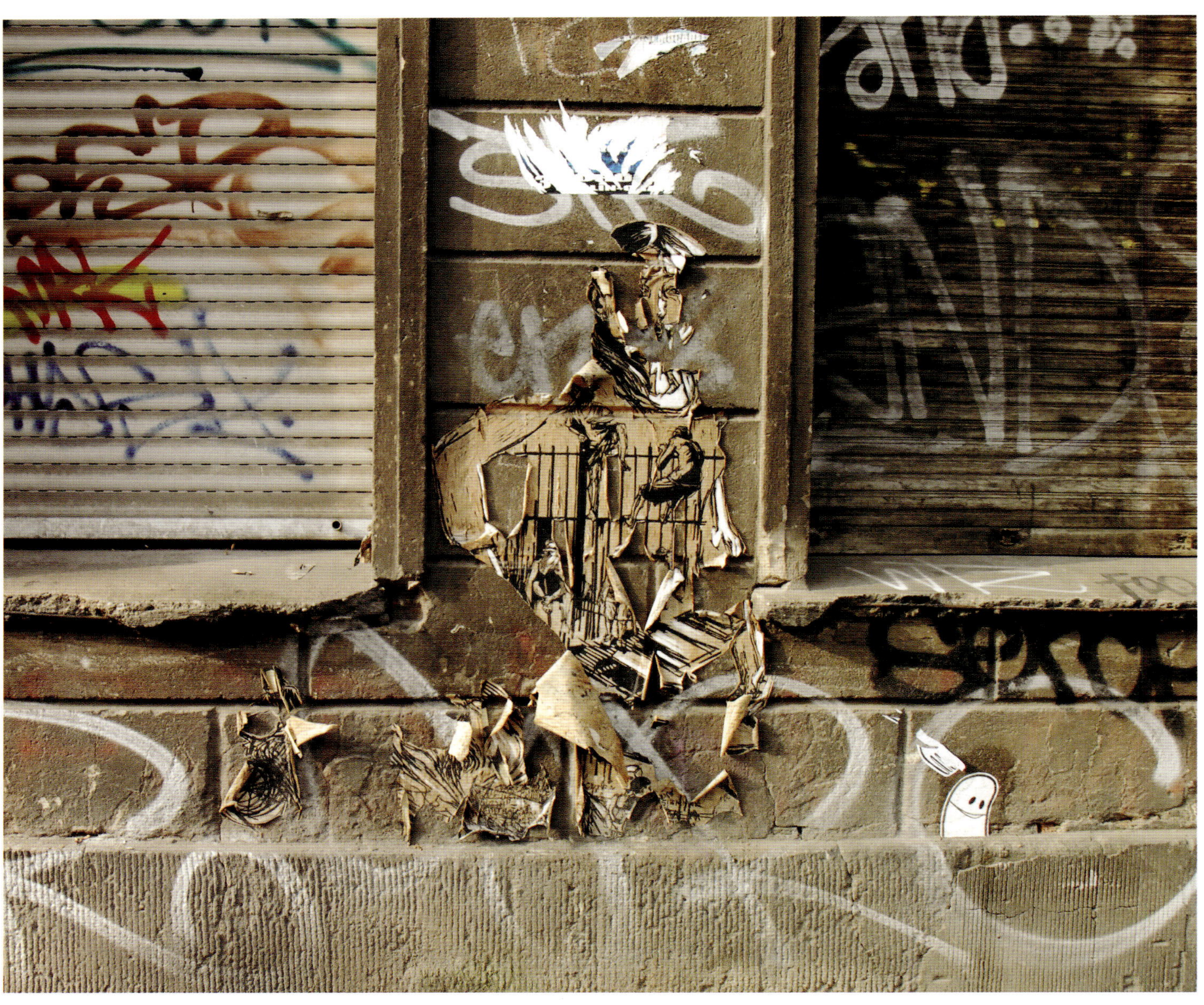

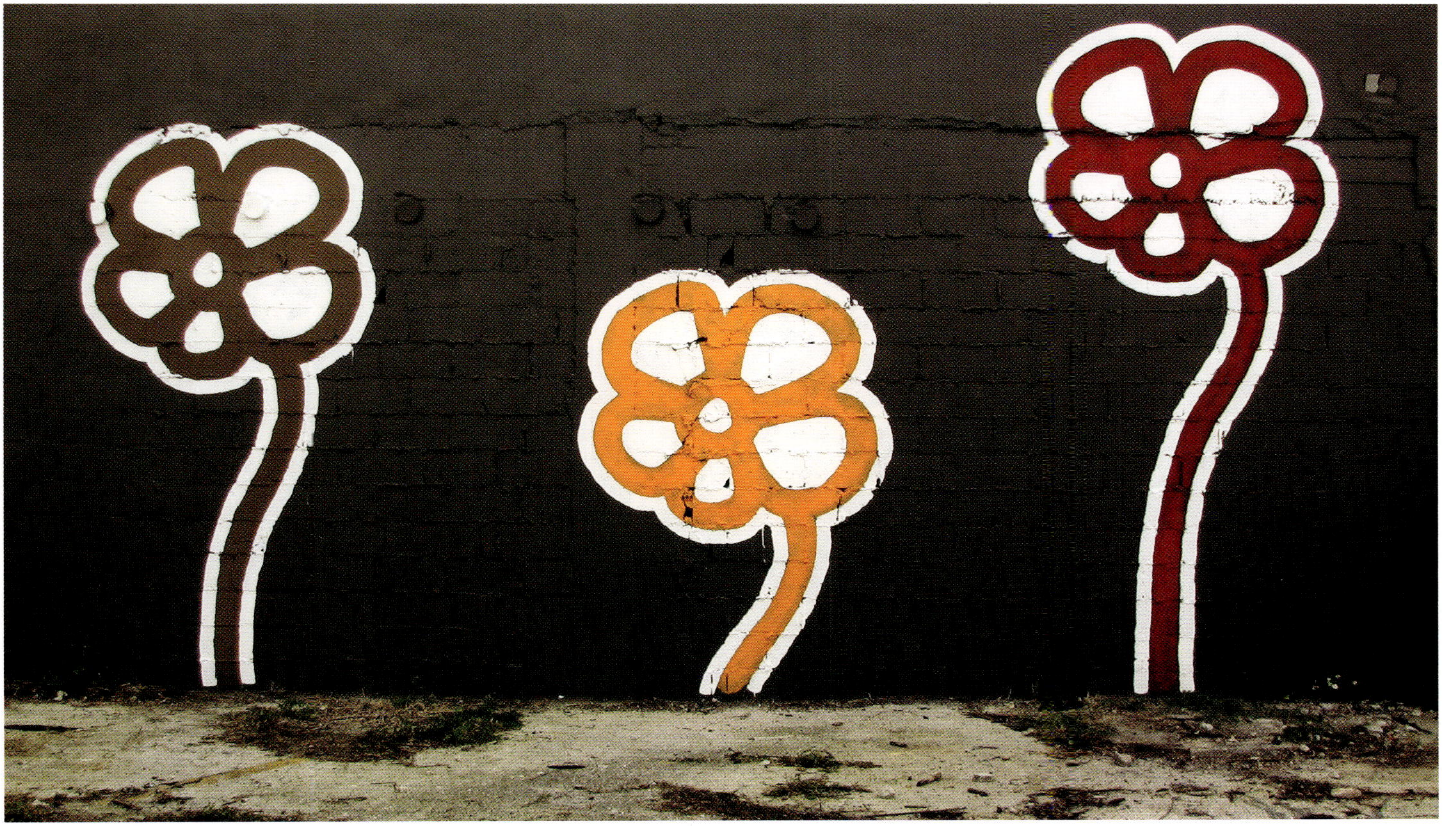

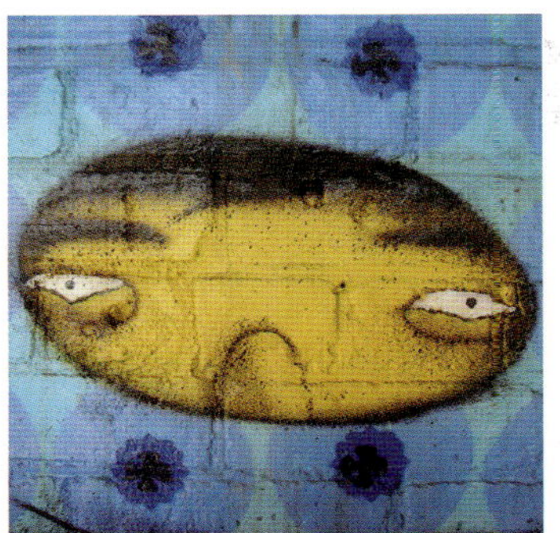

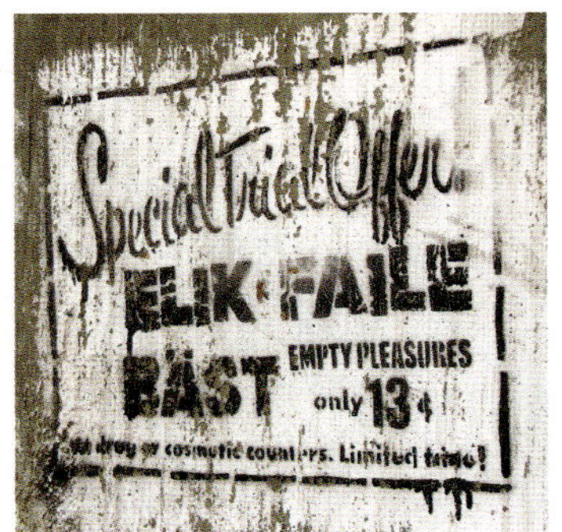

Special Trial Offer
ELIK·FAILE
BÄST
EMPTY PLEASURES
only 13¢
at drug or cosmetic counters. Limited time!


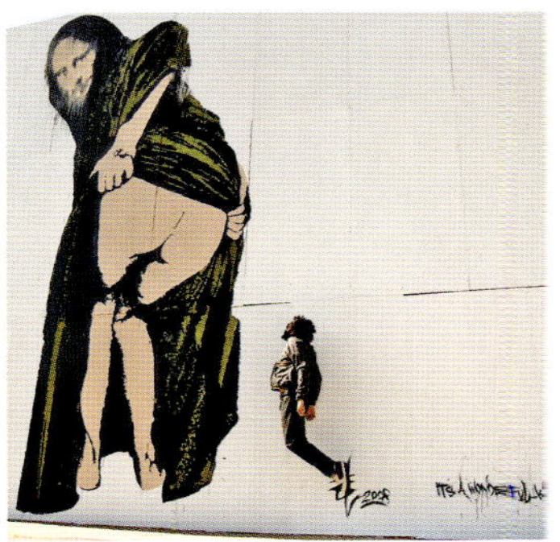

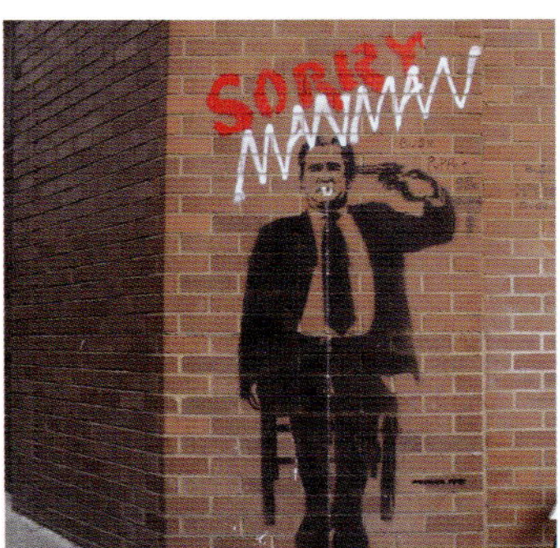

SORRY
MANMAN

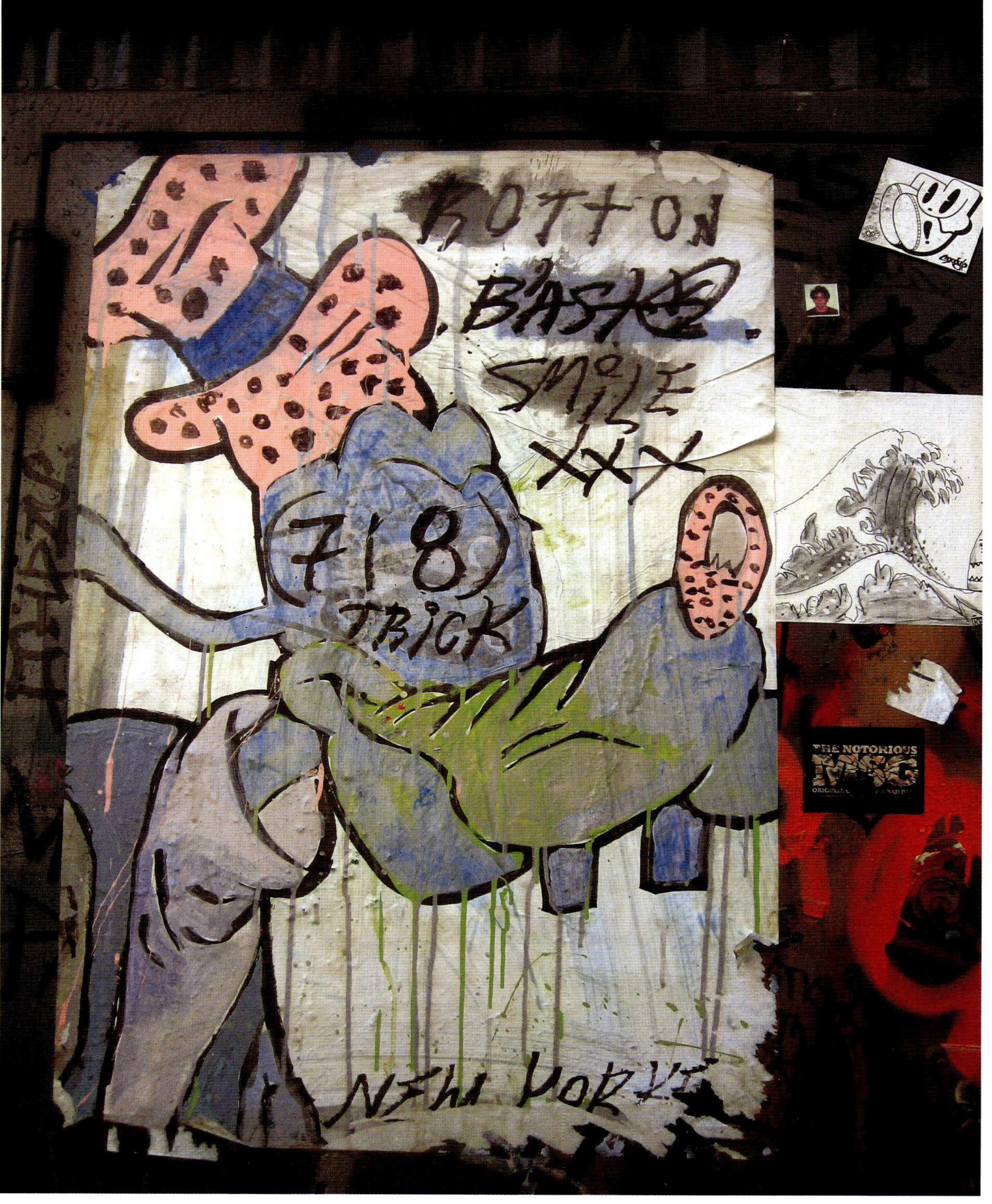

ROTTON
BASKO
SMILE
XXX
(718)
TRICK
NEW YORK
THE NOTORIOUS
MSG

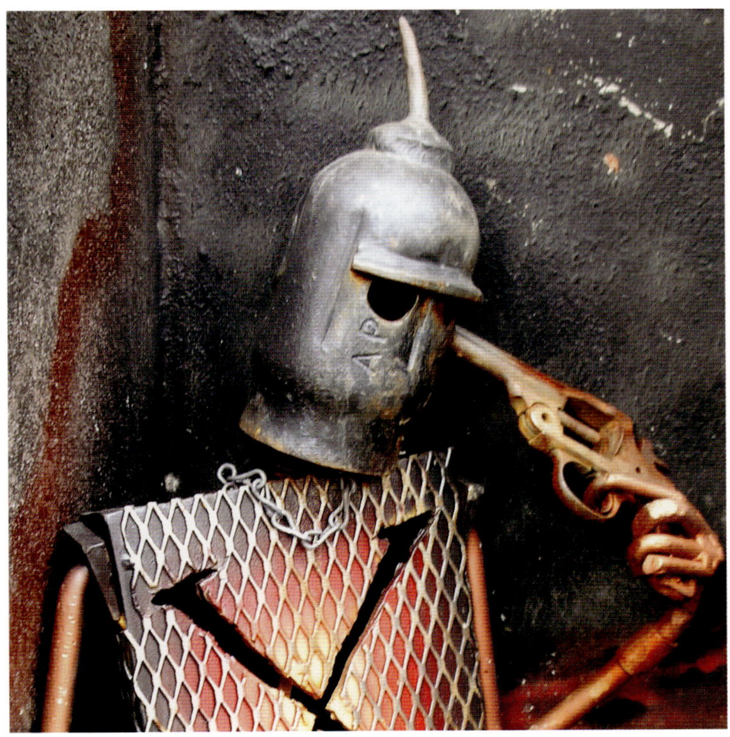

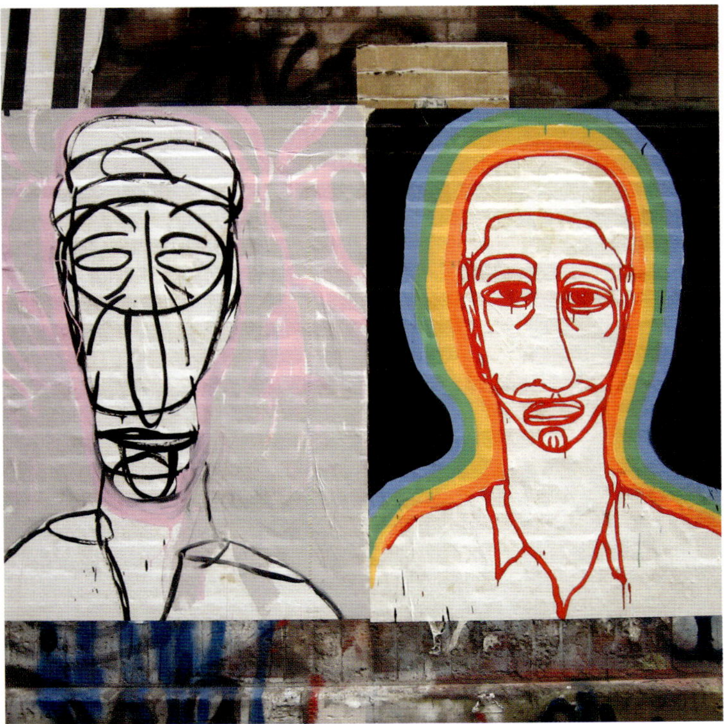

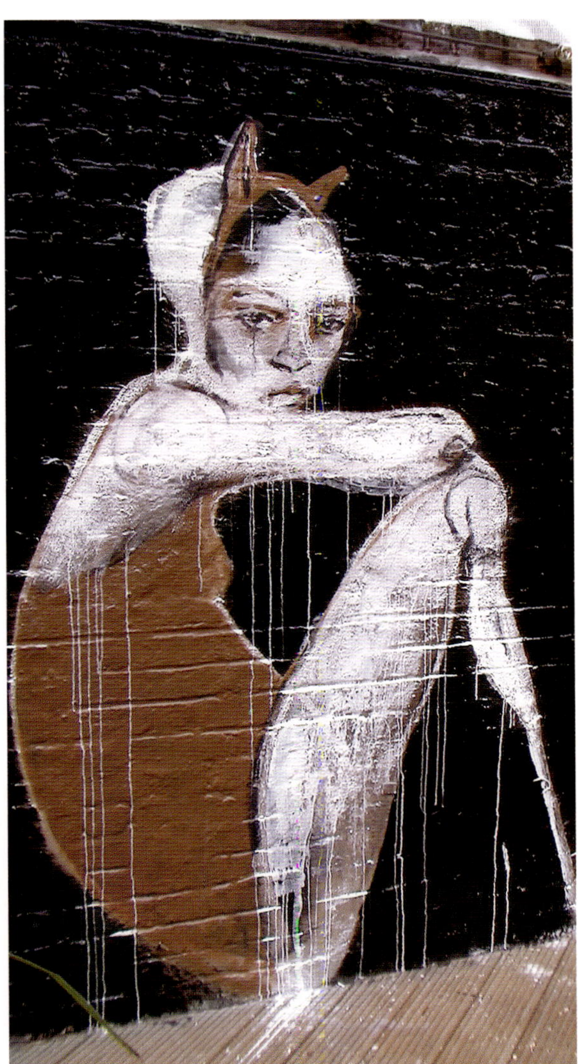

One wanders lonely as a cloud pondering ones inexorably rising debts, weak career position, the piles of threatening letters at ones door and the maze of bureaucracy one must face just to keep ones head afloat. A shaft of light breaks through the clouds, mottled by the winter branches and gently strikes a wall where a cloud of butterflies with the heads of minor celebrities has been painted in the night. The emperor isn't wearing any clothes. We do need to be reminded.

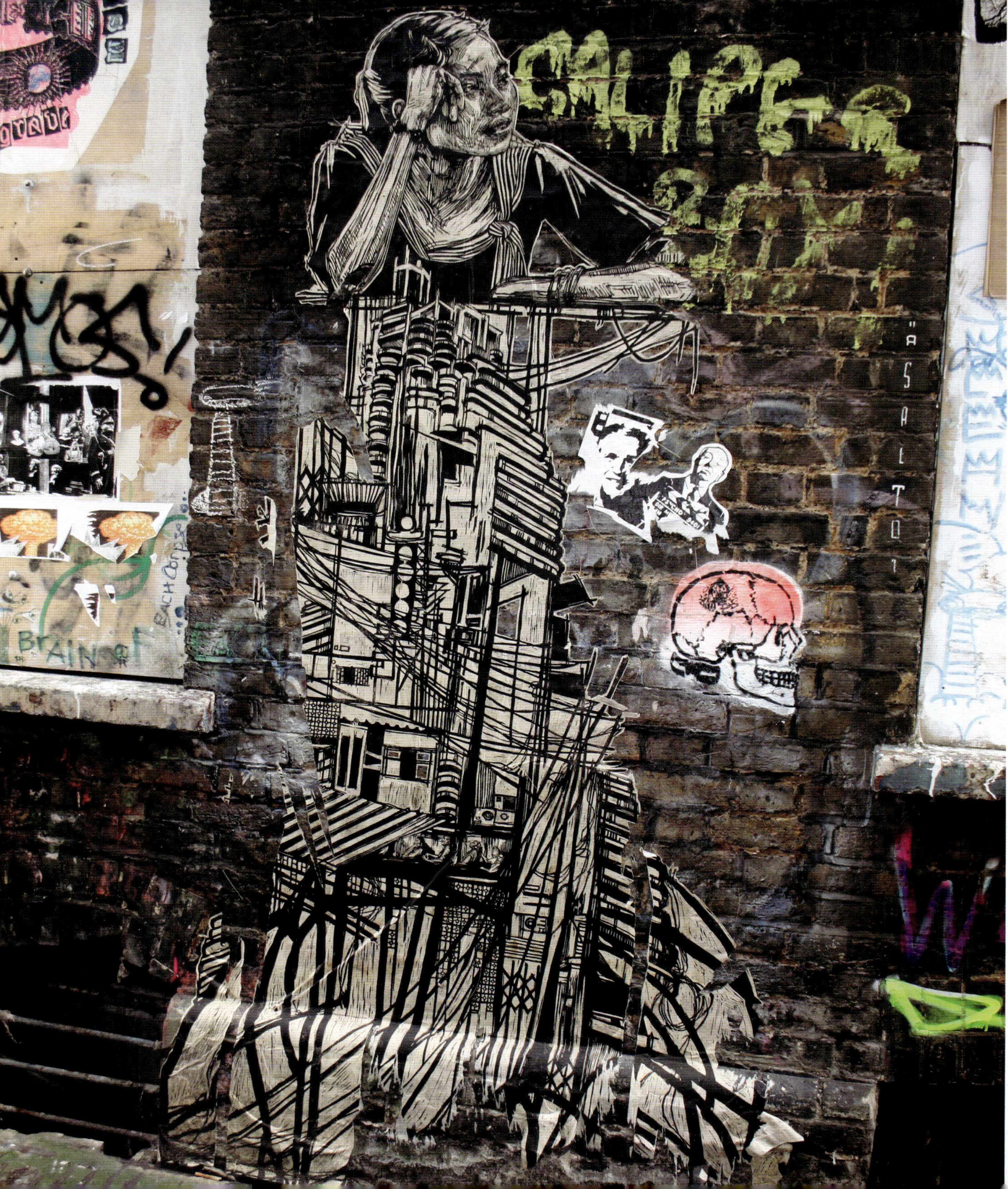
grave
BRAIN
"A SALTO"

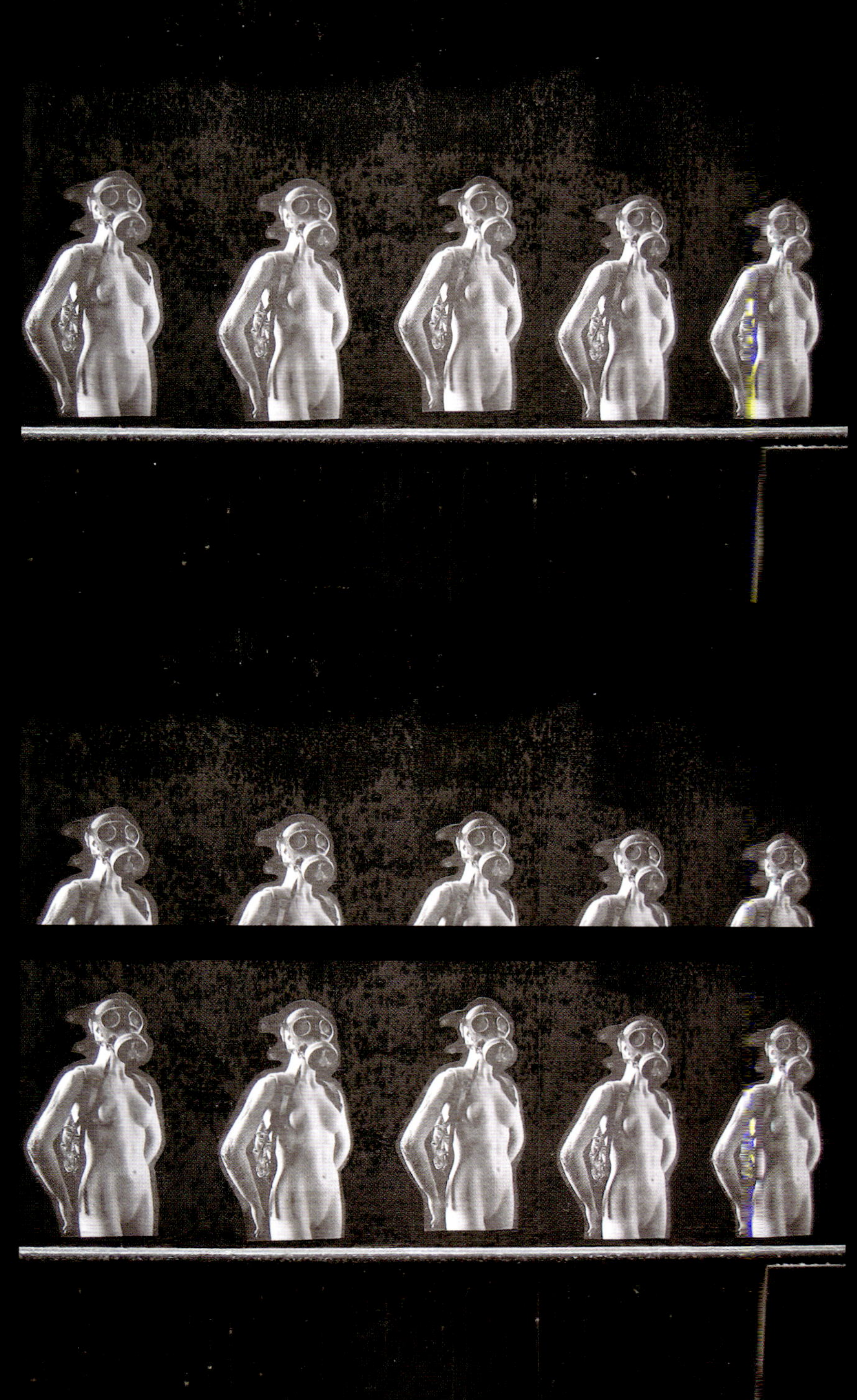

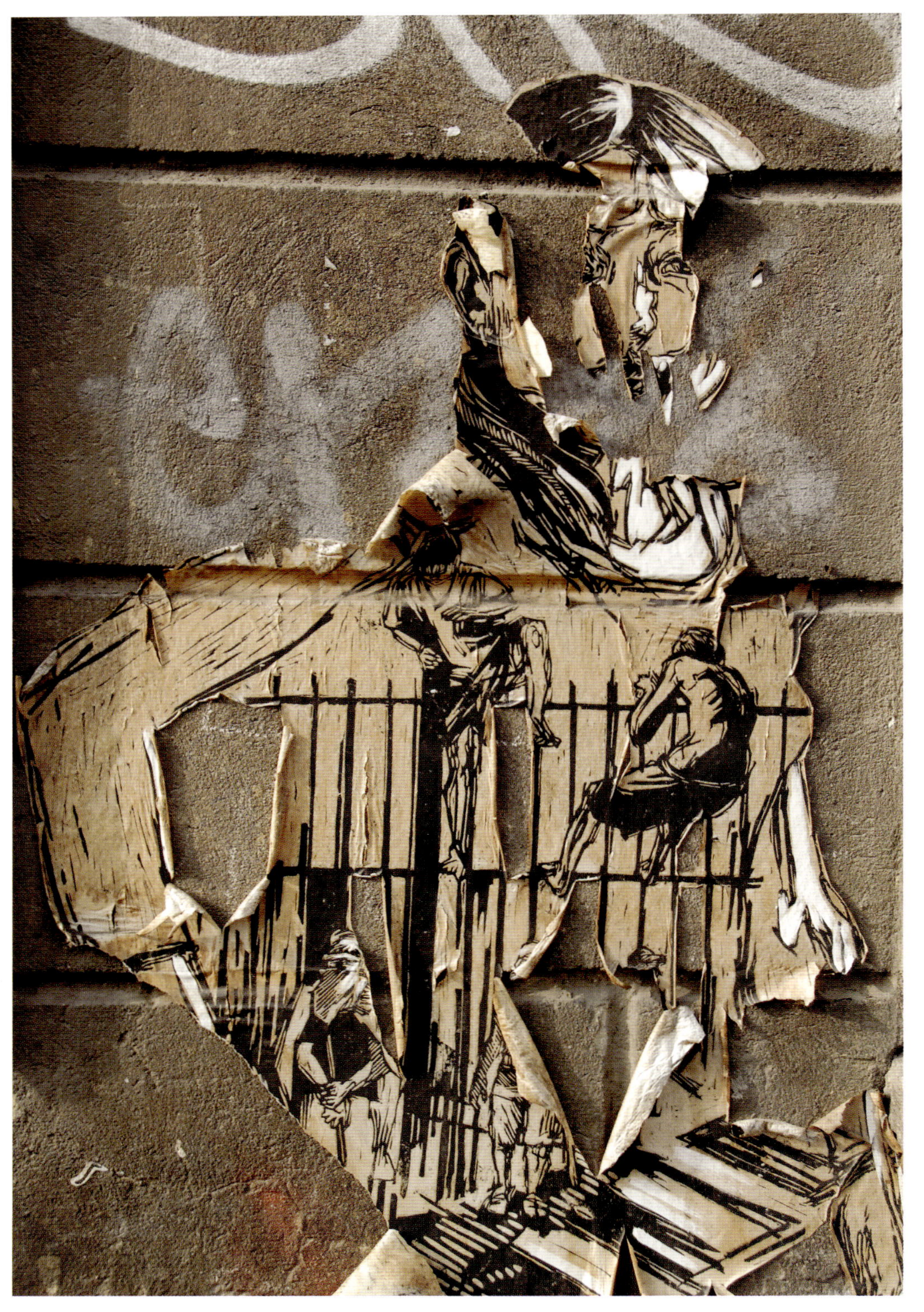

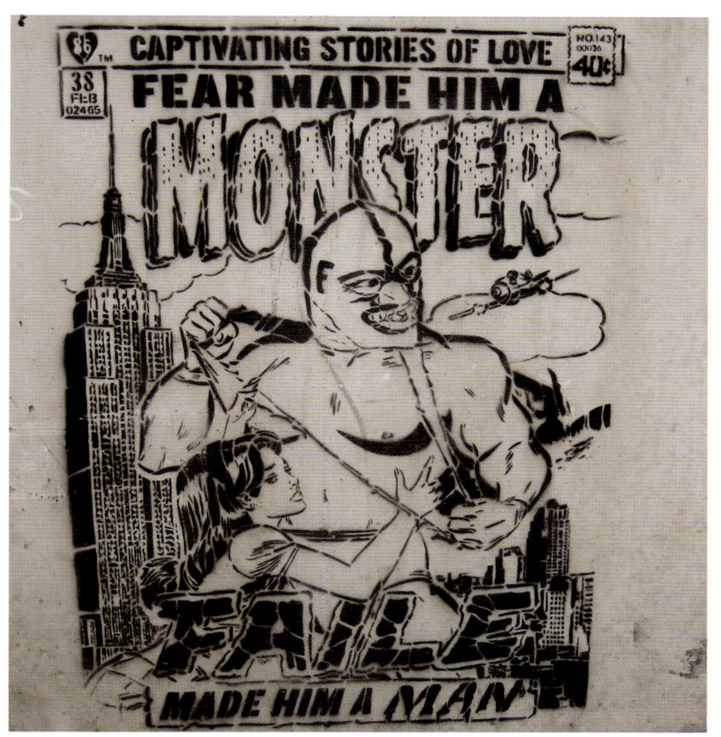


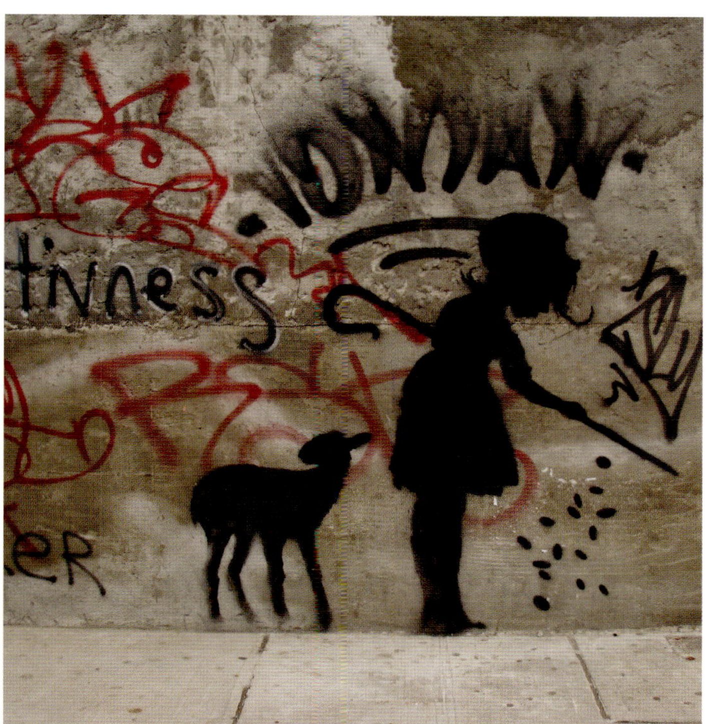


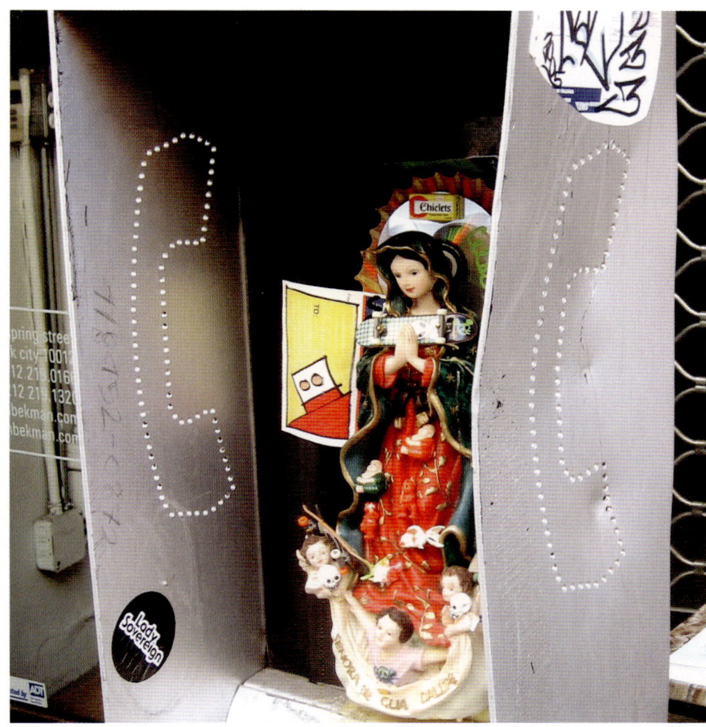


This caption is only here to annoy the photographs.

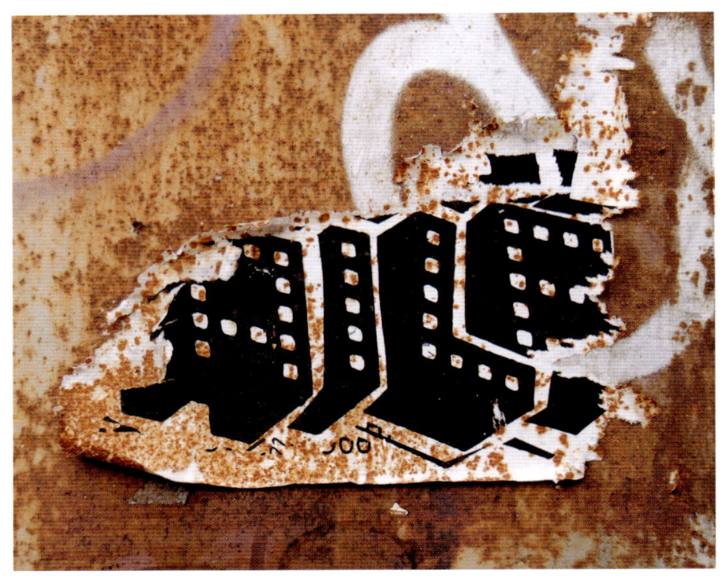
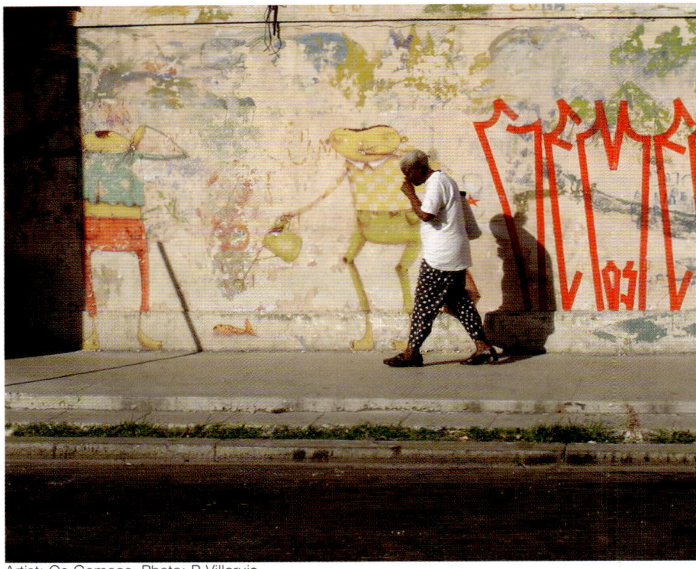

Artist: Os Gemeos. Photo: P. Villeruis

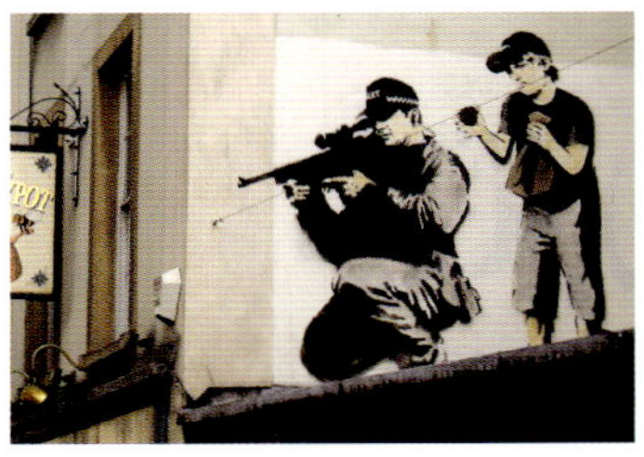
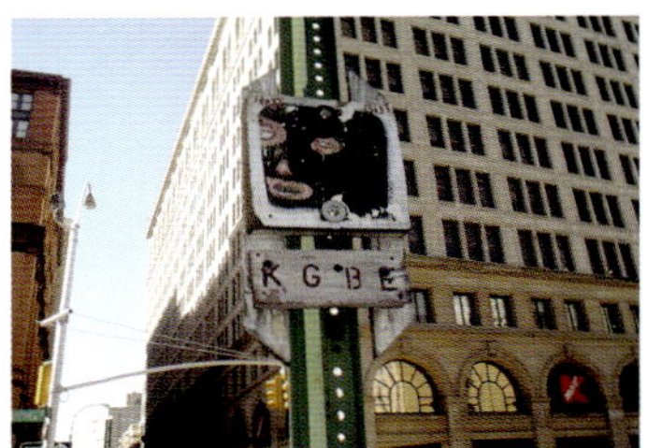
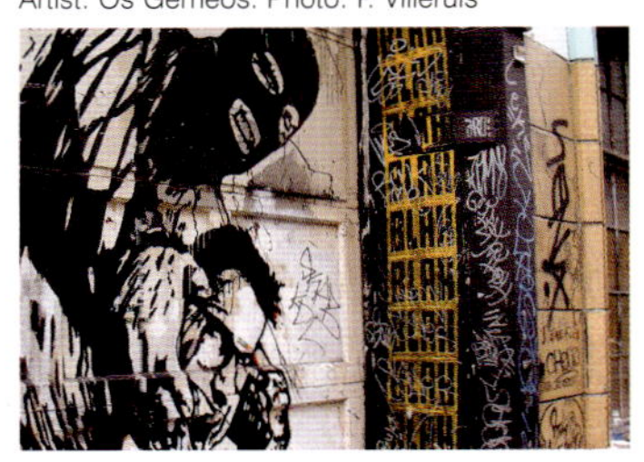
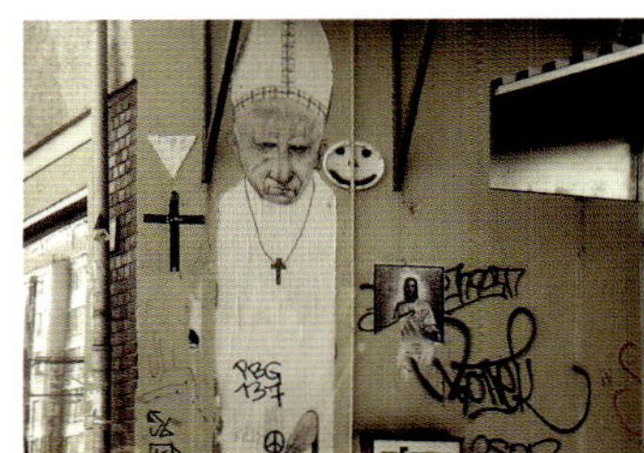

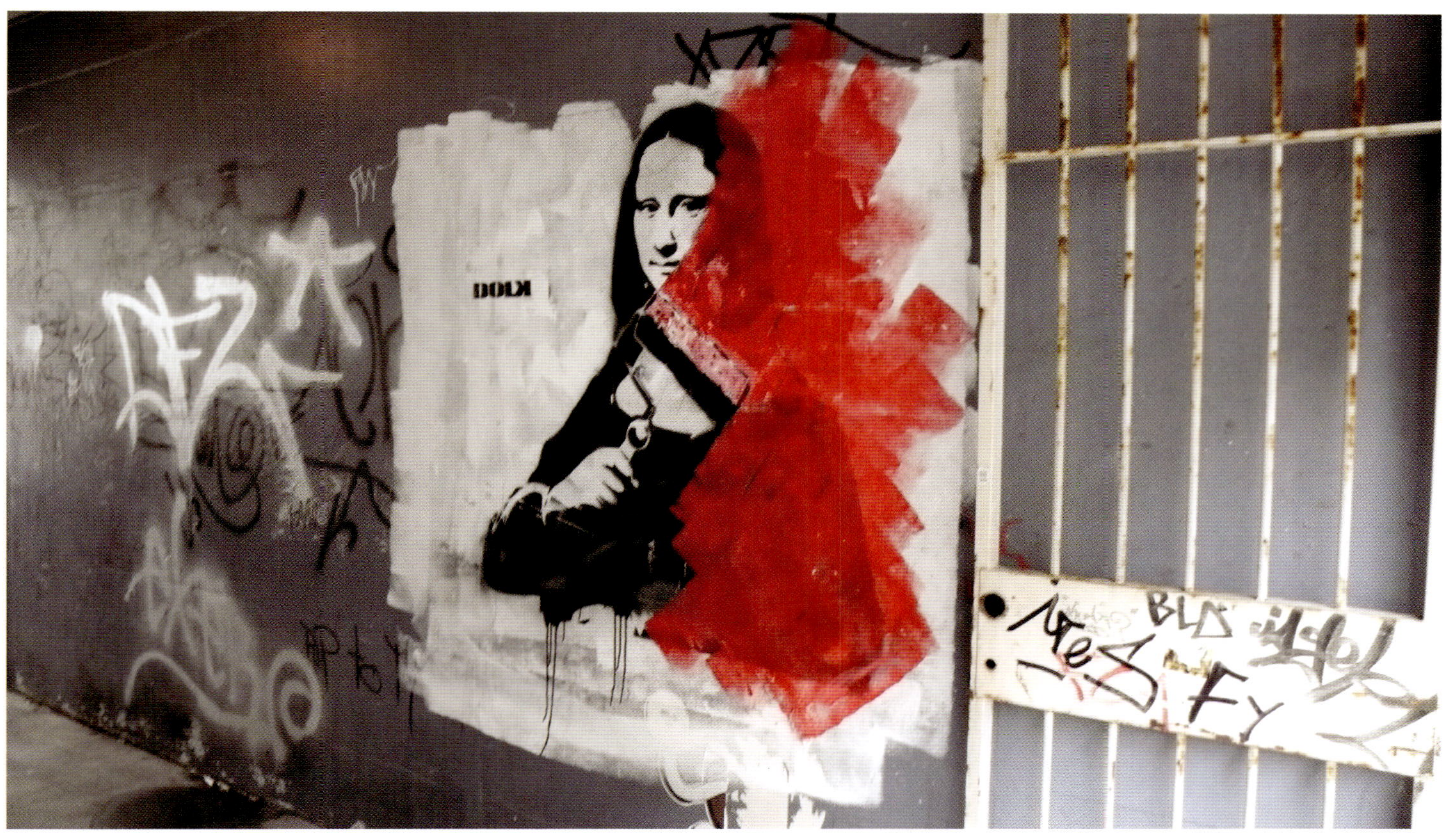



The only immediate feedback the artist gets is how long the image stays in place. Fortune, nature, other wild painters of the night and Bob from the council will decide the fate of the piece. It will never be around long enough to be stolen by comedy Nazis in some crazy third world war and kept hidden in a cellar in Belgium for fifty years only to be rediscovered by a delighted young couple from Norway. No priceless status for this Mona Lisa. Its days are brief like the life of the cicada.

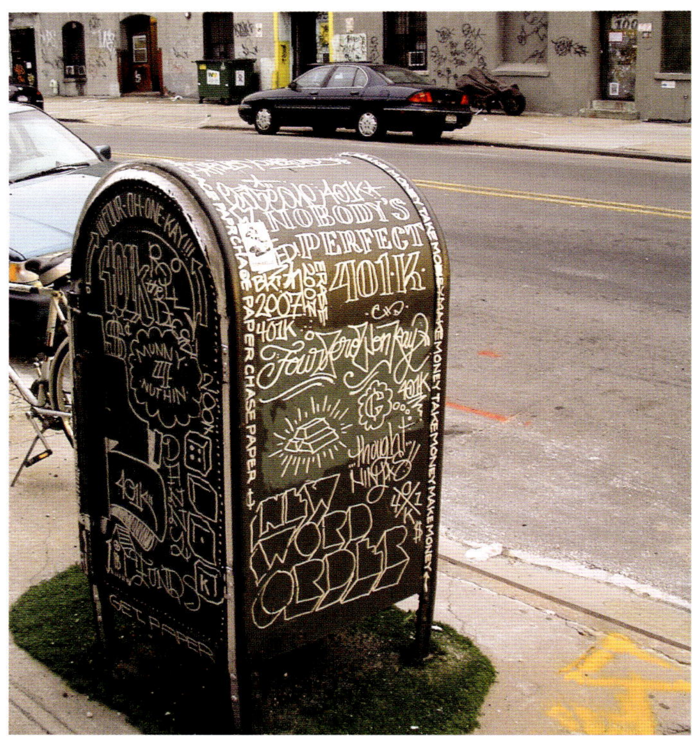

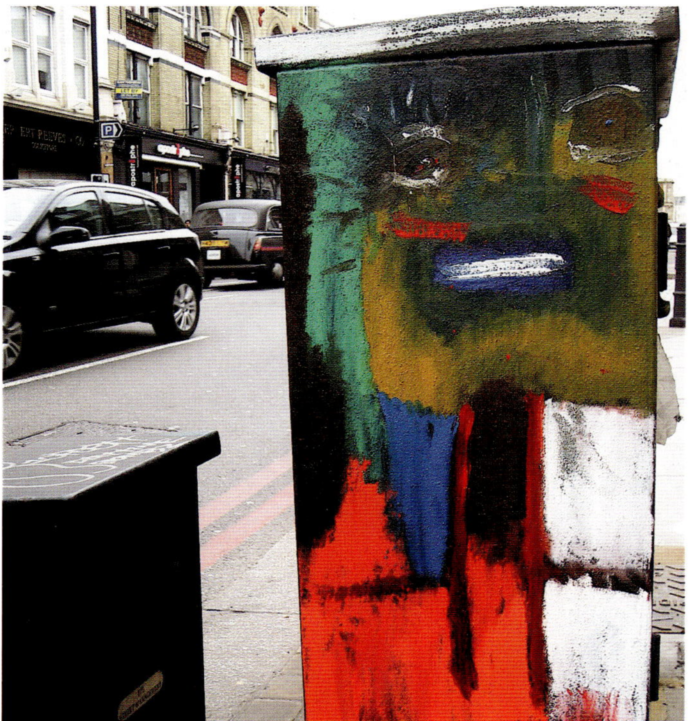

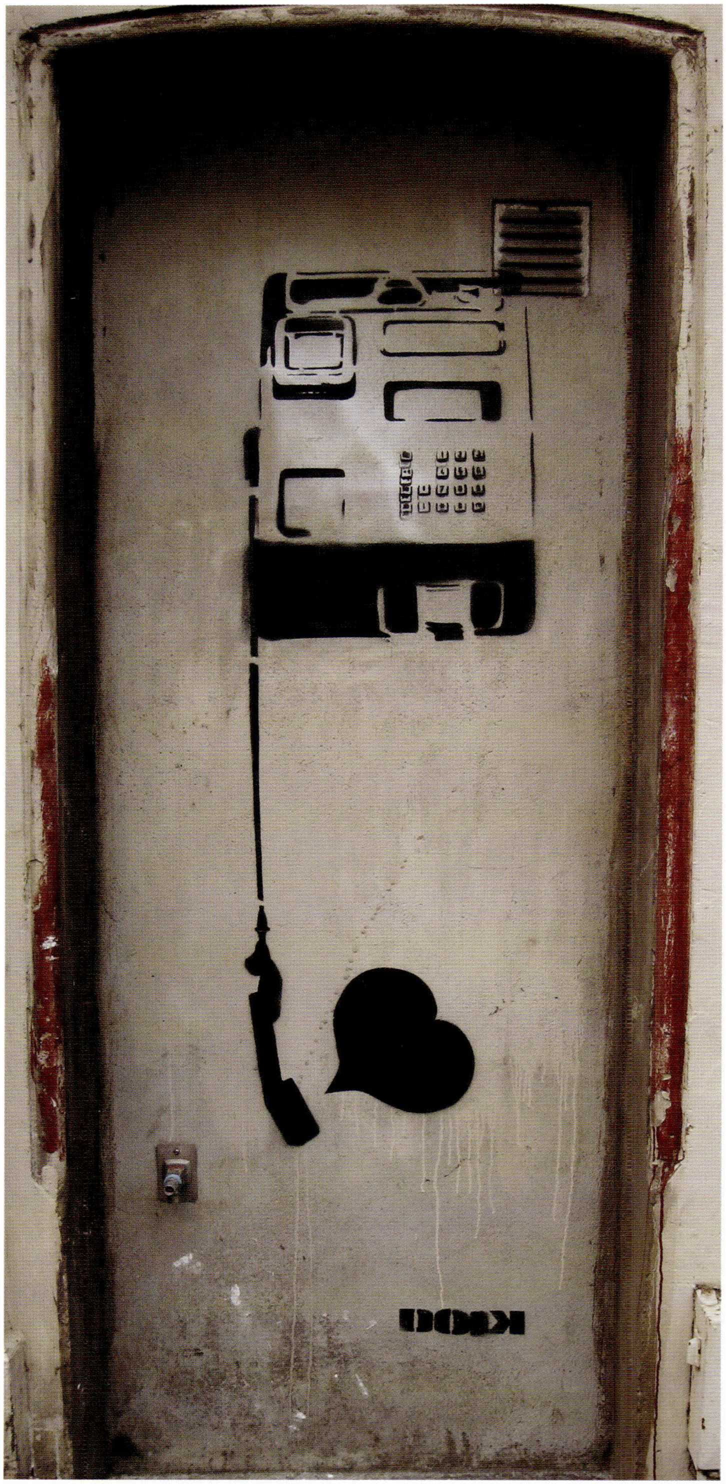

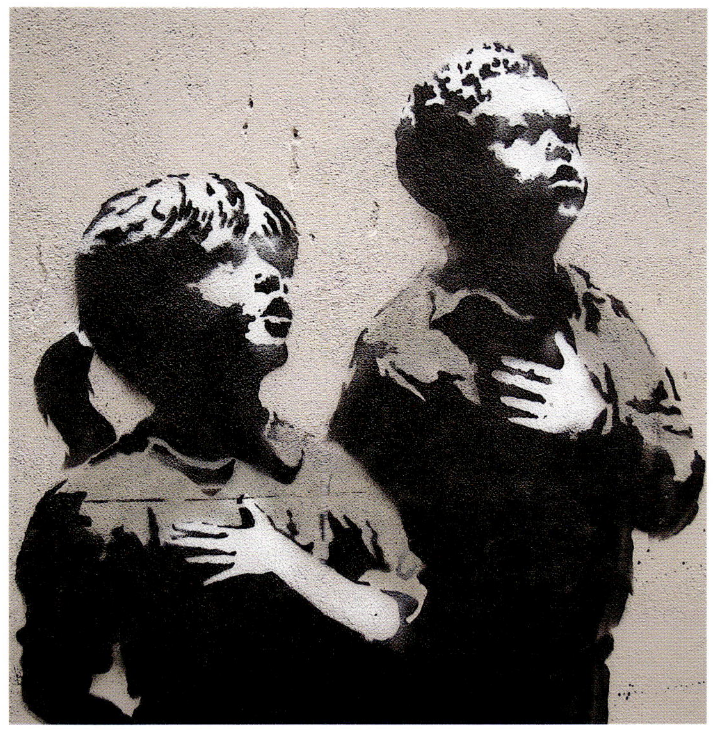 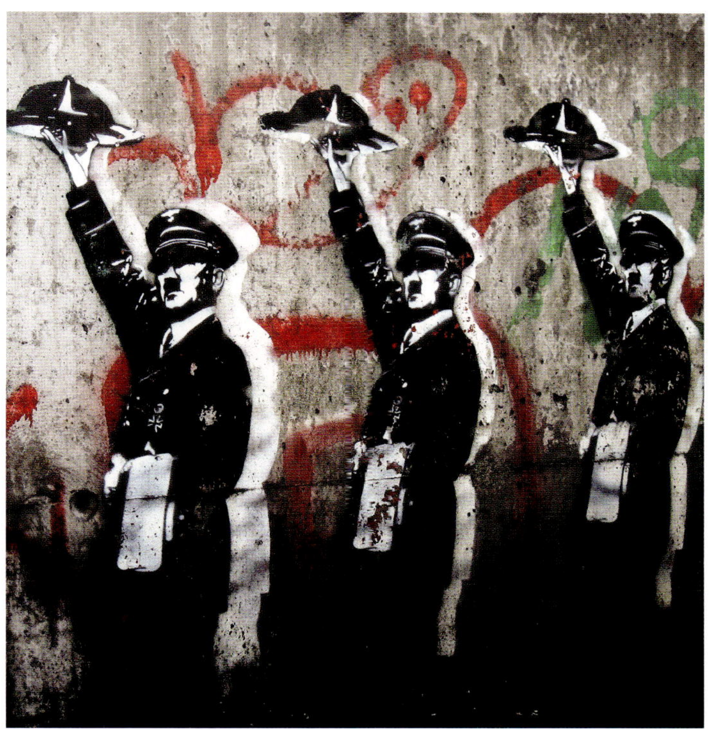

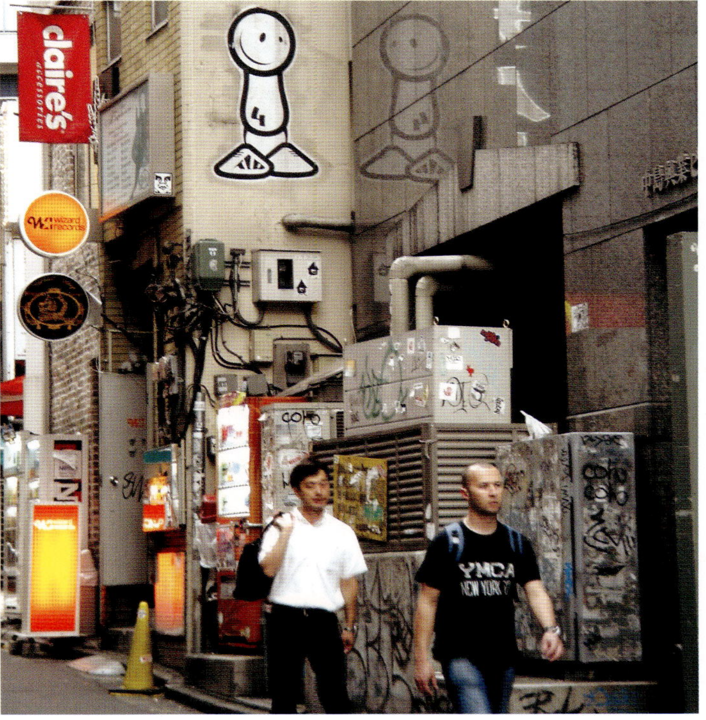

So when they put the flags on the
moon, how is that not lagging?

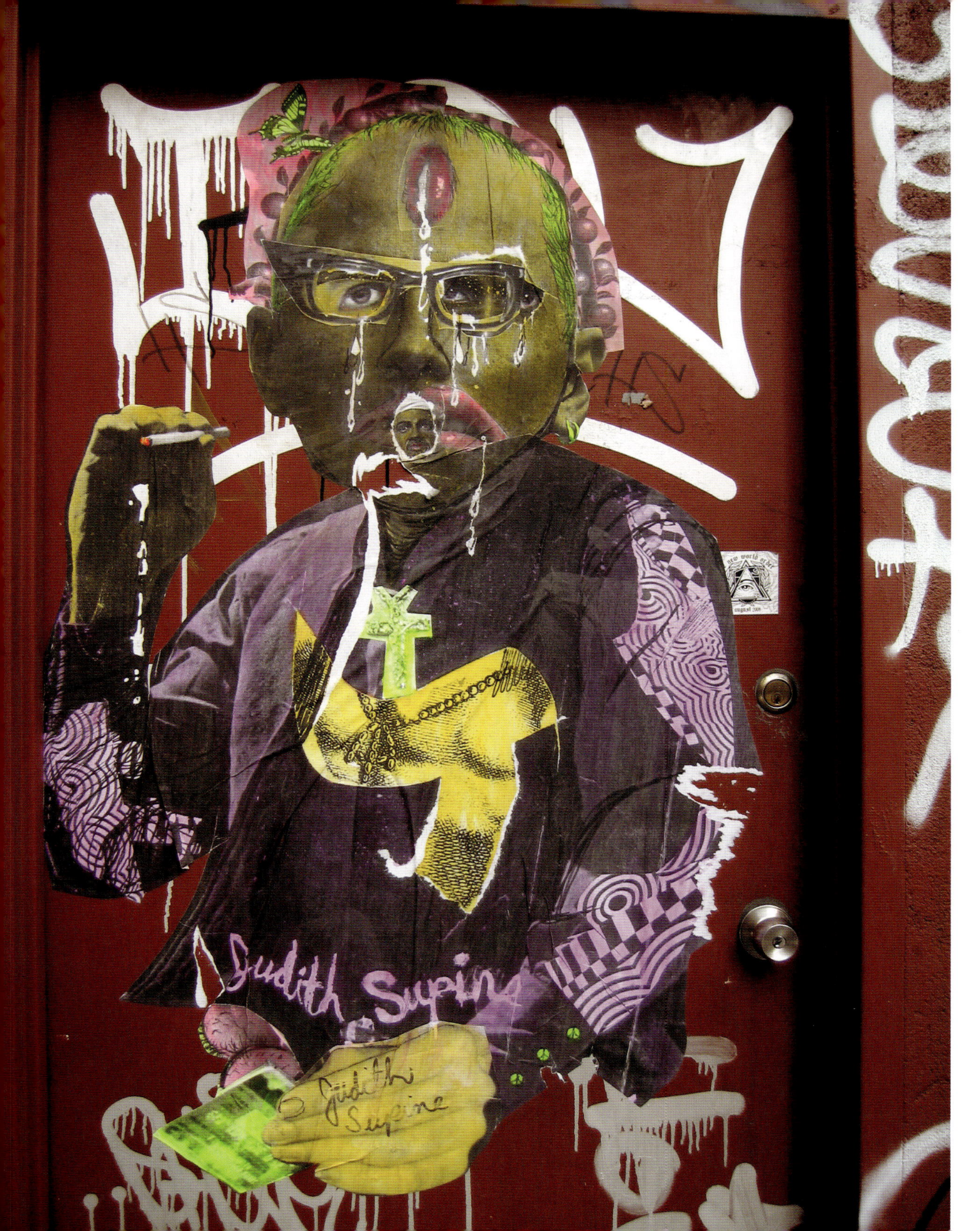

Judith Supine
Judith Supine

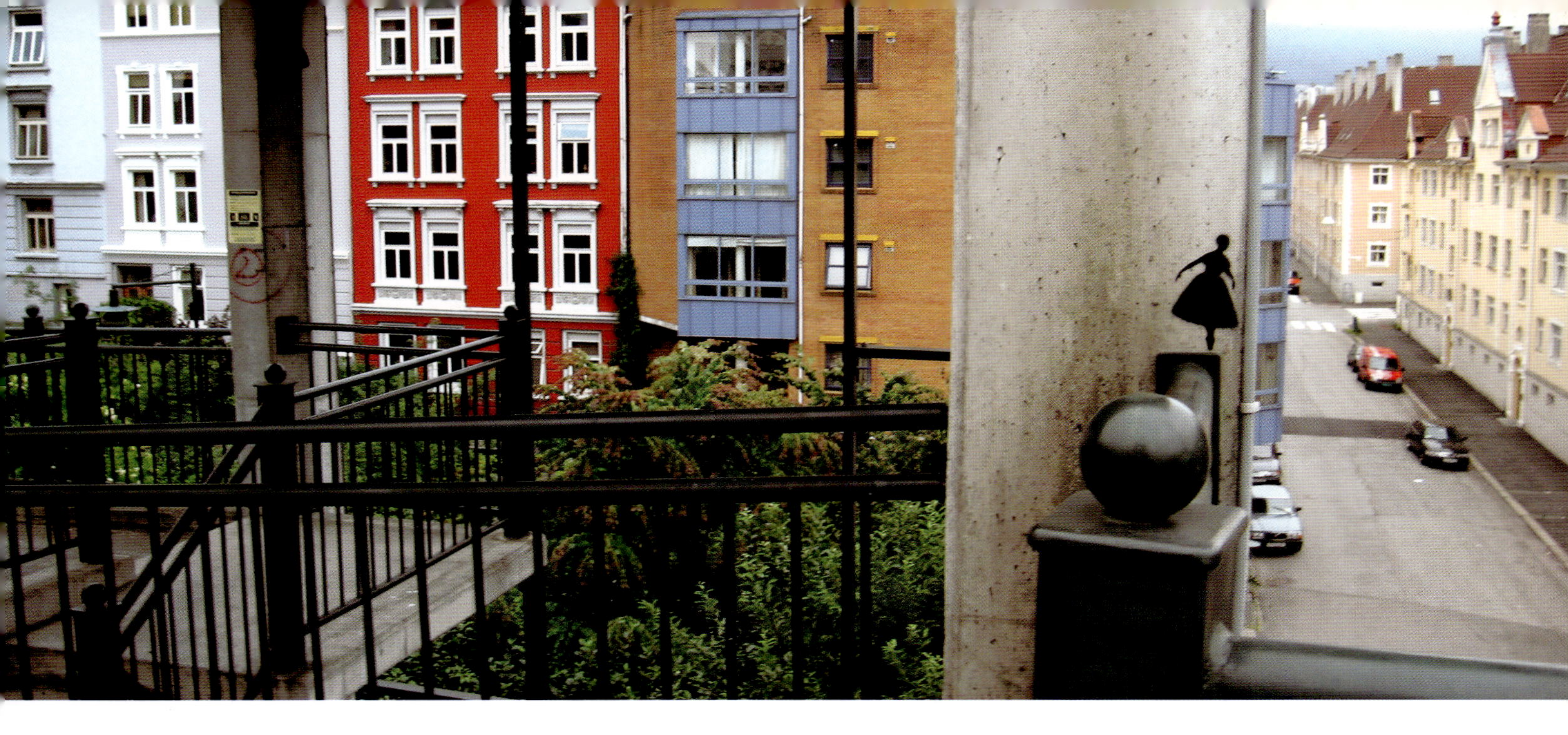

This page features no less than twelve thousand works by our featured artist STRAWBERRY FACE. See if you can spot them all.

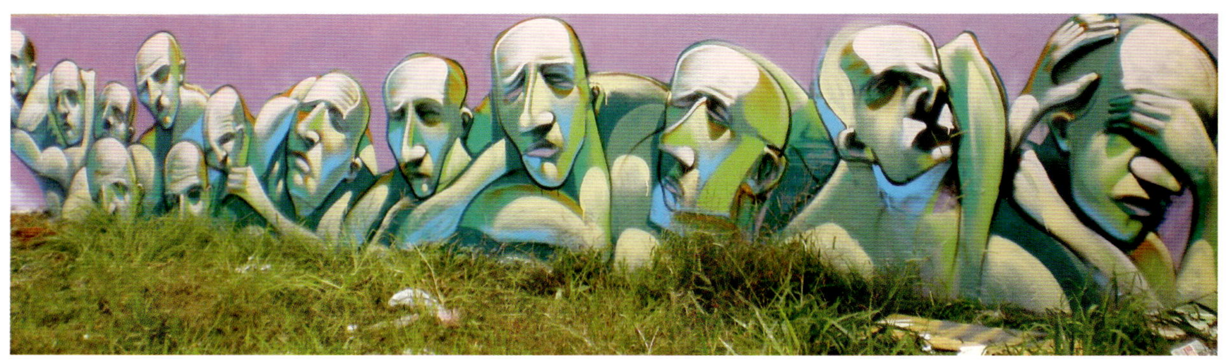

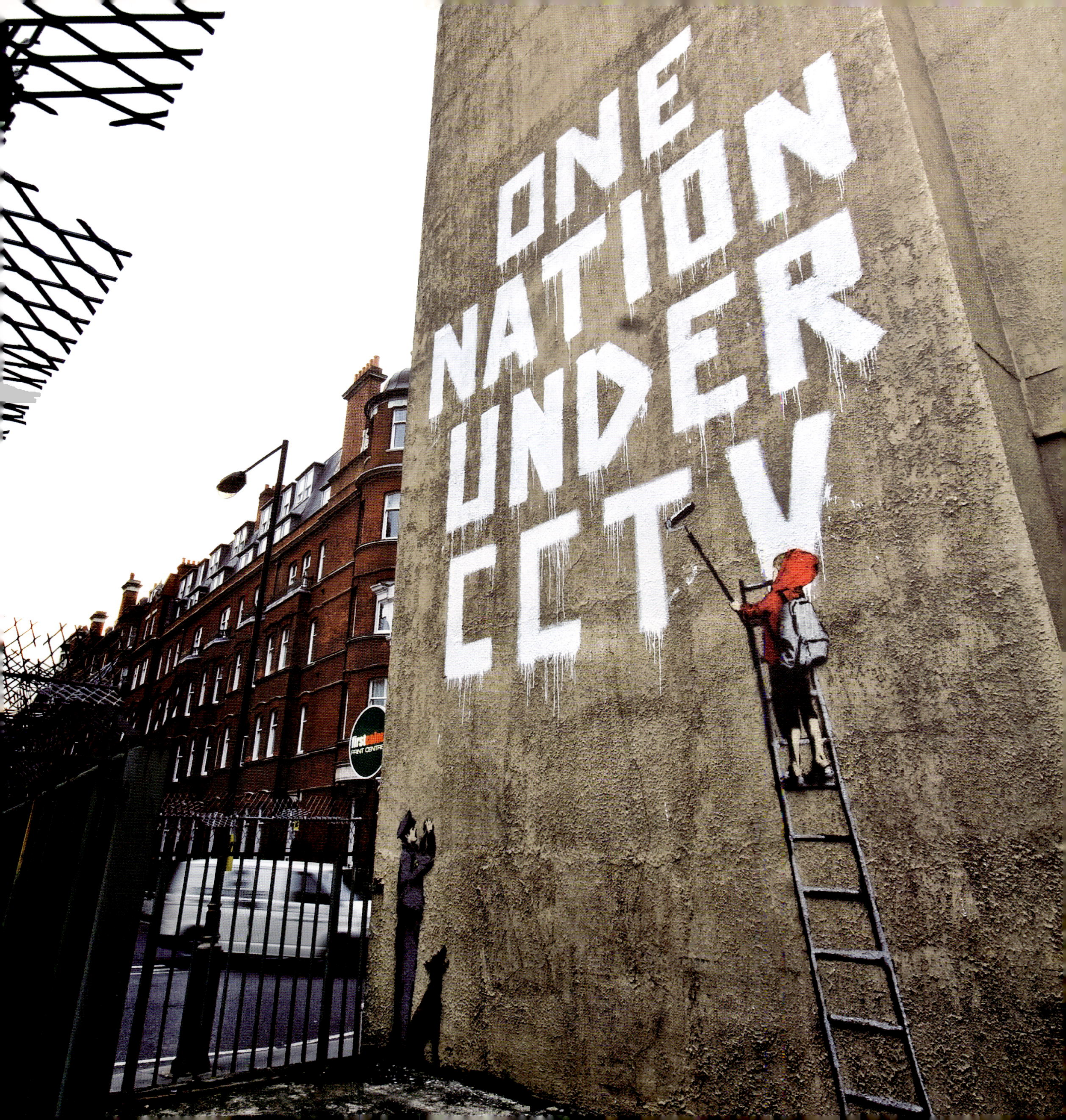

ONE
NATION
UNDER
CCTV
first colour
PRINT CENTRE

# Veni vidi vici

A fantastic display of ancient roman graffiti has been opened up to the public today at Hadrian's Wall in the North of England. Visitors can see the 2000 year old carved messages of bored soldiers stationed in the far flung reaches of the empire. These have been translated for the contemporary reader. Some of the most intact pieces include "What goes on tour stays on tour." And a huge piece of work that simply displays the name of its author; "DAVUS". A large bunch of Roman era copper keys found near the site are also on display. A museum spokesperson said, "We can't be certain, but it's likely a bunch of keys like these were used to create some of these works, perhaps even these keys here. It's tremendously exciting."

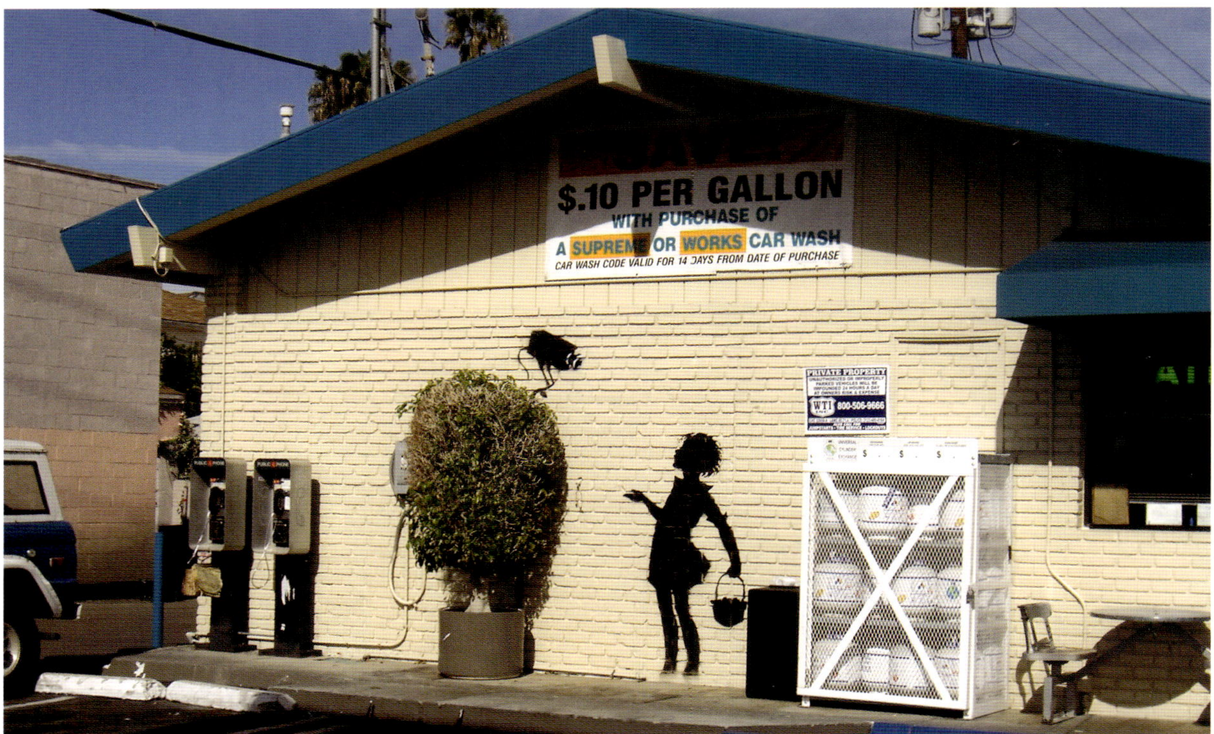

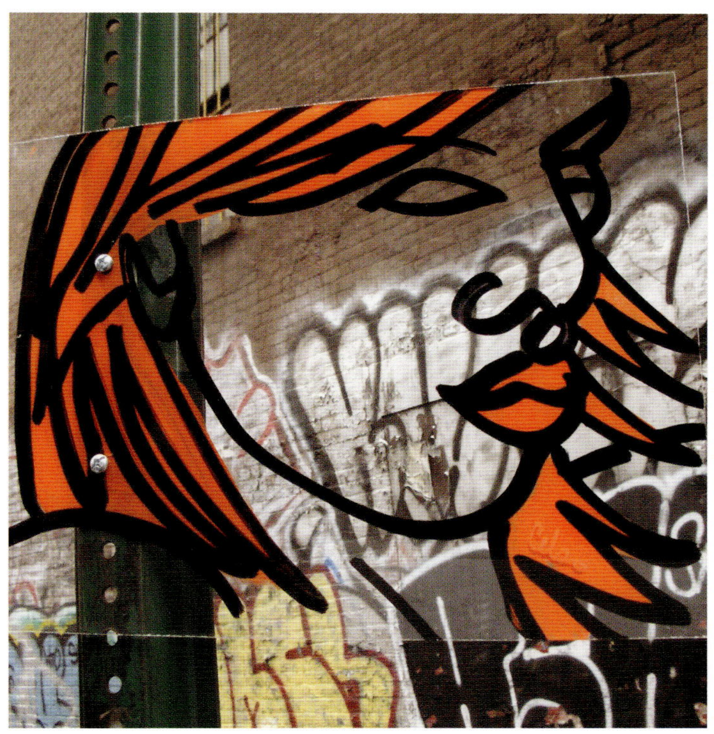 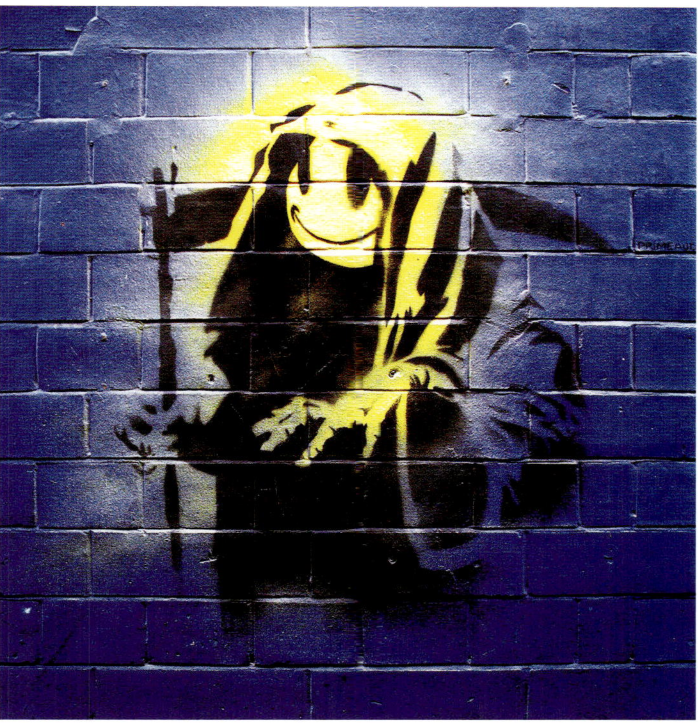

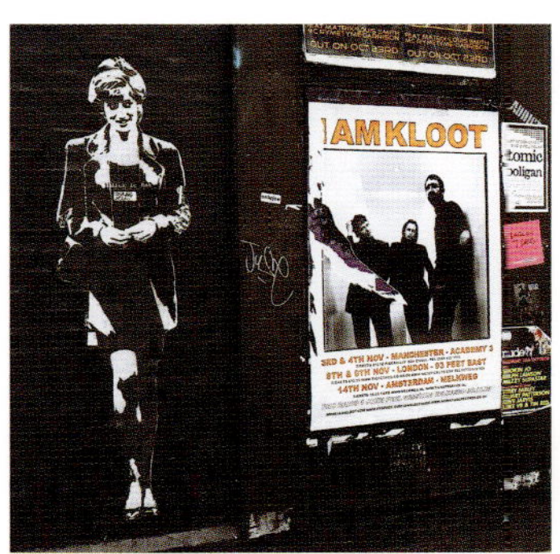 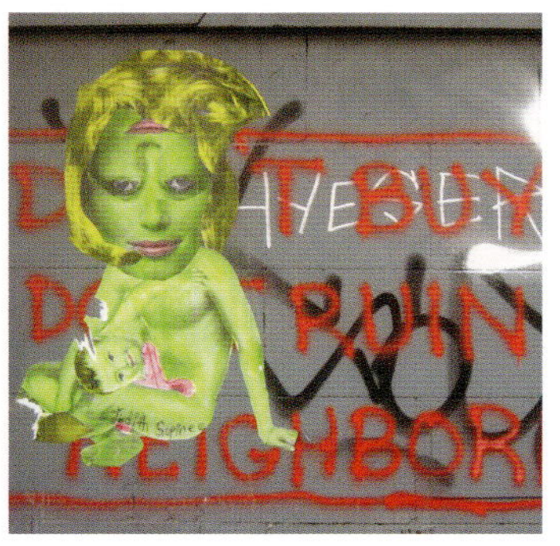 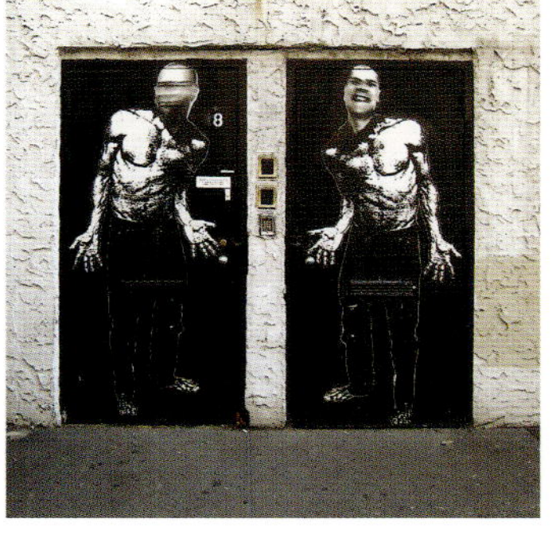 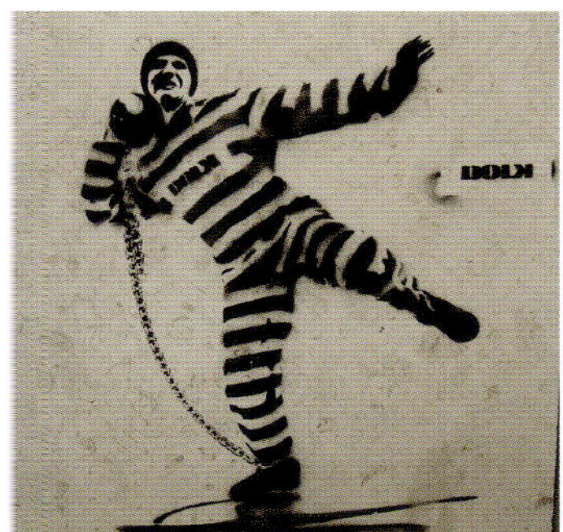

Tagging = know/like/trust. It's brand awareness gone mental!

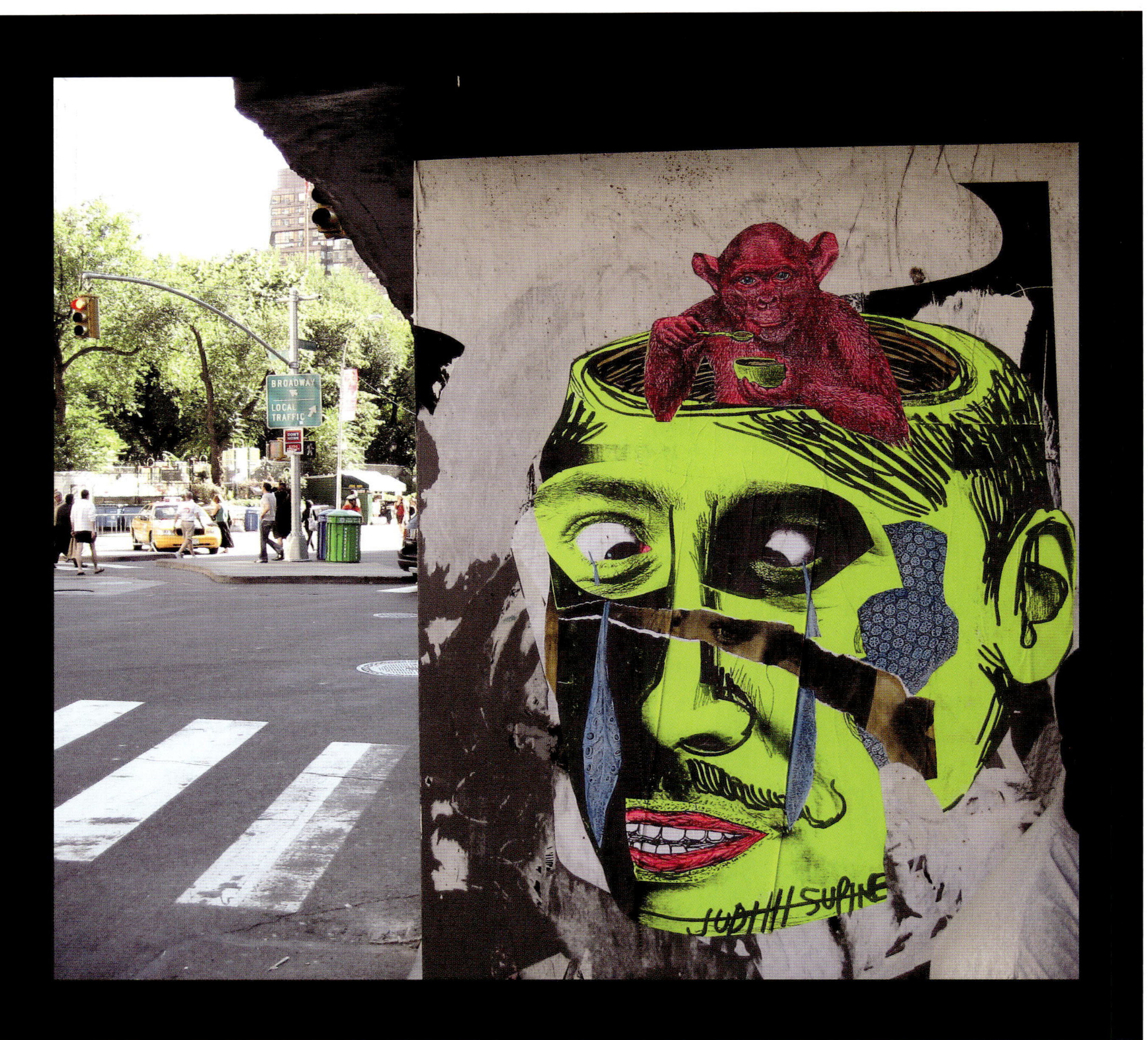

BROADWAY
LOCAL
TRAFFIC
JUDITH SUPINE

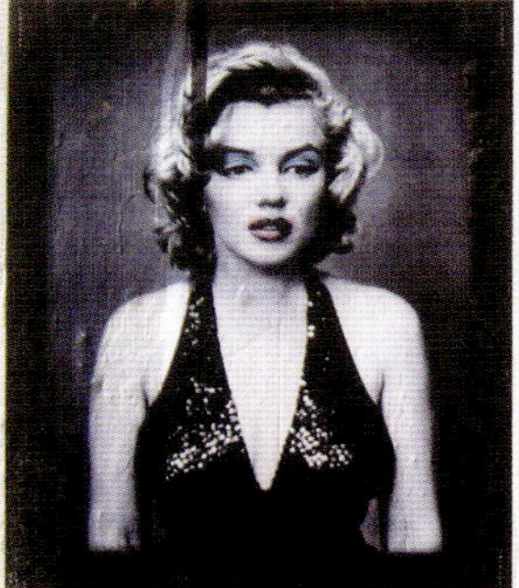

THEN IT HIT ME
im not going to be famous
i wont get to be a rock star
i am going to be stuck on the payroll
doing work that doesnt interest me
for a very long time


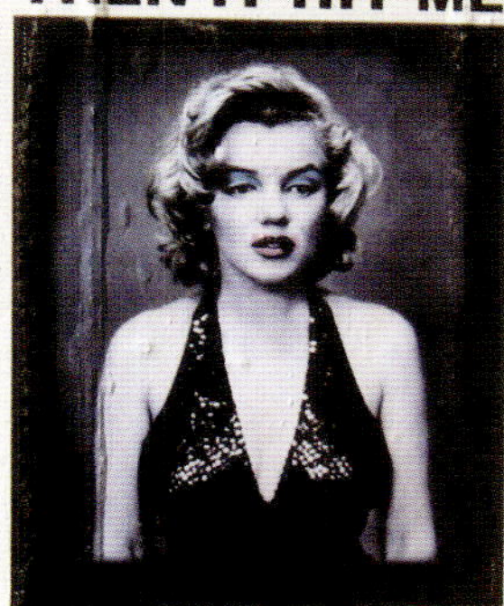

THEN IT HIT ME
im not going to be famous
i wont get to be a rock star
i am going to be stuck on the payroll
doing work that doesnt interest me
for a very long time

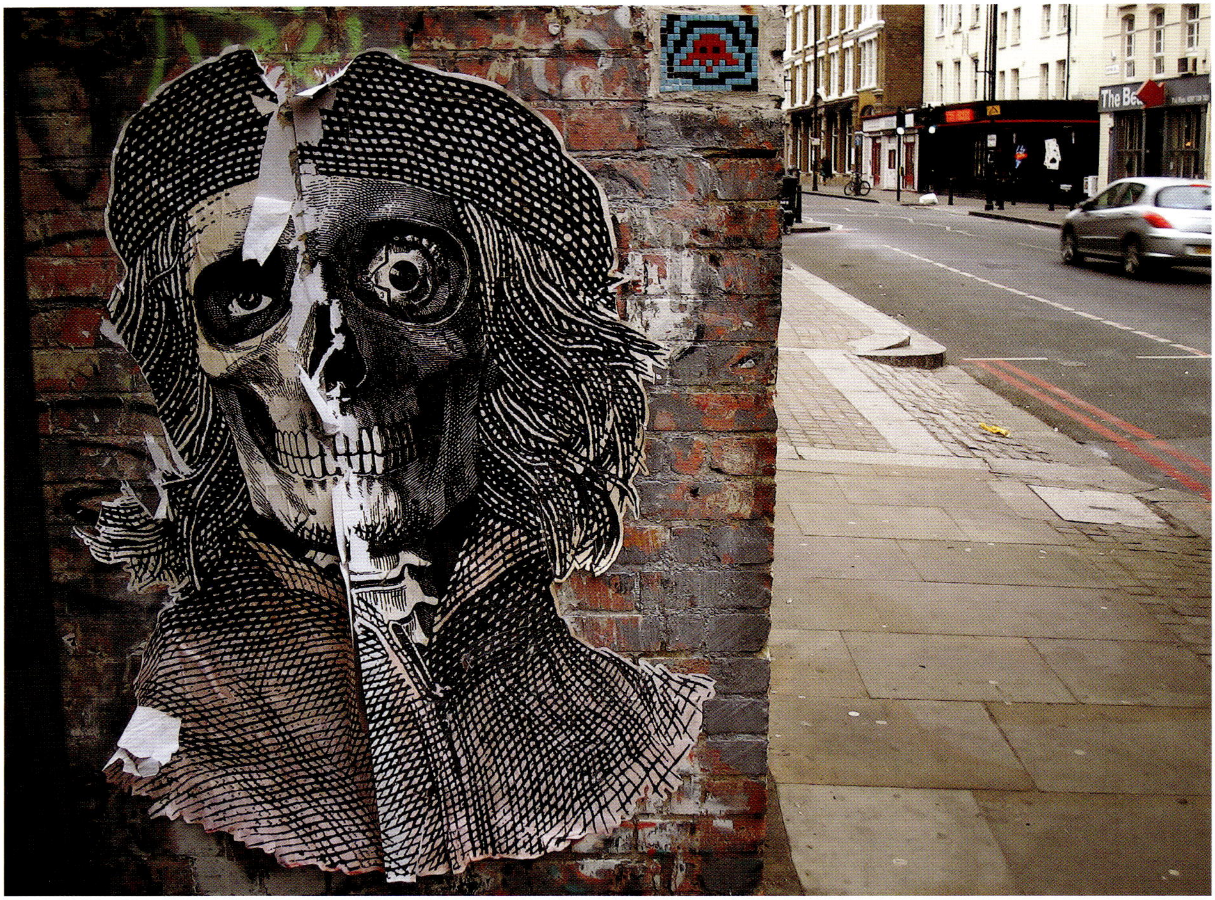

Colours are our currency and this is the redistribution of wealth.

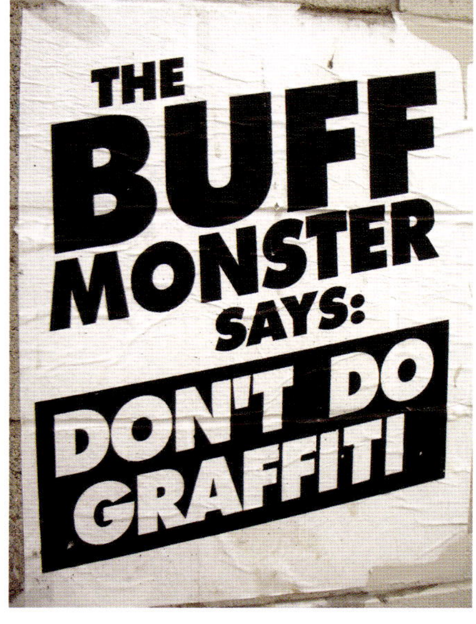

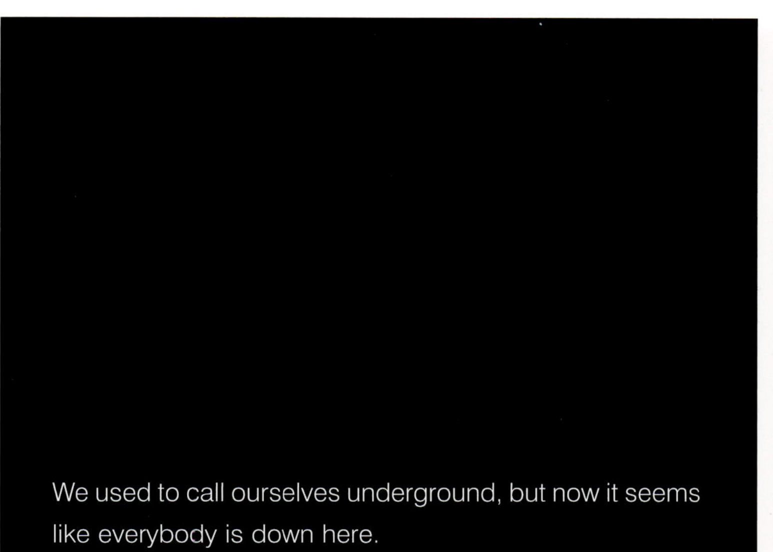


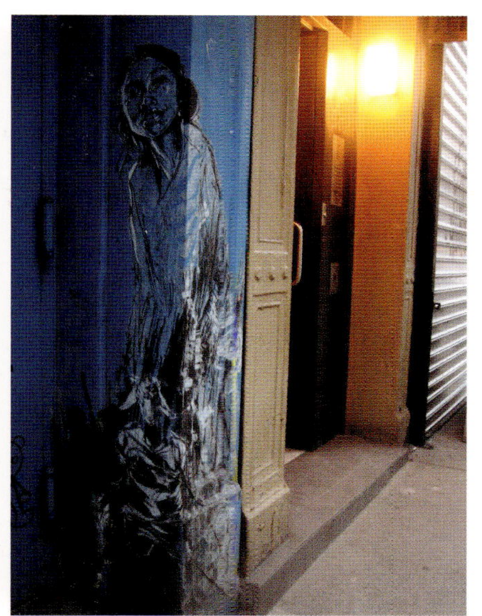

We used to call ourselves underground, but now it seems like everybody is down here.

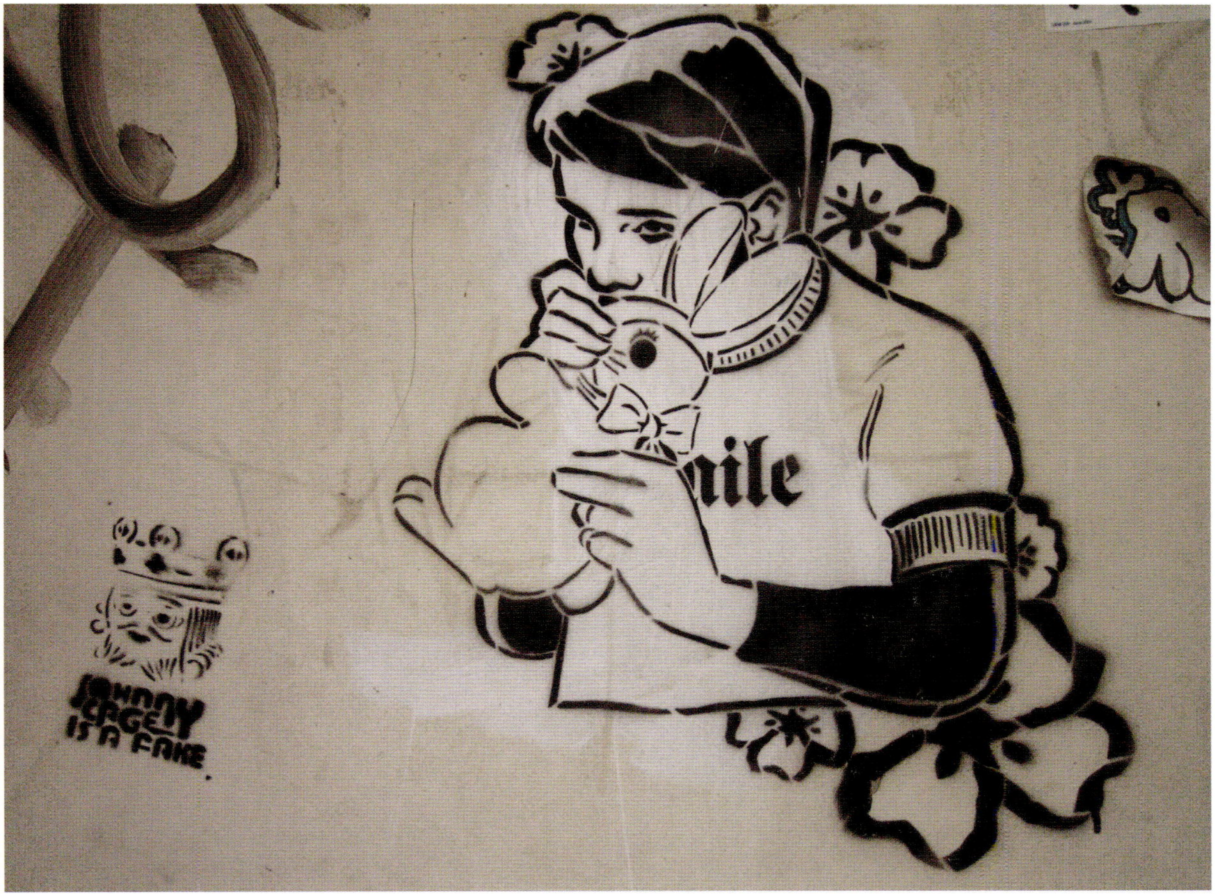

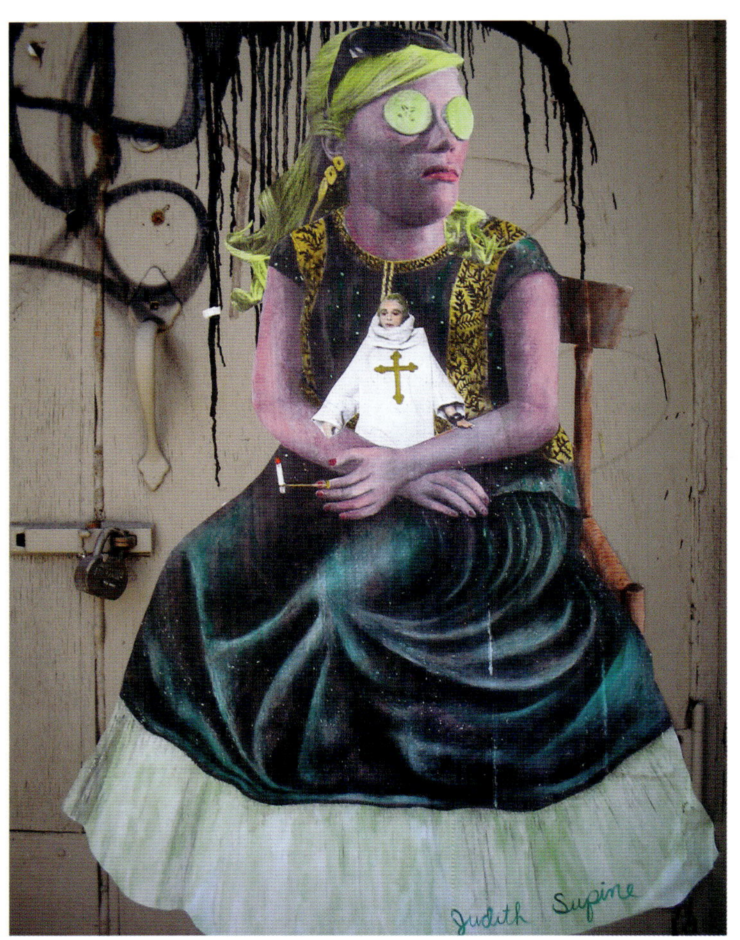
Judith Supine

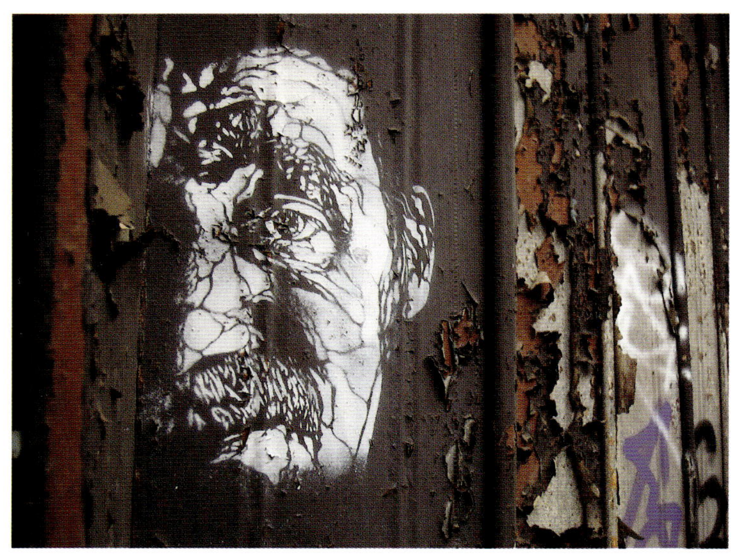

Graffiti is very much like
making love to a beautiful
woman. It's much easier to
sit at home and watch
other people doing it.

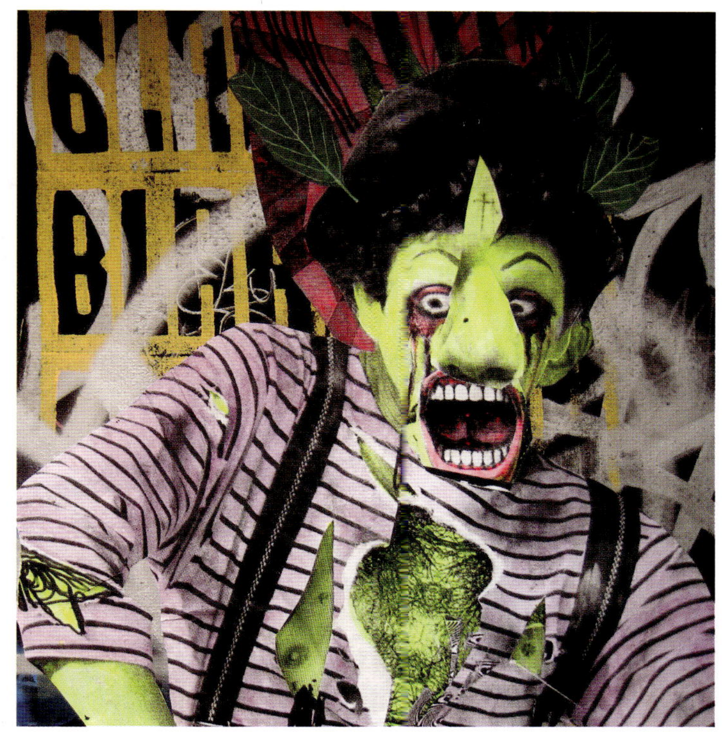

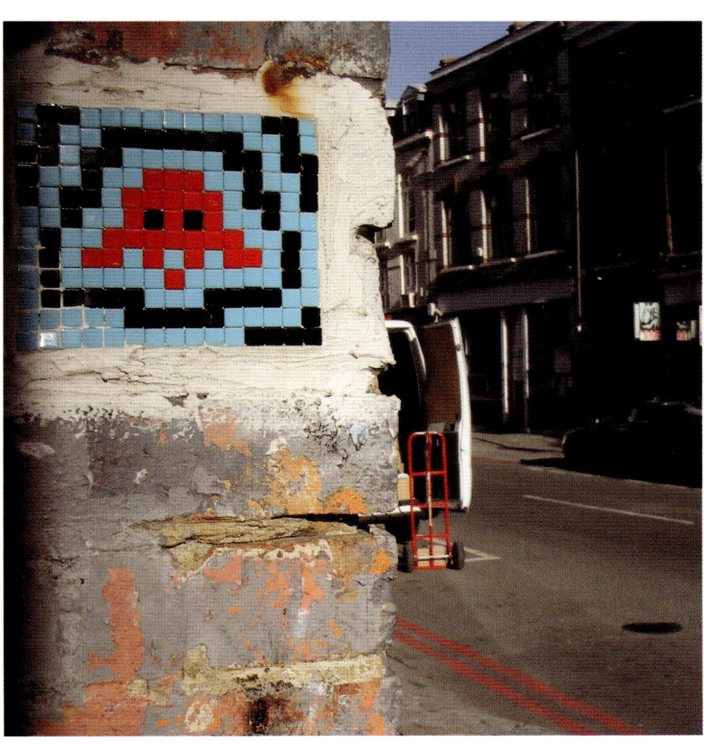

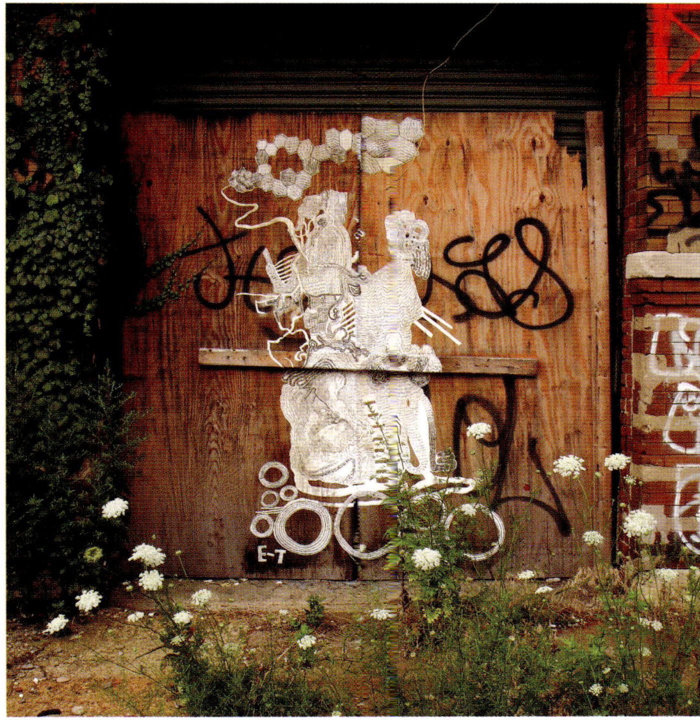

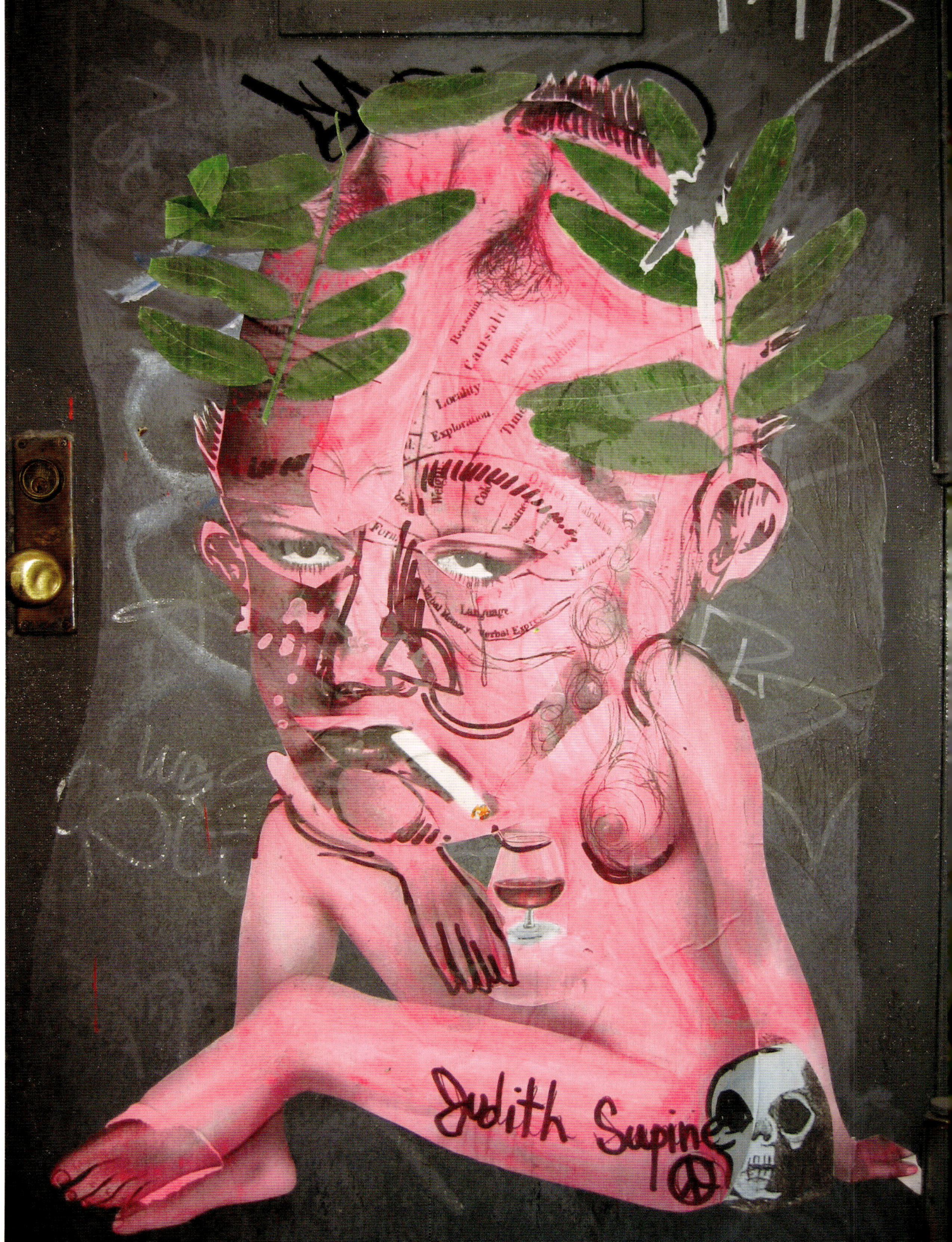

Judith Supine

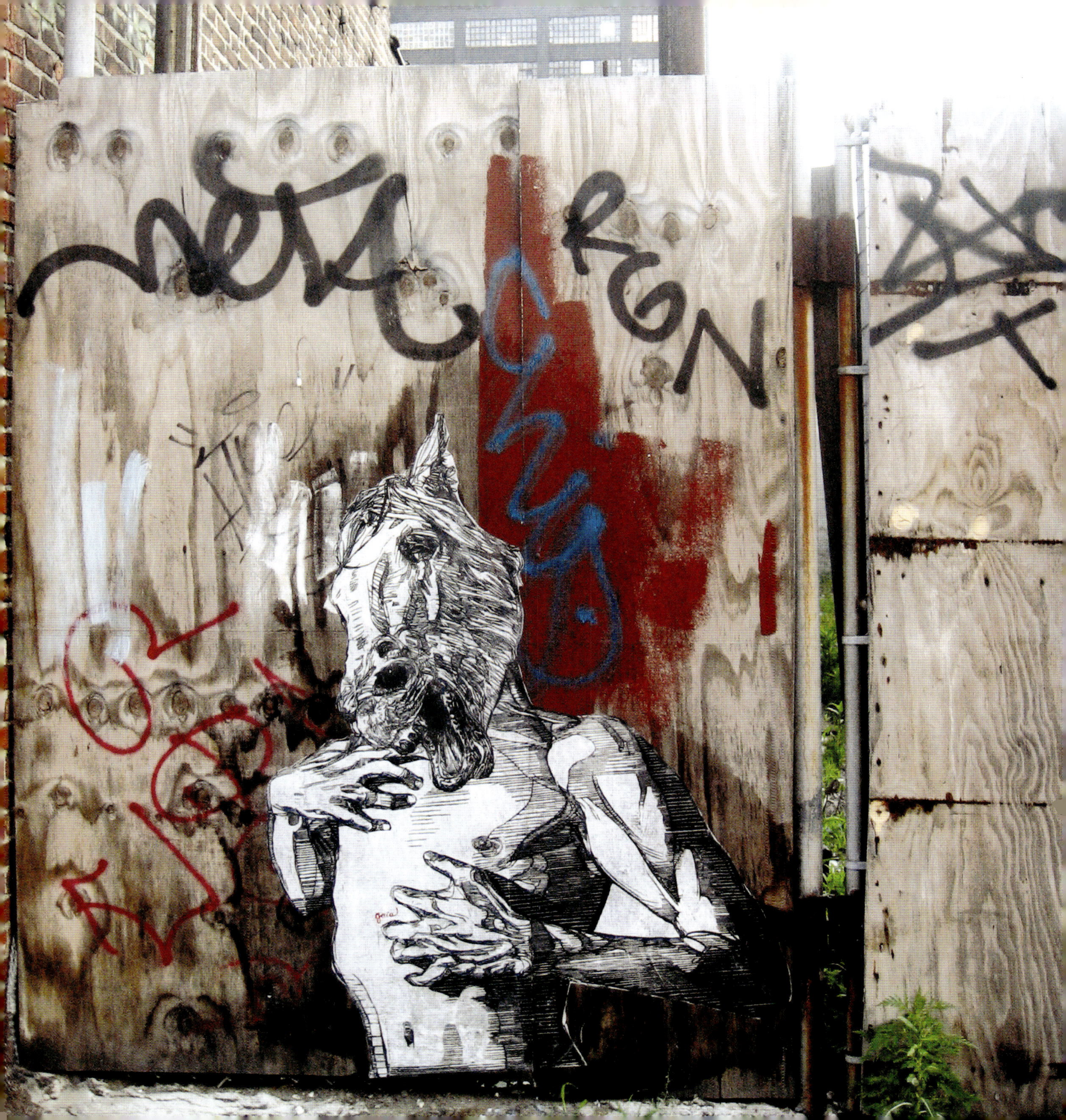

RGN

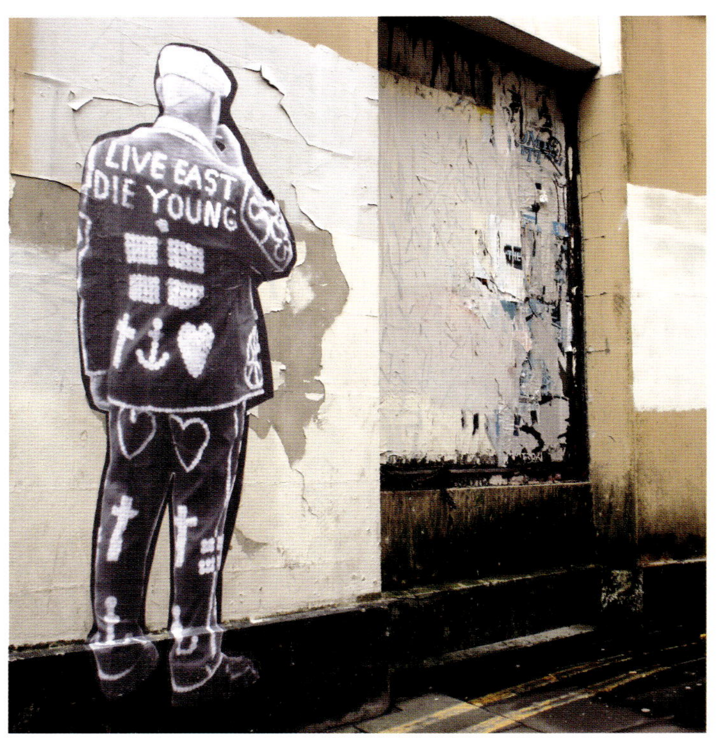

Is it fine to tag some working stiffs shop window? Dude works sixty hours a week keeping his little shop afloat and he gets up one day and there is Sod Capitalism all on his shutter. There he is scrubbing his fingers to the bone for hours. Is that sticking it to the man? Little kids walking by saying 'Mommy what's Sod Capitalism?' Hmm? Is that cool?

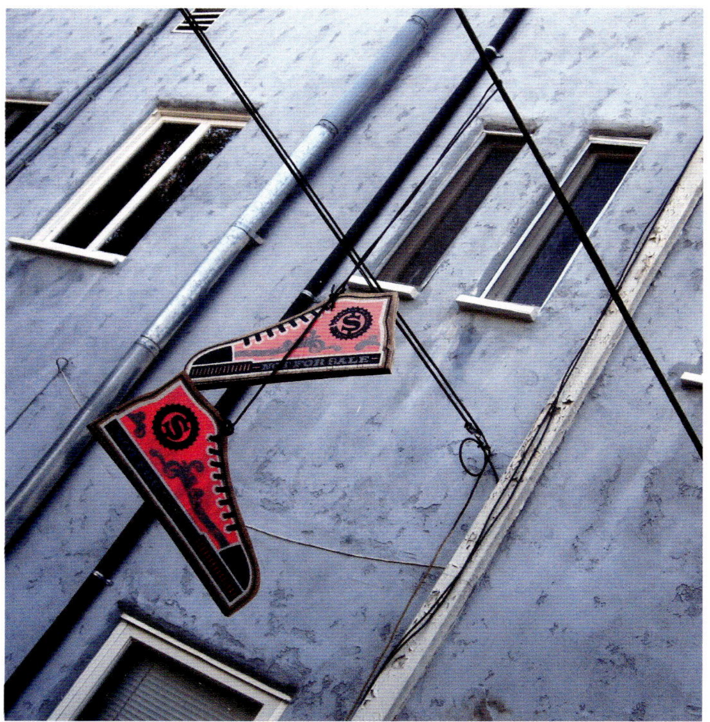

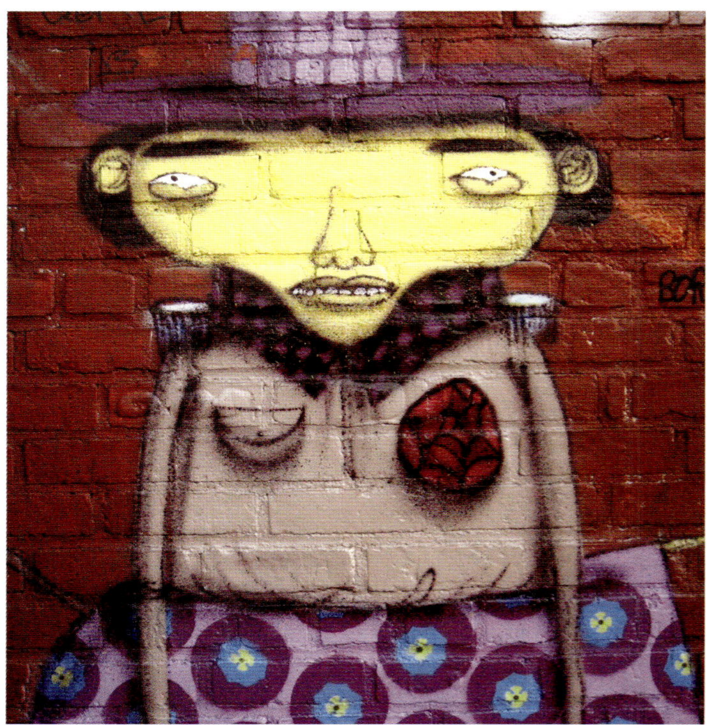

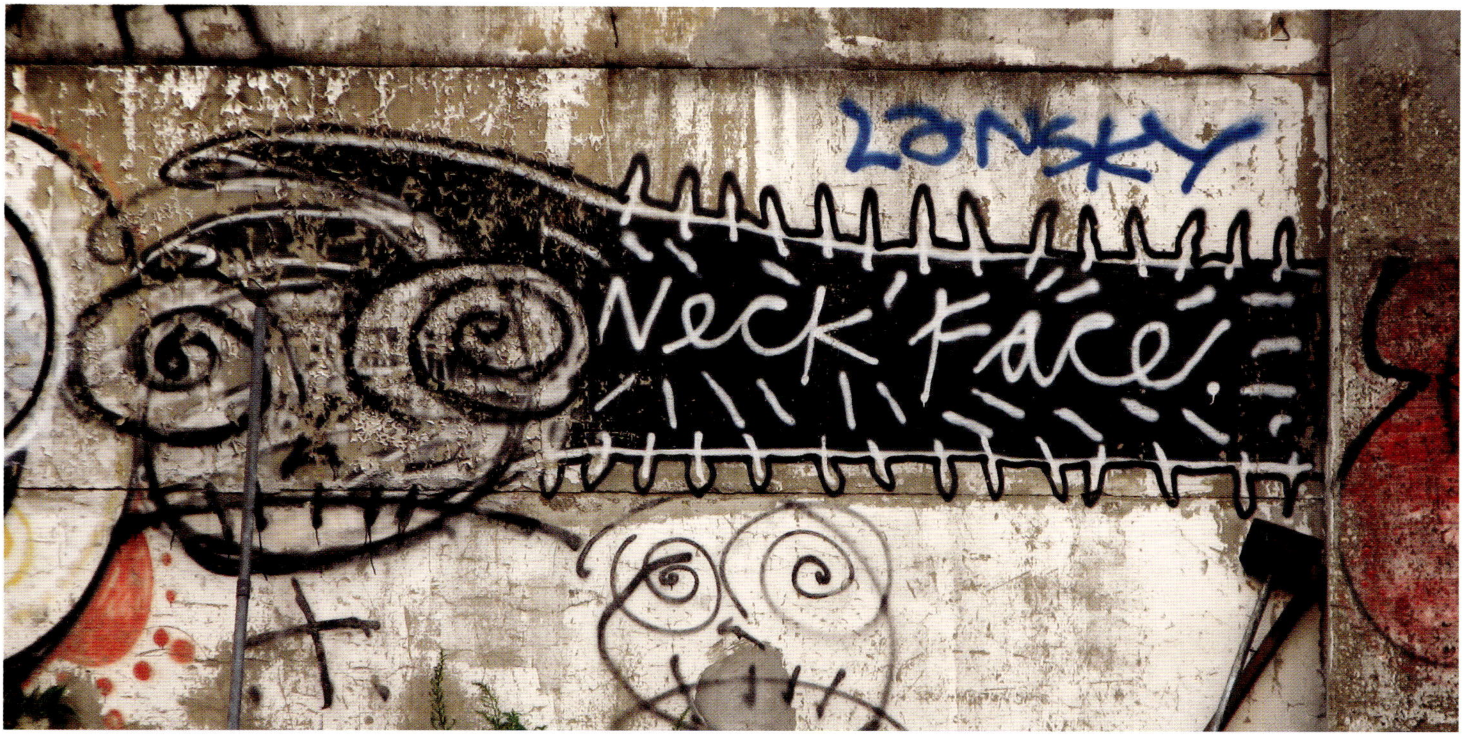

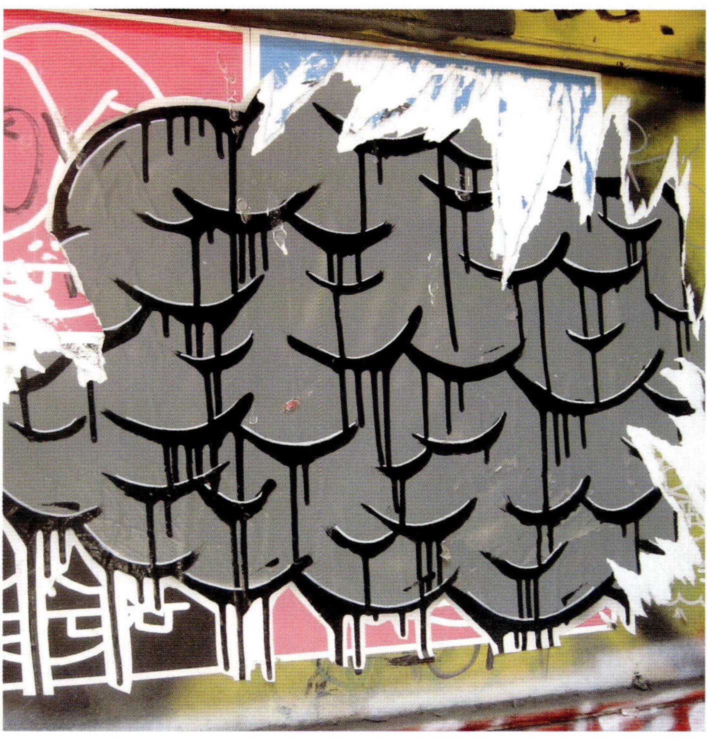

The moment that the paint hits the wall marks the transition between cultural consumer and cultural producer.

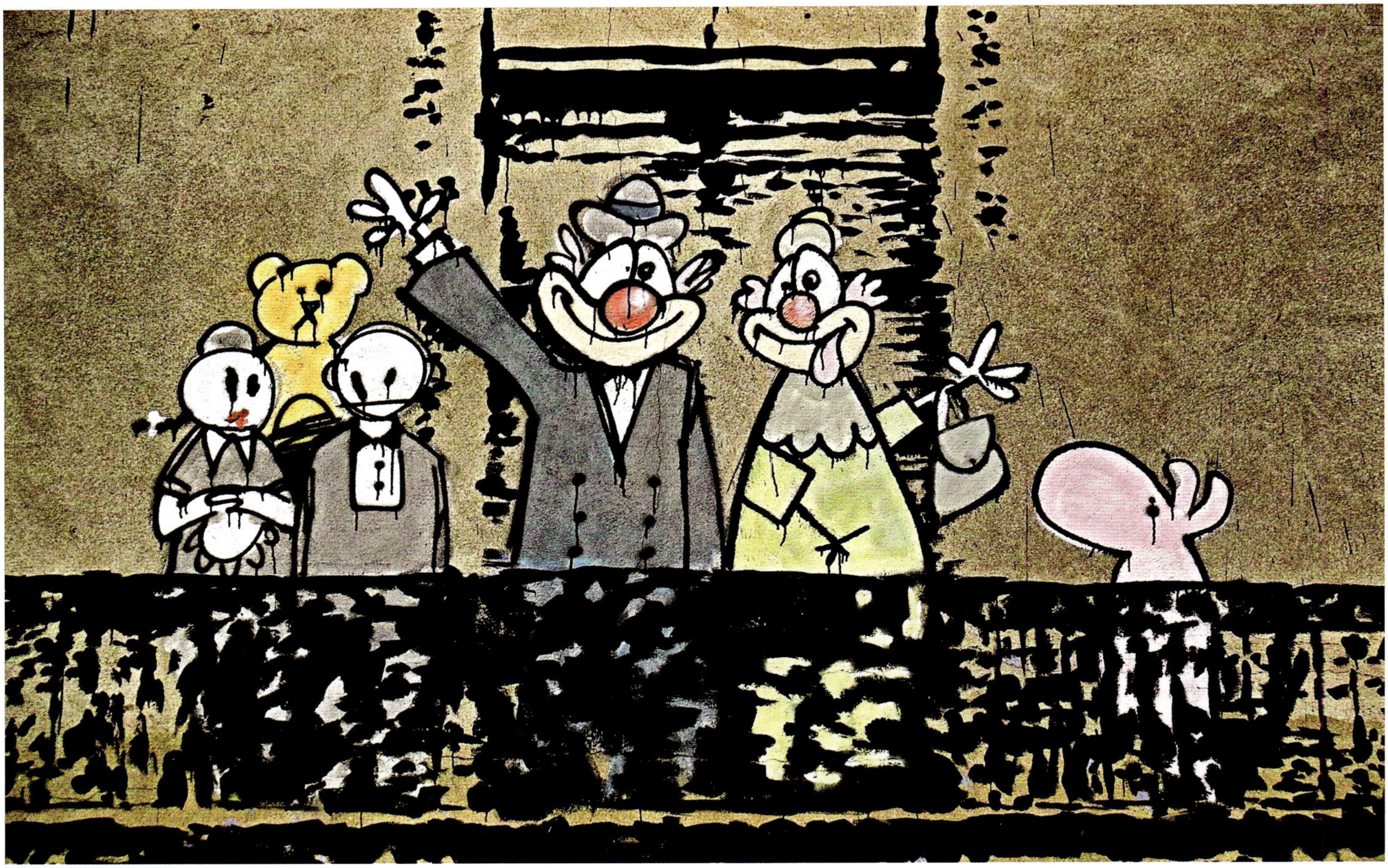

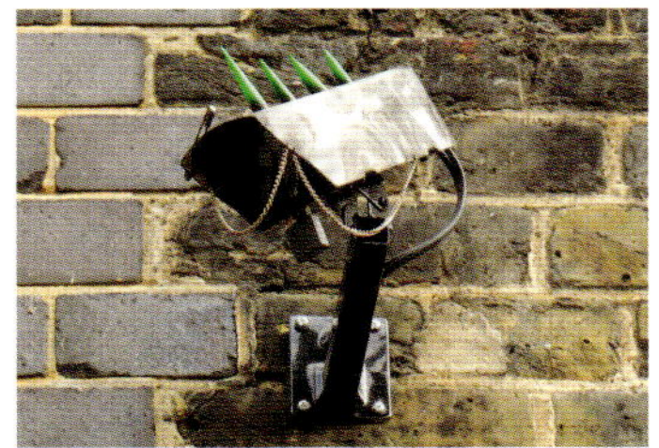 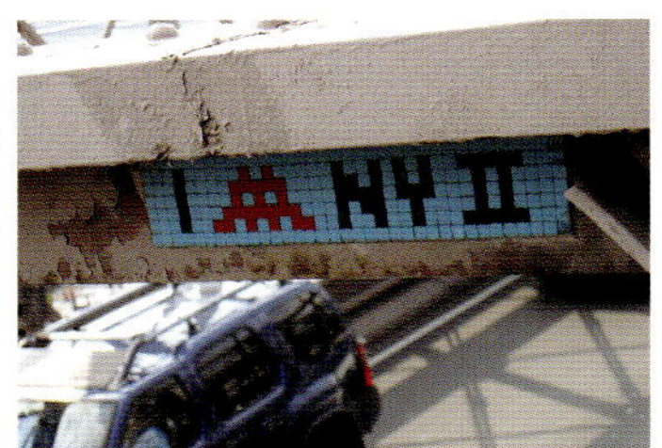 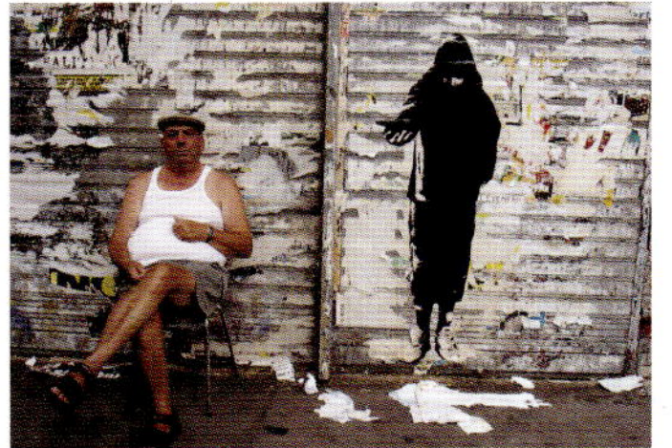 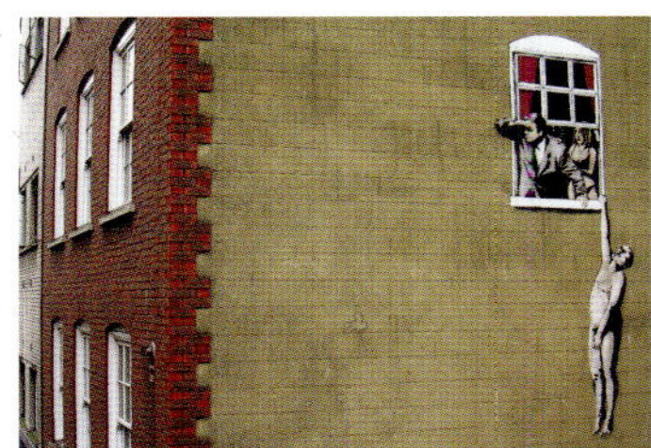

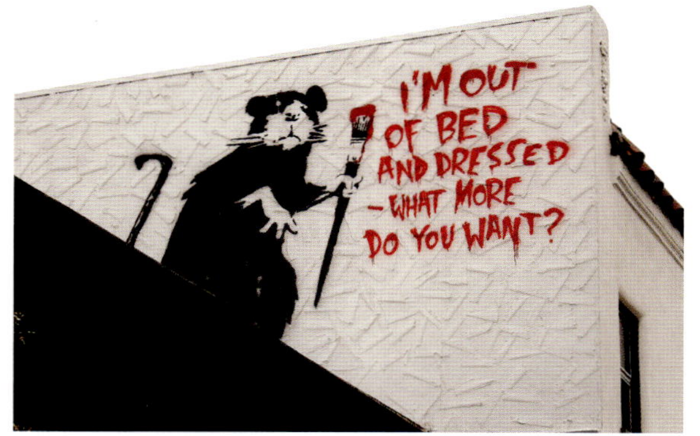

I'M OUT OF BED AND DRESSED — WHAT MORE DO YOU WANT?


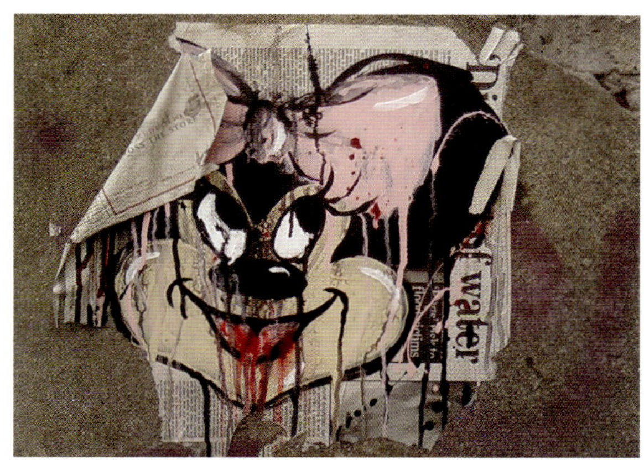

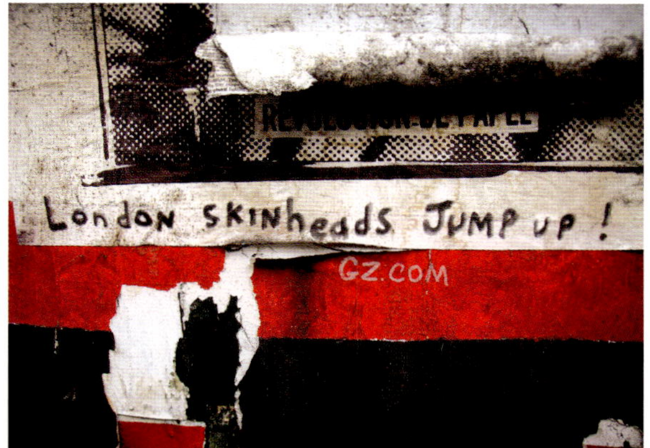

London skinheads JUMP up !
Gz.com


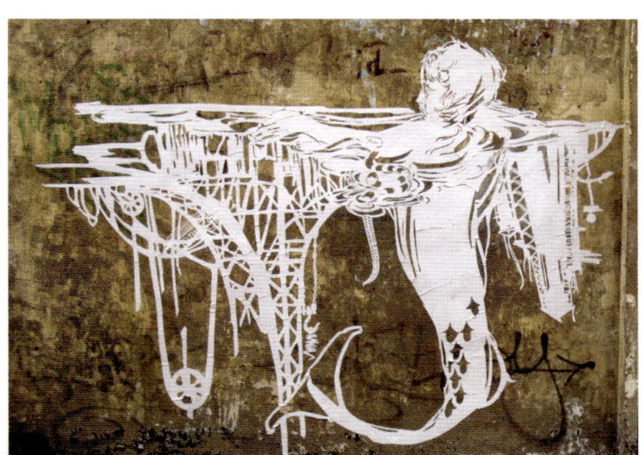

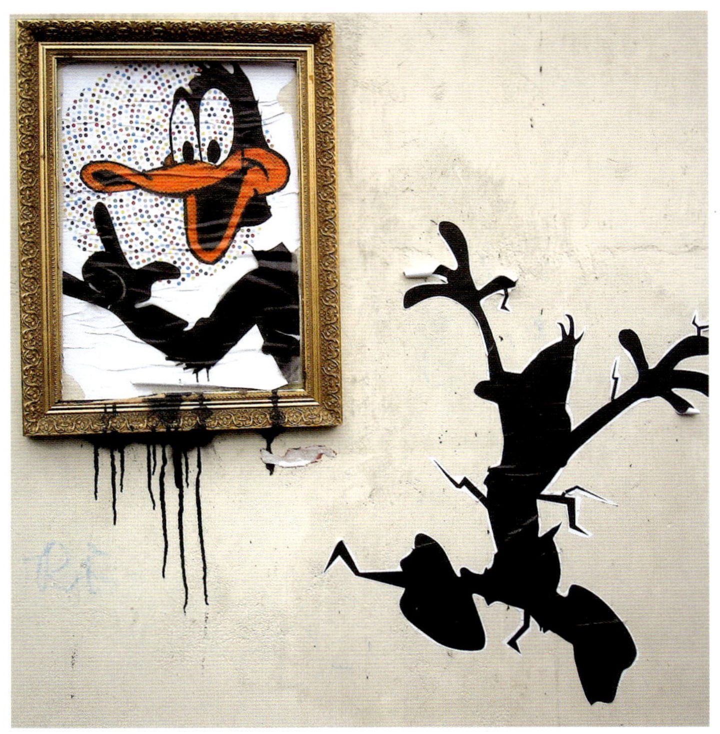

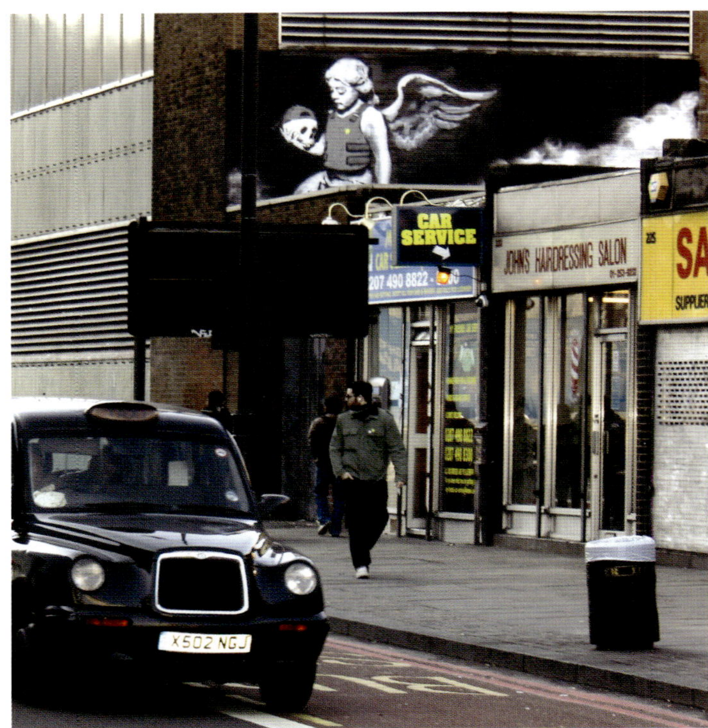



Some say that there is nothing on
earth that cries out to be defaced,
repainted and covered with graff
more than corporate art. Others say
that corporate art is a socially
responsible contribution to a
public space. Still others say that
corporate sculpture is usually
sweet for skating on.

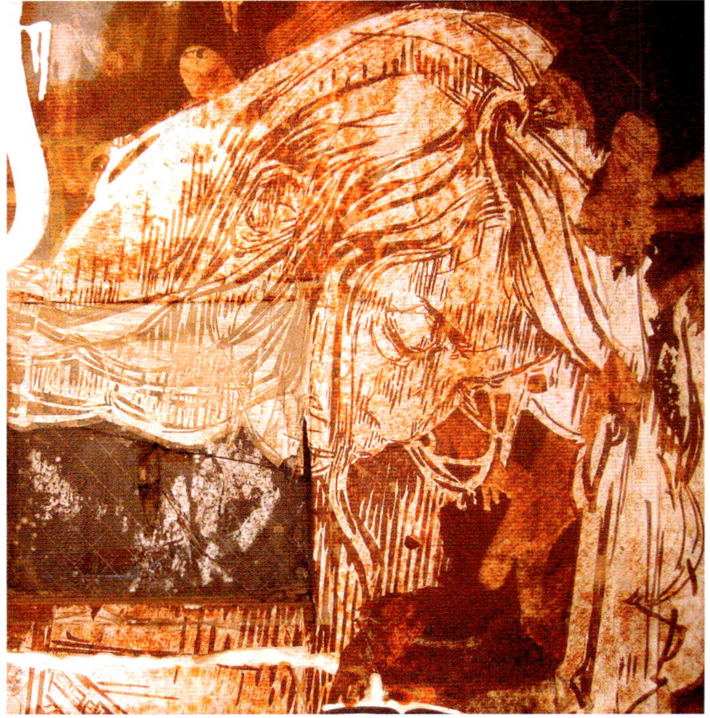

# How to Carpet Bomb Culture

The lone painter in the field is like the sniper. Yet one who deals in memes is like a pioneer of genetic warfare. Not that either of those roles is particularly inspirational. One shoots people in the head from great distances and the other is simply evil. But wait, these are 'metaphors'. The cultural monolith is not your friend. Use all weapons without mercy!

A meme is a unit of cultural replication, a phrase coined by Richard Dawkins to describe how ideas and culture might be thought of in terms of evolution. You will already be familiar with many memes. They already exist in street art.

Take space invaders for example. Invented by the shadowy 'Invader', these mosaics have cropped up all over the world like a rapidly spreading virus. The idea is to create something that begs to be replicated. To generate an idea that spreads.

Other memes include the OBEY project. Various artists have replicated and mutated the original OBEY meme which was itself intended to be replicated. Mutation is important in memetics. A meme will always be imperfectly transmitted as human communication is always at least slightly imperfect

Mutations will be more or less successful than one another and the less successful ones will die out (Clear coca-cola for example). This is genuine natural selection. Think of the music from Platoon when the good lieutenant dies. No one knows who wrote that tune but it continues to survive as a meme in its mutated form as 'that tune from Platoon when the good lieutenant dies.' Mutation is good. Mutation gives us the space invader made out of giant rubiks cubes.

The idea of the meme is not easy to get right. No one really understands why some memes are  successful and others aren't. An idea doesn't have to be good or even beneficial to its host to be a successful meme. Consider 'The Game', an enormously successful viral game where players can only win by forgetting that they are playing t. If you are a player you have just lost.

Despite the inherent difficulty of deliberately creating a meme it is still a possible ploy for an artist. Instead of thinking on the lines of creating a piece that expresses your individuality, think on creating an idea and distributing the means with which to re-create the idea rather than the final product. Who knows whether or not the group mind will accept or reject.

Your ideas of originality and your precious sense of authorship belong to the dark ages. Play with the human uni-mind! Imagine a proliferation of new memes sweeping the world like a plague   Smashing the boundaries between art and everyday life…

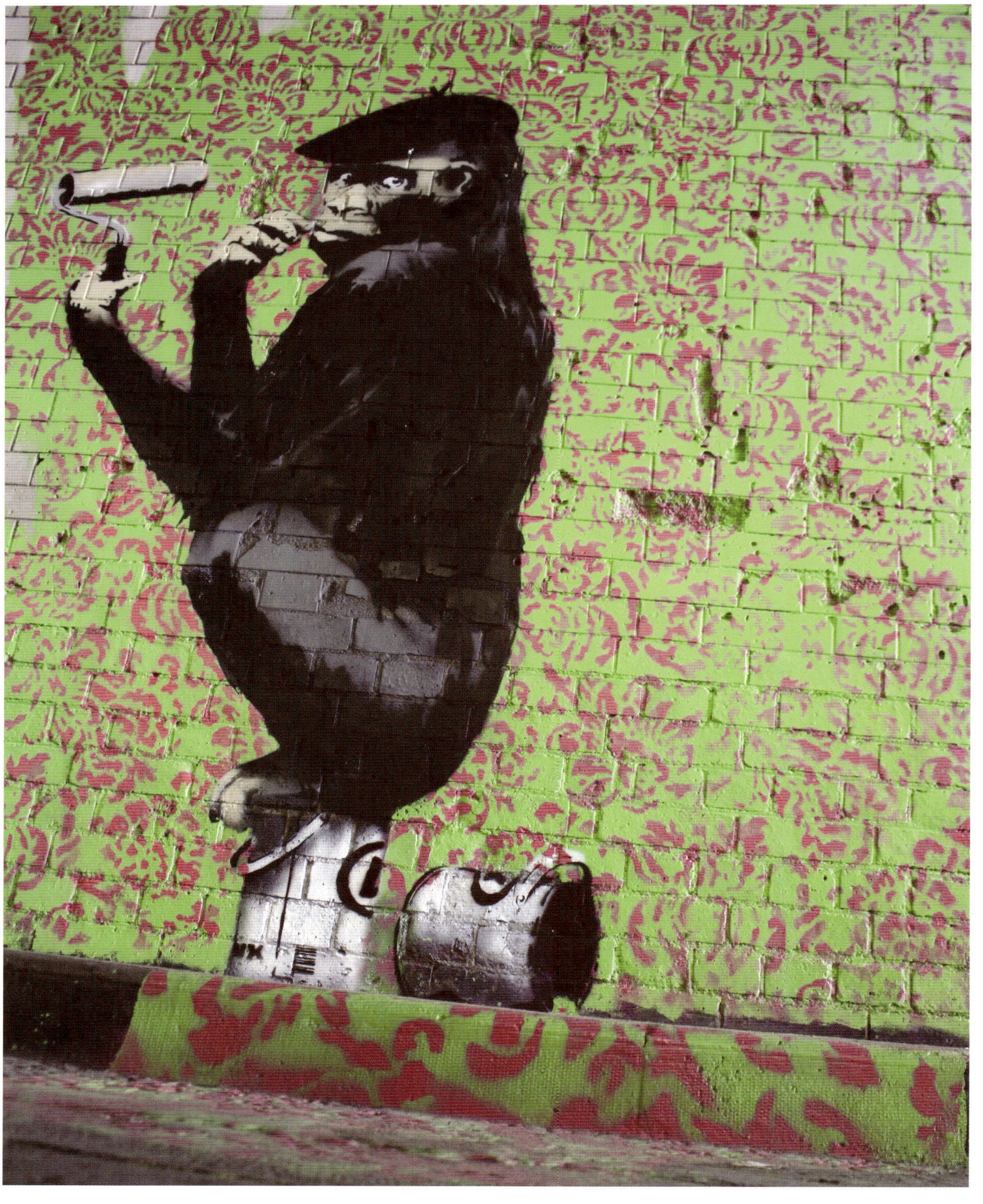

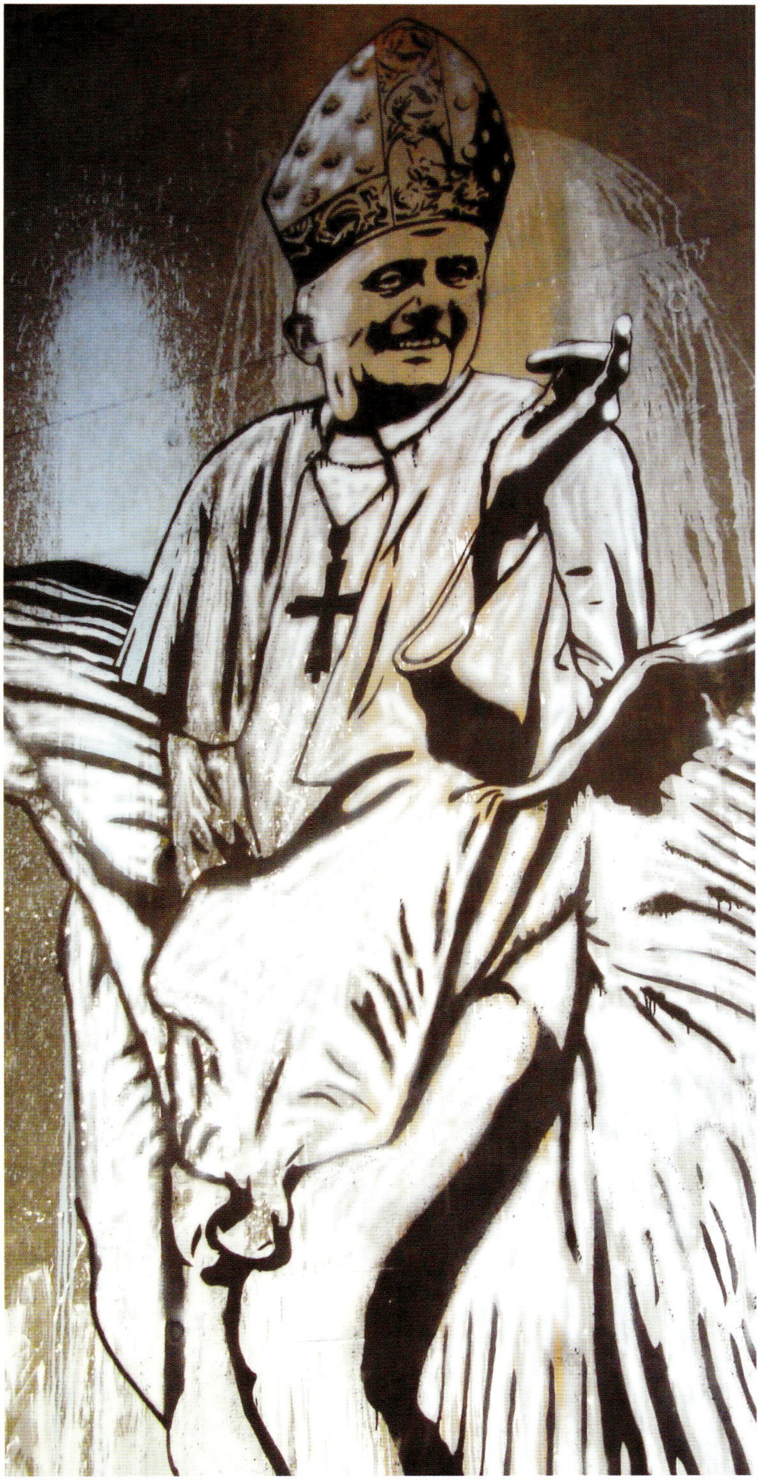

# The Cans Festival
## 3rd 4th 5th May 2008
## London

*Starring...*

| | |
|---|---|
| Dolk | Prism |
| Izolag | Danie Melim |
| Pobel | Altocontraste |
| M-City | Ananda Nahu |
| Vhils | Bandit |
| Btoy | Roadsworth |
| Nadie Crew | Artiste-Ouvrier |
| Sam3 | Blek |
| Faile | Sten |
| John Grider | Luclmaleonte |
| Logan Hicks | Lex |
| Pure Evil | Orticanoodles |
| Dot Masters | Kaagman |
| Banksy | |
| Dan | *...and a cast of* |
| Eelus | *thousands* |
| Bsas Stencil | |
| Run Don't Walk | |
| James Dodd | |
| civilian | |
| Vexta | |

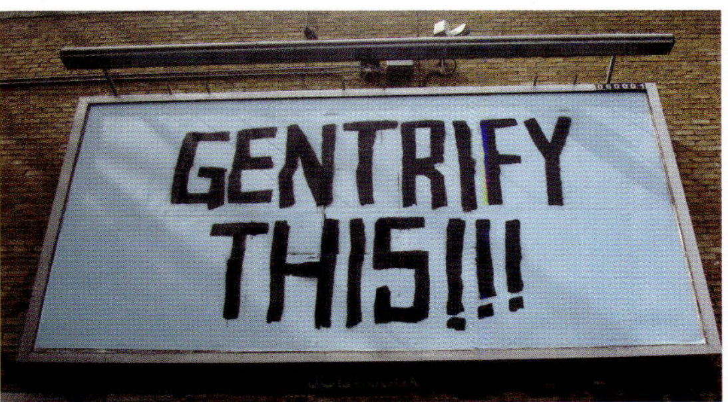

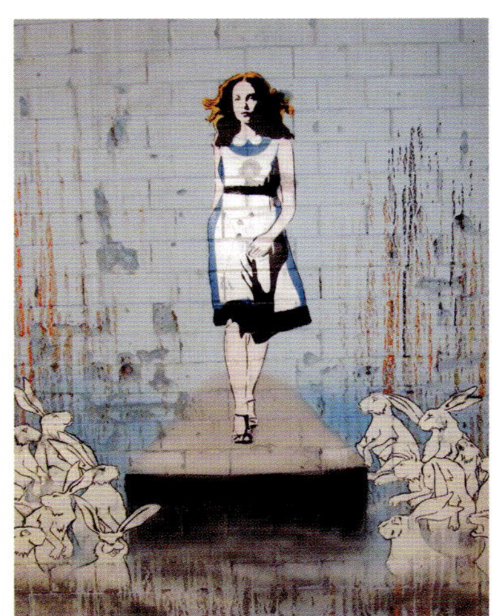
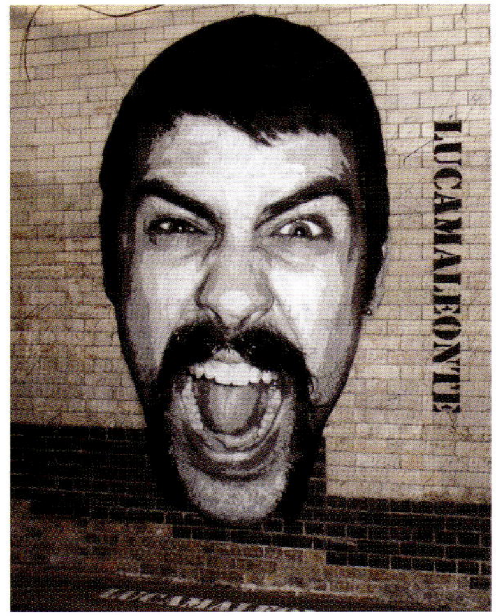

LUCAMALEONTE

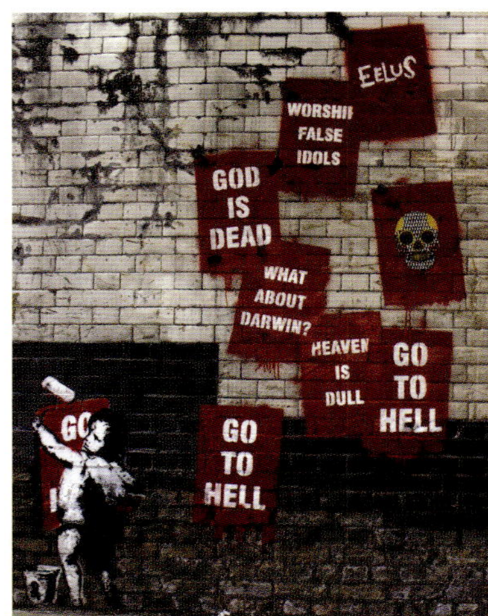

EELUS
WORSHIP FALSE IDOLS
GOD IS DEAD
WHAT ABOUT DARWIN?
HEAVEN IS DULL
GO TO HELL
GO TO HELL
GO TO HELL

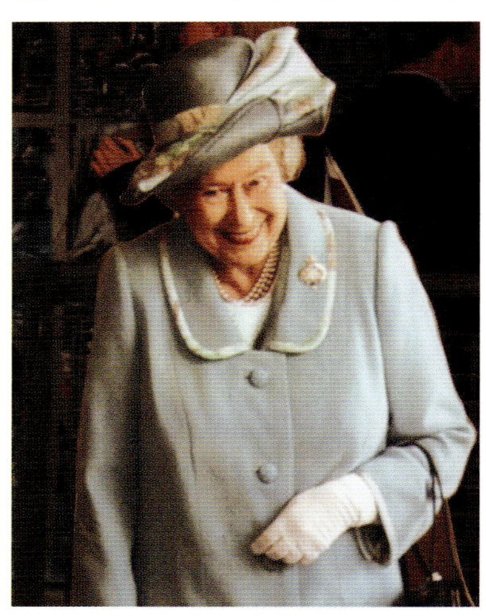

LIVE FAST DIE YOUNG

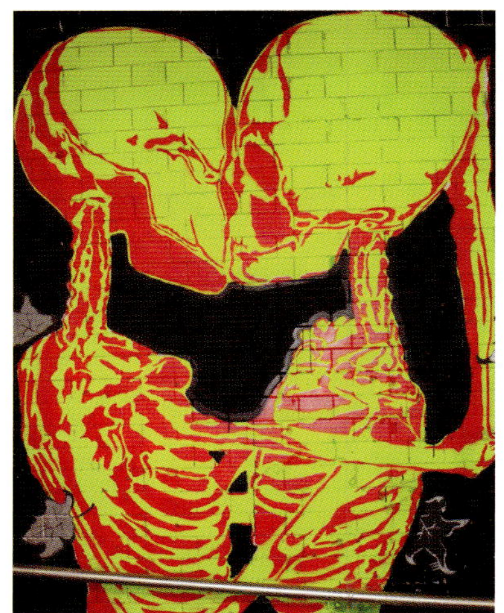
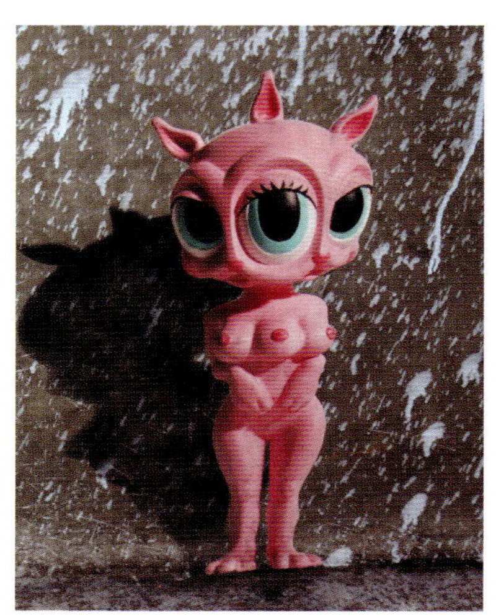
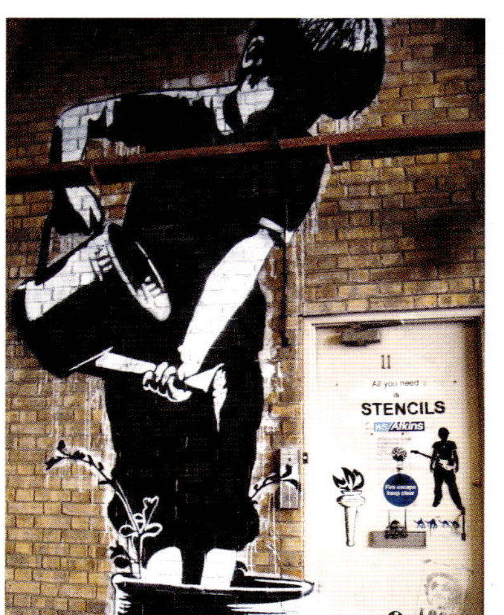

STENCILS

FAILE BITCH GODDESS
MISTRESS/SLAVE
KINKY FANTASIES
BIZARRE FETISHES
ALL AMERICAN
★ PHONE SEX ★
LIVE (212) 262-7122
She-males available

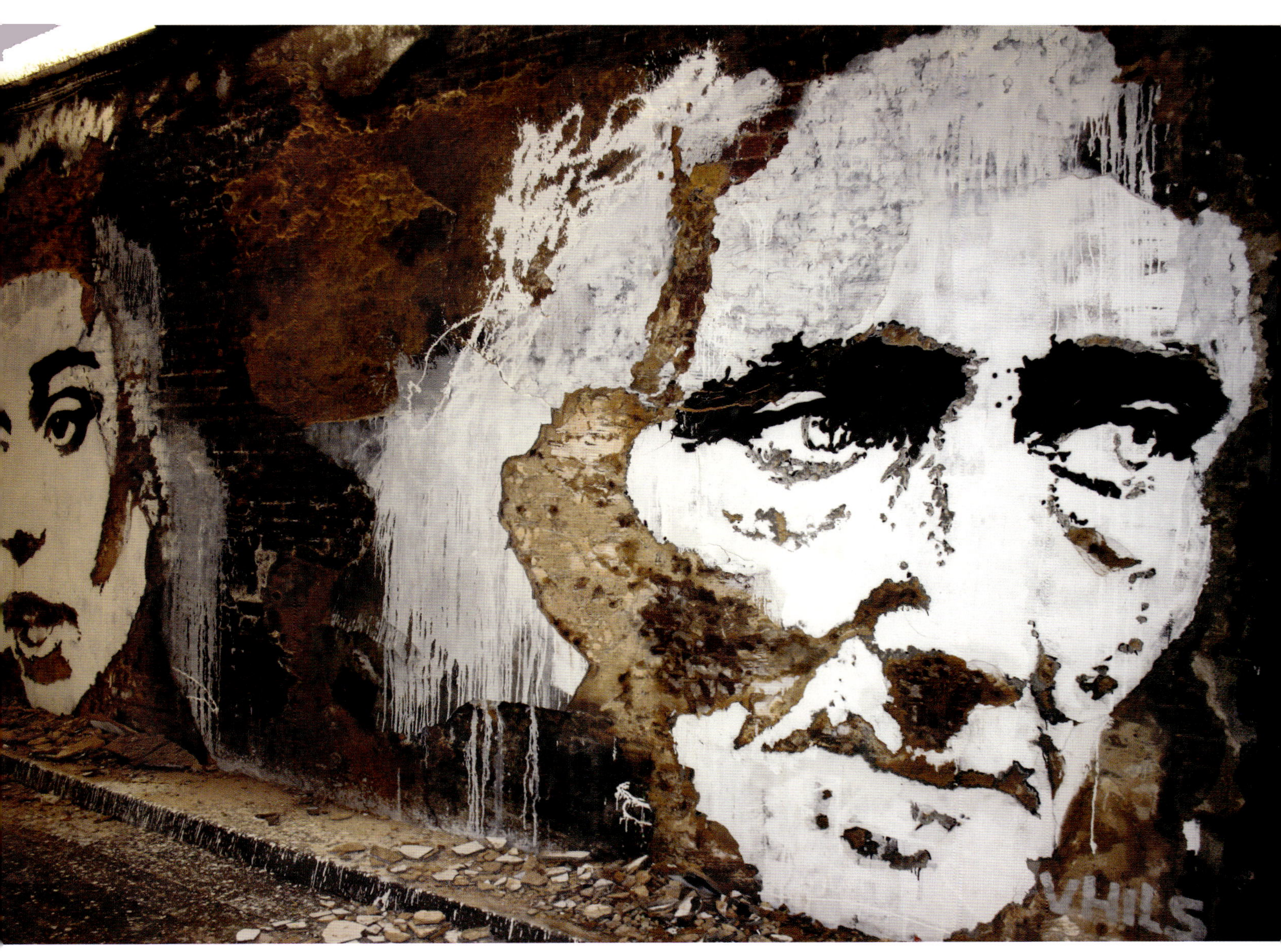

VHILS

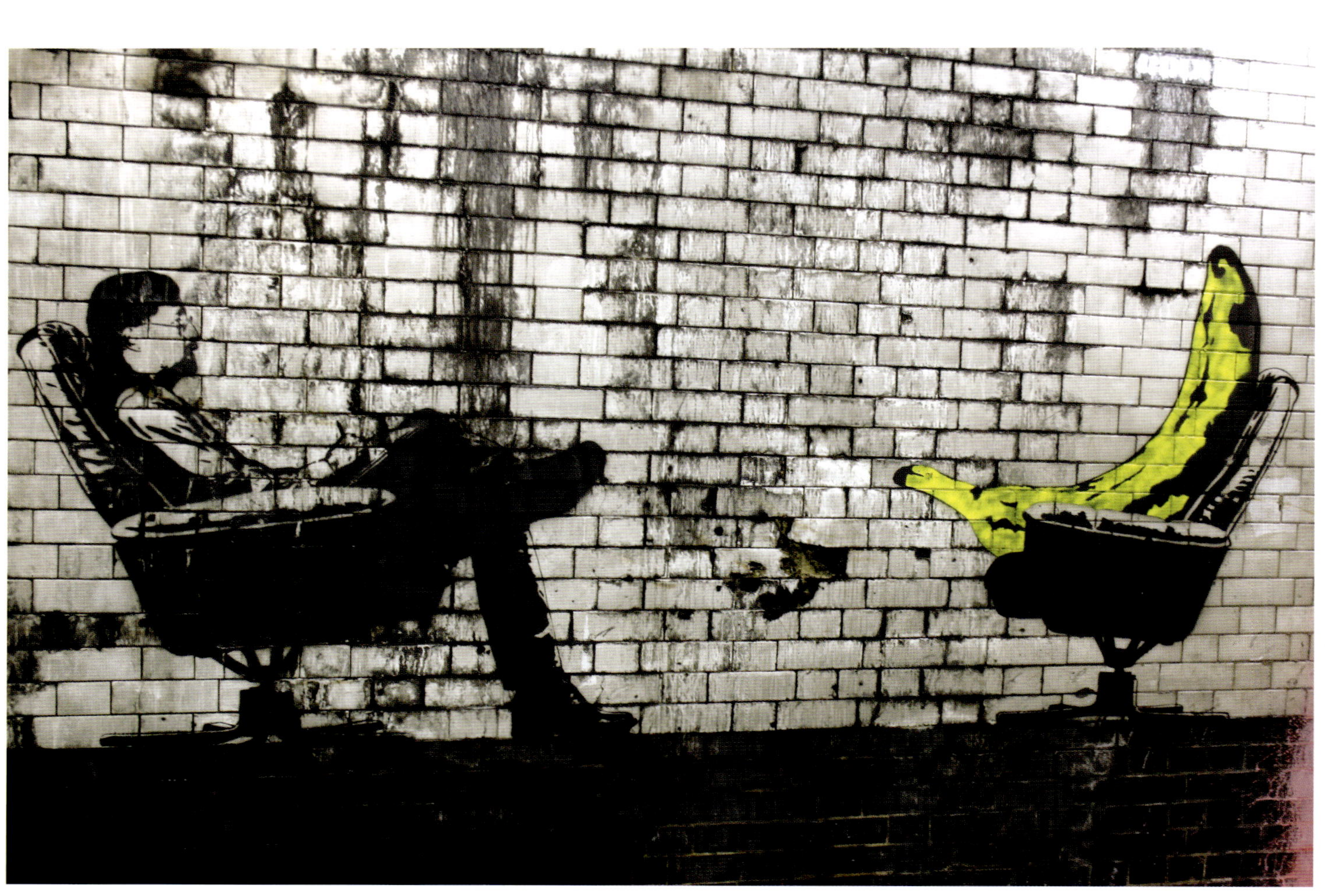

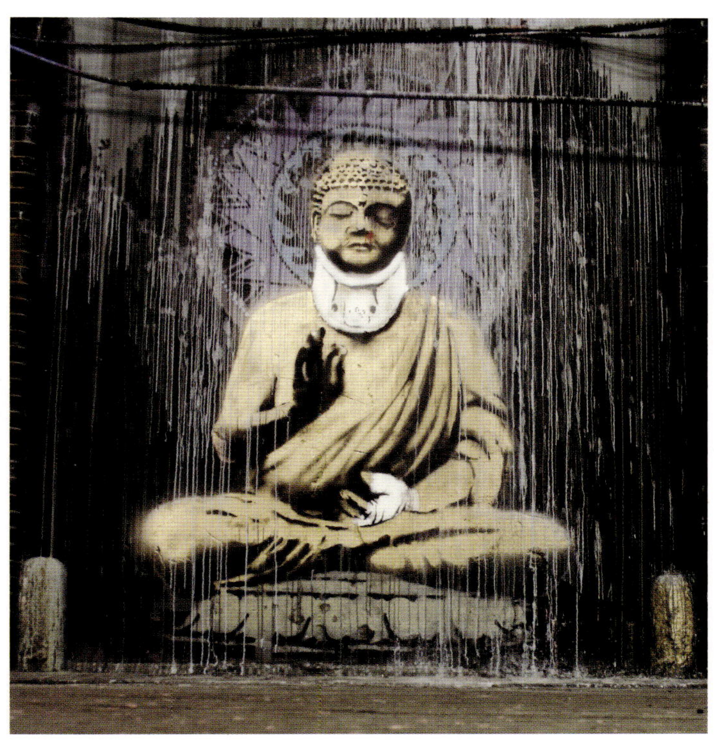

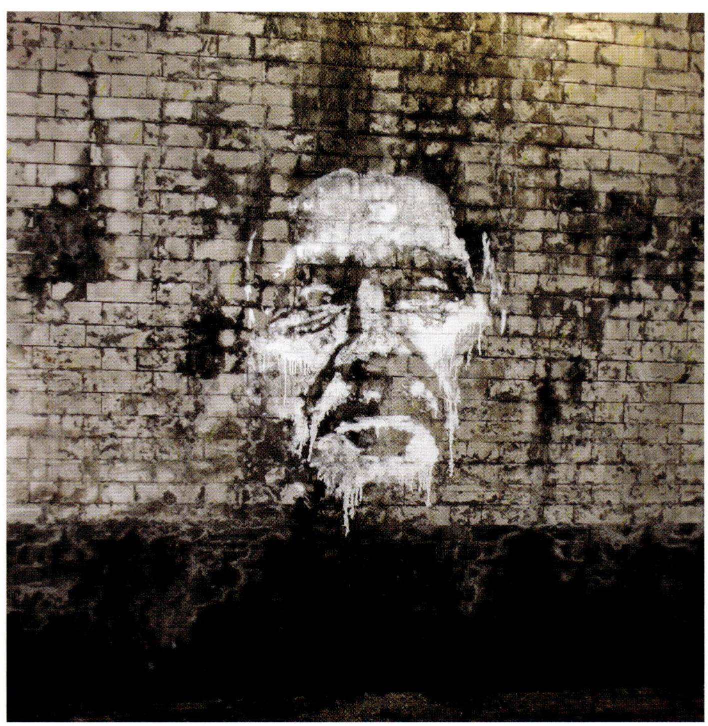

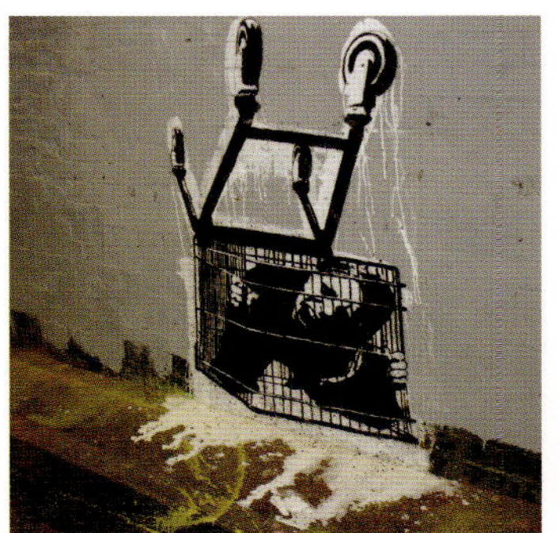

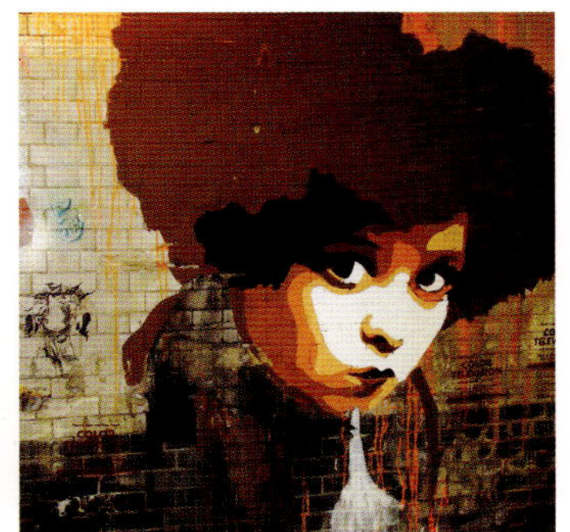

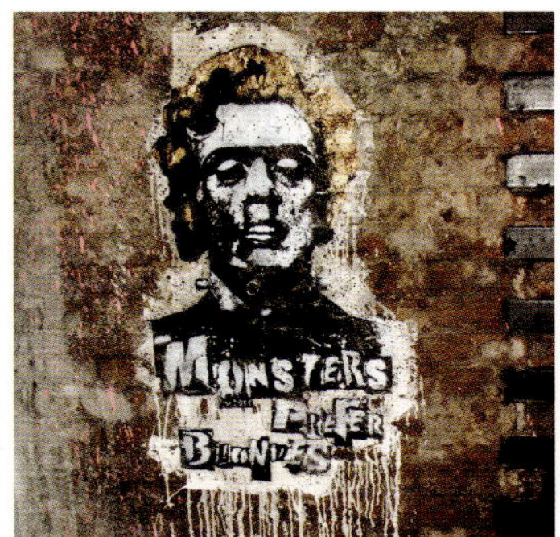
MONSTERS
PREFER
BLONDES

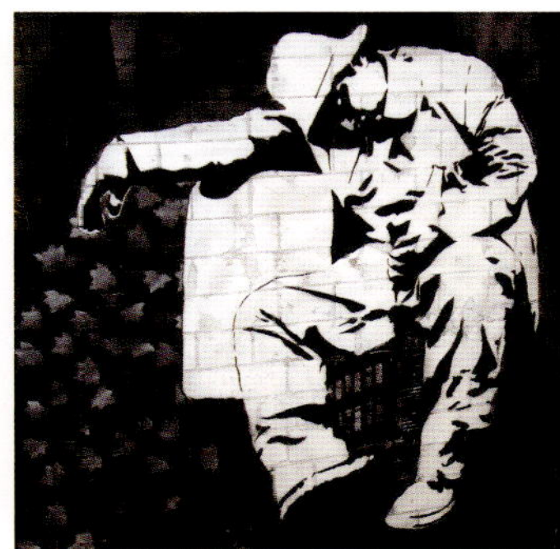

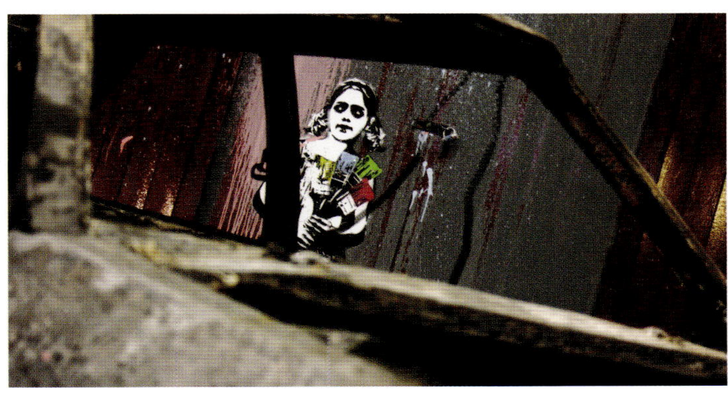

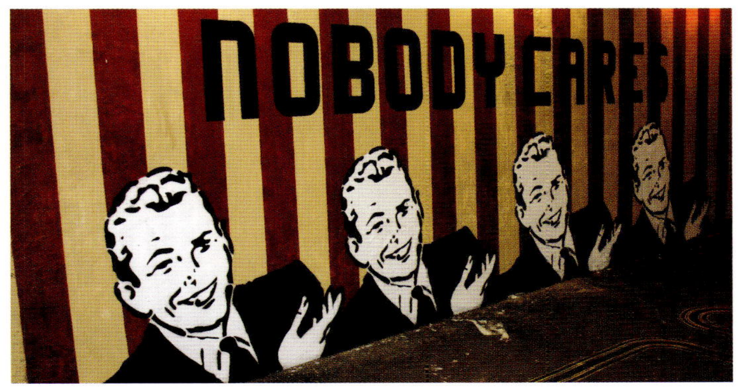
NOBODY CARES

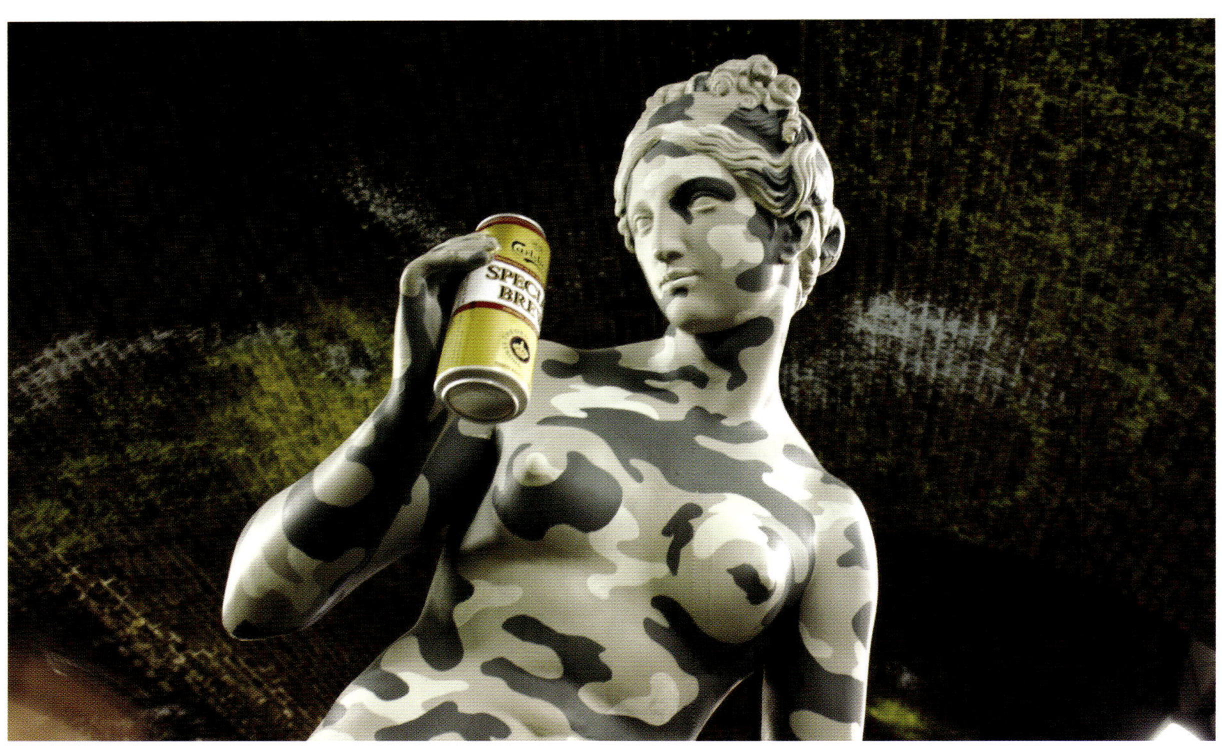
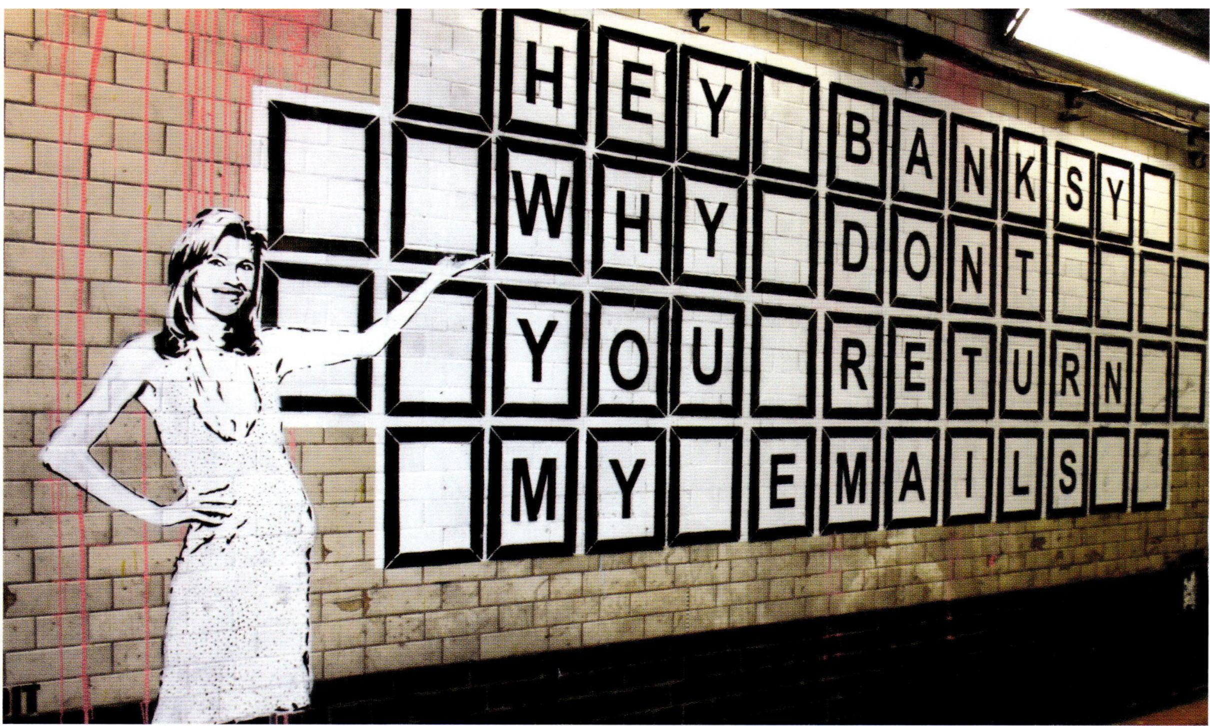
HEY BANKSY
WHY DONT
YOU RETURN
MY EMAILS

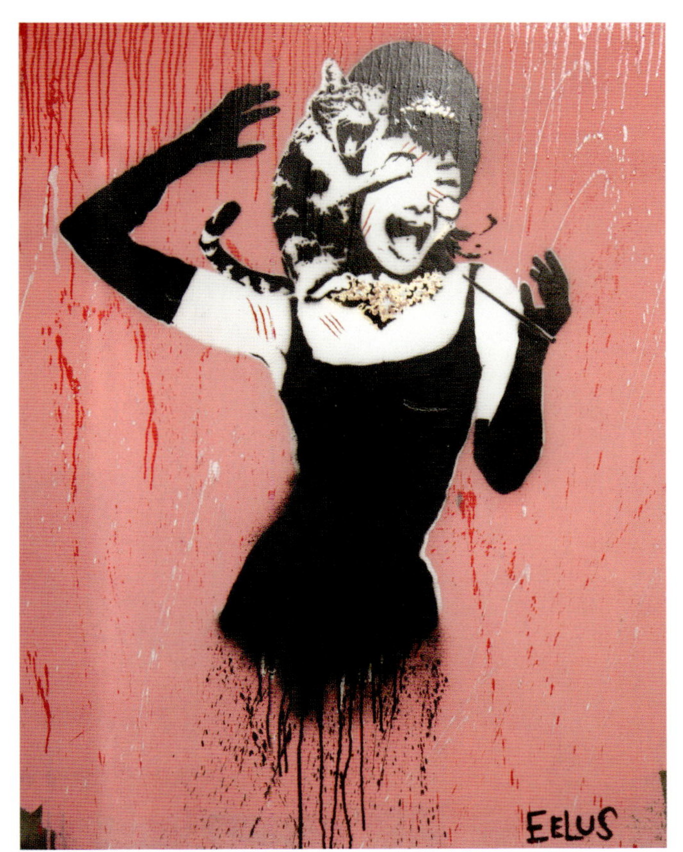
EELUS

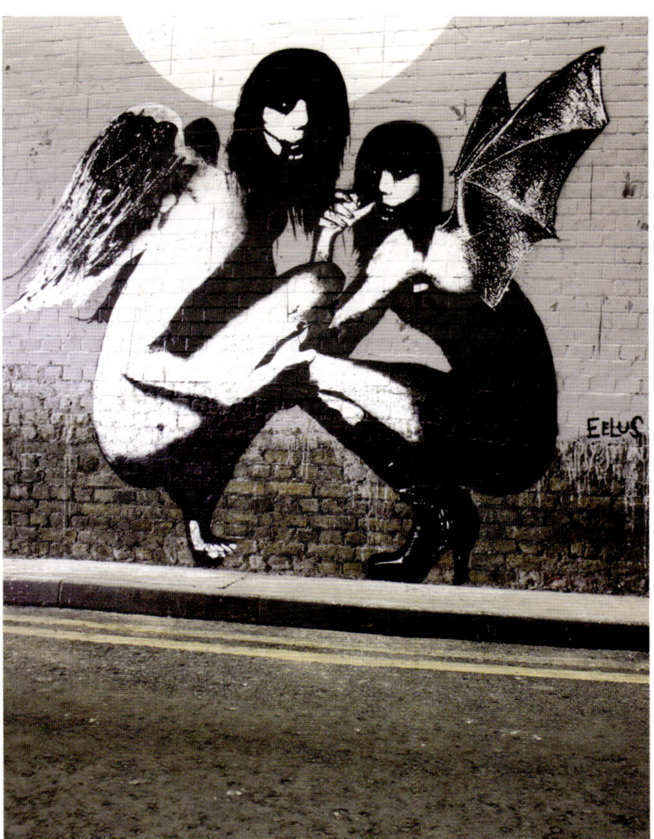
EELUS

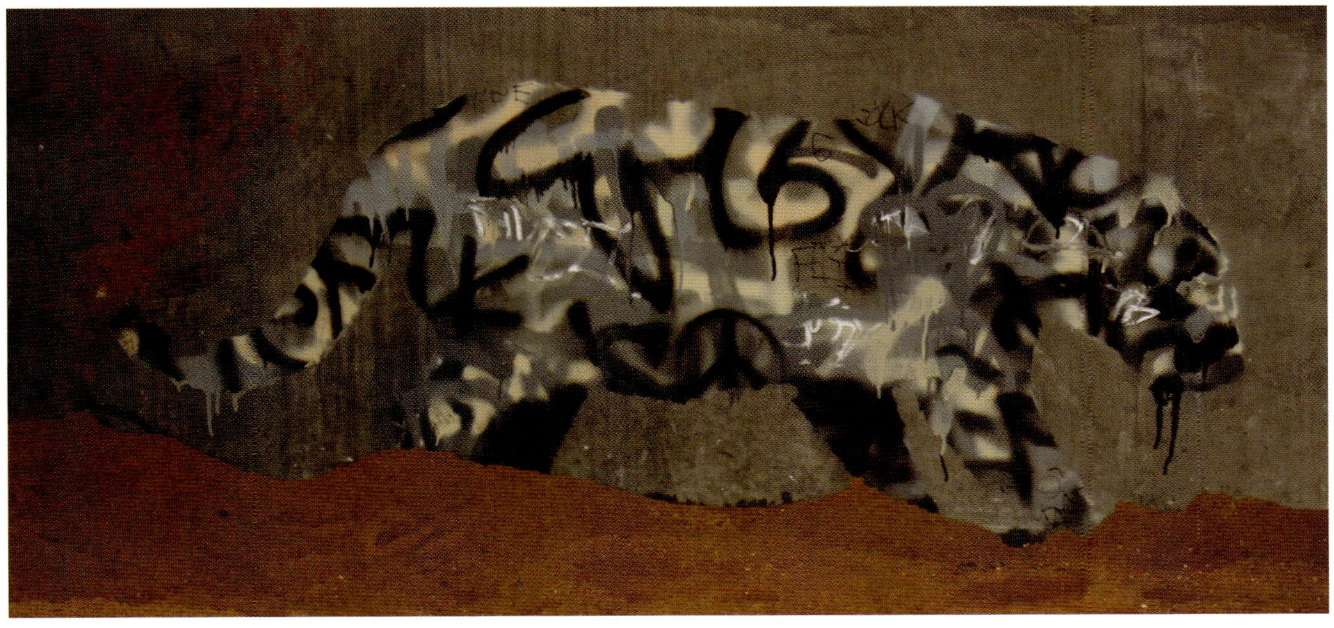

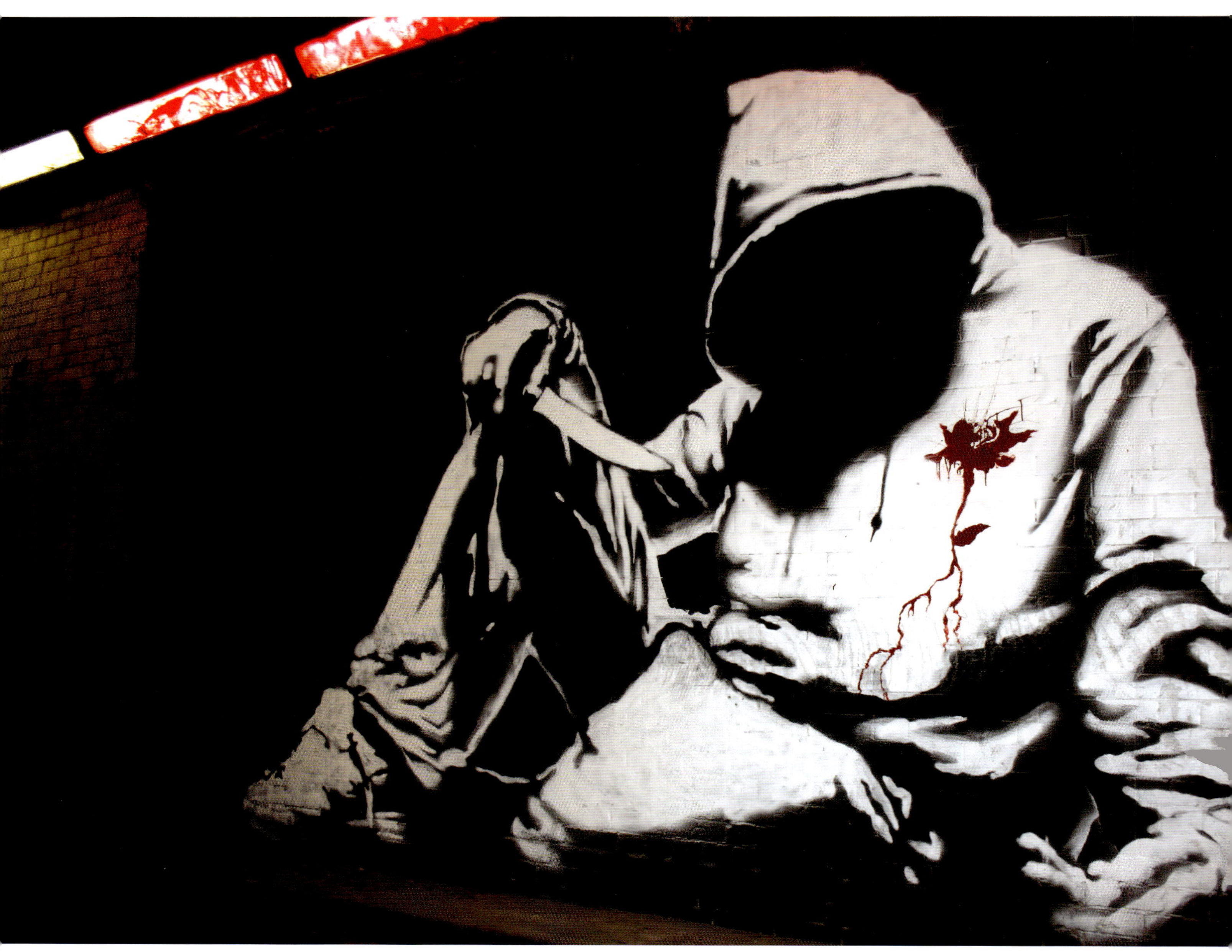

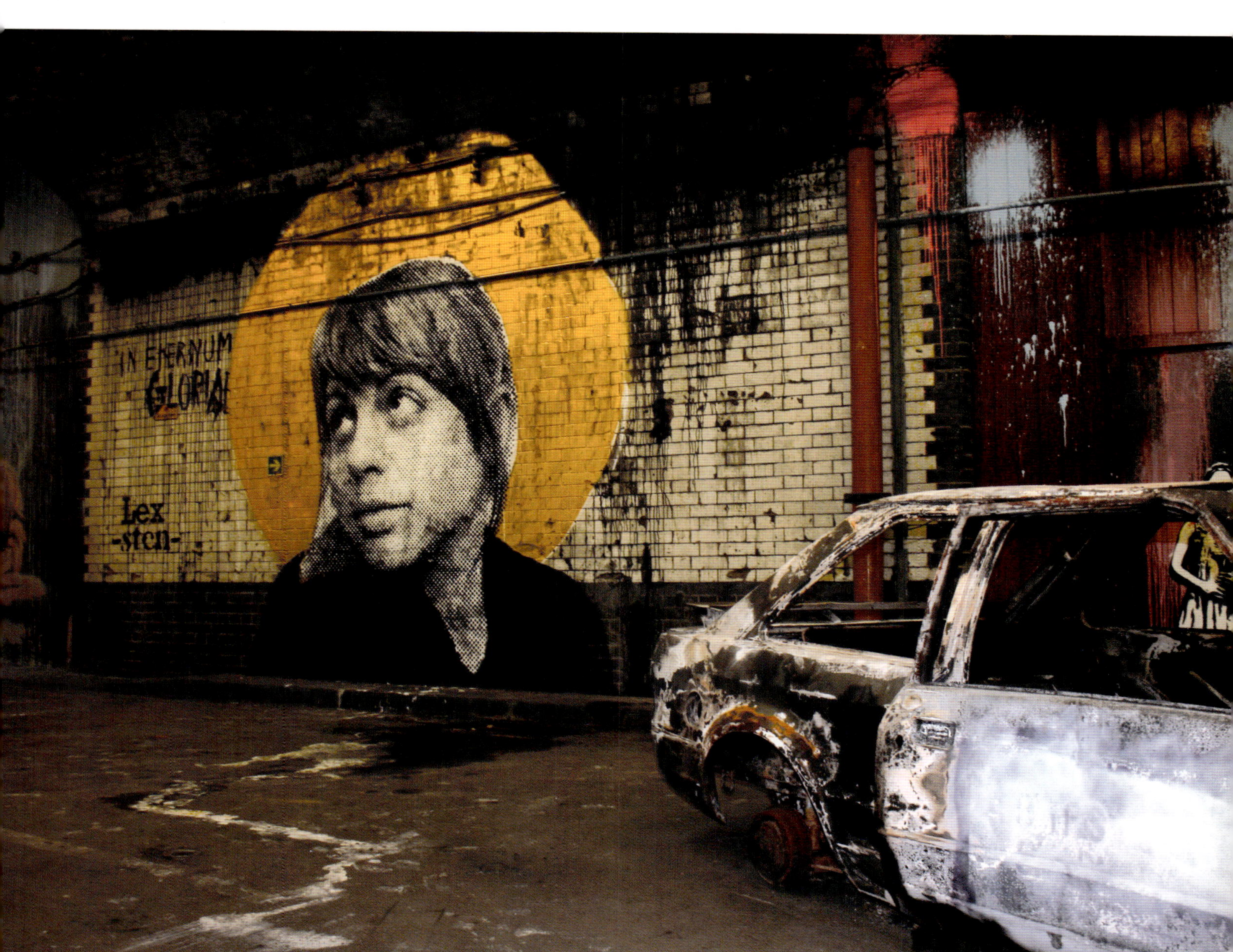
IN ETERNUM
GLORIA
Lex
-sten-

PICTURE CREDITS AND ATTRIBUTED ARTISTS:

p3 Dolk, Svenn Nevenn / p5 Banksy / p6 Banksy, Roland Peschetz / p7 Mir, Niki Molnar / p8 Elbowtoe NY, Elbowtoe / p9 Spring Street, C-Monster / p10 Spring Street, Clay Williams (www.ultraclay.com) / p10 Borf, Clay Williams / p10 Elbowtoe, Clay Williams / p11 Borf, Tracy Collins / p12 Spring Street, Clay Williams / p12 Michael de Feo, Clay Williams / p12 Faile, Clay Williams / p12 Adios Gringo, Clay Williams / p12 Spring Street, Clay Williams / p12 Swoon, Clay Williams / p12 Swoon, Clay Williams / p12 Swoon, Clay Williams / p12 Obey, L. Goggin / p13 Spring Street, Eugenio Garcia-Palacios / p14 Obey, Clay Williams / p14 DFace, Clay Williams / p14 Doze Green, Clay Williams / p15 Skewville, Clay Williams / p15 DFace, Clay Williams / p16 Banksy, Brian Garwood / p17 DFace / p19 Judith Supine NY, Judith Supine / p20 Gaia NY, Gaia / p21 Hush / p22 Maskerade, Maskerade http://maskerade.blogsome.com / p23 ilikecandy.co.uk, Beau / p24 Judith Supine NY, Judith Supine / p25 Banksy, Stew Dean / p26 Jeff Aerosol, Jeff Aerosol / p26 Dolk, Martin Isak Jansen / p26 Armsrock, Occam / p27 Blu, jACK TWO / p28 Dan Witz, Dan Witz / p29 Spazmat, C-Monster / p30 Banksy, Jake Dobkin / p31 Evol, Berlin 2004, photo: Antonia Schulz / p31 Gould, Basel 2008, photo Antonia Schulz / p31 Gould, New York 2006, photo: Antonia Schulz / p31 Various, Berlin 2006, photo Antonia Schulz / p32 Dolk, Nathan Rive / p33 Bast, C-Monster / p34 Blek le Rat, Holger Seidel / p34 Blek le Rat, Holger Seidel / p35 Visual Resistance, C-Monster / p35 Invader, Mat Sefton / p35 Borf Faile, Larry Lorca / p35 Banksy, Malcolm Chapple / p36 Faile, Mikkel Hermann Sorensen / p37 Bronco, Berlin 2007, photo: Antonia Schulz / p38 Banksy, Kriebel / p38 Banksy, Christopher Burgdorfer / p39 Skewville, Rebecca Fuller / p40 Elbowtoe, Elbowtoe / p41 Gaia, Gaia / p42 Invader, Phil Hilfiker / p43 Judith Supine, Judith Supine / p44 Ortica Noodles collab with Snub 23 / p45 Adam Neate, Neil Dowling / p46 Gaia, Gaia / p47 Obey, Steve Rhodes / p48 XoooX, Kathleen Waak / p50 Other, Other / p50 Other, Other / p50 Other, Other / p51 Dolk, Kevin Pollard / p52 Banksy, Kriebel / p53 Judith Supine / p54 Eine, Kriebel / p56 Banksy, Osmany Rodriguez / p57 Banksy, Romanywg / p58 Swoon, Tracy Collins / p59 Banksy, Sam Martin / p60 Banksy, Kriebel / p61 Faile, Jack Hynes / p62 Obey, Romanywg / p63 Gaia, Gaia / p64 Eine, Alistair Reid / p64 Elbowtoe, Romanywg / p64 Skewville, C-Monster / p65 Banksy, Dogbytedesign / p66 Swoon, Keith Puttnam / p67 Fauxreel, C-Monster / p68 Unknown, derMarkstein.de / p69 Banksy, David Stuart / p70 Banksy, Sam Martin / p70 Miss Van, Loso / p70 Other, Other / p71 Relax & WK Interact, C-Monster / p72 Banksy, Dogbytedesign / p72 Banksy, Dogbytedesign / p72 The Toasters, Eddie Dangerous / p72 Gaia, Gaia / p73 Banksy, Kriebel / p74 Elbowtoe / p74 Banksy, Martin Cleary / p74 Insect, Dogbytedesign / p74 Michael De Feo, Kaddischnitz / p74 Anthony Lister, Graham Turner / p74 Armsrock, Occam / p75 Michael De Feo, C-Monster / p76 Dolk, Kevin Pollard / p77 Know Hope, Know Hope / p78 Gaia, Gaia / p79 Swoon, Keith Puttnam / p80 Banksy, Will Denn / p80 Armstrock, Occam / p81 Copyright, Kriebel / p82 Unknown, Holger Seidel / p82 Bast, Loso / p82 Banksy, Phil Sissons / p83 Judith Supine, Judith Supine / p83 Dolk, Kevin Pollard / p83 The Nintendo Project, Frederik Mortensen / p85 Banksy / p86 JR / p88 Blu / p90 Banksy / p90 Bethlehem / p91 Erica Il Cane / p92 Know Hope, Know Hope / p93 Insect / p94 Insect / p95 Banksy / p96 Ame72 / p97 Banksy / p98 Insect / p99 Banksy / p100 Mark Jenkins / p102 Faile / p103 Bethlehem / p104 Erica Il Cane / p105 Insect / p106 Faile / p107 Erica Il Cane / p108 Sam3 / p109 Erica Il Cane / p110 Blu / p111 Faile / p112 JR / p113 Bethlehem / p114 Blu / p115 Gil Bensmana, Tofz4u / p115 Banksy, Eddie Dangerous / p115 Faile, Kathleen Waak / p116 Os Gemeos, Ric CheckDis / p116 Dolk, Cashen / p117 Judith Supine, Judith Supine / p120 Gaia, Gaia / p121 Dolk, berberechoproductions / p121 C215, Kriebel / p121 Banksy, Sam Martin / p121 Copyright, Eddie Dangerous / p121 C215 and Elbowtoe, Romanywg / p122 Nick Walker, Nuart / p123 DFace, Nuart / p124 Logan Hicks, Nuart / p124 Rene Gagnon, Nuart / p125 Nuart, Nuart / p125 Dolk, Nuart / p125 Eine, Nuart / p126 Unknown, Floortje Kinkhamer / p127 Bast & Billikid, Billikid / p129 Borf, Rik Goldman / p130 Banksy, Osmany Rodriguez / p130 Judith Supine, Piecemaker Design / p130 Pure Evil, Vincent Roman / p131 Gaia, Gaia / p132 Elbowtoe, Elbowtoe / p132 Os Gemeos, ISER 1 from Barcelona / p132 Obey, Clay Williams (www.ultraclay.com) / p132 Dolk, Mortsan / p132 Billikid, Billikid / p132 Skullphone, Dogbytedesign / p132 Sweettoof & Sickboy, Eddie Dangerous / p132 Swoon, Kathleen Waak / p132 Mir, Etienne Dessaut / p132 The London Police, Martijn Savenije / p132 PMP, Romanywg / p132 Dolk, Morten Oddvik / p133 Swoon, Kathleen Waak / p134 Banksy, P. Villerius / p134 Faile / p134 Bronco, Hamburg 2006, photo: Antonia Schulz / p135 Know Hope, Know Hope / p135 Above, TiDenis / p135 Banksy, Romanywg / p136 Eine, Kriebel / p139 Miss Van, Cristina Huguet / p140 Judith Supine and Tek13, Kriebel / p141 Elbowtoe, Corey Szopinski / p142 Unknown, Martin Isak Jansen / p143 WK Interact / p144 Swoon, C-Monster / p144 Jef Aerosol, Jef Aerosol / p144 Faile, Kathleen Waak / p145 Judith Supine, Judith Supine / p146 Bast, C-Monster / p146 Invader / p146 40 NYC, C-Monster / p147 Blu, Kathleen Waak / p147 Arte Jagua, C-Monster / p147 Revs, C-Monster / p148 Swoon, Kathleen Waak / p149 Nick Walker, Osmany Rodriguez / p149 Peeblitz, Alistair Reid / p149 Faile, C-Monster / p149 Michael De Feo / p149 Os Gemeos, C-Monster / p150 Bast, C-Monster / p151 Hera, Romanywg / p151 Revs, C-Monster / p151 Michael De Feo, C-Monster / p152 Swoon / p153 MikeMarcus, Romanywg / p154 Swoon, Kathleen Waak / p155 Celso, C-Monster / p155 Faile, C-Monster / p155 Banksy, Romanywg / p156 Banksy, Sam Martin / p156 kgbe Rotgut, Bruce Labounty / p156 Solovei, Lars Stadtbild / p156 WK Interact, Robert Capasso / p156 Faile, Kathleen Waak / p157 Dolk, Martin Isak Jansen / p158 NY Bin, Robert Capasso / p158 Dolk, Martin Isak Jansen / p158 Unknown, Romanywg / p159 Dolk, Sven Neven / p159 The London Police, Kathleen Waak / p159 Banksy, Romanywg / p160 Judith Supine, Judith Supine / p161 Unknown, Martin Isak Jansen / p163 Adam Neate, Panopito / p163 Banksy, Alistair Reid / p164 Banksy, J. Lisenbery / p165 Celso, C-Monster / p166 Judith Supine, Judith Supine / p167 Then It Hit Me, C-Monster / p168 DFace, Romanywg / 168 Buff Monster, C-Monster / p169 Faile, C-Monster / p169 Swoon, C-Monster / p170 C215, Romanywg / p170 Judith Supine, Judith Supine / p171 Elbowtoe, Elbowtoe / p171 Judith Supine, Judith Supine / p171 Invader, Romanywg / p172 Judith Supine, Judith Supine / p172 Gaia, Gaia / p174 Os Gemeos, C-Monster / p174 Skewville, C-Monster / p174 Pure Evil / p175 Dark Clouds, C-Monster / p175 Neckface, C-Monster / p176 Invader, Clay Williams / p176 Banksy, Luke Canvin / p176 Blek le Rat, Cicilie Fagerlid / p176 DFace, Kriebel / p177 Swoon, Kriebel / p177 Banksy, Dogbytedesign / p177 Bast, Issy Yu / p177 Unknown, Eddie Dangerous / p178 Miss Bugs, Romanywg / p178 Banksy / p178 Swoon, C-Monster / p180-189 The Cans Festival, London. 3rd-5th May 2008. Liam Shove / p190 Ree / p191 Artists Space, Holger Seidel / p192 Unknown, Alistair Reid. All other photos by Gary Shove.

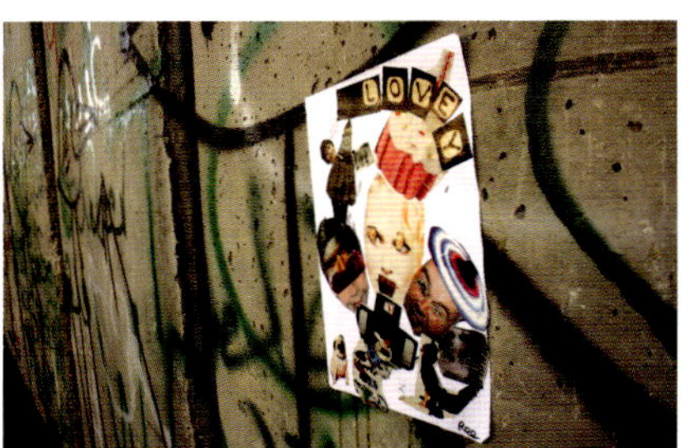

No mess, no fuss, just pure ipmact!

Many thanks to all the photographers who contributed worldwide.

All images are the copyright of their respective owner.

All artists recognised and acknowledged to the best of our (limited) knowledge.

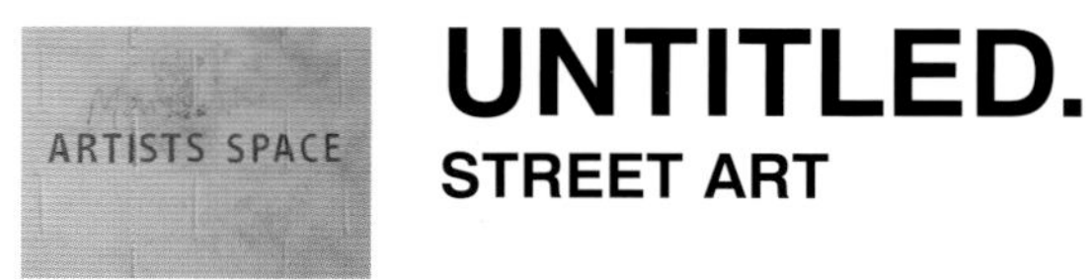


# UNTITLED.
## STREET ART

RESPECT TO ALL THOSE THAT MADE THIS BOOK POSSIBLE:

The artists (in no particular order): Banksy, Erica Il Cane, Insect, Ame72, Judith Supine, Os Gemeos, Nick Walker, Dolk, Blu, DFace, Elbowtoe, Faile, Swoon, Gaia, Skewville, The London Police, Obey, Blek le Rat, Know Hope, Mantis, Aerofish, Dan Witz, Eine, KGBE Rotgut, WK Interact, Bast, Michael de Feo, Copyright. Relax, Fauxreel, Jef Aerosol, Invader, Borf, Doze Green, Maskerade, Solovei, Bronco, Evol, Gould, Various, Gil Bensmana, Billikid, Miss Van, Skullphone, Sweettoof, Sickboy, Armsrock, Hush, Beau, Other, Mir, Above, Adam Neate, Anthony Lister, Miss Bugs, PMP, Orticanoodles/Snub23, Sam3, Pure Evil, Logan Hicks, Rene Gagnon, Hera, Revs, Arte Jagua, Peter Kennard/Cat Picton Philips, C215, Buff Monster, Neckface, Izolag, Pobel, M-City, Vhils, Btoy, Nadie Crew, John Grider, Logan Hicks, Dot Masters, Dan, Eelus, Bsas Stencil, Run Don't Walk, James Dodd, civilian, Vexta, Prism, Daniel Melim, Altocontraste, Ananda Nahu, Bandit, Roadsworth, Artiste-Ouvrier, Sten, Lucamaleonte, Lex, Orticanoodles, Kaagman ... *and a cast of thousands*.

SPECIAL THANKS TO:

All those from the North: Sharon, Patrick, Ali, Liam, Rhiannon, Calli, Stu, Mrs T, DK, Mom, Dad. Those across the pond: C-Monster, Clay Williams, Judith Supine, Elbowtoe, Dan Witz, Gaia, John, Osmany. Worldwide: Sam, Kriebel, Romanywg, EddieDangerous, K!wa One, Antonia, Dogbyte, Maskerade, Morten, Lars, Other, Keith, Jeff, Jack, Phil, Brian, Stew, Christopher, Svenn, Martin, Kriebel, Mikkel, Steve, Know Hope, Holger, Jake, Jack, Eugenio, Bruce, Nathan, Iser1, Vincent, Piecemaker, Mat, Loso, Goggla, Beberecho, Tofz4u, Izzy, Ric, Larry, Tracy, Robert, Deep6, Kathleen, Kaddischnitz, Etienne, Cristina, Martijn, Rik, Kevin, Martin, Panoptico, Graham, Shane, Floortje, Luke, P. Villerius, Occam, JackTwo, Holger, Martyn Nuart.

HEADS UP:

Check out 'Off The Street' by Stuart Mackenzie. The definitive guide to artists, galleries and collectors.

CONTRIBUTIONS:

If you'd like to contribute to UNTITLED. Vol2. drop an email to info@untitledstreetart.co.uk
Pics, thoughts, outbursts, rants are all welcome.

DISCLAIMER:

None of the words and spaces contained herein have any relevance to any of the photographs. They are only included to keep the pictures company and make us look cleverer than we actually are.

RESPECT COPYRIGHT: COLLABORATE AND CREATE. All images submitted by contributors have been supplied on the understanding that they as originator retain copyright and are credited.

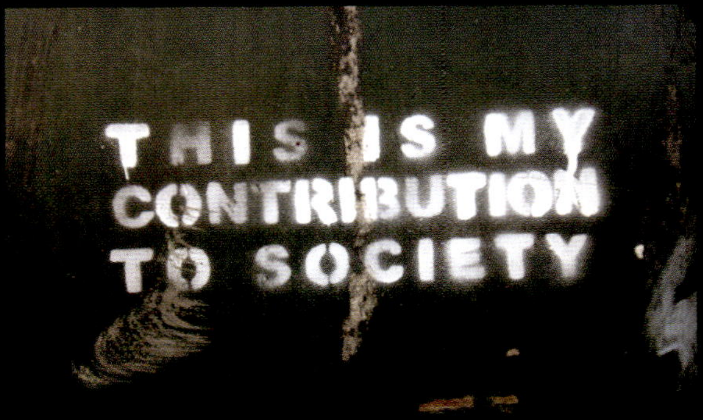

THIS IS MY
CONTRIBUTION
TO SOCIETY